THE CANING

Also by Stephen Puleo

Dark Tide: The Great Boston Molasses Flood of 1919

Due to Enemy Action: The True World War II Story of the USS Eagle 56

The Boston Italians: A Story of Pride, Perseverance and Paesani, *from the Years of the Great Immigration to the Present Day*

A City So Grand: The Rise of an American Metropolis, Boston 1850–1900

THE CANING

THE ASSAULT THAT DROVE AMERICA TO CIVIL WAR

STEPHEN PULEO

WESTHOLME
Yardley

Westholme Publishing, LLC
904 Edgewood Road
Yardley, Pennsylvania 19067
Visit our Web site at www.westholmepublishing.com

First Printing October 2012
10 9 8 7 6 5 4 3 2 1

ISBN: 978-1-59416-164-3

Also available as an eBook.

Printed in the United States of America.

To Kate

Forever the song in my heart

CONTENTS

INTRODUCTION

Deep in the locked vaults of the McKissick Museum, on the campus of the University of South Carolina in Columbia, sits a precious artifact that represents one of the most shocking and dramatic events in American history.

The gleaming silver goblet is truly a work of art: elegantly designed and crafted, a hexagonal body graced with ornamental chasing, a bedded molding at its lip and lead banding around the foot, its stem adorned with sculpted leaves and acorns. But those few museum visitors lucky enough to view and handle this five-inch-tall chalice—as I was—recognize that its true significance and irreplaceable value is derived from the flowery inscription engraved on one of its panels:

"To Hon. Ps Brooks From Citizens of Columbia, May 22, 1856."

Perhaps the date is most revealing. It is not the date Columbia residents presented the goblet to South Carolina Congressman Preston S. Brooks—the presentation ceremony actually occurred three months later at an enormous rally celebrating Brooks's triumphant return to the South after leaving Washington.

The inscription on the silver chalice immortalizes the date of a far more important event. Early in the afternoon of May 22, 1856, the ardently proslavery Brooks strode into the United States Senate chamber in Washington, D.C., and began beating renowned antislavery Senator Charles Sumner of Massachusetts with a gutta-percha cane. Brooks struck again and again—more than thirty times across Sumner's head, face, and shoulders—until his cane splintered into pieces and the helpless Massachusetts senator lay unconscious, covered in blood.

It was a retaliatory attack by Brooks. Forty-eight hours earlier, Sumner had concluded a speech on the Senate floor that had spanned two days, during which he vilified Southern slave-owners for violence occurring in Kansas and hurled personal slurs against Brooks's second cousin, South Carolina Senator Andrew Butler. Sumner also insulted the entire South for its support of and reliance on slavery.

The silver goblet presented to Congressman Preston S. Brooks by the citizens of Columbia, South Carolina to commemorate his caning of U.S. Senator Charles Sumner. (*McKissick Museum, University of South Carolina. All rights reserved.*)

Brooks not only shattered his cane during the beating, but also destroyed any pretense of civility between North and South. One of the most stunning and provocative events in American history, the caning hardened positions on both sides and convinced each that the gulf between them was unbridgeable; that they could no longer rationally discuss their sharp differences of opinion regarding slavery. The polar opposite reactions to the caning from the North and the South were clear omens about the nation's future.

In the North, the assault cemented the abolitionist view that slaveholders were barbarians; but of far greater consequence, it convinced moderate Northern voices that the South could no longer engage in reasonable debate about slavery and sectional differences. Even Northerners who deplored Sumner's vitriolic language in the Kansas speech, and who normally did not support his extreme antislavery views, were left with little choice but to stand with him and condemn the bloody beating.

Just as significantly, the newly formed antislavery Republican Party used the caning to seize dominance across the North; it was the caning of Charles Sumner that mobilized thousands to join the party that nominated Abraham Lincoln in 1860.

In the South, Sumner's Kansas speech, especially his personal attack on Senator Butler, enraged the entire region. Southern slave-owners, who already hated Sumner and all he stood for, had battled since the Missouri Compromise of 1820 to preserve a slave system that supported their region's economy and, as Brooks eloquently argued in the midst of the caning debate, fueled much of the North's economy as well. Brooks and his countrymen feared that elitists such as Sumner, whose antislavery views were among the most radical in the country and who expressed dangerous ideas about freeing the slaves, would, if not directly confronted, destroy the Southern way of life.

In addition, Sumner's use of inflammatory language, his superior attitude, and his personal attack on Andrew Butler cried out for revenge according to the Southern code of honor, by which Preston Brooks was bound. These precepts condoned, even demanded, physical confrontation when insults were hurled at a man's family or state, and Sumner's words served as the perfect provocation for Brooks to defend both his family and his region. Virtually the entire South cheered him for doing so.

Storm clouds gathered rapidly after the caning. Across the country, citizens pondered the questions Brooks's attack had raised: If physical violence could occur inside the U.S. Capitol between elected lawmakers and educated men, was there any hope of resolving sectional differences through discussion and compromise? Could the slavery debate ever be settled peaceably?

The merciless beating of the North's strongest and most eloquent antislavery voice ensured that all of these questions would be answered in the negative. The caning had a tremendous impact on the events that followed over the next four years: the increasing militancy of the abolitionist movement, the meteoric rise of the Republican Party, and the secession of the Southern states and the founding of the Confederacy. While Sumner eventually recovered, compromise had suffered a mortal blow and in its place came escalating tensions and violence.

Many factors conspired to cause the Civil War, but it was the caning that made conflict and disunion unavoidable five years later.

Others have written about the caning (see my Bibliographic Essay), but to my knowledge, this is the first treatment that fully develops the characters of Sumner *and* Brooks in the same book. Sumner has been the subject of numerous biographies, but even the most recent—and best, in my view—a masterpiece by historian David Donald, is more than fifty years old and offers only limited insight into Brooks. (Volume 1 of Donald's eventual two-volume epic, *Charles Sumner and the Coming of the Civil War*, which covers the caning episode, was published in 1960; the second volume, *Charles Sumner and the Rights of Man*, was published ten years later.) Indeed, historically, Brooks is often portrayed as a stereotypical cliché, a Southern ruffian whose attack on Sumner is seldom put into context. Sumner's history of provocation and Brooks's adherence to the Southern code of honor are generally not explored.

Sumner's virtues are many: moral courage, a deep belief in equality between races, honesty, clarity of thought, virtually unwavering in principle regardless of political consequences. Yet, his vices—narcissism, arrogance, deep insecurity, inflexibility, alienation from family, disrespect for the feelings of others, contempt for opinions different from his own, an unwillingness to compromise—all played a critical role in Brooks's bloody attack. Sumner was clearly the victim on May 22, 1856, but he could hardly be characterized as blameless.

Unlike Sumner, Brooks was a strong family man and regarded as a gentleman in every sense, but his personal rambunctiousness and latent proclivity for violence, long dormant until that fateful day in the Senate chamber, overcame him when he confronted Sumner. He and other slave-owners, who craved the order that plantation life had long represented in the South, saw that order come crashing down after the caning. Ironically, Brooks helped destroy the Southern order he cherished so much.

There is another irony that surrounds these two men. Brooks began his political career as a moderate amidst radical proslavery forces. Sumner began as a self-proclaimed antislavery fanatic, an abolitionist in all but name, representing a Massachusetts that was far more moderate. As time went on, Brooks veered closer to the extreme proslavery, "fire-eating" point of view, while

Massachusetts, and the rest of the North, moved closer to Sumner's utter disdain for slavery.

After May 22, 1856, these extremist views came to the fore and became mainstream and intractable. The two sides clung desperately to their positions, each convinced of their righteousness. Sumner and his Northern supporters demanded total, immediate, and uncompensated abolition, regardless of its impact on the Southern culture or economy. Brooks and his fellow Southern planters, and most of the South, wanted slavery to grow unfettered, uninhibited, and thriving, and would not even entertain the notion that black slaves were anything but subhuman in the evolutionary chain; thus, slavery's expansion presented them with no moral dilemma.

After the caning, the slavery question was transformed from a political and intellectual debate to a visceral maelstrom that pushed the country inexorably toward civil war.

PROLOGUE

May 19, 1856, U.S. Senate Chamber
Washington, D.C.

Even the Ladies' Gallery was filled to overflowing.

The sweaty Senate chamber crackled with tension and suffocating heat and the expectant murmurs of nervous lawmakers, but of all the indicators that big events were afoot, the most stunning was the number of women present. Normally, their section stood empty or contained a mere handful of occupants. This day, though, dresses clinging and hand-fans waggling in the stiflingly close quarters, women jostled for position and craned their necks for a better view of the drama. Their trip into the chamber had forced them into unladylike behavior: they had slogged through the thick mud on the streets outside; avoided squealing pigs that ran wild and feasted on garbage strewn across Pennsylvania Avenue; and covered their mouths with lacy handkerchiefs as they high-stepped through the dust-choked construction area, part of the Capitol building's renovations. But it was worth it to secure a spot in the Senate chamber on this potentially historic day.

The import and energy of the women's presence even eclipsed several other noteworthy and telltale signs that something special was in store: the throngs of eminent statesmen, former politicians, and ordinary citizens who clogged the aisles and doorways and anterooms; the many members of the House of Representatives, including South Carolina's Preston Brooks and Lawrence Keitt, who had ventured to the Senate chamber to witness the moment; the presence of Southern delegates, en route to the Democratic National Convention in Cincinnati, who detoured to the nation's capital to witness the day's events;

the fact that every journalist's chair was filled, and that virtually every senator was uncharacteristically seated at the session's outset, awaiting the words of a colleague. South Carolina's Andrew Butler, a notable exception, was home recovering from a stroke. One newspaper reporter later wrote that "the galleries were crowded with intellect, beauty, and fashion" for the occasion. Another added: "No such scene has been witnessed since the days of [Daniel] Webster."

Anticipation filled the room, too. The temperature in the chamber had soared above ninety degrees, but rather than induce lethargy, the heat, in the words of one correspondent, added to the "breathless suspense" that gripped senators and spectators alike.

Some of those in attendance admired the tall, broad-shouldered man who was about to speak. Many despised him. Still others simply wanted to catch a glimpse of one of Washington's most polarizing figures, who also happened to be one of the nation's most eloquent and incendiary orators. Whatever the reason, all eyes were focused on him.

The object of this attention, forty-five-year-old United States Senator Charles Sumner of Massachusetts, relished every moment. He was a complex man of immense contradictions—at once educated and pedantic, worldly and petty, principled and pious, cultured and close-minded, refined and arrogant, steadfast and stubborn, altruistic and narcissistic. Filled with self-righteousness, the humorless Sumner believed devoutly in his cause and, even more fervently, in assailing the stupidity and ignorance of his adversaries' positions.

He coupled this blind conviction with his legendary speaking style—contentious, caustic, sometimes cruel, but also animated, fiery, and persuasive. A prolific and careful writer, yes, but Sumner's greatest artistic gift was his soaring oratory. If the pen was mightier than the sword, Sumner believed the spoken word was the most powerful weapon of all. Whether wielded with deft precision or unsparing blunt force, the right words uttered by a skilled speaker could slice through deception, smash an opponent's spirit, or create a dazzling and unassailable argument from a shapeless block of blandness and ambiguity.

Onlookers flocked to the Senate chamber on this day, sensing that the grand setting and Charles Sumner's rhetoric would bring a white-hot intensity to the most combustible debate topic in Washington. The crowd would no doubt help the senator's delivery; as one reporter would later note, Sumner had an audience "to arouse all his faculties." That audience knew full well that Sumner would expend enormous energy attempting to persuade his colleagues and the nation to join him in rejecting the institution he so bitterly detested—slavery—and in denouncing the Southern planters and slaveholders who insisted on its continued and unchecked proliferation.

Sumner would deliver his message by focusing on the violence taking place in faraway Kansas, which for months had served as the crucible of the slavery firestorm between North and South; this much the spectators knew in advance. What caused the pensive stirring in the chamber was not so much what Sumner would say, but how he would say it. What explosive language would he employ? Whom would he anger or single out for criticism? Would he tweak his political opponents or insult them outright?

Sumner had anticipated the speech for weeks, and was thrilled when he found out days earlier that he would be permitted to deliver it. "I have the floor next Monday on Kansas, when I shall make the most thorough and complete speech of my life," he boasted to a friend. "My soul is wrung by this outrage, & I shall pour it forth." Another friend cautioned Sumner about his tone, predicting that an antagonistic speech could evoke "gnashing of teeth among the defenders of slavery. Be prepared, therefore, for the worst of their endeavors."

Undeterred and uncompromising, Charles Sumner paid no heed. He loved the big stage and he was just moments from the most memorable and controversial performance of his life.

Part I

ONE

BLEEDING KANSAS

Most of the nation's attention was focused on Kansas at the beginning of 1856. "My dear sir—help us," a despondent Hannah Ropes had written to Charles Sumner from Lawrence, Kansas, on January 22, 1856. "Where should the weak flee if not to strong heads and hands like yours?"

Months before Sumner prepared to deliver his dramatic speech in the U.S. Senate chamber, Kansas was suffering through a punishing winter and a desperate war for its very soul. Heavy snow blanketed the prairie, howling wind ripped across the plains, and temperatures plunged to thirty degrees below zero. All of this threatened "total destruction," Ropes wrote, but she was more frightened by the storm of wanton violence perpetrated by proslavery forces—lawlessness that caused "the most heroic hearts among us [to] cower." Lydia P. Hall agreed and pleaded to Sumner in her letter: "What will you do for us in Congress? We trust you will do a great deal."

For nearly two years, since the controversial passage of the Kansas-Nebraska Act in 1854—fashioned by Illinois Democratic Senator Stephen A. Douglas and signed by President Franklin Pierce—sectional strife, assaults, barbarism, and mayhem had rocked the territory. The sweeping, radical legislation repealed the portion of the Missouri Compromise of 1820 that forbade slavery in the former Louisiana Territory north of the 36° 30′ latitude parallel—except within the boundaries of the then newly admitted slave state of Missouri. Instead, the new Kansas-Nebraska Act stated that the future of slavery in those territories would be decided by the popular vote of residents.

The North was incensed, believing the Douglas-sponsored legislation recklessly and unnecessarily destroyed the delicate compromises on slavery that had existed since the nation's founding, and worse, opened vast new territories to slavery's expansion. When his bill was introduced, opponents held raucous public protest meetings throughout the North—three thousand attended one in Boston's Faneuil Hall and more than five thousand gathered in New York's City Hall Park. The Northern press vilified Douglas, and Northern clergy were unified in their exhortations against the bill.

While Douglas knew the legislation would spark acrimonious debate, he had both convictions and politics in mind when he proposed it and pushed for its passage. He believed strongly in the principle of popular sovereignty (self-rule by the citizenry), and he predicted that the residents of Kansas would choose to prohibit slavery, even though, he maintained, they had the right to allow it (similar to the way residents of California had petitioned Congress for admittance as a free state in 1850). On the political side, Douglas had ambitions to become president and would need the support of Southern Democrats to do so. He also sought a northern route for an envisioned transcontinental railroad, and hoped that its eastern terminus would be Chicago, in his home state, while Southerners favored St. Louis as the easternmost point. The Kansas-Nebraska Act of 1854 was Douglas's offer of tribute to the South for these political goals.

But Douglas never imagined the fury he would unleash, and the explosive hostility across the North distressed him. At mass meetings and rallies, speakers urged his removal from office, and in several places he was hanged in effigy. Never one to resist the pull of gallows humor—in this case literally—Douglas half-joked and half-lamented that he could have traveled the entire route between Washington, D.C., and his home in Illinois by the light of his own burning effigies. During debate on the bill, Charles Sumner said Douglas would suffer regardless of the outcome. "If he does not succeed in his plot, he will be kicked by the South; if he does, his brains will be dashed out at the North," he wrote. When Congress passed the Kansas-Nebraska Act in May 1854, the *Albany Evening Journal* wrote: "The crime is committed. The work of Monroe, Madison, and Jefferson is undone . . . we have seen the North crouch lower and lower each year under the whip of the slave driver."

Those who opposed the extension of slavery into the western territories—disillusioned Northern Whigs, Free-Soilers, and some Northern Democrats—even formed a new political party, "Republicans," who vowed to repeal the Kansas-Nebraska Act. "At last there seems to be an awakening of the North," Senator Charles Sumner declared. "Good!" Douglas asserted otherwise, saying the formation of such a party would mean "civil war, servile war, and disunion."

Predictably, Southern response to Kansas-Nebraska was much different, sometimes hailed, sometimes greeted with indifference, and occasionally even decried by those who thought it did not go far enough, the latter group insisting instead that Congress should simply permit slavery in the new territories without a popular vote. The more consistent and moderate view, expressed by the *Messenger* of Macon, Georgia, said the Kansas-Nebraska bill was "simply an effort to resist encroachments upon our rights, and establish the just principle of non-intervention."

South Carolina Congressman Preston Brooks chided the North for its hostility to the bill and its hypocrisy on the slavery question, pointing out that wealthy Northern textile magnates had become rich by transforming slave-picked Southern cotton into "thread, and wearing apparel, and umbrellas, and sun shades." It was hard to take seriously the North's pontifications against Kansas-Nebraska and slavery, Brooks declared, considering that, without slavery, millions in the North would face "bankruptcy, and ruin, and inutterable miseries . . . thousands who now live in contentment and comfort would beg for bread."

Almost immediately after the passage of Kansas-Nebraska, both antislavery Northerners and proslavery Southerners began the competition to win these regions for their sides. Nebraska was too far north to yield productive cotton, rice, or tobacco crops and, thus, it did not entice slave-owners, nor was there much doubt that its residents would reject slavery. But Kansas—whose soil and weather were not conducive to producing cotton but might allow for the growth of hemp and tobacco—quickly became the center of the sectional storm, a battleground between stalwart proslavery and fervent antislavery forces, and, unavoidably, the symbol of the country's very future.

The South was desperate to extend slavery and presumed Kansas was destined for slavery, especially after California was admitted as a free state as part of the Compromise of 1850, altering the national balance to sixteen free states and fifteen slave states. In addition, slave-owning Missourians feared that a free state on their western border would harbor escaped slaves. One Missouri newspaper even warned that "abolitionists would settle in Kansas and run off with our slaves."

Nor were these fears unfounded. The Massachusetts legislature had recently chartered the New England Emigrant Aid Company, incorporated under the guidance of founder Eli Thayer and treasurer and trustee Amos Lawrence. The company was established to send settlers with antislavery sentiments into the Kansas territory in an effort to secure its admission to the Union as a free state. Upon their arrival in Kansas, company volunteers established residences; helped to build homes, schools, churches, and mills; cleared land and planted crops; and secured reduced transportation fares for other emigrants traveling west.

Residents of the South in its entirety and Missouri in particular were outraged by what they perceived as long-distance interference. Missouri Senator David Rice Atchison urged his constituents to cross Missouri's western border and engage in illegal interstate voting. He said it was the most effective way slavery proponents could counteract antislavery emissaries, "fanatics and demagogues," who had arrived in Kansas from the East and were pouring money into an effort to "abolitionize Kansas." Atchison challenged his constituents: "What is your duty, when you reside within one day's journey of the Territory, and when your peace, quiet, and property depend on your action?" Atchison said he could send as many as five thousand men to cross the border into Kansas, "enough to kill every God-damned abolitionist in the Territory." Atchison supporter and proslavery activist Benjamin Franklin Stringfellow spoke just as bluntly to his western Missouri brethren: "I advise you, one and all, to enter every election district in Kansas . . . and vote at the point of the bowie-knife and revolver."

Nor would Missouri provide the only proslavery firepower. Atchison also sent out an appeal to other slave-owners to relocate their slaves to Kansas and urged armed men from the slave states to travel to the territory and fight for slavery. Troops arrived from Alabama, South Carolina, Georgia, Mississippi, and Tennessee; the Montgomery, Alabama, *Journal* noted that the South "stood ready at any moment to supply any balance of voters which may be necessary." Southern women gave up their jewels to help fund the cause, and several Southern railroads offered free passage to those willing to travel to Kansas. A proslavery committee in Abbeville, South Carolina, offered $200 to every "suitable person" who would emigrate to the divided territory. Another publication appealed urgently to Southerners: "Do not delay; come as individuals, come in companies, come by thousands."

The roiling on the plains reached a climax on May 30, 1855, when Kansas held its territorial elections.

Emboldened by the rhetoric of their elected officials, and supported by like-thinking people across the South, proslavery Missourians by the thousands, armed and ready for violence, crossed the border. Although only 1,500 men were registered to vote in Kansas, more than 6,000 ballots were cast, many of them by proslavery "border ruffians" from adjacent Missouri who flooded into Kansas to vote. They terrorized the few polling officials who dared to try to stop the outrage, and elected a bogus proslavery legislature that passed stringent laws protecting slavery in Kansas.

Known as the "black laws," they blatantly disregarded the Constitution and the Bill of Rights (one historian called them the most egregious violations of civil rights in American history) and mandated severe punishment for antislavery activity: two to five years of hard labor for anyone possessing an abolitionist publication and five years of hard labor for writers or publishers of antislavery writings. The laws also mandated the death penalty for those who induced slaves to revolt. "We now have laws more efficient to protect slave-property than any State in the Union," boasted Stringfellow.

The black laws proved so extreme as to be virtually unenforceable, but they created an atmosphere of violence and mayhem. Antislavery settler E. P. Brown was attacked by a crowd of border ruffians near Leavenworth, hacked with knives and a hatchet, and left at his cabin door. He died in his wife's arms and she went into shock. Proslavery men shaved the head of and tarred and feathered a Leavenworth lawyer named Phillips who had spoken out against the election frauds, and later shot him dead in his home. Thomas Barber, a free-state Kansan who lived ten miles outside of Lawrence, bled to death after he and his brothers were attacked and shot by a band of fifteen Missourians. In her letter to Charles Sumner, Lydia Hall described the impact of these episodes: "The cowardly murders . . . and the thousand nameless indignities offered in the same spirit have burnt deep into the hearts of our people."

In August 1855, opponents of slavery in Kansas known as "Free-Soilers" organized their own Free State convention to challenge the bogus legislature. A month later, Free-Soilers selected antislavery candidates, voted to oppose the black laws, and formed a committee for counting votes during elections. The convention passed a resolution stating that Free-Soilers would resist, with force if necessary, the "tyrannical enactments" of the proslavery legislature. The Free-Soilers drew up a constitution that prohibited slavery in Kansas, but at the same time also barred free blacks from the territory—they wanted Kansas free and white. They submitted the Topeka constitution to the territory's voters, who approved it by an overwhelming majority. The Topeka Free-Soil government then asked Congress to admit Kansas as a free state.

Kansas now had two competing legislatures: one allowing slavery, the other against. President Franklin Pierce threw his support behind the proslavery legislature and asked Congress to admit Kansas to the Union as a slave state. Advocates of slavery in Kansas were exultant and opponents mortified. A despondent Horace Greeley editorialized in his antislavery paper, the *New York Tribune*: "The Border Ruffians have been raised entirely off their feet by Pierce's extraordinary messages, which they regard as a complete endorsement of all their past outrages, and an incitement to persevere in their diabolical work."

Perhaps more foreboding were the words of militant abolitionist John Brown, who had arrived in Kansas by this time: "We hear that Franklin Pierce means to crush the men of Kansas. I do not know how well he may succeed; but I think he may find his hands full before it is over."

Throughout the winter months of 1856, despite frigid temperatures and brutal storms, antislavery men posted sentries in Lawrence to stand guard against possible attacks, but the weather temporarily dissuaded wide-scale bloodshed. With spring approaching, however, Kansas Free-Soilers expected fresh outbreaks of violence and additional armed incursions from the western counties of Missouri. "We are expecting open warfare, eventually," predicted Lydia Hall.

Indeed, as the weather warmed, more violence ensued across eastern Kansas territory, with shootings and hangings of antislavery men by proslavery forces. George Washington Brown, editor of the *Herald of Freedom* newspaper, was one of seven free-state leaders arrested in the spring of 1856, charged with high treason and held prisoner by federal troops near Lecompton. Proslavery leaders viewed Lawrence, the free-state capital, as a viper's nest of traitors, and their claims were bolstered when a judge, responding to President Pierce's proslavery stance, ordered a grand jury to indict members of the Free-Soil legislature for treason. A federal marshal claimed that rebels in Lawrence had interfered with the execution of the indictments. He called for "law-abiding citizens of the territory" to assemble for an attack on the town.

TWO

OMENS OF WAR

"My heart is sick," Charles Sumner despaired to a fellow abolitionist as the Senate began its debate over Kansas in March 1856, weeks before his Kansas speech. The violence on the prairie and in the towns of Kansas epitomized the monumental clash of differences between North and South. Sumner knew full well that the geographic center of the American continent also represented the center of the country's ongoing and increasingly bitter debate over slavery.

Sumner, whose long-held beliefs, writings, and speeches had cast him as the country's most eloquent and powerful antislavery voice, had paid close attention to the escalating violence in Kansas. He despised the proslavery forces who poured across the border from Missouri, describing them as uncivilized barbarians who were incapable of self-control, yet he sympathized with Emigrant Aid Company itinerants and other free-state sympathizers who had ventured to and settled in Kansas.

He heard from them frequently; they viewed Sumner as their savior. Hannah Ropes and Lydia Hall were not alone in pleading with him for assistance. For months in early 1856, Sumner's mail had been full of urgent letters about the ominous developments in Kansas, as antislavery settlers asked his help in recognizing the free-state government. As Sumner's correspondents told the story, the settlers in the remote frontier area were industrious, peaceable Northerners who had formed—as Sumner would later describe, perhaps naively—"an association of sincere benevolence . . . whose only fortifications are hotels, schoolhouses, and churches; whose only weapons are sawmills, tools, and books; whose mission is peace and good will." On the other hand, because the South was determined to create a new slave state once Kansas was admitted to the Union, Southern instigators had banded together "murderous robbers from Missouri" and "hirelings picked from the drunken spew and vomit of an uneasy civilization,"

In short, Sumner believed that a brutal and repressive proslavery government had been set up in Kansas with the endorsement of President Pierce—whose support disgusted Sumner—prompting Free-Soilers to establish their own government in Topeka. He feared for their safety and the future of the country. And he personally was appalled at a federal government predisposed to slavery. "The course of the Administration seems diabolic," he exclaimed in February 1856. "I have not been able to go near the Presdt." He also despaired that the turn of events in Kansas and the proslavery sentiments expressed in Washington had demoralized antislavery forces in Congress. "In the House, we are weak, in the Senate powerless," he wrote.

In March, as the Thirty-Fourth Congress began its debate on Kansas, Sumner summed up his feelings about Washington to a fellow abolitionist: "Truly—truly—this is a Godless place." In light of what appeared to be the forces of official Washington arrayed against a free Kansas, Sumner likely did not disagree when Henry P. Waters wrote to him from Topeka expressing "little reliance" on the government's ability to protect him and his neighbors. Sumner described the situation with far more urgency. Events in Kansas, he concluded, had caused the country to "shake with the first throes of civil war."

Sumner knew hours of debate lay ahead. "You will hear nothing but Kansas from this time forever," he communicated to his friend, Boston abolitionist Theodore Parker, in late February.

Later he acknowledged that he was confident Kansas eventually would be a free state, but he expected the upcoming passion play in Washington to produce debate in which "truth will be mocked and reviled."

In Sumner's view, the perversion of the truth started almost immediately. Rather than Congress offering relief to Kansas settlers for the outrages taking place in the territory, Southern fire-eaters (the Northern term for proslavery extremists) and Northern Democrats had outflanked Northern antislavery lawmakers by reducing the early debate to a critique of the Emigrant Aid Company. Were its members interfering unjustifiably in territorial affairs? If so, what should Congress do?

The Senate's Committee on Territories, chaired by Stephen Douglas, issued its *Affairs of Kansas* report on March 12, and devoted several pages to criticism of the Emigrant Aid Company for interfering in the internal affairs of Kansas and escalating the level of violence in the territory. The committee likened the interference of a Massachusetts company in Kansas—merely due to its "repugnance to domestic slavery"—to France or England doing the same thing in "Brazil or Cuba or in fifteen [slave] States of this Union." Similarly, the report argued, if one state could so blatantly influence the sovereignty of another simply because it disagreed with its laws and policy, then could not the United States interfere with "serfdom in Russia or polygamy in Turkey or any other obnoxious institution in any part of the world?" And what of foreign despots who viewed American democracy as despicably as some Massachusetts citizens viewed domestic slavery? Would they have the right to engage in a "common crusade" against America?

Sumner decried the report and the committee's strained logic, objected to the assault on the Emigrant Aid Company, and urged the North to hold protest meetings on a scale with those held two years earlier to protest the Kansas-Nebraska Act. He argued that the "slave oligarchy" would stoop to anything and stop at nothing to win the fight for Kansas; indeed, it had "staked its power in the national government" upon the territory's admittance to the union as a slave state. He implored Northerners to settle their past differences and rally together to prevent such an atrocity. "*Union to save Kansas, and Union to save ourselves*, should be the watchword," he declared.

Sumner's assessment of the South's goals for Kansas was no exaggeration. Still stung by the admission of California as a free state in 1850, but buoyed by the Kansas-Nebraska Act and President Pierce's support of slavery in Kansas, the South viewed any attempt to prevent slavery in the new territory as a direct assault on the region and its way of life. Southerners warned that any decision in favor of antislavery forces would mean the defeat of the Democrats in the 1856 November elections. One Georgia man warned his senator that if Kansas came into the Union as a free state, Southern masses would turn on their leaders in fury.

Congressman Preston Brooks and Senator Andrew Butler, both of South Carolina, the South's most ardent proslavery state (South Carolina candidates needed to own ten slaves just to run for Congress), issued warnings themselves as Congress readied to debate Kansas.

Brooks wrote a letter to a newspaper in which he first lamented that his state had not imposed a dollar-a-head tax on slaves and used the proceeds to send emigrants to Kansas. Brooks argued practically that if Kansas was to become free, the value of slaves in adjacent Missouri would drop by 50 percent. "Then abolitionism will become the prevailing sentiment. So with Arkansas; so with upper Texas." But his larger argument was far more solemn and momentous: "The admission of Kansas into the Union as a slave state is now a point of honor with the South," Brooks acknowledged. "It is my deliberate conviction that the fate of the South is to be decided with the Kansas issue."

Senator Butler, Brooks's second cousin, warned that "one drop of blood shed in civil strife" in Kansas territory "may not only dissolve this Union, but may do worse."

The stakes were so great, that at first, Charles Sumner was not sure how to proceed. Rock-solid in his antislavery convictions, his unwillingness to compromise left him less sure of what political steps he could take to bring the Kansas debate to a favorable conclusion. Fellow abolitionist Theodore Parker had urged him that the time had come "to strike a great blow. The North is ready—*if you err at all, let it be on the side of going too fast & too far*, not the other." But it was not immediately clear to Sumner exactly what form that great blow would take. It was one thing to speak forcibly, another to accomplish his goal of a free Kansas.

He sought the advice of orator, friend, and Unitarian clergyman Edward Everett Hale, who was then also vice president of the New England Emigrant Aid Company. Sumner asked Hale for a face-to-face "brief hour" conversation to discuss the numerous tentacles of the Kansas debate, whose complexity made it difficult to determine where to start. Should he ask for Congressional aid to bolster the free-state cause? How should free-state proponents handle the eventual Kansas application for statehood? What, if anything, should Congress do about the bogus proslavery legislature? Sumner was full of questions to Hale, and concluded in exasperation: "How shall these matters be dealt with? What next? Pray let me have yr counsels."

Hale crafted a cautionary and unsatisfying response to Sumner, urging him to remain patient, to "keep up a bold face" and to recognize that the Kansas issue would be decided—one way or another—within a few months. Hale was not upset at the delay in securing a government for the new territory, claiming that it was simply a matter of time, and he predicted that the question "would be settled in the valley of Kansas & not in Washington." He expected a continuance of antislavery emigration to Kansas, and fully believed that Kansas would enter the Union as a free state, pointing out that few slaveholders had actually picked up and relocated their farms or plantation operations to the territory. "No man carries any Negroes there, and you cannot make a Slave State without slaves," Hale declared to Sumner.

Frustrated by Hale's lack of outrage or even urgency on Kansas, Sumner suggested he at least respond directly to the Senate report that criticized the Emigrant Aid Company, lest "your company be gibbeted before the country as a criminal." In Sumner's opinion, Hale's calm reticence mirrored Washington's. "It is clear that this Congress will do nothing for the benefit of Kansas," he concluded. So he would do it on his own.

And he would do it with words. Sometime in late March 1856, Sumner concluded that the best way he could help Kansas—"that distant plundered territory"—was to deliver a major oration against both the Southern fire-eaters, and the Northern Democrats, the latter led by Illinois Senator Stephen Douglas, who advocated that individual states should make decisions about slavery. On March 17, Douglas had introduced legislation focused on popular sovereignty in the Kansas Territory, authorizing the people of the region to form a constitution and state government, and determine for themselves whether slavery would be permitted. New York's William Henry Seward, an antislavery senator, countered with a substitute bill that called on Congress to admit Kansas immediately as a free state.

The Congressional debate was officially under way at that point, and Sumner longed to be heard. "I shall speak on Kansas just as soon as I can fairly get the floor," he wrote to friend, physician, and abolitionist Samuel Gridley Howe, "& I believe you will be content with what I shall say."

Northern antislavery advocates welcomed Sumner's news. Since the beginning of the year, they had been waiting for him to speak out on Kansas. Sumner's acquaintance Francis Gillette said in February that he was "impatient to hear the senior Senator for Massachusetts . . . for he will let fly a bomb that will scatter confusion and terror in the hostile ranks." A Trenton, New Jersey, correspondent implored Sumner to "agitate more and more" against slavery, until the "cruel and accursed sin . . . shall never pollute another square foot of American soil." From Honolulu, Chief Justice of the Supreme Court of the Kingdom of Hawaii, William L. Lee, commended Sumner for "battling so nobly to stay the progress of human bondage!"

Once Sumner announced his decision and word circulated, advice poured in. Unlike Hale's admonitions to remain patient, most of Sumner's correspondence urged boldness. "It is time for us to show that we mean to submit to thc Southern bravado no longer," said Boston's Dr. LeBaron Russell, a member of the Emigrant Aid Company. Russell admitted that he had always felt "humiliated" with the conciliatory, even deferential, tone expressed by Northern lawmakers on the slavery debate. Up until now they had "yielded everything . . . never daring to assert their rights or exercise their true power to crush these fellows into submission." It would be up to Sumner to change that. Eli Thayer "rejoiced" that Sumner would be speaking, reminding the senator that he "had a very important mission to perform."

With this type of encouragement, in the midst of the grandest of debates, Sumner plunged into preparing his speech with a near religious fervor, determined to exchange the cloak of mere antislavery crusader for the mantle of freedom's messiah. He assured Theodore Parker that he would "use plain words" in his speech, but boasted—perhaps signaling the invective that would be contained in those words—that he intended to "pronounce the most thorough philippic ever uttered in a Legislative body."

To abolitionist William Jay, Sumner promised to "expose this whole crime at great length," and vowed to do so "without sparing language." It was a vow that would contain dire consequences for Sumner personally, and lead to an explosive thunderclap that would reverberate across the land.

Two integral and essential components of Charles Sumner's character drove his preparation for his upcoming oration—one easily defined and virtuous, the other complex and dark.

Without question, Sumner's antislavery convictions glistened with the sheen of nobility. Where others preached compromise and moderation, he never wavered in denouncing slavery's evils to all who would listen and demanding that it be wiped out of existence. Where others muttered insipid platitudes, his voice was clarion clear and strong. Where others wilted under the onslaught of political attack, he stood tall and fearless, a bulwark against the slings of Southern slaveholders who targeted him. He was beholden to no one, sought no ill-gotten gains, and had little interest in currying favor to advance his own political fortunes. By 1856, the abolition of slavery, pure and simple, was the driving force in his public life.

Yet Charles Sumner's dark side was every bit as influential in shaping and feeding his persona. Egotism and narcissism consumed him, and his sneering arrogance was well known to friend and foe alike. He cared little for the opinions or feelings of others, exhibited a coldness of heart even to his family, dripped with condescension when he issued advice, and was intolerant of criticism and nearly incapable of conciliation. As such, he had few close friends, and—in a profession that depended upon relationships—only tepid political alliances. Formally educated, brilliant in some ways, he possessed little in the way of street smarts and instinctual savvy, and was oblivious to the personal interactions often needed to lubricate the levers of power. Reaching across the political aisle was anathema to him; his opponents despised him—and even his allies found his elitism exasperating. Those who professed to like him often complained of his moody self-centeredness, and some could only spend short amounts of time around him. His lack of empathy rendered him uncomfortable around most people, awkward with most women, and clumsy in most relationships; and he was either irritatingly unaware or cruelly uncaring of how deeply his unfiltered words—his "unsparing language"—could wound. In short, the inspirational music of Sumner's antislavery message was often drowned out by the tone-deaf insolence of the messenger.

For those who knew him, these observations would come as no surprise. His great strength had been part of Charles Sumner's core personality for nearly two decades; his weakness for most of his life.

THREE

THE SPREAD OF SLAVERY

Charles Sumner was shocked, but hardly sympathetic, when he saw his first slaves in 1834 at the age of twenty-three. Fresh out of Harvard and Harvard Law School, Sumner was traveling away from Boston for the first time, and making his inaugural trip by steamboat and train, to New York, Philadelphia, and eventually, Washington D.C. He wrote breathlessly to his parents on the magnificence of modern technology and transportation, the physical vastness of the two big northeast metropolises ("Boston is but a baby compared with the size of these two places," he wrote from Philadelphia), and a "Capitol that would look proud amidst any European palaces."

It was while riding by stagecoach from Baltimore, through the "barren and cheerless country," upon the "worst roads" Sumner had ever traveled, that he spotted his first group of slaves. In the same letter in which he lamented to his parents that he wished he had brought an additional twenty dollars with him, Sumner apparently saw no irony in his belittling description of slaves, who were not only forbidden to earn or possess anything, but were owned by other men: "My worst preconception of their appearance and ignorance did not fall as low as their actual stupidity," he wrote. "They appear to be nothing more than moving masses of flesh, unendowed with any thing of intelligence above the brutes. I have now an idea of the blight upon that part of our country in which they live."

Sumner learned a great deal about politics on the trip. He attended debates in Congress and the Supreme Court, heard Henry Clay deliver a "splendid and thrilling" oration, and was introduced to a number of senators by Massachusetts' own Daniel Webster. He heard the "rugged language" of South Carolina's John C. Calhoun, who made a "strong impression" on his audience. And, the more he saw and heard, the less he liked the political maneuvering. He declared that he had little interest in pursuing politics as a profession—he would become a lawyer instead, opening a practice with a friend in 1834—and predicted he would "never come to Washington again."

Strangely, Sumner did not write home about slaves again. If the brutality of their condition affected him, if he even gave them a second thought while witnessing the American government at work in Washington, he remained silent on the subject. But clearly he began taking a deeper interest in the subject of slavery soon afterward. Sumner's father, Charles Pinckney Sumner, had strong antislavery sentiments, and though Charles and his father were not close, the elder Sumner's convictions carried some sway over his son's thinking. In 1835, young Charles denounced proslavery mob violence in the South and he began reading William Lloyd Garrison's abolitionist newspaper, *The Liberator*, the first publication to which Sumner subscribed. Sumner credited Lydia Maria Child's *An Appeal in Favor of that Class of Americans Called Africans*, first published in 1833, with convincing him of the injustice of slavery and racial discrimination during these formative years.

And he was outraged at the South's bullying tactics as it sought to discredit and silence antislavery voices. Early in 1836, South Carolina Governor George McDuffie described abolitionists who circulated antislavery literature as "wicked monsters and deluded fanatics" and advocated capital punishment because the agitators were "enemies of the human race." The twenty-five-year-old Sumner wrote that the attempts by slave-state sympathizers to "abridge discussion," the conduct of the South generally, and McDuffie's scathing remarks in particular "have caused many to think favorably of immediate emancipation who never before inclined to it."

Sumner was far from an antislavery champion in his mid-twenties, but he wrote a prescient letter to his friend Francis Lieber, then professor of political economy at South Carolina College and an antislavery sympathizer in the heart of slave country: "We are becoming abolitionists in the North fast," Charles Sumner observed.

Not fast enough, apparently, for Europeans, who watched America's ongoing slavery debate with amazement and contempt. And they let Charles Sumner know about it on his first trip to Europe in the late 1830s, a pilgrimage that accelerated his antislavery education and hardened his beliefs.

From Paris to London to Rome to Munich to Vienna, Sumner toured museums, attended university lectures, debated statesmen, dined with royalty, studied foreign languages, and, in his words, "travelled with all sorts of people, gentlemen, scholars, soldiers, priests, monks, saints & devils." And for more than two years, Europeans told him repeatedly that American slavery was a disgrace unbefitting a civilized nation.

What gave him pause—even more than the opinions of the political, social, and academic elites in his host countries—were the things Sumner saw with his own eyes. On a freezing January day in Paris ("My hair is so cold that I hesitate to touch it with my hand," Sumner wrote), he attended a lecture at the Sorbonne and spotted "two or three blacks" in the audience. Sumner was surprised that they had the "easy, jaunty air of men of fashion, who were well received by their fellow students," and even more surprised that while they were standing in the midst of their classmates, "their color seemed to be no objection" to the group. While Sumner was "glad to see this," he acknowledged that such a scenario would be unlikely in America.

It was at that moment—in France in 1838 at the age of twenty-seven—that Sumner recognized the full import of what he was witnessing and reached the conclusion that would anchor his antislavery philosophy. In his opinion, the camaraderie displayed between students of different races at the Sorbonne could only mean one thing: "that the distance between free blacks and whites among us is derived from education, and does not exist in the nature of things."

Later, in Italy, Sumner spent time near Alban Lake at the Convent of Palazzuoli, whose members included an "Abyssinian very recently arrived from the heart of Africa, whose most torrid sun had burned upon him." Nonetheless, among Italians, the man's color provoked little more than "added interest," not bigotry. Sumner observed that "it was beautiful to witness the freedom, gentleness & equality which he mingled with his brethren," a sharp contrast to the "prejudices of colour which prevail in America."

Throughout Europe, people whom Sumner admired often had strong abolitionist opinions and were not shy about expressing them. In London, the Duchess of Sutherland (whom Sumner called "the most beautiful woman in the world") was unsurpassed among English nobility in using her position to argue against American slavery. Judge and former Parliament member Lord (Thomas) Denman, a vociferous opponent of slavery and the slave trade, impressed Sumner with his strength and "justice-like countenance," and was "as honest as the stars." And in Paris, Sumner met lecturer and author Jean Charles Léonard de Sismondi, who talked "much and with great ardor of slavery." Sumner declared Sismondi a "thorough abolitionist" who was "astonished that our country will not take a lesson from the ample page of the past and eradicate slavery, as has been done in the civilized parts of Europe." Sismondi compared slaves to the serfs of the feudal system, explaining to Sumner that the system had "entirely disappeared" and English society was better for it.

By the time he returned from Europe in 1840, Charles Sumner was unequivocally convinced that American society would also be far better if slavery were abolished. And if Southern congressmen continued their "infamous bullying" of

Northern members, Sumner had an answer. "Dissolve the Union," he wrote.

Since his return to the United States, Sumner had devoted himself to what he referred to as social justice issues, including peace ("For myself, I hold all wars unjust and un-Christian"), prison reform (he was appalled that the "idiots, feeble-minded, and the insane" were herded into Massachusetts jails with hardened criminals), and—ever more firmly and powerfully—the antislavery movement. "I think slavery a sin, individual and national," he declared, "and think it the duty of each individual to cease committing it, and, of course, of each State to do likewise."

He had begun to articulate legal and constitutional arguments that focused on the equality of all men and the moral wrong of extending slavery beyond the current states that now allowed and depended on the institution, and on refuting the notion that blacks were inherently inferior and thus could not become citizens. On the latter point, Sumner questioned how those who argued in favor of black inferiority reconciled their support for the U.S. Constitution. "If it be urged that the African cannot be a citizen of the U.S., it may be asked if the Constitution was intended to apply only to the Caucasian race," Sumner concluded. "Is the Indian race also excluded? Is the Mongolian excluded?"

As for slavery itself, while Sumner personally favored its eradication, he initially argued publicly that it was a local institution—governed by local and municipal laws—that must be contained within the states that already allowed it. He argued that slavery laws only held sway in those areas in which slavery was currently legal. He added that, while the Constitution did not prohibit a state from inflicting "injustice" upon its own citizens, a state was not permitted to extend that injustice to citizens of another state. In Sumner's view, this protected free

Northern blacks anywhere in the country—the slavery issue was not unique to race, per se, but to the race within the boundaries of a particular state. "The free negro, born in Massachusetts, & still retaining his domicile there, wherever he finds himself, may invoke the protection of his native state," Sumner wrote.

Sumner believed the best way to stop slavery was to "surround the Southern States with a moral blockade," in which people in all walks of life—the "moralist, the statesman, the orator, and the poet"—all expressed their disapproval of slavery. In addition, while the national government could not constitutionally reach into a slave state to abolish the institution, it could establish antislavery laws within the District of Columbia, in territories, and as part of interstate commerce and coastal trade.

There was also one other possibility, Sumner argued, a position that would one day send a chill through slave-owners and the Southern states. "The Constitution may be amended," he wrote, "so that it shall cease to render any sanction to slavery."

Up to this point, the evolution of Sumner's beliefs and his writings were almost academic in nature—certainly important in his own development as an antislavery voice, but circulating only on the periphery of the national slavery debate. He put forth his opinions in letters to friends, associates, and newspapers, but he remained largely on the sidelines of the political battle; he was relegated even more so to spectator status when he suffered a debilitating illness due to exhaustion in 1844.

But then came Tyler's strategy—later continued by President James K. Polk after his election in 1844—to annex Texas, which would almost certainly lead to war with Mexico. Sumner viewed this as a national emergency and crisis. It violated both his antiwar and antislavery principles, and, in the words of Sumner's biographer years later, "shocked him out of his complacency and brought him actively into politics." In May 1844 a despondent Charles Sumner wrote in response to President John Tyler's plan "Folly, *dementia* & vulgar weakness now rule the country." Sumner viewed the move as nothing more than a power grab by the proslavery Tyler to extend human bondage hundreds of miles west. "By welcoming Texas as a slave state we make slavery our own original sin," Charles Sumner admonished a huge anti-

Texas crowd that had gathered at Boston's Faneuil Hall on a stormy November night in 1845. "Let us wash our hands of this great guilt."

As his views about blacks and slavery evolved, Sumner's increasing militancy often placed him at odds with Massachusetts Democrats, who depended on good relations with the South for business and trade reasons, and even with antislavery Whigs, who had eyes on the White House in 1848 and would need Southern support to be successful. Conservative Massachusetts merchants, for example, were leery of overly strident anti-Texas-annexation voices for fear of alienating Southern congressmen at precisely the time President Polk was proposing a reduction in a trade tariff that was hindering New England manufacturing.

Sumner, the political amateur, cared nothing for these arguments; for him, it was enough that the annexation of Texas was wrong. And in his Faneuil Hall speech—the first political oration of his career—he argued that to admit slaveholding Texas to the Union would implicate Massachusetts in that wrong. On that November night in 1845, he employed the rhetoric and passion that would become the hallmark of his career, language that would frighten his opponents and even cause uneasiness among his allies.

"God forbid that the votes and voices of Northern freemen should help to bind anew the fetters of the slave," he thundered. "God forbid that the lash of the slave-dealer should descend by any sanction from New England. God forbid that the blood which spurts from the lacerated, quivering flesh of the slave should soil the hem of the white garments of Massachusetts."

His pleas were in vain. In December, Texas was admitted to the Union as a slaveholding state. In April 1846, General Zachary Taylor's men, marching through territory claimed by both the United States and Mexico, were fired upon. President Polk had announced that war with Mexico was under way.

A furious Charles Sumner declared that "an unjust war is the greatest crime a nation can commit," and believed it was his duty to oppose it, "even if he stood *alone.*"

Livid over the Texas annexation and the hostilities with Mexico, Charles Sumner became consumed with the antislavery fight by the late 1840s. "In Sumner's alphabet just now there are only two words: Slavery and the Mexican war," wrote his friend George Hillard in 1847. "Business he utterly neglects and the only persons he sees with any interest are those with whom he is in communication on these points." Sumner's law practice languished and his interest in law virtually disappeared.

He continued his battles with more moderate voices from Massachusetts, joined the ardently antislavery Free-Soil Party, and campaigned for it in the 1848 elections. While the party did not win any states or a single electoral vote, Sumner found the experience satisfying, declaring that "the public mind has been stirred on the subject of slavery to depths never before reached."

Nonetheless, he again angered Massachusetts merchants when he accused Southern slaveholders and New England textile manufacturers—"the lords of the lash and the lords of the loom"—of conspiring to bring about the nomination of Zachary Taylor, a charge that alienated even Sumner's close friend Henry Wadsworth Longfellow. Sumner was undeterred, writing to his brother George that the "abuse" and "bitter attacks" he had suffered from many in Boston society were the price he paid for unwavering principles. He consoled himself by recalling the words of his friend and former president John Quincy Adams: "No man is abused whose influence is not felt."

If Texas and the Mexican War exacerbated sectional tensions in the 1840s, the first half of the 1850s sent shock waves through the North and South. Another series of stunning national events soon changed the political landscape in Massachusetts and across the country, pushed the political mainstream ever closer to Charles Sumner's point of view, and ultimately cleared the way for a man who had never held political office to be elected to the United States Senate.

Ironically, it was the incumbent U.S. Senator from Massachusetts and political legend Daniel Webster who made it all possible; the seemingly unrelated discovery of gold at Sutter's Mill in northern California in January 1848 provided the impetus.

The California Gold Rush attracted tens of thousands of intrepid fortune-seekers from Europe, Asia, Australia, South America, and the East Coast of the United States to seek riches. Thousands embarked on the grueling overland journey across the American continent, battling severe weather, starvation, bandits, Indian raiding parties, loneliness, fear, and second-guessing in their quest to reach California's rivers of gold.

By nature and definition, those who faced and overcame enormous odds on their trek, and populated California in two short years, possessed self-reliance, independence, courage, determination, and a deep reservoir of optimism and resilience—qualities that influenced their outlook and their politics. They moved quickly and decisively, virtually skipping the territory stage, ratifying a governing document, and petitioning Congress for statehood in early 1850.

But controversy swirled almost immediately, for California sought admission to the Union as a *free* state. By itself, this request would have been objectionable enough to the South, but the impact was exacerbated by simple mathematics. As Congress considered California's request, the American Union consisted of thirty states—fifteen slave and fifteen free—a delicate balance that both sides had worked to achieve. If and when California joined the Union as the thirty-first state, Northern antislavery elements—abolitionists and even moderates—would rejoice, believing that slavery's future was doomed; that the newly acquired territories of New Mexico and Utah would follow suit, that Southern power would be irreparably weakened, that slaveowners would become further isolated, and that the peculiar institution, unlikely to spread further, would eventually wither and die. Southerners believed all of the same things; thus, they viewed with a sense of foreboding the admittance of a free California.

The nation was at a crossroads. Whatever Congress did with California's petition would have profound consequences. The admittance of the far-western state threatened to shake both North and South.

With the stakes so high, the nation looked to the Senate, and three men in particular for answers: Henry Clay of Kentucky, John C. Calhoun of South Carolina, and—the senator whose remarks and opinion would generate the greatest interest among Boston's abolitionists and merchants (and Charles Sumner)—Daniel Webster of Massachusetts. The trio had worked together before on sectional compromises, and though aging (all three would be dead within two years), each commanded the respect of his colleagues and the population at large. These three giants in the Senate, men whose reputations transcended politics and defined them as statesmen, assumed familiar leadership roles in what would become the Compromise of 1850. Debate on the momentous measure began in March—Webster made a passionate and famous plea for its passage on March 7—and several components made up the compromise, including, of course, California's admittance as a free state.

One other controversial element was seen as the counterweight to the California decision, the component of the legislation that would most placate the South, shush the whispers of secession, and perhaps hold the Union together. Southern slave owners demanded it and Northern antislavery men dreaded it: a harsher and more stringent Fugitive Slave Law.

"I might call him [Daniel Webster] Judas Iscariot or Benedict Arnold," Charles Sumner wrote to his brother George in response to Webster's March 7, 1850 speech in support of the strengthened Fugitive Slave Law. "I have been glad to observe the moral indignation which has been aroused against that speech."

The tougher law mandated harsh summary enforcement over civil liberties, but, Sumner's outrage aside, Webster understood that its very strictness was the only way to ensure Southern support. He thought that even the most fervent proslavery lawmakers would recognize the new bill's good-faith concessions to Southern interests. The law would allow a slave owner or his

From left to right, Senators Henry Clay of Kentucky, John C. Calhoun of South Carolina, and Daniel Webster of Massachusetts. All three senators were instrumental in the passage of the Compromise of 1850. (*Library of Congress*)

agent to reclaim a fugitive slave by securing a warrant beforehand or arresting the runaway on the spot. The case for returning the slave to his master would be heard by a federal judge or a court-appointed federal commissioner, who would be paid ten dollars if the certificate of removal was issued, but only five dollars if the claim was denied. (Abolitionists would later decry this measure as virtually bribing the commissioner to return an individual to bondage.) No jury could be called during court proceedings, testimony from the fugitive was prohibited, and the commissioner's decision could not be appealed. Municipalities and local governments were mandated to work with slave-hunters to return runaways. Finally, the law called for stiff penalties—a $1,000 fine and up to six months in jail—for anyone aiding a fugitive or interfering with his or her return to slavery, a component that chilled and infuriated antislavery advocates.

Webster, who loved the Union as much as any man, believed the Compromise would preserve it, and agreed to support the measure regardless of the consequences he might face in the North. Above all, he thought, the Fugitive Slave Law might succeed in holding together a nation that was fraying at the seams. He was fully aware that he would anger many Northerners and that his hopes for a future presidential run would evaporate. But for him, preserving the Union outweighed any sectional loyalties.

For weeks after his speech, Webster felt the wrath of abolitionists; radicals of every type "plied a whip with scorpions," in the words of one historian. Abolitionists took him to task on the issue and vilified him personally with the venom reserved for traitors and turncoats. William Lloyd Garrison launched a petition drive to convince the Massachusetts legislature to censure the senator whose "degrading" betrayal ranked him beside Benedict Arnold. In his entire career, Garrison said no speech "had so powerfully shocked the moral sense, or so grievously insulted the intelligence of the people." Ralph Waldo Emerson spat, "The word *liberty* in the mouth of Mr. Webster sounds like the word *love* in the mouth of a courtesan." Charles Sumner spoke of "Webster's elaborate treason."

But the die had been cast. Debate continued throughout the spring and summer, but Webster's March 7 speech had put the Compromise of 1850 on a road to passage. Millard Fillmore's ascension to the presidency after President Zachary Taylor's death from typhoid fever on July 9 buoyed proponents due to Fillmore's expressed support for the Compromise.

Fillmore also chose Webster as secretary of state in his new cabinet, meaning Webster would have to resign his Senate seat; ironically, despite a final speech in support of the measure on July 17, Webster, the Compromise's most articulate and passionate defender, would not cast a final vote on its passage in early September.

On September 18, 1850, President Fillmore signed the Compromise and the Fugitive Slave Act into law. On October 2, Daniel Webster wrote: "We have now gone through the most important crisis that has occurred since the foundation of this government, and whatever party may prevail, hereafter, the Union stands firm."

Then Thomas Sims came to Boston.

FOUR

THE FUGITIVE SLAVE ACT

Twenty-three-year-old Thomas Sims, a runaway slave from Savannah, Georgia, was captured by slave-hunters in downtown Boston on April 3, 1851, imprisoned, and after court proceedings, ordered returned to slavery. In the early-morning dampness of April 12, he stood alone at the center of a "hollow square" of federal troops and Boston police, who surrounded him, and marched him to a ship moored in Boston Harbor. As the glimmer of dawn broke across the water, and a contingent of Boston abolitionists watched in shame and humiliation, Sims was ushered aboard. At just after 5:00 A.M., the vessel set sail. Boston, the birthplace of the struggle for America's liberty seventy-five years earlier, had for the first time sent a free man in the North back to slavery.

Distraught Boston abolitionists, who shared an abhorrence of slavery with Charles Sumner, were even more chagrined when word arrived from Georgia that, upon his arrival in Savannah, Sims was whipped in the public square. He was administered thirty-nine lashes across his bare back, the penalty for running away.

The Sims case shook Boston to its core. It galvanized abolitionists, transforming them from speechmakers to men and women of action, and cemented Boston's reputation nationally and internationally as a leader of antislavery activity. Perhaps even more important, the Sims case began to change the thinking of moderates, who, while wincing at the uncompromising views of radical abolitionists, were uneasy with the official legal and enforcement apparatus of their city that had returned a human being to bondage. But perhaps the most stunning sign that the Fugitive Slave Law and the Sims case had changed Boston and the Commonwealth came just two weeks after the fugitive slave's departure.

On April 24, 1851, the Massachusetts legislature, on its twenty-sixth ballot and after an exhausting political battle, elected Charles M. Sumner to the United States Senate (U.S. senators were not yet elected directly by the people). Sumner filled the vacancy left by the departed Daniel Webster, now secretary of state. The irony was not lost on Massachusetts or the nation: Webster, the consummate compromiser, had been replaced by a man who—especially on the subject of slavery—believed compromise was simply another word for weakness.

"If you could have heard the swearing, your hair would have stood on end," wrote Edmund Quincy on April 28, 1851, describing the reaction of Boston merchants and business leaders to Sumner's election. More than one hundred years later, historian Allan Nevins recounted the reaction this way: "On State Street, faces were long and scowls were black." In contrast, abolitionists celebrated with bonfires, bell ringing, cannon firing, and public meetings. With half the Massachusetts population rejoicing and half embittered at Sumner's election, it was clear that it never would have happened without the Sims episode. "The election of Charles Sumner . . . practically followed from it [Sims's misfortune]," wrote minister and abolitionist Thomas Wentworth Higginson.

Sumner traveled to Washington in November to begin his first session of Congress, one of three Free-Soil senators, a tiny minority that would face derision and ridicule for its strong antislavery views. Sumner knew the road would be difficult, and again, immodestly cast his election and his duty to serve as part of the greater good: "For myself, I do not desire public life," he wrote to his sister Julia. "I have neither taste nor ambition for it; but Providence has marked out my career, and I follow."

He was dedicated and studious, dutifully walking the mile between his lodgings and the Capitol each day, and paying close attention to debates. Ironically, Sumner became close with some Southerners, including South Carolina Senator Andrew Pickens Butler, whose seat adjoined Sumner's. Butler frequently asked Sumner to verify classical quotes that he would use in his speeches, and Sumner acknowledged, with condescension for sure, that if Butler had been "a citizen of New England [he] would have been a scholar, or at least, a well educated man."

Sumner bided his time, declining to speak on the slavery issue right away, feeling that "by strengthening myself on other subjects," he would be viewed as more than a one-issue senator, and ultimately, would stand on firmer ground when he was prepared to tackle slavery. This strategy alarmed his Massachusetts constituents, and some felt they had sent the wrong man to Washington. William Lloyd Garrison assaulted Sumner in his abolitionist *Liberator* newspaper, pointing out that after four and a half months in the Senate, Sumner had "yet to utter his first word of disapproval of slavery in general, or the Fugitive Slave Law in particular."

An annoyed Sumner felt he had nothing to prove and asserted that his antislavery credentials were as strong as any man's. He urged patience and, despite being a political neophyte, argued that his approach made the most political sense. "With pain I learn the impatience of some of my friends because I have not spoken on slavery," Sumner wrote. "This subject is always in my mind and heart, and I shall never be happy until I have expressed myself fully upon it." But, Sumner said, his silence had been "deliberate" and his plan was to speak about slavery "late—very late" in the session.

Finally, on July 27, under enormous pressure from his constituents, Sumner made a motion to repeal the Fugitive Slave

Law of 1850. But when he asked for permission to speak under Senate rules, his fellow senators denied him. South Carolina's Butler said his resolution was purely political, "merely a pretense to give him the opportunity to make an oratorical display before the Senate," and perhaps worse, "to wash deeper and deeper the channel through which flow the angry waters of agitation." Another Southern senator said Sumner's motion was "equivalent to . . . a resolution to dissolve the Union." Even Northern Democrats opposed him. Stephen Douglas said he would not extend the courtesy to speak to "any gentleman to fan the flames of discord that have so recently divided this great people."

Sumner's request to speak was denied by a vote of thirty-two to ten. It was a stunning defeat on a routine procedural vote that left Sumner "mortified and dejected." Afterward, Virginia Senator James M. Mason told Sumner: "You may speak next term." When Sumner said he must speak in the current term, Mason said: "By God, you shan't."

In August, Sumner finally did get to address his colleagues, through a circuitous parliamentary route. When a budget bill was put forth to cover the expenses of executing the Fugitive Slave Act, Sumner quickly proffered an amendment asking that the money not be appropriated and calling again for repeal of the act. Because his amendment was tied to the original bill, he was allowed to speak. He launched into his nearly four-hour "Freedom National" speech, in which he reiterated his argument that slavery was a sectional institution, but freedom was national in scope, a concept embodied in the country's founding and the Constitution, and one that epitomized the very heart and soul of America.

"Slavery . . . is not mentioned in the Constitution," he argued. "No 'positive' language gives to Congress any power to make a slave or to hunt a slave." During his speech, spectators crowded the gallery and Daniel Webster, ill and within two months of his death, also came to listen. Sumner later crowed that he, not the secretary of state, was now the spokesman for Massachusetts. In the fiery speech, Sumner spoke of the "unutterable wrong and woe of slavery," an institution "I must condemn with my whole soul." He told his colleagues that God's

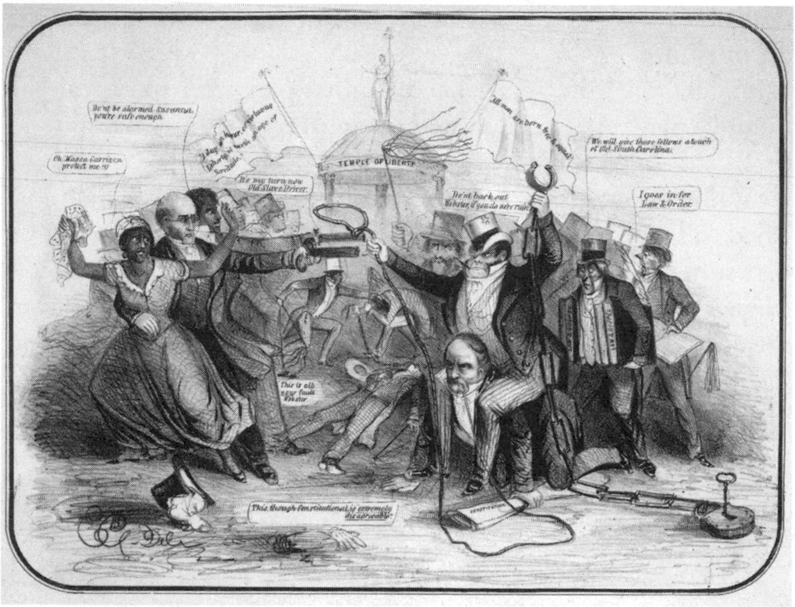

"Practical illustration of the Fugitive Slave Law," published in Boston in 1851, satirizes the antagonism between abolitionists and northern politicians who supported the enforcement of the law. Abolitionist William Lloyd Garrison is at left with a slave woman, while a slave catcher rides Daniel Webster on the right. (*Library of Congress*)

law and the Constitution made him "bound to disobey this [Fugitive Slave] Act. Never, in any capacity, can I render voluntary aid in its execution. Pains and penalties I will endure, but this great wrong I will not do." He concluded by urging his fellow senators: "Repeal this enactment. Let its terrors no longer rage through the land."

When Sumner finished, irate members responded. Stephen Douglas said Sumner was not attacking the Fugitive Slave Law, he was assaulting the Constitution. Senator John Weller of California said that while Sumner's speech was eloquent, he saw no purpose to it unless it was to incite riots in Northern states. Senator Jeremiah Clemens of Alabama urged his colleagues to simply ignore Sumner's remarks and not reply at all. "The ravings of a maniac may sometimes be dangerous, but the barking of a puppy never did any harm," he said. The Senate considered the Fugitive Slave Act a finished topic, part of a compromise designed to preserve the Union; Sumner's arguments bordered on treason.

Finally the vote was taken. Sumner's motion to repeal the Fugitive Slave Act was defeated by an overwhelming margin, 47 to 4.

While Sumner believed his speech was a triumph ("I am satisfied to labor in the cause and not in vain"), in one summer he had suffered two indignities in the U.S. Senate. First, his colleagues humiliated him by denying him permission to even speak on the slavery issue. Then, when he finally got the floor, his motion went down to a defeat perhaps more crushing than even he could have imagined. Charles Sumner would not forget either slight.

"The threats to put a bullet through my head and hang me—and mob me—have been frequent," Charles Sumner wrote in mid-June 1854. "I have always said: 'let them come: they will find me at my post.'"

Many of Sumner's utterances since his arrival in the Senate could have prompted such threats, but this reference was to a midnight speech he delivered on May 25 in opposition to the Kansas-Nebraska Act and the repeal of the Missouri Compromise, his final attempt to kill the measure. For months he had railed against it, again and again criticizing Douglas for offering it and slaveholders for adding it as the third unacceptable component in their list of sins behind the admittance of Texas as a slave state and the barbaric Fugitive Slave Act ("I will not call it 'law,'" Sumner asserted). Castigated by the South and Northern Democrats throughout the debate, Sumner was emboldened by support from Massachusetts, even the more conservative merchants and mercantile Whigs, many of whom supported the Fugitive Slave Law, but now, four years later, felt duped by what they saw as a further power grab by the slaveholding South.

In his midnight speech, "standing at the very grave of freedom in Nebraska and Kansas," Sumner welcomed Northern agitation and forewarned of future "civil strife and feud"—indeed, encouraged it—once Kansas-Nebraska became law. Predicting dire consequences from the bill, Sumner nonetheless recognized that it had set up a grand showdown between freedom's good and slavery's evils, calling the Kansas-Nebraska bill "at once the worst and best which Congress ever acted." It was the worst, for obvious reasons—it provided slave-owners with yet another victory. But, Sumner added, "it is the best bill . . . for it . . . annuls past compromises with slavery and makes all future compromises impossible. Thus it puts Freedom and Slavery face to face, and bids them grapple. Who can doubt the result?"

The next day an answer came from Boston, in a celebrated episode that Northerners interpreted as an illustration that slave-owners had gone too far and Southerners blamed on Sumner. Three years after the Thomas Sims case, Boston, unbelievably, was about to send its second runaway slave back to bondage. But reactions would be different this time around.

When runaway slave Anthony Burns was arrested in Boston on May 24, 1854, on a warrant that he had escaped a Virginia master, Boston abolitionists did more than howl in protest as they had in the Thomas Sims case. Burns's incarceration occurred during debate of the Kansas-Nebraska Act, "at the most combustible moment imaginable," one historian wrote.

On May 26, a day after Sumner's speech in Washington, militant Boston abolitionist Thomas Wentworth Higginson led a group of rioters, armed with axes, on a courthouse assault in his city. "We hammered away at the southwest door . . . before it began to give way," he wrote. A few men squeezed inside and were met by a half-dozen policemen wielding clubs, "driving us to the wall and hammering away at our heads." A shot was fired—it was impossible to say by whom—and a guard named Batchelder was killed.

Sumner's enemies blamed him for inciting the riot and for Batchelder's homicide, ignoring the fact that telegraphic reports of his speech did not reach Boston until the day after the Burns riot. They held Sumner personally responsible for what was called an assassination of an officer of the government in the discharge of his duties. One Southern newspaper charged him with "giving the command" and the "word which encourages the assassin . . . in citing his constituents to resist federal laws." The *Washington Star* accused Sumner of "counseling treason" to the country's laws and inciting "the ignorant to bloodshed and murder."

New Englanders welcomed the fight. The seizure of Burns and the attempt to intimidate Sumner had unified "the good men of all parties in a common hostility to the encroachments of the slave power." Moderate Boston merchant George Livermore was even more direct, writing to Sumner: "Let the minions of the Administration and of the slaveocracy harm one hair of your head, and they will raise a whirlwind which will sweep them to destruction."

Sumner was heartened by the support of his constituents and he paid little attention to negative newspaper coverage or Southern threats, even when Southerners insulted him in a restaurant at which he regularly dined. "The howl of the press here against me has been the best homage I ever received," he concluded. To friends who urged him to take precautions, he replied: "I am here to do my duty and shall continue to do it without regard to personal consequences."

After the unsuccessful riot to free him, runaway slave Anthony Burns remained imprisoned, and after his trial, he was marched down State Street to the docks in a route eerily similar to the one Sims had followed. This time, though, more than 50,000 Boston residents jammed the streets and rooftops on June 2, 1854, to protest Burns's return to slavery. As Burns marched toward Long Wharf, surrounded by one thousand U.S. soldiers and militiamen, the Brattle Street Church bell tolled, the crowd booed, hissed, cursed, and cried, "Kidnappers, Kidnappers." Black bunting draped office buildings in Boston's mercantile and financial districts, and the accompanying symbolic props were telling. From one building a coffin was suspended with the word "Liberty" printed on its side; at the

Merchants Exchange, a petition calling for the repeal of the Fugitive Slave Law was signed by many of Boston's commercial elite, proving that "the most solid men of Boston . . . are fast falling into the ranks of freedom," abolitionist Theodore Parker wrote. Indeed, many Webster Whigs, among the strongest pro-Union voices in the country, felt betrayed by the South. Yes, they had commercial interests and economic ties to consider, but most found both slavery and the Fugitive Slave Law distasteful.

An 1855 poster featuring a portrait of Anthony Burns surrounded by events in his life, including (clockwise from lower left) his sale at auction, his arrest in Boston, his departure from Boston under escort by federal marshals, and his imprisonment. (*Library of Congress*)

Now, Kansas-Nebraska was another bitter pill to swallow—perhaps the South had overstepped. Merchant Amos Lawrence wrote on the impact of the Burns case: "We went to bed one night, old fashioned, conservative, compromise Union Whigs and waked up stark mad Abolitionists."

For Sumner, the Burns episode, which made him feel "humbled in the dust," along with final passage of the Kansas-Nebraska Act, and the Southern threats simply fortified his desire to renew his war on slavery. He planned to again demand the repeal of the Fugitive Slave Act and seek "the complete annulling by the North of all other compromises" on the odious institution. He promised Theodore Parker: "Slavery will be discussed with us as *never before*."

"I find myself a popular man," Charles Sumner wrote upon his return to Boston in the late summer of 1854. "If my election to the Senate were now pending before the million [*sic*] of educated people whom I now represent, I should be returned without any opposition."

He had battled hard throughout the final debate on the Kansas-Nebraska bill. In June, he launched into a fresh and ferocious debate on slavery when, in the wake of the Burns case, nearly three thousand Massachusetts citizens petitioned Congress for the repeal of the Fugitive Slave Law. He said he would never support it, again prompting Southern retorts that he refused to uphold the constitution. "I recognize no obligation in the Constitution of the United States to bind me to help to reduce a man to slavery," he retorted during debate. They labeled him a fanatic, a charge he welcomed, saying Bostonians were familiar with the label. "It is the same which opposed the execution of the Stamp Act, and finally secured its repeal; it is the same which opposed the Tea-tax; it is the fanaticism which finally triumphed on Bunker Hill." When another Southerner said Boston was filled with traitors, Sumner said the charge was nothing new. "Boston of old was the home of Hancock and Adams. Her traitors now are those who are truly animated by the spirit of the American Revolution."

During the debate over the Massachusetts petition, Sumner spoke in bitter personal language, intending from the outset to be "as severe as the overseer's lash." He singled out South Carolina's Butler and Virginia's Mason for special treatment, rebuking their "plantation manners" and claiming both men viewed the United States Senate not as an august body, but as a "plantation, well stocked with slaves, over which the lash of the overseer has full sway." Furious Southern senators explored the possibility of expelling Sumner for perjury and treason, but realized they could not gather the votes.

Sumner attained new stature during the summer of 1854. He proved to his supporters that he was more than an intellectual; he could fight back and stand tall against criticism, even when outnumbered. "You have done gallantly," his friend Richard Henry Dana wrote. "You don't know how rejoiced I am that a Northern gentlemen and scholar has met them in the true spirit of a cavalier." Sumner returned to Massachusetts with new purpose.

He was further buoyed in September when he addressed the regular nominating convention of the new Republican Party, an antislavery coalition of former Free-Soilers, Whigs, and even some Democrats. He blasted the national proslavery administration, branded the Kansas-Nebraska Act as an atrocity, and said federal authorities had shamelessly run roughshod over the law and Boston in the Burns case; the courthouse was guarded by a "prostituted militia" who saw that the "precious sentiments, the religion, the pride of glory of Massachusetts were trampled in the dust." He viewed the new Republican Party, fledgling though it was, as the only antidote to the slave power, arguing that neither Democrats nor Whigs could effectively carry on the fight, especially against the "unutterable atrocity" that was the Fugitive Slave Act.

He was greeted with a thunderous ovation from the immense throng and was triumphant at the response, though Sumner's elation may have been premature. The Republican Party had few followers and would not be a real factor in Massachusetts politics for close to two years. For now, though, what it lacked in numbers and political clout, it made up for in enthusiasm. "The people were tired of the old parties & they have made a new channel," he wrote.

Charles Sumner himself would eventually be responsible for the growth of the Republicans on a national scale, though neither he nor anyone else could ever have predicted how.

Twenty years after he had seen his first slaves, Charles Sumner had become the nation's strongest, clearest, and most resolute antislavery champion. He had started his Senate career as a mere thorn in the side of Southern slaveholders; by 1855, he had emerged as their most formidable and dangerous opponent.

At the same time, Sumner helped lead and now represented the mood shift that had occurred in Massachusetts in five short years. Once solidly moderate and governed quietly by its State Street merchant and business interests, once tolerant but suspicious of abolitionists, once opposed to the *extension* of slavery but ambivalent about its continued existence in its current locations, Massachusetts had moved closer to Sumner. Webster's political pandering, the constant bullying by slaveholders, the sordid Sims and Burns cases, the threats against Sumner, and Douglas's opportunism in proposing the Kansas-Nebraska law—all conspired to spread the seeds of abolitionism across a much broader swath of a state that considered itself the birthplace of liberty and freedom.

Abolitionism still was not the mainstream philosophy in Massachusetts, but it would not take much to make it so. Southerners now correctly identified Sumner and Massachusetts as the twin pillars supporting activist antislavery sentiment throughout the North.

If Southerners felt contempt for Sumner the antislavery activist, they also despised Sumner the man. His acerbic language, his air of superiority, and his rudeness all rankled Southern sensibilities and violated the Southern code of how a gentleman should behave. It was not only what Sumner said that infuriated the South, but *how* he said it. Debate was expected and acceptable—personal insults were not. These irritating character traits that had shaped Sumner's personality for years made him more than a political target. They made him an enemy.

FIVE

THE MAKING OF CHARLES SUMNER

If psychoanalysis had been part of the American vocabulary in 1811, it would be easy to conclude that Charles Sumner's difficulties empathizing with and relating to others could be traced almost literally to the day he was born.

On January 6 of that year, Charles and his twin sister, Matilda, entered the world prematurely, struggling to survive, each weighing barely three and a half pounds. They were the eldest of the nine children who would eventually be born to Charles Pinckney and Relief Jacob Sumner of Boston. Charles was nursed by his mother, but Matilda was turned over to a nurse's care.

Relief Sumner's decision to separate the children appeared to have long-standing consequences; Charles and Matilda were not close and never shared the deep and inexplicable bond that is so often associated with twins. Sumner barely mentions Matilda in any of his writings, and when she died at age twenty-one from tuberculosis after a year's illness, her twin brother, who wrote fiery letters expressing his outrage on many topics, reacted with only cool detachment. "My grief, whatever it may be, has not the source that yours has," he wrote to a college chum who had expressed sympathy. "I have lost a sister; but I still have other sisters and brothers, entitled to my instructions and protection. I strive to forget my loss in an increased regard for the living."

Sumner explained to another friend that his understanding of his sister's disease was that it carried "no decided pain," and that it often deceived its victims into believing they may regain their health. He admitted that he was not sure whether Matilda felt this way—he never asked her and "she seemed as studiously to avoid" the topic. Sumner described his normally cool and reserved father as greatly distressed over Matilda's passing ("More than once I saw tears steal from his eyes"), and his mother as "dejected and comfortless," but young Charles expressed no such emotions, saying simply: "She is now beyond the show of my affection and regard." Almost inconceivably, in the same letter in which he dismissed his friend's sympathy over Matilda's death, Sumner declared himself in excellent health. "I never was better," he wrote.

His feelings toward his twin sister carried over to most of the rest of his family. Sumner grew up in a loveless home, raised by a stoic, distracted mother who was unable to express affection (it was not until after her death that Sumner learned that she had kept a lock of his baby hair), and a rigid, demanding father who tolerated little in the way of mistakes or underachievement. Sumner resented his younger brothers, whom he viewed as rivals for his father's affection, and determined that most of his sisters were incapable of making decisions or getting through daily life without his wise counsel. Sumner's unhappy home experience and lack of emotional ties to his family, manifested primarily by his inability to please his father, had a profound impact on his behavior throughout his life. His unpleasant family situation laid the foundation for his self-centeredness, his paranoia, his often desperate desire for praise, his lack of empathy and concern for the feelings of others, his inability to employ humor and self-effacement, and his eagerness to wear the martyr's mantle. These characteristics contributed to irrational petulance in many of his relationships, a reflexive intolerance for criticism or opinions that differed from his own, and a deep need to resort to invective in his speeches and writings—he was either oblivious to, or uncaring about, the wounding power of his venomous words.

The aloofness and lack of affection that marked Sumner's relationship with his family deeply influenced his interaction with others and ultimately had an enormous impact on the nation.

"I have a son, named Charles Sumner, in his fifteenth year, and large of his age, but not of so firm and solid a constitution as I should wish him to have," Charles Pinckney Sumner wrote to Captain Alden Partridge, commander of the American Literary, Scientific, and Military Academy in Middletown, Connecticut. Although young Charles had good grades, at the time his father could not afford to send him to college, and, he stressed to Captain Partridge, "The life of a scholar would be too sedentary and inactive for him."

It was clear early that Charles Pinckney had questions about his son's ability to transition to manhood. Despite his strong academic performance at Boston Latin School, young Charles was uncoordinated and had no interest in sports or games. Boys nicknamed him "Gawky Sumner" and a friend later pointed out that he "never, so far as I know, fished or shot or rowed; he had no fancy for dogs and horses; and in a word, was without all those tastes which are almost universal with men of his age."

Maturity and accomplishment were paramount in his father's eyes. The Sumners could trace their Massachusetts lineage to the 1630s and they took great pride in their deep roots and their contributions to the commonwealth. Charles Pinckney did not demand so much of his other sons; but Charles, bearing his father's name, carried a special burden to uphold the family's reputation. "Charles," his father said, "upon your discretion and good deportment the happiness of my life will in no trifling measure depend. If any persons entertain a favorable opinion of you, I hope you will never disappoint them." Young Charles resented his father for setting this impossible goal.

Charles Pinckney's fortunes improved when he became sheriff of Suffolk County, a position that paid more than $2,000 a year, and he was able to send young Charles to Harvard. Despite the fact that Charles had vacated his father's Beacon Hill home to study in Cambridge, the elder Sumner did not let up on his son. He wrote a long send-off letter to Charles urging him to "preserve . . . a good character [and] associate with those who have it; shun those who have no good character of their own." He required Sumner to report every week on what happened at school and kept meticulous watch of his son's expenses. Anything less than perfection was unacceptable. One of Sumner's biographers points out that, despite young Charles's absence for only three of 580 classes and chapel exercises during his first year of school—a remarkable attendance record—his father was far from impressed. "It is of little avail to have expensive and learned professorships established at college if a scholar does not devote his whole times to the duties prescribed," Charles Pinckney admonished his son.

Charles Pinckney wanted his son to achieve an exalted and perhaps impossible well-roundedness. The elder Sumner loved the scholarly life, but as the son of a Revolutionary War hero himself, he also wanted young Charles to excel physically and attain the proud bearing and strength of character that military training often produces. When Charles paid a visit to West Point during a Harvard recess, his father wrote a letter of introduction to the commander of the military academy in which he lamented that his son was "somewhat deficient in strength." Without a doubt, Charles Pinckney wrote, had Sumner been under the commander's tutelage for the past three years that he spent under "mere literary men," his son would now be "as strong as a soldier of Bonaparte."

Even after he graduated from Harvard and contemplated his future course in life, Charles complained to a friend that his father offered "nought by way of encouragement. He seems determined to let me shape my own course, so that if I am wise, I shall be wise for myself; and if I am foolish, I alone shall bear it." Expressing his gratefulness for his friend's support, Charles contrasted that with his own family's lack of interest in his future fortunes, which left him "despondent." When Charles went to Europe later, he made a point of not corresponding with his father. "Where Charles is now and what his designs [are] I am ignorant," Charles Pinckney confessed in 1839.

To compensate for his inability to please his father, Charles Sumner sought the company and mentoring of other men who were contemporaries of his father—former president John Quincy Adams; Joseph Story, at various times speaker of the Massachusetts House, Supreme Court Justice, and Harvard law professor; and Unitarian reformer William Ellery Channing. It was under their tutelage that Sumner gained self-confidence, honed his ideas, and entered the world of Boston's elite. Story, especially, was everything Sumner's father was not—warm, affectionate, complimentary. It is telling that Sumner, who does not mention his father in his autobiography, writes of Story: "Who could forget his bounding step, his contagious laugh, his exhilarating voice, his beaming smile, his countenance that shone like a benediction?" Sumner remembered Story as a man "whose face was never turned to me, except in affection." When Story died, Sumner wrote that the loss created "a chasm which I shrink from contemplating."

Sumner's own father's death created no such chasm. Charles Pinckney raised a son who feared making mistakes, desperately needed the acceptance of other men, and craved public attention and affirmation, all in response to a dreary upbringing and an iron rule at home. When Charles Pinckney died in April 1839, at the age of sixty-three, it was almost a relief to his son. Young Charles was traveling in Europe and opted not to return from Rome, "for I do not see any particular thing in which I could be useful." To his friend George Hillard, he admitted that his father's death "has caused me many painful emotions—not the less painful because [it is] beyond the reach of ordinary sympathy." Hillard knew of Sumner's strained relationship with his father, which prompted Charles to add: "To you . . . I need say nothing." To another sympathizer, he wrote: "I cannot affect to feel entirely the grief that others have on such a bereavement." Nonetheless, his father's death—indeed, the memory of their relationship—was a source of "unfeigned sorrow" to Sumner, "[which] has thrown a shadow across my Italian pleasures."

Other friends tried to reassure him. "You were a good son," wrote Francis Lieber in his condolence letter. Henry R. Cleveland, who knew all the circumstances of Sumner's home life, added frankly, "That your duty to him was fully done must now be a source of infinite satisfaction."

And then Cleveland added a brutally honest assessment that even Sumner may have been afraid to state: "What your father has been to you, you have not disguised from me." Thus, it was not surprising that Sumner was "not as deeply afflicted by his death as you would have been if he had been like a father to you."

Charles Sumner's personal travails started with his father but did not end there. His relationships with virtually all of his siblings were marred by clumsiness and coldness for most of their lives. With one exception—his sister Mary—Sumner constantly and alternately lectured, admonished, tolerated, or outright ignored his siblings. Often he was as domineering as his father, reproaching his brothers and sisters for what he perceived as their shortcomings and lack of discipline. He did not include them in important moments in his life, made scant references to any of them in his autobiography, and penned letters to them that were professorial, preachy, condescending, and tedious. For all but Mary, he had little to say when his siblings died, and when he did mention them—as he did when Matilda passed—his words carried either the impersonal musings of the philosopher or the arm's length observation of a stranger. Expressing love was a rarity for Charles Sumner.

Occasionally, he seemed to recognize his shortcomings and his inability to correct them. On his first trip to Washington, D.C., he wrote a letter to twelve-year-old Mary. After a particularly lengthy and dense recap of his day ("I have found time to read an able work . . . and to run my eyes through a law book, and to prepare a law-argument of four pages"), Sumner finally seems to realize that the letter's content was not suitable for his young sister. "My dear Mary, I am ashamed of addressing such a letter as the above to you," he concluded. "It contains nothing,

I feel, adapted to your age, and should rather be addressed to father." After a similar missive to fourteen-year-old Jane, he wrote: "Pardon the above dissertation."

A youthful portrait of Charles Sumner at the Frederick Douglass House in Washington, DC. (*Library of Congress*)

Sumner was full of weighty advice for his young siblings, too. In the same letter from Washington, he urged Jane to study Latin to "discipline your mind," and read books that will become "constant friends to relieve you from lonesomeness and perhaps sorrow." He pointed out that his advice in the letter consisted of "incoherent hints," and offered—in a gesture that must have frightened his young sister—to "expand them into a treatise." Five years later, he wrote to his fourteen-year-old brother, Horace, from London and acknowledged that he simply couldn't resist imparting mundane advice and exhorting the young man to study hard. "You will, I fear, think me a dull preacher, and will dread my letters as much as the minister's sermon," he wrote, "but I cannot take my pen to write any of you without, forthwith, falling into this vein." While Horace might find his older brother's words "irksome" at this point in his life, Sumner was sure that "if we both live, you will thank me hereafter."

Nor did things change much as the years passed. Sumner's brother George, who traveled to Russia and Europe extensively and at one point did not see Charles for fifteen years, nevertheless could not escape his older brother's incessant advice and nitpicking. After George announced that he planned to write a book about his travel adventures, Charles launched into a torrent of suggestions and asserted smugly: "I shall criticize you in order to save you from the criticism of others." He urged his brother to "study your subject thoroughly" and suggested that he think long and hard before he put words to paper: "You may imagine that you have the subject well digested in your mind.

Believe me, you will see it more clearly two years from now." He admonished George for using the word "swill" in a letter instead of "dirt," warning him against using such crass words and reminding him that a "pure and undefiled English style" could only be achieved from conversing with the best authors and "considerable practice."

As for his travel habits, Charles reminded George to "engage an instructor" to learn the language of the country he was visiting, to change his shirt once a day on the European continent ("every day should be clean-shirt day"), and to bathe "once or twice a week or oftener." When George announced that he would be visiting France and England, Charles confided to a friend that, brother or not, he would not introduce George to his acquaintances in those countries "unless I feel assured that he is *entirely presentable*."

All of his advice, Sumner assured George, was "written in a brotherly spirit of love" and was not meant to insult or hurt. Perhaps realizing that his words could be construed as overly harsh, Sumner added: "I wish I could talk with you for one half-day; I could explain my views . . . in a way that should avoid mistake."

Occasionally, a sibling hinted that Charles's constant pillorying and his inability to show affection might actually have masked his true feelings. His sister Julia said: "There was a world of love and tenderness within him—often hidden under a cold exterior, or apparently crusted over with a chilling coat of reserve."

At no time was Sumner's chilling reserve more apparent than on the occasions of most of his siblings' deaths. His unemotional response to his twin Matilda's demise notwithstanding, at least he acknowledged it. But when his sister Jane died in 1837 at age seventeen from typhoid, Sumner was excitedly preparing to sail for Europe and mentioned nothing about the loss. He feuded with his brother, Henry, for years and remained silent upon his death in 1852, even as the sectional debate over slavery was heating up. In November 1856 (as Sumner was attempting to recover from his beating by Preston Brooks), Charles did not comment when his brother Albert, his wife, and their only daughter, Catherine, age fourteen, were killed in a tragic shipwreck sixty miles from Nantucket Light.

Earlier, his brother, Horace, died in a separate shipwreck off Fire Island in New York in 1850, and Sumner did offer comment, but again found it difficult to express sympathy. Horace, who had been an invalid for much of his life, was returning from a trip he had taken to Italy in an effort to restore his health. His ship, the *Elizabeth*, ran aground and broke up—Horace tried to swim ashore and was never seen again. Charles told his friend, Samuel Gridley Howe, that Horace was returning to America "full of hope" and that his mother and sister Julia were anxiously awaiting his return and his stories. Sumner recounted the feelings of both women, but again, remained guarded about his own thoughts: "To them especially it is a bitter thing to lose him," Sumner said. "All who knew him speak warmly of his gentle, loving & utterly unselfish nature." Julia was Horace's constant companion—the two attended concerts and went horseback riding together—and Charles admitted he could not find the words to console his sister. "I feel painfully my own inability to supply her loss, by sympathy or companionship."

Surprising, given his lack of relationship with Horace, Sumner did visit the site of the shipwreck, and walked the beach, which was "strewn for miles with fragments of the wreck." Sumner said that because of the "rage" of the sea in the area, it seemed "unreasonable to expect" that his brother's body would ever be found. "My brother was an invalid, & has passed away from a life of suffering," was all Sumner could reveal of his own feelings.

The one exception to Sumner's unemotional reactions to his siblings' deaths was the deep sadness that consumed him when Mary died of tuberculosis in October 1844 at the age of twenty-two. Mary's demise was long and painful, and as the end neared, the thirty-three-year-old Charles—suffering his own emotional and physical breakdown from exhaustion—was bedridden in the room adjacent to his terminally ill sister. Some believed Charles was near death, too; his closest friends, George

Hillard, Henry Wadsworth Longfellow, and Cornelius Felton, who visited Charles, were shocked when he made a full recovery.

Whether it was Mary's inherent gentleness, her long illness, or Charles's witnessing of her daily suffering even as he recovered from his illness, she was the only member of the family with whom Charles developed a deep attachment. He was devastated when she died. "I had long expected this blow," he wrote, "but no preparation could render it other than bitter." No other death, before or after, affected him so deeply. "I dwell often on the image of her beauty, of her sweet nature, and of her most serene soul," he wrote a few months after her funeral.

The normally staid, cool, self-centered Charles Sumner even admitted he would have traded places with Mary. "I feel that it would have been far better had the health, which was unexpectedly renewed in my veins, been bestowed upon her in my stead," he wrote.

It was the one time Charles Sumner expressed unconditional love for a family member.

Charles Sumner's friends—and he had many, especially in his younger days—were also familiar with his brooding, self-righteous, and introverted manner.

They enjoyed discussing politics and issues with him, but worried about his inability to relax and engage in pleasant conversation. "Though he was an interesting talker, he had no lightness of hand," William Story wrote, pointing out that Sumner was "totally put off his balance" by good-natured banter, and when friends tried to joke with him "his expression was one of total astonishment." He had no sense of humor "and little sense of it in others." Indeed, Story said, during verbal jousting with his companions, Sumner was "never ready [with] a retort, tacked slowly, like a frigate" and was "almost impervious to a joke."

Dr. Oliver Wendell Holmes described Sumner as "pleasant, affable, and cheerful," but added he had "little imagination, wit, or sense of humor." Holmes recalled that Sumner's group of friends teased him about his inability to enjoy or even recognize mirthfulness, joking that "if one told Charles Sumner that the moon was made of green cheese, he would controvert the alleged fact in all sincerity, and give good reasons why it could not be so."

With women, especially, Sumner exhibited great awkwardness. His dark, wavy hair and rugged good looks were more than offset by his dourness and insecurity. Strong, intelligent women intimidated him, yet because of his social standing, this was precisely the type of potential wife he was expected to pursue. He had grown up in a home in which letting down his guard was a sign of vulnerability, and this extended to his relationship with women—fear of rejection and humiliation accompanied him his entire life. Julia Ward, who later married Sumner's friend, Samuel Gridley Howe, claimed Charles had "no heart." An indignant Sumner protested: "I have a heart—it is not my fault if all its throbbing had been in vain." Holmes declared that Sumner was "less at ease with women" than with men. Once at a social gathering, his friends noticed him talking uneasily to an attractive woman and wagered how long it would take for Sumner to turn away and revert to his more comfortable surroundings—talking to men. They roared with laughter when it happened in a matter of minutes. Frustrated with his own lack of success in dealing with women, Sumner exclaimed: "I would walk on foot around the earth to find a woman who would love me with . . . truth."

Perhaps women sensed Sumner's self-centeredness more acutely than his male friends. In the matter of relationships, even when they did not involve him directly, Sumner made his own feelings paramount. When Howe announced he would marry Julia Ward in 1843, Sumner's primary emotion was not happiness for the couple, but despair for himself. He wailed: "I am *alone—alone*. . . . My friends fall away from me. I lead a joyless life, with very little sympathy. What then will become of me?" When Henry Wadsworth Longfellow announced his impending marriage the same year, Sumner was distraught; the two men had shared long conversations and spent hours in each other's company. "What shall I do these long summer evenings?" Sumner wondered to Longfellow. "Howe has gone . . . now you have gone, and nobody is left with whom I can have sweet sympathy." Taking pity on Sumner, Longfellow and his wife, Fanny (Appleton), allowed Sumner to accompany them on their honeymoon to the Catskills.

As Sumner struggled with all of these relationships, he continued to express an acute sense of loneliness, and he increasingly adopted and relished the martyr's role of standing alone against perceived injustices, personal and public. Both his narcissistic tendencies and his position on issues hardened, and the personal nature of his public utterances became more intense. Upon his return from Europe, and throughout the 1840s, he was more convinced than ever of his rightness on the slavery issue—and on virtually everything else. He was defined by his grandiose self-image, his desire for recognition, and his harsh response to almost any criticism. "Once Sumner suspected a slight," biographer David Donald wrote, "he magnified every occurrence, real or fancied, into an assault."

Sumner's aggressive personal attacks on public figures first occurred in the mid-1840s. During debates about the condition and methods of Boston's prison system, Sumner launched into several diatribes against Louis Dwight, secretary of the Boston Prison Discipline Society. Rather than simply disagreeing with Dwight's positions, Sumner angrily denounced Dwight's reports as "lies" and "willful and unwarrantable perversions of the truth." Later he described Dwight as lazy, inefficient, and extravagant, and publicly denounced one Dwight-authored report on the Boston prison system as "flimsy" and a waste of money. Waving the pages of Dwight's report above his head during a meeting, Sumner said, "Our three thousand dollars have been wrapt here as in a napkin."

Dwight battled back, but he was no match for Sumner and the public ridicule took its toll; the prison administrator suffered a nervous breakdown, though he remained secretary until his death in 1854. For his part, Sumner believed he had contributed to the overall improvement of the penal system by pointing out the flaws in Dwight's leadership. He also showed no sympathy for Dwight's emotional condition, informing his brother George, "Mr. Dwight, the secretary, has become insane, whether incurably so or not, I do not know."

Members of Boston society, including influential leaders on Beacon Hill, were shocked at Sumner's intemperate attitude and vituperative language. Some stopped speaking to him. Others were mystified that he chose anger and personal insults as his debate weapons. His actions against Dwight cost Sumner a chair at Harvard Law School; in the opinion of the scholar who got the job, the conservative Corporation of Harvard College "consider Sumner in the Law-school, as unsuitable as a Bull in a china shop."

Sumner next felt the full brunt of Boston society's alienation when he trained his sights and his scalding tongue on respected Massachusetts Congressman Robert C. Winthrop after the representative voted in favor of the Mexican War in 1846. An apoplectic Sumner described Winthrop's action as "*the worst act that was ever done by a Boston representative.*" Sumner said the congressman's actions could not be "forgotten on Earth [and] must be remembered in heaven." Comparing Winthrop to a modern Pontius Pilate, he added: "Blood! blood! is on the hands of the representative from Boston. Not all great Neptune's ocean can wash them clean!"

An angry Winthrop responded with a letter that terminated relations with Sumner for the next sixteen years. He declared that Sumner's words were full of "the grossest perversions" because they attacked not just Winthrop's actions but his integrity. Winthrop was hurt on a visceral level, and believed it "inconceivable" that a man who had professed to be his friend "should turn upon me with such ferocity, denounce me so publicly and grossly, and pursue me with such relentless malignancy." Entirely unaware of the power of his own words, Sumner was surprised by Winthrop's angry reaction.

Again, much of Boston, including most of his close friends, turned against Sumner after the personal vitriol he exhibited against Winthrop. His friend Cornelius Felton ventured that

Sumner was becoming so intolerant that he believed the "difference from his opinions can only proceed from a bad head or a corrupt heart." Sumner was totally alone. "There was a time when I was welcome at almost every house within two miles of us," he remarked while riding down Beacon Street in Boston. "But now hardly any are open to me." One member of Boston's wealthy elite who knew Sumner said: "His solitude is glacial. He had nothing but himself to think about." Despite his isolation, Sumner interpreted his condition as a type of social martyrdom, the price to pay for the sake of adhering to principle. He derived enormous satisfaction from "doing his duty."

Sumner continued his ways as the 1850s began, eviscerating Daniel Webster and branding him a "traitor" for his role in the Compromise of 1850. After his election to the Senate, Sumner had an argument about slavery with his friend, Francis Lieber, while Lieber was teaching in South Carolina. Sumner blasted Lieber for his views on the subject at hand, but he did not stop there. He accused his old friend of becoming "the apologist of slavery." Incensed and hurt, Lieber had to remind himself that "Sumner uses words as boys do stones," to "break windows and knock down flowerpots, while he all the time plays the offended." As if to prove Lieber's point, in 1853, Sumner called the Congress of which he was a member "the worst—or rather it promises to be the worst—since the Constitution was adopted. It is the Devil's own."

None of this ferocious language or personal bitterness was accidental. Sumner intensified it during the rancorous debate over the Kansas-Nebraska Act, often citing his intentions to shock his opponents with the sharpness of his words. He could never admit that he was wrong or that his tactics were mistaken. In his view, his critics almost always demonstrated poor judgment. Nor could he grasp why they would take offense to criticism that questioned their moral character, their virtue, or their integrity.

As storm clouds gathered over Kansas during the winter and spring of 1856, Sumner's personal attacks continued, particularly against Southern leaders. "Bleeding Kansas" became his rallying cry and he blamed the slave oligarchy for spilling that blood. He expressed utter disdain for the South, especially South Carolina, the staunchest of the slaveholding states. During his preparation of "The Crime Against Kansas" speech, he planned all along to pepper his arguments with personal attacks as a way to call attention to his larger themes. Aside from pointing out the injustices taking place in Kansas, he could not resist insulting his opponents, believing it was necessary to "say something of a general character, *not belonging to the argument*, in response to Senators who have raised themselves to eminence on this floor in championship of human wrongs."

As Senator Charles Sumner approached the biggest speech of his career in May 1856, his attitude of superiority, his need to render judgment, antagonized and infuriated the South and even irritated most of his Northern colleagues. As historian Allan Nevins would write years later, by the spring of 1856, Sumner's arrogance had cloaked him with the unofficial but nonetheless befitting title of "the best-hated man in the chamber."

All that was missing when Charles Sumner entered the Senate chamber on May 19, 1856, was a fanfare of trumpets. The throngs awaiting his words, the intense heat, the grand stage, the sectional tension, the magnitude of the moment, the nation's eyes upon him—all of this lent a drama that suited Sumner's thirst for attention and his irresistible desire to preach and moralize to the masses, all in the name of their enlightenment. He felt the occasion was "the greatest . . . that has ever occurred in our history," a categorization that presumably referred to the future of slavery and the events swirling in Kansas, but likely also served as a less than subtle reference that *he* would be addressing these issues.

As always, Sumner was prepared. He laboriously wrote out his speech, which, in printed form, would span 112 pages; his remarks were being set in type on the day of his speech and printed copies would be available within a couple of days. As was his custom, he committed the speech to memory, practicing for hours on end, so he could speak without referring to the text. Senator Stephen Douglas later mocked Sumner's theatrics, saying his Massachusetts colleague had "his speech written, printed, committed to memory, practiced every night before the glass with a Negro boy to hold the candle and watch the gestures, and annoying the boarders in their neighboring rooms until they were forced to quit the house!"

Douglas may have been exaggerating, but Sumner did practice in front of New York Senator William Henry Seward and his wife, Frances, forcing them to sit through the entire address—ostensibly to get their advice, but more likely to provide Sumner with a live audience. Frances Steward strongly advised Sumner to remove the stinging personal attacks in the speech, and her husband disapproved of his "gratuitous assault against the honor of South Carolina."

Sumner ignored them both. Two decades of hardening antislavery views coupled with a lifetime of ignoring the feelings of others left little doubt about his course of action. He had promised "unsparing language," and he would deliver. Violence on the plains, high drama in Washington, acrimony between North and South. It was upon this canvas that Charles Sumner prepared to apply slashing and scarring brushstrokes, designed to enrage and inflame, setting in motion a series of events that ultimately would lead America to the edge of the abyss.

At one o'clock in the afternoon, in a packed and stifling Senate chamber, Charles Sumner of Massachusetts rose to denounce and demand redress for "The Crime Against Kansas."

SIX

THE CRIME AGAINST KANSAS

A profound occasion and a dramatic setting called for a powerful opening and Sumner did not disappoint. "A crime has been committed," he began, "which is without example in the records of the past. . . . It is the rape of a virgin territory, compelling it to the hateful embrace of slavery." Only a handful of Senators were absent (the ailing Butler of South Carolina was one of them); the rest listened intently as Sumner promised to strip bare the proslavery conspiracy against Kansas in all its brutality, without, in the words of one correspondent, "a single rag, or fig-leaf, to cover its vileness."

Sumner's speech would cover a total of five hours over two days—three hours on the first day—and one New York antislavery correspondent described him as "animated and glowing throughout, hurling defiance among the opposition, and bravely denouncing the Kansas swindle from first to last." Without doubt, in that writer's view, some of Sumner's passages "electrified the Chamber, and gave a new conception of the man."

Sumner's vitriolic opening castigated the slave power and its crime against Kansas, "a wickedness which I now expose," fueled not simply by any "common lust for power," but rather "in the hope of adding to the power of slavery in the National Government." Sumner charged that the power employed by proslavery forces "compelling Kansas to this pollution, all for the sake of political power" represented, again, "an essential wickedness that makes other public crimes seem like virtues."

Indeed, Sumner argued to his colleagues, the violence perpetrated by proslavery men in Kansas had forced the citizens of Lawrence to arm themselves before they slept, and despite the bitter winter, deploy "sentinels" to keep watch at night against surprise attacks. "Murder has stalked—assassination has skulked in the tall grass of the prairie," he said. Worse, this violence was originating outside of Kansas, imposed by men who relied on brute force to accomplish their lawless ends because they could not achieve their goals peaceably. The Kansas violence had brought the entire nation to the brink, Sumner contended. "The strife is no longer local, but national," he warned. "Even now, while I speak, portents lower in the horizon, threatening to darken the land, which already palpitates with the mutterings of civil war."

For the rest of his oration on Monday, Sumner outlined the four "Crimes Against Kansas" and the four apologies offered for the crimes by their perpetrators. The first crime was the passage of the Kansas-Nebraska Act—a "swindle" in Sumner's view—which repealed the Missouri Compromise and opened the Western territories to slavery. The legislation made a mockery of Douglas's popular sovereignty, instead bringing about "popular slavery." The second crime was proslavery sympathizer President Franklin Pierce's decision to appoint a territorial official in Kansas who enforced the "tyrannical usurpation" of freedom by Southern slave mongers. Third, Sumner claimed that proslavery forces in Missouri organized associations to intimidate Northerners from settling peacefully in Kansas. And fourth, the most heinous aspect of the crime was when slavery had gained "entry to free soil" because of the willingness of the "Slave Power" to use force against antislavery advocates already living in Kansas. The conspiracy of the "reptile monster," slavery, was led by Senator David Atchison of Missouri.

A daguerreotype of Charles Sumner taken in 1855. (*Boston Public Library*)

"Slavery now stands erect, clanking its chains on the Territory of Kansas," Sumner roared, "surrounded by a code of death, and trampling upon all cherished liberties, whether of speech, the press, the bar, the trial by jury, or the electoral franchise."

Almost as egregious as the "crime," in Sumner's opinion, were the four apologies for its perpetration—the Apology Tyrannical, the Apology Imbecile, the Apology Absurd, and the Apology Infamous. The Apology Tyrannical was the approval by Kansas territorial Governor Andrew Reeder of the "usurping" legislature that the Missouri border ruffians had successfully established. The Apology Imbecile was the reply to the salvo Sumner fired against President Pierce, who claimed he had no power to intervene in Kansas, a position which encouraged the border ruffians. Under the full control of the slave power, Pierce was "ready at all times" to do or "not to do precisely" as it dictated. Indeed, Sumner declared Pierce not merely an imbecile, but an "idiot."

Sumner said the Apology Absurd referred to an accusation by Southerners that a secret organization existed in Kansas that was promoting the total abolition of slavery and the admittance of the territory to the Union as a free state. According to the rumor, the organization's secret charter was pulled from the mouth of one of its founders as he was attempting to swallow it rather than be caught with the document on his person. Finally, the Apology Infamous, according to Sumner, was the Southern denunciation of the New England Emigrant Aid Company, which the slave power saw as a collection of wealthy interlopers from the North conspiring to dictate policy in Kansas. Not so, said Sumner, who argued that the company served a noble purpose to help foster "human progress" in Kansas by investing in schools, churches, and other institutions.

It was on this last point that Sumner angered the South further by claiming that Massachusetts was on the side of the angels in the slavery debate, and that his Massachusetts roots, grounded in freedom and liberty, provided him with the moral nourishment to plead the case for a free Kansas, "a cause which surpasses in moral grandeur the whole war of the Revolution." It was Massachusetts, he declared, with its spiritual, intellectual, and moral superiority that would transmit the light from its "far darting rays whenever ignorance, wretchedness, or wrong prevail."

On the second day of his speech, Sumner spoke for an additional two hours on the four "Remedies" available to stop the violence in Kansas: the Remedy of Tyranny, the Remedy of Folly, the Remedy of Injustice and Civil War, and finally, the Remedy of Justice and Peace.

The Remedy of Tyranny was President Pierce's proclamation that the government would enforce the laws of Kansas. Sumner argued that because the legislature "elected" by Kansas was illegal, any laws it passed were illegitimate, and to enforce such laws would constitute tyranny. The Remedy of Folly was the suggestion by South Carolina Senator Andrew Butler that the people of Kansas should be disarmed, which Sumner argued would blatantly deprive them of their constitutional rights under the Second Amendment. The Remedy of Injustice and Civil War referred to Senator Stephen Douglas's bill arguing that Kansas should be admitted as a state to the Union when it reached a certain population, which would ensure that it would be a slave state in the view of most with the infusion of border ruffians from Missouri and settlers from other Southern states. At various times in the speech, Sumner referred to the Missouri invaders as "murderous robbers" and men who had "renewed the incredible atrocities of the Assassins and the Thugs."

No clear-thinking, rational person could countenance any of these choices for Kansas, Sumner contended. That left only the Remedy of Justice and Peace to reverse the outrage against the Territory of Kansas, which was for the Senate to wield the "angelic power" of freedom and approve Senator Seward's proposal to admit Kansas immediately as a free state.

Throughout the two-day, five-hour speech, Sumner's language was bold, confrontational, even incendiary, but not out of the ordinary for the speaker. Senators from the North and South were accustomed to his outspoken, sometimes strident, sometimes exaggerated proclamations. If "The Crime Against Kansas" had contained nothing more, history would have regarded the speech as powerful, even noteworthy, but certainly not transformational or even overly controversial for the time—certainly not "among the Senator's most notable productions," in the words of Sumner's biographer.

But Charles Sumner could not stop with a recitation of the issues and their possible resolution; nothing in his history or his personal constitution suggested he was capable of doing so. He simply could not help himself. He had promised much more in the way of shock and impact; specifically, language of a "general character, not belonging to the argument" designed to vilify those senators who have "raised themselves to eminence on this floor in championship of human wrongs."

In addition to laying out the issues that led to "The Crime Against Kansas," Sumner called out as villains two Southerners, Senators Andrew Butler of South Carolina and James Mason of Virginia, and one Northerner, Stephen Douglas of Illinois, author of the Kansas-Nebraska Act. Not surprisingly, he reserved his most vicious and insulting verbal attacks for the man least able to fight back—the elderly, ailing, absent Butler—and for the state from which he hailed.

On the first day of the speech, Monday, he delivered one of his most highly charged passages—what would become one of the speech's most frequently referenced and most famous lines—when he berated Butler. Despite their past friendship, their relationship had cooled as the slavery debate intensified, especially after the Kansas-Nebraska Act. Sumner, who had once escorted Charles Dickens through Boston's cobblestone streets and toured the great cities of Europe to further his education, considered Butler neither his moral nor his intellectual equal. Thus, Sumner had no compunction about belittling the man as a way to weaken the man's argument.

He began by comparing Butler to the fictitious Don Quixote (Sumner had borrowed *Don Quixote* from the library to prepare his speech), a man who believed himself to be a chivalrous knight, but who was actually deluding himself—a true knight who practiced genuine chivalry would have resisted the temptation of slavery, but Butler could not. Instead, Sumner charged, Butler "has chosen a mistress to whom he has made vows, and who, though ugly to others, is always lovely to him; though polluted in the sight of the world, is chaste in his sight—I mean the harlot, Slavery." He labeled Douglas "the squire of Slavery, its very Sancho Panza, ready to do all its humiliating offices." Douglas, pacing at the back of the Senate chamber, later recalled saying to himself, "That damn fool will get himself killed by some other damned fool."

South Carolina Congressman Preston Brooks was in the Senate chamber for some of Sumner's first-day speech and was deeply offended to hear Butler, his second cousin, compared to a foolish old Don Quixote who embraced his wench, the harlot slavery. In fact, Sumner's repeated sexual references in the speech, his use of words like "harlot," "virgin," and "rape" were likely particularly galling to Southern slaveholders who repeatedly chafed at stubborn rumors (many proven true after the Civil War) that they sometimes engaged in sexual relations with their slaves and even sired children. Sumner's choice of language was designed to cut to the quick about this most controversial and sensitive topic.

Preston Brooks was not in the Senate chamber for Sumner's second-day attacks against Butler and South Carolina, utterances that were not as inflammatory as his "harlot" remark, but were in some ways more personally cruel, biting, and—Southerners would later say—cowardly, because they were directed against a defenseless opponent. As a result of his stroke

From left to right, Senators Andrew Butler of South Carolina, James Mason of Virginia, and Stephen Douglas of Illinois. Sumner charged each of his three colleagues with promoting slavery through their support of the Kansas-Nebraska Act. (*Library of Congress*)

and a slight facial paralysis it had caused, Senator Butler now slurred his speech. Ridiculing this affliction, Sumner accused Butler of arguing against the admission of Kansas as a free state "with incoherent phrases [that] discharge the loose expectorations of his speech." Sumner described Butler as a buffoon, telling a shocked Senate chamber that the South Carolinian "touches nothing which he does not disfigure with error . . . he shows an incapacity of accuracy, whether in stating the Constitution or in stating the law, whether in details or statistics." In an outrageous conclusion to this set of insults, Sumner declared that Andrew Butler "cannot open his mouth but out there flies a blunder."

Sumner also taunted Butler for his state's reliance on "the shameful imbecility of slavery" and ridiculed him for questioning the value and contributions of Kansas Territory when his home state had so much to be ashamed of. "Has he read the history of the State which he represents?" Sumner shouted. "He cannot forget its wretched persistence in the slave trade . . . or in its constitution, republican only in name, confirming power in the hands of the few," including containing the requirement that legislators from South Carolina own an "estate of five-hundred acres of land and ten Negroes."

Sumner labeled "madness" Butler's attempts to diminish Kansas by comparing it to South Carolina. "In the one is the long wail of slavery; in the other the hymn of freedom," he said. Sumner added that there already was more "educated talent" in Kansas than in Butler's "vaunted" state. "Already in Lawrence alone, there are newspapers and schools, and throughout this Territory, there is more academic mature scholarship . . . than in all South Carolina." Sumner told his Senate colleagues that if the entire history of South Carolina "were blotted out of existence," civilization would lose less than it "has already gained by the example of Kansas in that valiant struggle against oppression." In short, Sumner's message to Butler was "that Kansas, welcomed as a free State, will be a ministering angel to the republic, when South Carolina, in the cloak of darkness which she hugs, lies howling."

Virginia's Mason and Illinois's Douglas also felt Sumner's wrath, though they were not subjected to the same scorching language as Butler. Sumner said that Mason, a key author of the Fugitive Slave bill—"a special act of inhumanity and tyranny"—also suffered from the "bitterness of a life absorbed in support of slavery." Mason did not represent the "early Virginia," the Virginia of Jefferson and Washington, but instead represented the "other Virginia, from which Washington and Jefferson avert their faces." This was the Virginia "where human beings are bred as cattle" and people were imprisoned if they read the Bible to "little [slave] children." Considering Virginia's reputation, it was "proper" that Mason should "rail against free Kansas."

Douglas, too, was one of the "natural enemies" of Kansas, and Sumner lambasted him for declaring as "traitors" those who opposed the unlawful Kansas legislature. "If this be treason," Sumner asserted, "make the most of it." And if Douglas favored hanging those who were convicted of treason, so be it, Sumner said—"not the first time in history will a scaffold become the pedestal of honor."

Coyly, Sumner said he singled out Butler, Mason, and Douglas with "reluctance," but felt it was his duty to help "the country understand the character of the hostility to be overcome."

His entire speech, including his recitation of the issues in Kansas and his personal attacks upon his three Senate colleagues, culminated with emotional closing remarks on the second day. As the clock approached three in the afternoon, after five hours of oration over two days, a drained Sumner begged his fellow Senators to consider a free Kansas. He appealed to them to admit the territory as a free state in "just regard for free labor; in Christian sympathy for the slave . . . in dutiful respect for the early Fathers . . . in the name of the Constitution . . . and, in the name of the Heavenly Father, whose service is perfect Freedom."

When Sumner finally sat down, the storm broke forth in the stunned Senate. Northerners expressed their displeasure first.

Michigan's Lewis Cass, the dean of the Senate and the man who formally presented Sumner to his colleagues for his swearing-in ceremony after his election by the Massachusetts legislature, rose to criticize Sumner first. In solemn tones, he declared that Sumner's speech was "the most un-American and unpatriotic that ever grated on the ears of the members of this high body . . . I hope never to hear again here or elsewhere." According to former Massachusetts governor Edward Everett, Sumner's speech had raised the stakes and deepened the bitter rancor between North and South. "Language equally intemperate and bitter is sometimes heard from a notorious parliamentary blackguard," a shocked Everett said, "but from a man of *character* of any party I have never seen any thing so offensive."

Douglas responded angrily after Sumner finished on the second day, kicking off a heated exchange with the Massachusetts senator. He accused Sumner of "a depth of malignity that issued from every sentence," and deemed his speech "obscene and vulgar . . . unfit for decent men to read," and more worthy of "those haunts where ladies cannot go, and where gentlemen never read Latin." He objected to Sumner's verbal assaults on the absent Butler. "He will be here in due time to speak for himself, and act for himself too," Douglas said. Douglas took great umbrage at Sumner's description of the Kansas-Nebraska Act as a "swindle" and failed to understand why Sumner felt compelled to use personal attacks in his speech. Was it to foment political strife? Was it Sumner's object to "drive men here to dissolve social relations with political opponents?" Was it to "turn the Senate into a beer garden, where Senators cannot associate on terms which ought to prevail between gentlemen?" Or, Douglas wondered, was it simply Sumner's goal "to provoke some of us to kick him as we would a dog in the street, that he may get sympathy upon the just chastisement?"

Sumner regained the floor to respond, shouting that Douglas had best remember that "the bowie-knife and bludgeon are not the proper emblems of senatorial debate." Sumner followed by saying that "no person with the upright form of a man can be allowed—" but then he hesitated and did not finish his sentence.

"Say it!" Douglas taunted him.

Sumner complied: "No person with the upright form of man can be allowed, without violation of all decency, to switch out his tongue the perpetual stench of offensive personality. Will the Senator from Illinois take notice?"

A steaming Douglas retorted: "I will, and therefore will not imitate you, sir."

Undeterred, Sumner replied that "again, the Senator has switched his tongue, and again he fills the Senate with his offensive odor."

Virginia's Mason, whom Sumner had personally attacked in the speech, told his Senate colleagues that listening to Sumner was to hear "depravity, vice in its most odious forms," something he would not tolerate outside of the Senate, but was forced to listen to in the chamber because of the "necessity of my position under a common Government." Under Senate rules, Mason lamented, he was required to "recognize as an equal, politically, one whom to see elsewhere is to shun and despise."

As the encounter ended late in the afternoon of the second day, some of Sumner's allies crowded around him and congratulated him for taking the fight to his opponents; one newspaper correspondent in attendance later called Sumner's remarks "majestic, elegant, and crushing."

But several of Sumner's Republican colleagues also feared for his safety, especially troubled that Douglas's reference to kicking Sumner "as we would a dog in the street" could provoke violence. Representative John A. Bingham, a Republican from New York who attended the second day of the speech, warned Sumner's fellow Massachusetts senator, Henry Wilson, to protect his colleague. He believed Douglas's remark was "designed to produce and encourage an assault," and predicted that "there will be an assault upon him." Wilson and Ohio's Ben Wade both regretted the vindictiveness of Sumner's language, and believed that others who felt the same could take action against him. "I am going home with you today—several of us are going home with you," Wilson told Sumner. Believing the proposed precautions were totally unnecessary, Sumner replied: "None of that, Wilson." He slipped out a side door of the Capitol and walked to his lodgings alone.

Beyond the walls of the Senate chamber, reactions to Sumner's speech also began almost immediately, with equal intensity expressed on both sides of the Mason-Dixon line.

Northern antislavery stalwarts felt as though Sumner had finally issued a long overdue clarion call against the deteriorating situation in Kansas and slavery in general. Proslavery Southerners concluded that Sumner's extreme views and his personal attacks, especially against Butler, were just additional examples of the radical, destructive, and uncompromising beliefs of abolitionists and evidence of their desire to obliterate the Southern way of life.

On one end of the reaction continuum were the gushing remarks by Northern antislavery newspapers such as the *New York Tribune* ("Mr. Sumner has added a cubit to his stature") and compliments from Sumner's loyal friends: including poet Henry Wadsworth Longfellow ("A brave and noble speech . . . the greatest voice on the greatest subject that has ever been uttered"), abolitionist William Lloyd Garrison (who called the speech "invincible in its truthfulness), and genteel antislavery champion Lydia Maria Child (who found nothing in Sumner's speech "which offended either my taste or my judgment"). Child, who normally eschewed personal invective, found the speech "magnificent" and filled with "intellectual strength and moral heroism."

The South was deeply aroused, too, but in an overtly hostile way. Most Southerners objected to Sumner's overall message, but were far more infuriated at the personal insults levied against Butler. One Tennessee congressman announced that Sumner "ought to be knocked down and his face jumped into." The *Richmond Enquirer* was outraged by his language and tone and denounced him for daring to speak his words while American ladies were present in the gallery. With his obscenities, Sumner acted as "the public insulter of female delicacy, sensibility, and refinement." The cowardly Sumner stood in stark contrast to the "honorable, courageous and manly" Andrew Butler. The *Washington Star* wrote that Sumner's "personal vilification and abuse of Senator Butler . . . caused a blush of shame to mantle the cheeks of all present" in the Senate chamber.

Most political moderates, Northerners and Southerners alike, expressed dismay at Sumner's harsh tone, sensing that the Massachusetts senator had crossed a Rubicon of sorts on the subject of slavery, sensing also that recriminations were likely.

Sumner's speech was printed at once in leading newspapers in many Northern cities, and large pamphlet editions were soon made available in New York, Boston, San Francisco, and Washington, D.C.—more than one million copies of the speech would be distributed within a couple of months. Sumner himself picked up final copies of the speech from the printer on May 21, one day after he had concluded his five-hour oration.

On street corners, in offices, and in homes across Washington—a city filled with proslavery interests—Southerners seethed at Sumner's insults and discussed retaliation. They denounced the speech and Sumner again and again, and one man, South Carolina Congressman Preston Brooks, interpreted Sumner's caustic words as a personal affront to his family, his region, and his manhood. To Brooks, part of a new breed of young Southern congressmen who fiercely defended their region's way of life, despots such as Sumner represented a dangerous group of radical Republicans whose rhetoric threatened the South, her sense of order, and her most cherished institutions. Sumner's uncompromising and strident calls for the immediate, unconditional, and *uncompensated* emancipation of slaves posed a grave danger to the Southern economy and the region's orderliness. If a man could be forced by the federal government to surrender his assets—human or otherwise—then that government, and the people who advocated this abuse of power, must be stopped.

Sumner had compounded his sins by personally insulting Brooks's physically impaired second cousin, Senator Andrew Butler, and his home state, South Carolina, on the United States Senate floor and in front of an entire nation.

When Butler returned to the Senate two weeks after Sumner's speech, he revealed to his colleagues that in the thirty-six hours after "The Crime Against Kansas," his cousin Brooks was tormented everywhere he turned. "He could not go into a parlor, or drawing-room, or to a dinner party, where he did not find an implied reproach that there was an unmanly submission to an insult to his State and his countrymen," Butler said. The South Carolina senator added: "It was hard for any man, much less for a man of his temperament, to bear this."

As Brooks bristled under these reproaches, he considered his options. Though Sumner's remarks were slanderous, legal action was out of the question. No Southern gentleman considered a lawsuit the proper redress for a slur upon his good name or that of a family member. According to the normal code of Southern chivalry, Senator Butler would be obliged to flog Sumner—but Brooks's elder cousin was now sixty years old and infirm, and Sumner was a physically large and powerful man. Thus, after two sleepless nights, Preston Brooks had made a decision. Later he would say, "I felt it to be my duty to relieve Butler and avenge the insult to my State."

Part II

SEVEN

NOTHING BUT A CANE

As Representative Preston Brooks, gold-headed cane in hand, approached an unsuspecting Senator Charles Sumner on Thursday, May 22, 1856, the Southerner was thankful that the waiting was finally over.

During his lifetime, Brooks had been seriously wounded in a duel, contracted and recovered from typhoid fever, lost a brother in action during the Mexican War, buried his first wife, and watched his three-year-old daughter die from illness in 1851—yet in some ways, the days and hours after Charles Sumner's speech were the longest of his life.

He had been contemplating action against Sumner since Tuesday, even before the Massachusetts senator had concluded his offensive oration. Brooks was in the Senate chamber to hear Sumner's Monday tirade against Senator Butler, and while he was not present for the conclusion of Sumner's speech, he had heard plenty from his colleagues about the disparaging and insulting language the arrogant Massachusetts lawmaker again had used to describe Butler and South Carolina.

On Wednesday morning, he met his friend Representative Henry Edmundson of Virginia and told him that he planned to punish Sumner—"to relieve Butler and avenge the insult to my state"—unless the Senator apologized for his utterances. He asked Edmundson to wait with him to witness, but "take no part in," the confrontation. "Sumner may have friends with him, and I want a friend of mine to be with me to do me justice," Brooks explained. He told Edmundson that "it was time for Southern men to stop this coarse abuse used by the Abolitionists against the Southern people and States." He believed that Sumner deliberately provoked Butler and South Carolina, and Brooks would "not feel that he was representing his State properly if he permitted such things to be said."

Brooks and Edmundson had sat on a bench in the blistering heat near the walkway leading from Pennsylvania Avenue to the Capitol and awaited Sumner's arrival. Edmundson reminded Brooks of persistent rumors that Sumner had armed himself in anticipation of an attack and asked Brooks what preparations he had made for such an occurrence. Brooks replied simply: "I have nothing but my cane." After fifteen minutes of waiting and no sign of Sumner, Brooks and Edmundson concluded that either they had missed their quarry or that Sumner was not going to show. Much to Brooks's frustration and dismay, the two Southern congressmen made their way to the House chamber.

The same afternoon, Wednesday, Brooks had an opportunity to read the text of Sumner's speech, which stoked his rage anew. That evening, he told his close allies from South Carolina, Representatives Lawrence M. Keitt and James L. Orr, that he planned to "disgrace" Sumner with a "flagellation," though he stated neither the time nor the place. Angry that Sumner had escaped his wrath that day, smoldering from the senator's repeated insults, Brooks barely slept and awakened early Thursday morning. Again, he carried his wooden gutta-percha cane and again he met Edmundson at the western end of the Capitol, which provided him with a wide view of the approach Sumner was likely to take. He planned to assault Sumner there if the senator walked to work; if he came by carriage, Brooks planned to cut through the Capitol grounds, run up a series of stairs, and intercept Sumner behind the building where the carriages stopped. Edmundson advised him against this course of action, arguing that Brooks would become fatigued climbing so many stairs and would thus be physically incapable of overpowering the larger, stronger Sumner.

Perhaps Brooks agreed with Edmundson's logic, perhaps he felt Sumner had eluded him again. In any case, he and Edmundson walked toward the Capitol, and Edmundson recalled later their conversation "was in relation to other matters."

But when they arrived at the door entering into the rotunda, Brooks abruptly headed toward the Senate chamber. Edmundson turned toward the House, but shortly thereafter, once the House adjourned, "casually" made his way to the Senate—both houses of Congress had planned to adjourn early to mourn the recent death of a representative from Missouri, and the House broke session first. Edmundson said he wanted to hear the remaining Senate eulogies for the Missouri congressman, but he also admitted that he expected an "interview" to take place between Brooks and Sumner, and "perhaps that influenced me in remaining longer in and near the Senate Chamber than I otherwise should have done."

The Senate adjourned at 12:45 P.M.

On the day he would unknowingly alter the course of American history, Brooks squirmed in his seat and silently cursed the attractive woman who stood chatting a few feet from him. Agitated and sleep-deprived, Brooks was out of patience. He needed the woman to leave—now. He could hardly carry out his mission to avenge his kin and his region in the presence of a lady. It would violate the code of honor he lived by as a Southern gentleman. He had already tried, but failed, to get the sergeant-at-arms to remove the woman.

So Brooks waited, seething. He sat in the back row of the Senate chamber with Edmundson. Earlier, they had encountered Keitt, who had also made his way from the House to the Senate chamber. Sensing trouble ahead, Edmundson had proposed that they all leave the chamber, but Keitt said: "No, I cannot leave till Brooks does." Keitt now stood nearby.

Although the Senate had just adjourned, a few senators milled about. Brooks paid them no notice. His eyes were fixed on Sumner, whom Brooks regarded as one of the most arrogant boors he had ever come across—and one of the most dangerous threats to the future of the South.

Brooks knew from the conversation around him that Sumner was signing copies of "The Crime Against Kansas," a speech that Brooks viewed as a crime in itself. Sumner, whom Brooks and his Southern colleagues considered the most radical of the Boston antislavery leaders, had delivered his usual fanatical tirade against slavery, but this time he had gone too far. Not satisfied with merely focusing on the issue, Sumner had resorted to vicious personal attacks on Brooks's second cousin, an insult compounded by Senator Andrew Butler's absence from the chamber and inability to offer his own defense.

Worse, the reason for Butler's absence was that he was home recovering from a stroke that had paralyzed a portion of his face and hindered his ability to speak; shockingly, Sumner had used his speech to mock Butler's affliction, too. Sumner had also insulted Brooks's home state, and by extension, the people of South Carolina—and added a blistering, unprovoked attack against the Southern way of life.

The crime against Kansas? No, Brooks believed the real crime was Sumner's attack against Brooks's family and his beloved home state. Sumner had crossed a line, and Brooks would make him pay—as soon as the woman vacated the Senate chamber. "She's pretty," Brooks said to Edmundson, "but I wish she'd leave."

Restless and anxious, Brooks rose and he and Edmundson walked out of the main chamber and into the adjoining vestibule. Keitt, meanwhile, stood near the clerk's desk at the rear of the chamber. Brooks had been in the Senate chamber for an hour now. He considered sending a note to Sumner asking the Massachusetts senator to meet him outside, but Edmundson convinced him that Sumner would simply invite Brooks to come to his desk.

Finally, the woman finished her conversation, turned, and walked directly past Brooks and Edmundson and out the Senate chamber door. Brooks waited another moment, his eyes boring into Sumner, who seemed oblivious to anything except the speech copies he was signing. It came as no surprise to Brooks that Sumner was completely absorbed in his own duties; his ego was well known across the Washington political establishment. Justice demanded that he be brought down a peg.

Brooks glanced at Edmundson, nodded, and began walking toward Sumner with his usual pronounced limp, the result of an old bullet wound that Brooks had sustained during a duel in 1840. In his hand, Brooks carried the gold-headed gutta-percha cane that he often leaned on for support, though today he needed the cane for another reason. Brooks made his way up the aisle toward Sumner, later saying he did so "under the highest sense of duty." He stepped closer. Sumner still had his head bent toward his desk, writing feverishly.

Clutching his cane, Brooks reached Sumner's desk where the Senator sat behind a large pile of documents, "writing very rapidly, with his head very close to the desk" completely unaware of Brooks's presence. Sumner's chair was drawn up close and his long legs were entirely under the desk.

"Mr. Sumner . . ." Brooks began.

Sumner did not stand, but raised his head to identify his visitor.

Brooks tightened his grip on the cane.

Later, another South Carolina congressman would say that Preston Brooks felt a "high and holy obligation" to step forward and avenge the insults Sumner directed toward his kin and his state. Anything less would have humiliated Brooks—as a man, a slave-owner, a proud South Carolinian, and a passionate advocate for the Southern way of life.

Brooks saw no alternative; years of adhering to the twin Southern virtues of honor and order demanded retaliation against Sumner.

EIGHT

A SON OF SOUTH CAROLINA

"The South has been the goose of the golden egg to the North," thundered Preston Brooks in March 1854, during the congressional debate over the Kansas-Nebraska Act, "which Free-Soilers, [with] their . . . fanatical tampering, are threatening to destroy."

It was Brooks's first speech since his election to Congress in 1853. Unlike Charles Sumner, Preston Brooks sought neither fame nor limelight when he arrived in Washington, but interwoven with his service was a deep desire to attain glory and uphold honor for himself and his state. In the same way that Sumner's Boston upbringing and dysfunctional family life shaped his antislavery views and his invective in speeches and debates, Preston Brooks's steadfast loyalty and devotion to family, state, and Southern mores and customs fueled his staunch proslavery views. They combined to ensure that, at this particular moment in history, he—more so than anyone else—would be the one to retaliate against Sumner for his insulting speech.

Thanks to his actions after "The Crime Against Kansas" speech, the man whose political outlook and sentiments were once considered overly moderate and "a little too national" in the eyes of his Edgefield, South Carolina, constituents, would become the standard-bearer and the avenging angel for the most radical elements of the slaveholding South.

In the weeks following the pivotal event of his life, Preston Brooks would be almost unanimously vilified by Northerners as "Bully Brooks," "hotheaded," "evil," "hot-tempered," a "dastardly ruffian," "black and wicked," a "coward and an assassin," even "mentally unbalanced," all characterizations that were understandable in light of his actions, but mostly inaccurate.

In fact, with the exception of his rambunctious college years and the two years leading up to May 22, 1856—commencing with the debate on Kansas-Nebraska in 1854—the South Carolina congressman had spent most of his adult life building a reputation as a reasonable, even gentle, moderate who judged men on their character and issues on their merits.

Virtually everyone who knew Brooks described him as amiable and unselfish. Newspapers described him as a man "of kind heart and the most tender sensibilities" who maintained an "imperturbable dignity" and was "considerate and kind" in his relations with others. One publication referred to him as "earnest, sincere, so full of enthusiasm, that few could resist the influence of his spirit." A political colleague called him "generous, kind, and even gentle in his nature," taking more pleasure in repairing "a wrong done by himself than in one inflicted on him by another." Another ally pointed out that even during a period of "unusual party bitterness," Brooks maintained many warm friendships among his political opponents.

Brooks himself deplored acts of needless violence. He warned a friend that defending honor through violence was "the bane and plague of humane society." After he was wounded in a duel, he pledged to the doctor who treated him that he would never again engage in dueling "for in my conscience I do think it to be wrong." He intervened to prevent duels and, after becoming a member of Congress, suggested that any member who brought a concealed weapon into the House of Representatives should be expelled.

Even at a young age, he developed a reputation for prudence and sound judgment. As a twenty-five-year-old aide-de-camp to

South Carolina Governor James Henry Hammond, Brooks volunteered and was selected to discreetly remove Massachusetts lawyer and politician Samuel Hoar from Charleston. Hoar was an uninvited emissary of the Massachusetts legislature who had come to South Carolina to investigate the treatment of black seamen who were Massachusetts citizens. The South Carolina legislature asked Hammond to remove Hoar and gave the governor "unlimited power for that purpose."

Hammond, fearing mob violence against Hoar, felt it was "of the greatest importance that all should be concluded decently and with such a tone of quiet and air of dignity," and above all, wanted the expulsion to occur without violence (though he did authorize the use of force to remove Hoar). The governor wanted to "show the world that we are acting more from principle than impulse." As for the man he selected for the delicate mission, Hammond said: "Brooks is young and ardent, but not without judgment."

Politically, Brooks was a moderate, at least in South Carolina, and he supported the national Democratic Party from his first days in the House. He opposed his state's so-called "Irreconcilables," who believed South Carolina's interests were not served by the national Democrats, and whose most extreme members advocated immediate secession from the United States.

His reputation as a moderate followed Brooks upon his election to Congress. After a speech, one constituent said he was "pleased with the nationality of his address" and impressed with the way Brooks "repelled all local prejudices and sectional jealousies." During debate about the transcontinental railroad, and in particular, whether the massive project should be built along a Southern or Northern route, Brooks pleaded with fellow members of Congress to "suppress all sectional feelings," arguing that "sectional jealousies are the bane of national advancement." While some loyal South Carolinians found his national legislative positions unnerving, Brooks held the view that "my devotion to my state . . . requires not to be propped by cultivation of sectional sentiments."

Northerners were impressed with Brooks's moderate demeanor and willingness to seek common ground. New York abolitionist Gerrit Smith found Brooks to be a "frank, pleasant man." The *National Era*, an antislavery journal, said Brooks was "always a Southern gentleman" when he expressed his opinion, and the *New York Times* described Brooks as "a man of generous nature . . . warmly attached to his friends" who was "by no means relentless or vindictive towards his foes."

A cabinet photo of Preston Brooks about the time of his election to Congress in 1853. (*Edgefield, South Carolina County Archives*)

Preston Brooks's reputation as an even-tempered moderate soon had colleagues looking to him to broker discussions and agreements among those with more entrenched views. This often thrust Congressman Brooks into the diplomat's role—something his former college faculty members would never have believed possible.

Perhaps Preston Brooks sought to fashion himself as a political peacemaker to atone for the pugnacity of his university years. College life revealed impulsive and even violent components of Brooks's personality that bubbled to the surface in the mid-1850s after years of dormancy. He learned to control these emotions as he matured, but these latent tendencies influenced his behavior years later, and they were an important part of his unfolding persona.

Brooks's rebellious antics deeply irritated the staff and faculty at South Carolina College in Columbia. Indeed, after his fellow Edgerfieldian, Louis Wigfall, graduated in 1837, Brooks became the leading troublemaker at the school, the "chief disturber of faculty peace . . . destined for [a] spectacular career in the realm of violent personal conflict," according to the college historian. While his solid scholarship and good grades protected him in some cases, he had poor study habits, enjoyed the taverns in Columbia a little too much, and was never far from expulsion.

Brooks was first called before the faculty as a freshman for traveling far from the college without permission, but because of his high class rank, he was not disciplined. As a sophomore, he was suspended for missing too many classes and church services. Upon his readmission, Brooks was reprimanded several times for "drifting up town to Briggs' Tavern and other attractive, though forbidden, haunts."

In South Carolina, dueling was a common way to settle differences, but ironically, it was Brooks's *refusal* to duel that led to his first campus fight. In January 1838, Brooks was seeking the presidency of the school's Clariosophic Society, a prestigious debating club. A fellow student, Lewis R. Simons, had promised not to run against Brooks, but apparently went back on his word. Brooks told acquaintances that Simons was a "falsifier" and Simons challenged Brooks to a duel. Brooks refused, pointing out that college rules prohibited duels. He agreed to give Simons a "boy's satisfaction," a fistfight. The following day, as Brooks walked to meet Simons, his friends informed him that Simons had armed himself with a pair of pistols and that Brooks should do the same. He refused at first, but then he accepted a gun from a friend.

When the two met, Simons again challenged Brooks to duel. When Brooks refused again, Simons pulled a horsewhip from beneath his cloak and began to strike Brooks, who drew his pistol. Simons cried that he was unarmed. Brooks tossed away his pistol and the two engaged in fisticuffs. The faculty expelled Simons, the instigator of the incident, and suspended Brooks to "reflect on the matter" until the following April.

When Brooks returned, he continued to frequent taverns and was careless about attending class, but easily passed his final exams in November 1839. Presumably, graduation lay just a few months ahead.

But another incident interfered. This time, Brooks received an exaggerated and perhaps incorrect report that his brother had been detained in a Columbia jail and was suffering from "ignominious treatment." Brooks rushed to the guard house brandishing pistols and threatened to shoot police who had mistreated his brother. Officers quickly disarmed him and sent him on his way, but the exasperated South Carolina College faculty had had enough. Weary of his belligerence and his casual attitude toward his studies, they voted to expel him. His fellow classmates and the former governor of South Carolina petitioned on his behalf, but to no avail. The future congressman never received his bachelor's degree.

It was this last college incident that offered a telltale glimpse of Preston Brooks's distant future. He had rushed headlong and rashly to assist a family member against insurmountable odds—armed officers—based on little more than a rumor. He had to know that his actions, combined with his previous transgressions, would further sully his reputation at the college and perhaps jeopardize his standing. Yet, in Preston Brooks's world, virtually nothing trumped fierce loyalty to family in importance, risks be damned.

Like many Southerners, Preston Brooks viewed family as the most important unit in his life. As strained as Charles Sumner's relationship was with his father, as aloof as Sumner behaved toward his siblings, Preston Brooks lived at the opposite end of the familial spectrum. A devoted son, brother, husband, and father, Brooks was deeply committed both to his immediate family and to extended kin. By all indications, Brooks was happiest with his family; again, in sharp contrast to Sumner. "Family meetings are the purest and to me the most delightful of human enjoyments," he wrote. He was married twice; for two years to Caroline Means Brooks, who died after a lengthy illness (one report called her "always delicate in health"), and then to her cousin, Martha C. Brooks, with whom he had four girls. "God bless these children," he wrote. "I love them all as the apple of my eyes, and their sweet mother more than all."

Brooks showered his wife with affection and attention. When a pregnant Martha suffered a fractured leg in a buggy accident in August 1849, Brooks stayed by her side and attended to her care unceasingly. Martha was brought to her mother's house to heal and Preston stayed for a week, showing her how to use crutches and tending to her needs. After two months, with Martha showing little improvement, Preston enlisted the services of a Columbia doctor who operated on Martha's leg. Brooks then cared for his wife every day afterward. Two weeks after the surgery, Martha could walk by herself and Preston took her home. She gave birth to a healthy daughter, Caroline, after this ordeal. Brooks prayed that "God bless and preserve to me one of the best of wives." He often referred to Martha as "my precious wife," and "my beloved wife," and repeatedly asked God to protect and heal her.

In July 1851 Preston Brooks had watched as his three-year-old daughter, Sallie, fought desperately for her life. It wasn't that the death of children was so unusual in South Carolina during the early 1850s—sadly, it was not. But as Sallie, whom Brooks also called Yettie, had been born when Brooks was away at war in Mexico, he developed a deep and tender bond with the child upon his return. He was jubilant that Yettie's first word was "papa," and she captivated him from the time father and infant laid eyes on each other. As she neared death, there was only a deep pall over the Brooks household.

"My child is now dying," Brooks wrote, after Yettie had caught cold and became feverish. He recounted that only days earlier, "Yettie had said to her mother . . . that she had such a bad cold that she could not say her prayers." In his diary, a devastated Brooks wrote: "It is hard, very hard to give up one so sweet. Her mother is unconscious of her present condition and is asking the poor babe if she knows her. My heart bleeds . . . My God I pray to Thee to let this affliction prepare my heart and make it acceptable to Thee." When Yettie died, Brooks recalled tenderly: "Poor sweet 'Yettie' was the [most] fearless and sweetest tempered child we had." Brooks described Yettie as "amusing" and added: "If a child can be said to be humorous at 3 years and 3 months of age, she was so—dearest Sallie has been all we could desire." A pained Brooks wrote of watching as Yettie's nurse "closed both [the child's] eyes" and took "our poor babe from us."

A loving husband and father, Brooks was a deeply caring son, too. As the health of his father, Whitfield Brooks, Sr., deteriorated in 1851, Preston prayed for his well-being and wrote: "A better husband and Father never lived. . . . He is a noble man in virtue and generous tender parent." At Christmas, Preston realized that the holiday would be the last with his father; Whitfield was not even well enough to come to the dinner table. When his father passed, Preston wrote: "I was with him during the last day and a half and he died in my arms. A kinder parent never lived nor a juster man." Later, Brooks wrote that he hoped God would bless Whitfield's spirit and "preserve his memory fresh in our hearts." Doing so would "enable us to emulate his example and appropriate his principles to our conduct." Preston hoped his father's wisdom and character would serve as inspiration to future generations: "Sacred be the page wherever his name be mentioned," he implored.

Martha's buggy accident and the deaths of Brooks's father and daughter were followed in April of 1853 by more bad news, a miscarriage—a relatively common occurrence for the time, but still deeply saddening for the Brookses, who had hoped to have another child after Yettie's passing. In the early morning of April 12, Martha had become ill and "threatened with a miscarriage," Brooks wrote. At first light, he sent for a doctor, but the physician's efforts proved fruitless. Just after 9:00 A.M., Martha "lost a perfectly formed baby boy." Brooks described the tragedy as "a sore disappointment as we have never before had a son." Yet, he refused to become mired in self-pity, focusing instead on the blessings he had received in life. "God has been good to me," he wrote. "I know how very much more of good I have received than was deserved. [I] believe that an habitual dependence upon the providence of the Almighty . . . is real wisdom." Such an outlook allowed Brooks to "very much [be] inclined toward thankfulness, even when overtaken by what the human mind would regard as a calamity."

Martha's miscarriage, which prompted Brooks's philosophical and spiritual reflection on hardship, came at the conclusion of six years of personal pain for the Brooks family, beginning when Preston's brother, Whitfield, Jr. was killed in action in Mexico in 1847. A devastated Brooks buried Yettie next to Whitfield, Jr.—Brooks noted in his diary the ironic juxtaposition of Whitfield's death and Yettie's birth during the war. Whitfield, Jr.'s death was crushing to Preston, who was home from battle recovering from typhoid fever when his brother died. Preston was consumed with guilt when he learned of Whitfield, Jr.'s death, believing that by leaving his combat post, *he* had not adequately discharged his duty and thus had let his brother down.

These deep familial relationships were part and parcel of Preston Brooks's South, and more specifically, of South Carolina's Edgefield district, where the bonds of kin and region were intertwined and virtually unbreakable.

Insults to his parents or siblings obviously cried out for vengeance, but even indignities inflicted upon his extended family demanded rapid redress and justice. Like any self-respecting South Carolinian, Brooks would never tolerate the belittlement of his region or his state. "Whatever insults my state insults me," Brooks declared. In some ways, this devotion was among Preston Brooks's most admirable character traits. In other ways, this unswerving loyalty would prove to be a curse.

Like Charles Sumner, Preston Brooks had deep roots in his home state and region. His grandfather, Zachariah Brooks, fought with a South Carolina regiment in the American Revolution. His father, Whitfield, who had some training as a lawyer, ultimately became one of Edgefield's most respected planters, and was described as "a man of science, of liberal education and polished manners." The Brooks family estate, Roselands, was located near the village of Ninety Six in the northern part of the Edgefield district (it became a county in 1868) and was one of the community's largest plantations.

Located on South Carolina's western border—part of its lower Piedmont district, about midway between the Blue Ridge Mountains and the Atlantic Ocean, separated from Georgia by the Savannah River—Edgefield prided itself on its deep influence and leadership statewide. Edgefield residents saw themselves as representatives of South Carolina and the South, strongly espousing the complex Southern ideals of honor, self-reliance, paternalism, classism, loyalty, local governance, and the virtuousness of agriculture, community, and leadership. By the Civil War, the Edgefield district had produced five governors (the region has produced ten governors to this day), two United States senators (including Butler), and was one of the most powerful regions in South Carolina. Edgefield was also home to two Civil War governors and Confederate General James Longstreet. In the words of one historian: "As South Carolina led the South—first in nullification, then in proslavery and prosouthern arguments, and later in secession—Edgefield led South Carolina." The town of Edgefield, which would become the county seat, boasted South Carolina's oldest newspaper, the *Edgefield Advertiser*, and a classic municipal centerpiece, the Edgefield Court House, which was built in 1839 and anchors the town square, the community's gathering space for civic events and commerce.

Some of the state's staunchest proslavery, pro–states' rights, and promilitary voices emanated from Edgefield, as did many of its most daring and rebellious troublemakers. One editor applauded Edgefield as having "more dashing, brilliant, romantic figures, statesmen, orators, soldiers, adventurers, daredevils, than any other county in South Carolina, if not of any rural county in America." Families like the Brookses, the Butlers, and the Pickenses "gave to their village and county a character that was South Carolinian, more intense, more fiery, than was found elsewhere. . . . They seemed to be harder riders, bolder hunters, more enterprising and masterly politicians."

For Preston Brooks, Edgefield provided a strong training ground for his political future and the foundation from which to pursue public office. Here, he strengthened already deep family bonds—the Brookses were related through marriage to the most important families in the district, including the Butlers and the Pickenses; became devoted members of the elite in the Episcopal Church; and forged a leadership position among the wealthy planter class that owned the majority of slaves in

Edgefield. Brooks loved Edgefield; its history, its people, its sense of community, its streak of independence and roguishness; its boldness and brashness.

Nearly 40,000 people, 60 percent of them black, lived in the Edgefield district, which was larger than all Southern cities save for Charleston and New Orleans. Yet for Brooks and other members of the planter elite, the region had the distinct feel of a small, close-knit town. Unlike Boston and other industrial cities of the north, with their factories, railroads, tenements, crowded and disease-ridden immigrant neighborhoods, crime, prisons, impersonal way of life, and utter lack of control, Brooks saw Edgefield as a paragon of pastoral orderliness, a hard-working agricultural district where stately mansions and enormous plantations stood adjacent to small homes and one-mule farms; an intimate setting where extended families and personal relationships defined the community's essence, and where business was conducted face-to-face; a place where, even after people moved away, they often returned to visit.

Of course, Edgefield relied on the strength of one other critical economic and social system that wove its way throughout the district's orderly tapestry, one that existed throughout South Carolina and throughout the South, the ingredient that also distinguished it markedly from Northern cities like Boston. Preston Brooks's economic fortunes depended on it, and he supported it, was defined by it socially and culturally, and in his own way, loved it every bit as much as he loved Edgefield and South Carolina.

The South embraced it and was sustained by it. The North sometimes denounced it, but more often wrestled with how to justify it. And it presented the single most vexing contradiction to the nation's promise that all men were created equal. In the South, its oft-used euphemism was "our peculiar institution." Stripped of verbal niceties, its actual name bespoke the stark rawness of the issue that had divided and haunted America since her founding.

Slavery.

NINE

VALUABLE PROPERTY

"The institution of slavery, which is so fashionable now to decry, has been the greatest of blessings to this entire country," Preston Brooks told his House colleagues during debate over the Kansas-Nebraska Act in 1854. "Slavery has been the strongest bond of union between these States."

Not only did "every section of the Confederacy" benefit from slave labor, Brooks pointed out, but the sweat of the African slave gave "employment to the shipping interest of the East, wealth to the manufacturer of the North, and a market for the hemp and live-stock of the West." Brooks declared that slavery had given the United States "a commerce which excites the admiration and jealousy of the world," and a power "greater than armies and navies."

Without any doubt, Brooks said, "enough has been shown to prove the indebtedness of every quarter of the nation to the humble slaves"—the whole country owed a debt of gratitude to the institution of slavery and to the South, which perpetuated its existence and promoted its broad expansion.

In fact, he warned at the time, because slavery benefited every corner of America, failure to enact the Kansas-Nebraska Act—which would breathe new life into the slave-power—would place the country at "greater danger of disunion than at any time since the formation of this government."

As much as it derived its identity from the bonds of family, the formal customs of Southern gentility, and the virtues of agriculture and religion, Preston Brooks's Edgefield district was undeniably defined by slavery. If South Carolina was the South's staunchest proslavery state, Edgefield stood as its sentinel, fiercely defending the institution against all detractors and attackers, and proudly espousing slavery's contributions, not just on behalf of white Southern agriculturists, Northern industrialists, and Western landowners who profited from it, but to society as a whole, including (so the reasoning went) the slaves *themselves.* Slaves may have been shackled and subjugated, but, Edgefield's white residents believed, this was the natural order of things; didn't slaves also enjoy the beneficence of orderly plantation life and the benevolence of protective owners?

The Edgefield argument was the South's argument: slavery was inherently good—for the owners and the owned; for the nation's business; for the overall community. Economic and civil order was best maintained and advanced, and life was richer both materially and morally, with a robust, thriving, and unencumbered system of human slavery.

Cotton was king in Edgefield by the mid-1850s, and black slaves served the monarch well. Thanks to its large plantations and large number of slaves, Edgefield district, with the fourth largest population in South Carolina, led the state in the number of cotton bales produced. Slavery was the basis of economic prosperity in Edgefield, and those with slaves profited most. Historian Orville Burton points out that nearly 63 percent of white households owned land and nearly 66 percent of landowners had at least some slaves. With slaves as collateral, planters could obtain credit from cotton factories and could rent or sell slaves if they needed cash. And slaves helped the community at large too—taxes levied on slave-owners provided Edgefield and other districts with revenue to repair roads and provide other services.

Slavery was so woven into the fabric of Edgefield and South Carolina that virtually no white planter could imagine life without it. Not only was it considered essential to the economy, it was viewed as integral to the overall moral and social order of the region and the strength and stability of the entire country; most slave-owners believed the institution of slavery elevated society and civilization in general. A well-run plantation, with an unambiguous and authoritative patriarchal relationship between owner and slave, symbolized an orderly and morally upstanding community. "No Republican government can long exist without the institution of slavery incorporated into it," declared one minister. The sentiment was echoed by Thomas Green Clemson, the Northern-raised son-in-law of John C. Calhoun, who said: "Slaves are the most valuable property in the South, being the basis of the whole southern fabric."

Preston Brooks agreed completely, choosing to scold abolitionists and Free-Soilers when he reminded them that they "know nothing of the Negro [slave] character, or of his intimate and inseparable connection with the moral, social, and political condition of the South." Whites and blacks working together—one as master, one as slave—was best for all involved, Brooks believed. His parents were large slave-owners at their Roselands plantation, and at his own Leaside Plantation near the town of Ninety Six, Brooks owned more than eighty slaves, whose value in 1857 exceeded $50,000. This was in an era when a set of blacksmith tools was valued at $5, Brooks's two-horse wagon was priced at $35, and Columbia lodging-seekers could rent a seven-room apartment, complete with "heat, hot water, and janitor services," for $45 per month. Slaves were by far a planter's most precious commodity—far outdistancing the plantation owners' next most valuable property, mules and grains, the latter used as feed and sold at market.

To those from the North who sought to interfere in the system of slavery or in black-white affairs in general, Brooks said simply: "If you wish either of us well, let us alone." This feeling was so pervasive in South Carolina that the mere hint of dissent was, at best, discouraged, and at worst, punished. Vigilance and safety committees were established across the state (and the

South) to resist and crush any antislavery sentiments and to root out abolitionists who roamed the South, secretly or overtly spreading their message. The committees often opened mail of those with suspected abolitionist leanings, and while some Southerners objected to this practice on First Amendment grounds, most supported any efforts to blunt the impact of abolitionist thinking. In Mississippi, any "free person" who incited slaves to rebel faced a death sentence. In his early days as a congressman, South Carolina's John Henry Hammond warned abolitionists, "ignorant, infatuated barbarians that they are," that if they were caught in his home state, they could expect "a felon's death." He viewed it as an offense against heaven *not* to kill abolitionists.

Years later, in Hammond's home state, the town of Spartanburg arrested a New York man, posing as a researcher, after he was caught carrying abolitionist pamphlets among his materials. While he awaited trial, public sentiment overwhelmingly favored the ultimate penalty for his transgression: death. But Spartanburg officials delayed his trial, instead using the New Yorker as an example to heighten public awareness about the dangers of abolitionism. Later, cooler heads prevailed, and the man was released and allowed to flee to the North unharmed.

The Southern hatred of abolitionists had deep roots that went well beyond economic concerns. It was a hatred fueled by a visceral fear that abolitionism had the potential to destroy the South's way of life, but—even worse—that the South would become as decadent, disorderly, and godless as the North.

At the heart of Southerners' fear of abolitionism, at the core of the entire planter-plantation-slave dynamic, was the nearly universal and unshakable belief among elite white slave-owners that blacks were inherently inferior.

Plantation owners believed blacks, slaves in particular, were incapable of caring for, providing for, or—God forbid—governing themselves. Slaves required guidance and discipline, in much the same way parents would shelter or reprimand innocent or insolent children. Most planters had convinced themselves that the plantation model was both the best way to protect blacks from themselves and the best way to protect white society from blacks. Hence, the plantation's strict prohibition against blacks learning to read or write; its religious instruction to save blacks from their heathen tendencies; its detailed written rules governing the whipping, hobbling, and other severe punishment of slaves for a slew of transgressions. James Henry Hammond believed that the black race had been created to be a "mud-sill" upon which a higher level of society could be built. Without such a lower-class foundation, "you might as well attempt to build a house in the air," he wrote.

Preston Brooks grew up in an environment whose entire structure depended on absolute adherence to and reliance on these beliefs, an agricultural society in which the principle of black inferiority was constantly reinforced. As much as Charles Sumner believed emancipation was virtuous in the eyes of God, Preston Brooks believed any talk of freeing slaves was heresy. How could blacks care for themselves? How could they survive?

"The history of the African contains proof upon every page of his utter incapacity for self-government," Brooks told his fellow congressmen in 1854. "His civilization depends upon his contact with and his control by the white man." Brooks asserted that abolitionists who sought liberty for the black man not only were threatening the entire Southern economic structure, but were threatening the well-being of the very people they were allegedly trying to help. Abolitionists were well aware, Brooks said, that "when he [the black man] is left to his own government, he descends to the level of the brute."

One need look no further than Jamaica, which had emancipated its black slaves in the mid-1830s, to see the constant chaos and mayhem that existed on the island, Brooks argued. If abolitionists had "one drop of genuine philanthropy . . . in their veins, they would guard [the black] population . . . from the evils of such a liberty." Slave-owners repeatedly employed this argument of protectionism to mask the brutality of human bondage and repel calls for emancipation. For Brooks and others, the thought of thousands of free blacks roaming the South represented the most frightening disorder imaginable. The *Edgefield Advertiser* warned its readers of the dangers of abolitionism and emancipation: "Insolent free negroes would thrust themselves into society and make proposals of marriage with their [white] sons and daughters."

Southerners were also appalled at Northern abolitionist hypocrisy—not just for enjoying the fruits of economic prosperity that Southern slavery had helped create in the North, but for decrying the mistreatment of slaves at the same time immigrants in Northern cities subsisted in squalor. In the mid-1850s, while Charles Sumner demanded that the federal government force planters to emancipate slaves across the South, Irish immigrants in Sumner's Boston were living in horrendous conditions, suffering from hunger, disease, unsanitary housing, abject poverty, and unceasing religious and ethnic bigotry, the latter often perpetrated by the very class of people to which Sumner belonged.

Preston Brooks and his Southern compatriots repeatedly mocked the North for its failure to recognize the irony. Indeed, slave-owners argued, Northern capitalist greed, manifested by the growth of factories and the unstoppable wheels of industry, had exploited and crushed poor white workers to a much greater extent than slavery had subjugated the black man. South Carolina Congressman Lawrence Keitt scoffed: "The tower of Massachusetts civilization, which hypocritically nestles the . . . African to her bosom, thrusts aside thousands of the children of her loins, who can scarcely draw the support of their existence from an overtasked industry!"

And what of the obvious and most glaring distinction between slaves and poor immigrants: that slaves were nothing more than property in the South, owned by planters who bought and sold human beings as the business required, who, like Brooks, listed their slaves among their plantation assets, along with plow horses and kitchen china? Why, that was the very point, Southern slaveholders argued; because slaves were the most valuable property on a plantation, their well-being was paramount. Plantation owners had invested far too much capital in their slaves to allow those assets to deteriorate or suffer harm.

According to Preston Brooks and his slaveholding counterparts, this level of investment created a system of dictatorial benevolence on the plantation that simply did not exist in the ruthless industrial world of the North. Slaves were often considered an extension of the family, albeit vastly inferior members, while in the North, the relentless pace ground workers to dust, and they were simply replaced by others who would soon suffer the same fate. Even punishment of slaves—sometimes mild, sometimes horrific—was simply a means of maintaining order on the plantation and in society, a way of protecting the owner's investment. Virginia author and slavery advocate George Fitzhugh saw slavery as the most mild and humane form of exploitation, a system that was essential for Southern civilization to flourish.

Beyond Northern hypocrisy, Southerners believed they had one more argument on their side: a constitutional one. Notwithstanding the intensity of slavery debates during the Constitutional Convention seventy years earlier, the fact that the Founders had virtually ignored the slavery question in the final document proved not only that it was just and legal, but that the institution was intrinsically important and valuable to the success of the republic.

It also proved, de facto if not explicitly, that the Declaration's claims that "all men are created equal," endowed by their Creator with the inalienable rights of "life, liberty, and the pursuit of happiness," simply did not and could not extend to black slaves.

For abolitionists to argue differently, Southern slave-owners said, demonstrated a profound and dangerous ignorance, of both the Founders' intentions and God's plan.

As deeply as they cherished slavery—for cultural, moral, social, economic, religious, and societal reasons—Southerners hated Charles Sumner for his unabashed and brazen efforts to tear down the institution, an unforgivable offense.

His very name was "the synonym of all that is base and odius," one letter-writer proclaimed to Brooks. A Memphis newspaper called Sumner a "low groveling wicked demagogue, whose character stinks in the nostrils of all rational men." Another Brooks friend claimed Sumner was hiding behind his "Senatorial robes which he has for so long disgraced" to "shoot his poisoned arrows and fling his filthy" foul-mouthed abuse.

Brooks's second cousin, South Carolina Senator Andrew P. Butler, asserted that Sumner represented a movement "uncontrolled by responsibility and unregulated by intelligence." He viewed Sumner's constant attacks on slavery as far from principled; Southern planters and politicians believed that the arrogant senator from Massachusetts simply desired to destroy the moral and social order of the South.

That Sumner sought to obliterate the South's most sacred values—love of family, loyalty to region, reliance on slavery—provided enough reasons for Preston Brooks to respond forcibly to the acerbic tone and inflammatory content of "The Crime Against Kansas" speech. But overlaying all of these was one more reason, one that governed and defined the way Preston Brooks lived, loved, and managed his life. Even more important than the sense of order that he held dear was an ingrained and powerful concept that lay at his core.

TEN

THE SOUTHERN CODE OF HONOR

On an island in the middle of Georgia's Savannah River in 1840, twenty-one-year-old Preston Brooks felt the searing pain as the bullet from his opponent's pistol tore into his thigh. But Brooks's own bullet had found its mark too; his Edgefield rival, Louis T. Wigfall, fell to the ground after being struck in the hip. Both men had missed with their first shots; both suffered serious wounds in the second exchange of fire.

The duel had been a long time coming, as complicated political and social divisions between the Brooks and Wigfall families were well-known in Edgefield. The tensions between Preston and Wigfall finally came to a head during the heated gubernatorial election of 1840, in which the two families supported different candidates and traded vicious charges and insults. Wigfall challenged Whitfield Brooks to a duel according to the Southern *code duello*, a series of complex rules governing dueling, but the elder Brooks refused. Under the same dueling code, Wigfall let Whitfield Brooks know that he would post a placard that afternoon labeling him a scoundrel and a coward. Preston's uncle J. P. Carroll and his cousin Thomas Bird went to the courthouse where Wigfall had posted the notice and asked him to remove it. Wigfall refused and Carroll tore the placard down. Bird, thinking Wigfall would shoot Carroll for the offense, drew a pistol and fired at Wigfall, but missed. Wigfall fired two shots back; the second mortally wounded Bird, who died two days later. To avenge his cousin, Preston Brooks challenged Wigfall to a duel, and Wigfall—desirous to kill another member of the Brooks family—eagerly accepted.

The *code duello* was a subset of a code of honor that governed virtually every aspect of a white Southern gentleman's life and character. Firmly established by tradition, it governed how to behave, both at home and in social situations; how to treat and speak to women; how to manage his plantation, including the proper way to interact with slaves; how to serve his country and community; and how to avenge personal insults, slights, or slander against him or his kin. It helped define for men the notion that strong, sincere beliefs were worth fighting and dying for; strong moral character, fierce family loyalty, knightlike chivalry, and unswerving courage were among the code's hallmarks. Often, perception was more important than reality—a man's reputation in the community was defined by a complex set of mores and values, and if others perceived that he was living up to these standards, he was accorded public respect and his honor remained intact.

Outright violence was a violation of the code, but dueling provided an outlet that allowed gentlemen to channel their aggressions according to well-defined and mutually agreed upon rules. As historian Steven Stowe wrote: "The code of honor and the duel itself were a bulwark against social chaos rather than a form of violence."

By virtue of his upbringing, his personality, and his social standing, Preston Brooks was bound by the code of honor, and though he felt obligated to adhere to its rules, obligation alone did not govern his actions. He was a willing participant in the code because he believed fully and unequivocally in its principles and its rituals. For a Southern planter, acting honorably was, in fact, the *natural* order of things. And in Edgefield, honor defined a man's moral worth.

Preston Brooks's experience during the Mexican War made him question the strength of his character and whether he had embarrassed his family, and by extension, violated the Southern honor code.

Unlike Charles Sumner and most abolitionists, who were outspoken opponents of the war, Brooks and virtually all of Edgefield were strong supporters of the action in Mexico. Recruitment swelled after General Zachary Taylor won rapid and decisive victories; men wanted to travel to Mexico to get a taste of the glory that could accompany heroism in combat. Patriotism and defense of the republic were concepts embodied in the Southern honor code. "I devoutly pray that I may be in at least one battle," Preston Brooks wrote.

Like many from Edgefield, Brooks volunteered and was named captain of Company D of the Palmetto Regiment, also known as the "Old '96 Boys" (from the village of Ninety Six). In late 1846, after Brooks led his troops into the public square accompanied by "The Star Spangled Banner," he pledged to the gathering to bear the flag honorably, to "bear it aloft in triumph, or perish beneath it in glory." Colonel Pierce M. Butler praised the "gratitude and patriotism" of Brooks and others from Edgefield, including Preston's youngest brother, Private Whitfield B. Brooks, Jr. Butler also expressed satisfaction that his district had supplied its quota of volunteers quickly, writing to Brooks: "I am much gratified at the spirit & Patriotism evinced by yourself & other officers. From old Edgefield nothing less was expected."

Edgefield sent its sons off to war with a commemorative dinner, where they recalled the glory of the American Revolution, toasting "Capt. P. S. Brooks, in whose veins run the blood of our revolutionary sires. We believe he will lead 'The 96 Boys' wherever duty, honor, or patriotism require." Anxious to prove himself in battle, Brooks led his company to Mexico, arriving just as

Veracruz was being occupied. He then marched his troops to the city of Alvarado.

In June 1847, he contracted typhoid fever, became seriously ill, and was forced to leave his troops and return to South Carolina. The humiliation and disgrace he felt was greater than had he fallen on the battlefield—literally, a fate worse than death. A bullet or a bayonet would have brought Brooks glory, but illness connoted weakness. Brooks feared that he would disappoint his community and his family, especially his father.

Those fears were exacerbated when his brother, Whitfield, Jr., died in action. "Thus is fallen one of my dearest sons," wrote the elder Whitfield. "Mysterious are the ways of God." In a letter to a friend, where he recounted his family's contributions to the Mexican War, Whitfield, Sr., called his namesake "the noblest son that a father ever raised." In another letter, he wrote that because Whitfield, Jr., was a "noble specimen of a man," and his future held so much promise, "the severity of the bereavement is increased by [a] thousand." His son had died "like a chivalrous knight in the cause of his country," and perhaps the one consolation is that Whitfield, Jr.'s violent death had occurred "while his heart was yet pure and untouched by selfishness, and unsullied by vice." Whitfield, Jr.'s heroic legacy was further burnished when his commanding officer recalled the young Brooks's dying words on the battlefield: "Have I discharged my duty?" His commander's reply: "Yes, like a man; you are an honor to yourself, your family, and your country." Those last words were chosen for his Edgefield tombstone. Whitfield, Jr. was later immortalized in a poem by William Gilmore Simms, one of South Carolina's literary legends.

His brother's heroic death and his father's subsequent grief caused Preston to agonize while recovering from his illness during the summer of 1847. Though he was assigned as a recruiting officer, the work proved unsatisfying and boring. So many Edgefield men had already volunteered that not many recruits remained. Many others were discouraged by the reports of the intense Mexican heat and heavy rains by returning troops. "The disasters of the climate . . . have quite destroyed the spirit of volunteering," Brooks noted.

Feeling utterly inadequate and embarrassed, he pleaded to go back to Mexico to reunite with his troops. Fearful that he would be branded a coward, Brooks wrote to Palmetto Regiment surgeon Dr. James Davis, who had treated him, asking for "professional and personal testimony" to the citizens of Edgefield as to the seriousness of his health and the need for him to return from Mexico. Desperate to save face, to avoid disgrace of his fellow townspeople, to preserve, or perhaps regain, his reputation and standing, Brooks fired question after question in his letter to Dr. Davis: "Did not Col. Butler and yourself urge me to return home from Vera Cruz because of my ill health?" "Did I not refuse to resign or take leave of absence and go to Jalapa at the peril of my life—saying that I would try that climate before I would consent to return?" "Was I not at Death's door on this journey?" "Did not Col. B and yourself again insist on my return, and did you not tell me that my life depended on it?"

It was imperative that Davis answer each question fully and accurately, Brooks insisted, "before the people of my District [deny me] the confidence and respect of which I value more than life itself." The tone of his questions bespoke an irony that Brooks apparently failed to recognize—that begging for respect, in and of itself, demonstrated a lack of the honor that he so craved. Southern honor was earned, not simply granted if one pleaded enough.

Nonetheless, pressured to respond in a manner that would place Brooks in a favorable light, Davis wrote a detailed letter in October 1847 outlining Brooks's illness. Brooks likely had the letter hand-copied and circulated, since a notation on the letter's exterior reads: "Copy of Letter to Dr. David No. 5 Preserve this" and paraphrased versions of its content appeared in later newspaper accounts.

Dr. Davis emphasized that Brooks was "laid bare with a roasting typhoid fever, a disease extremely fatal in our country, and almost certainly fatal to our soldiers under the climate of Mexico." Yes, Brooks had fought strenuously against the doctor's advice, fought to remain at his post, to lead his men, to engage in combat, but Dr. Davis asserted: "I candidly told him that if he persevered in going on with the army, or in remaining in

Mexico, he would die." Brooks "at last yielded" to the doctor's entreaties to return to South Carolina, "only after the doctor insisted the soldier was near death." Indeed, Davis repeated in his conclusion, had Brooks remained in Mexico, "he would not have been at this time among the living."

Brooks finally returned to Mexico in December 1847, but many of the great battles were over. His troops welcomed him back, but the Palmetto Regiment was assigned the relative inglorious role of occupation army. Brooks was distraught, believing, as the company declared in its welcoming resolution, that had he remained in Mexico over the summer, "he would have added another name to the list of the heroes of Edgefield." Instead, because of his illness and the orders he received to return home "he was deprived of the honor of participating in the glorious achievements of an army."

Brooks wrote to his father asking for help in obtaining a more exciting post by appealing to South Carolina Congressman James H. Black. Preston conceded that "every officer in my regiment [says] had I not gone home, I would have died." Nonetheless, "I will never be satisfied without a fight." The senior Whitfield complied with his son's request to write to Congressman Black, noting that Preston "deeply and sorely feels the loss sustained by being absent in the great battles." Whitfield recounted for Black that Preston said "he will never return home until he has been in a battle," and concluded that his son "now pants for an opportunity of doing something to repair what he conceives he has lost."

Despite his best efforts, Preston Brooks did not achieve glory or honor on the battlefields of Mexico, one of his great regrets. He was haunted by the effects of his own illness, which itself could be perceived as a sign of weakness even before it drove him from the battlefield, and by his brother's gallantry and sacrifice. Preston was humiliated again on July 4, 1849, when Edgefield held a ceremony to honor its heroes of the Mexican War, but did not include him among the recipients of commemorative swords to herald their bravery, a slight about which he felt "unjustly neglected." Brooks took some consolation in December when members of Company D presented him with a "handsome sword' to honor his service, which they hoped he would "transmit to your children." Still, even in his remarks thanking his men, Brooks alluded to Edgefield's earlier snub during the Fourth of July sword presentation ceremony.

Historian Harlan Gradin called Brooks's wartime illness and feelings of failure "one of the most profound psychological traumas in his lifetime." Brooks would need to find another way to achieve recognition and glory; another way to honor his family, his state, his region, and all that his way of life stood for.

PART III

ELEVEN

THE CANING

Many factors—love of family, loyalty to region, reliance on slavery, adherence to the code of honor—weighed heavily on Preston Brooks as he approached Charles Sumner's desk in the Senate chamber on May 22, 1856.

But the growing bombast and all-out assault by abolitionists and their ilk also drove him. Since the passage of the Kansas-Nebraska Act two years earlier, when Southerners openly talked of secession if the legislation failed, Northern abolitionists had only grown bolder and more radical. They denigrated the South and her way of life at every turn, they preached emancipation without compensation, they portrayed Southern planters as brutes and criminals, they encouraged insurrection by slaves—and now, with Sumner as their vocal spokesman, they assailed efforts by Southerners to admit Kansas to the Union as a slave state. The situation was perilous; the South's right to exist as a slave society was in jeopardy. "If abolitionism be successful in Kansas," warned one Southern newspaper, "we believe the battlefield of Southern rights will be brought to our own doors in less years than the life of a man."

These overall attacks, plus Sumner's "gross insult to my State . . . and uncalled for libel . . . on my blood" left Preston Brooks with little choice. Later he would say that he would have "forfeited my own self-respect, and perhaps the good opinion of my countrymen," if he had not "resented the injury enough" to call Sumner to account.

Despite his loathing for Charles Sumner, Preston Brooks did not intend to kill him. A fellow congressman would later say that had Brooks decided to make Sumner pay by "pulling his nose" or "slapping his face," events might have turned out much differently. But the irate Brooks viewed Sumner's sins as demanding a more severe form of punishment. A duel was a possibility, but two factors caused him to dismiss this idea: first, Sumner was not a man of honor and thus was unworthy of such a gentlemanly form of settling disputes; second and most important, Brooks feared Sumner would brush aside a challenge to duel and institute embarrassing legal proceedings against Brooks for "sending a hostile message," in addition to any injuries Sumner suffered in a duel. Brooks noted that these charges would "subject me to legal penalties more severe than would be imposed for a simple assault and battery."

Brooks also thought about using a horsewhip or cowhide to flog Sumner, but feared the larger, stronger Sumner would wrest either weapon from his hand. "[He] is a very powerful man and weighs 30 pounds more than myself," Brooks told his brother. If Sumner disarmed him, Brooks perhaps could be forced to draw a pistol and "been compelled to do that which I would have regretted the balance of my natural life."

Instead, to "expressly avoid taking [a] life," Brooks decided to punish Sumner using an ordinary, easy-to-grip cane made of gutta-percha wood, which a friend had given him three months earlier. The cane weighed eleven and a half ounces, had a gold head, and tapered from a thickness of one inch at the large end to three-quarters of an inch at the small; it had a hollow core of about three-eighths of an inch. Because the cane was not solid, it was likely to splinter if and when it struck the head or torso.

Vanity prevented a nearsighted Charles Sumner from wearing glasses, so when he heard his name spoken, he looked up and squinted at the tall, blurred and indistinct figure standing before

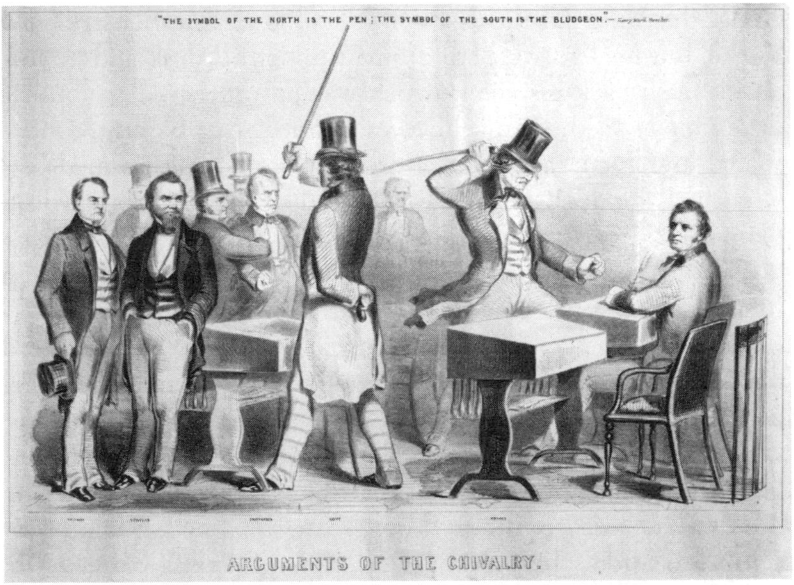

"THE SYMBOL OF THE NORTH IS THE PEN; THE SYMBOL OF THE SOUTH IS THE BLUDGEON."
ARGUMENTS OF THE CHIVALRY.

Winslow Homer's dramatic illustration of the caning from a northern point of view. Shown, from left to right are, Georgia Senator Robert Toombs, Illinois Senator Stephen A. Douglas, Kentucky Senator John J. Crittenden (being held by an unidentified man), South Carolina Representative Lawrence M. Keitt (cane raised and holding a pistol behind his back), Preston Brooks, about to stike, and Charles Sumner, seated. (*Library of Congress*)

his desk. Sumner had never met Brooks and would not have recognized the South Carolinian even if he had been wearing spectacles.

"Mr. Sumner, I have read your speech twice over carefully," Brooks began in a low voice. "It is a libel on South Carolina and Mr. Butler, who is a relative of mine." Sumner moved as if to rise, and Brooks stopped speaking and struck him on the top of the head with the smaller end of the cane, a blow simply "intended to put him on his guard." The force of the blow so shocked Sumner that he lost his sight immediately. "I no longer saw my assailant, nor any other person or object in the room," he recalled. "What I did afterwards was done almost unconsciously, acting under the instincts of self-defense."

Sumner threw up his hands to protect himself and Brooks struck him again and again on his head and face with the heavy end of the cane. For the first five or six blows, Sumner struggled to rise, but his legs were still pinned under his desk and he forgot to push back his chair, which was on rollers. After about a dozen blows to the head, his eyes blinded with blood, Sumner roared and made a valiant effort to rise and his trapped legs wrenched the desk—which was bolted to the floor by an iron plate and heavy screws—from its moorings.

Sumner staggered forward down the aisle, arms outstretched in a vain attempt at defense, now an even larger and easier target for Brooks, who continued to beat Sumner across the head with the cane "to the full extent of [my] power." He rained down blows upon the Massachusetts senator. "Every lick went where I intended," Brooks said later. "I plied him so rapidly that he did not touch me."

As he pounded Sumner, Brooks's cane snapped, but he continued to strike the senator with the splintered piece. "Oh, Lord," Sumner gasped, "Oh! Oh!" He stumbled and reeled convulsively around the seats in the Senate chamber, tearing another desk from its screws as he began to fall to the floor. But Brooks showed no mercy and would not let Sumner escape that easily—he had discarded his initial plan to simply teach Sumner a lesson and now did seem intent on killing him. He grabbed the helpless Sumner by the lapel and held him up with one hand while he continued to strike with the other. Brooks would later state that he did not stop hitting Sumner until he had thrashed him with "about 30 first-rate stripes." Witnesses later testified that they heard shouts of encouragement for Brooks, including, "Go, Brooks!" and "Give the damned Abolitionist hell!" Near the end of the beating, Sumner was "entirely insensible," though before he succumbed, he "bellowed like a calf," according to Brooks.

Finally, others in the Chamber responded to the uproar. *New York Times* reporter James W. Simonton ran forward with a group of other men, seemingly determined to stop Brooks, but as they got near the action, Brooks's friend Congressman Lawrence Keitt rushed in, his own cane raised high over his head, yelling, "Let them alone! Goddamn, let them alone." With his other hand hovering near his holstered pistol, Keitt threatened anyone who interfered. His tactics worked. Brooks would later say in his account of the beating: "I repeated it till I was satisfied; no one interposed and I desisted simply because I had punished him to my satisfaction."

New York Congressmen Ambrose Murray and Edwin Morgan finally entered the fracas as it wound down. Murray seized Brooks by the arm and tried to draw him back, but Brooks's arm slipped from Murray's grasp. Later, conflicting reports emerged about this singular moment—some witnesses said Brooks's brief escape from Murray allowed him to beat Sumner once or twice more as the senator lay motionless, lodged against a toppled desk; others, including Brooks, denied it vehemently. As Murray struggled again with Brooks, Whig Senator John Crittenden from Kentucky ran up the aisle and warned Brooks, "Don't kill him," and helped pull him away from Sumner. Brooks, perhaps realizing he had gone too far, muttered, "I did not intend to kill him, but I did intend to whip him."

Robert Toombs of Georgia, standing close by, did not help subdue Brooks; indeed, he hoped that Brooks would renew his assault on Sumner. "I approved [of] it," Toombs said later. Stephen Douglas, who had run from the anteroom when he heard sounds of the struggle, also chose not to interfere. He thought about trying to end the attack, but reconsidered, believing "that my [strained] relations to Mr. Sumner were such that if I came into the Hall, my motives would be misconstrued, perhaps, and I sat down again."

Meanwhile, Morgan caught a dazed Sumner, whose torso had begun slipping from the desk toward the floor, "saving [him] from falling as heavily upon the floor as he otherwise would have done." Morgan cradled the fallen Sumner, who, head and face covered in blood, "lay at the side of the center aisle, his feet in the aisle." Morgan heard Sumner groan piteously at first and then go silent, "as senseless as a corpse for several minutes, his head bleeding copiously from the frightful wounds, and the blood saturating his clothes." Morgan's shirtsleeves were soaked with blood from Sumner's head wounds.

With Sumner now unconscious, and several pieces of Brooks's cane splintered across a floor slippery with Sumner's blood, friends led Brooks toward a side room; along the way, Crittenden gently took the nub of the broken cane that the South Carolinian still clutched. Brooks surrendered the remnant of his weapon without resistance, but asked Crittenden to find and retrieve the cane's gold head. Brooks later boasted to his brother John Hampden "Ham" Brooks, "I wore out my cane completely, but saved the Head which is gold." Other Southerners picked up pieces of the splintered cane; later, these scraps would be fashioned into rings that many Southern lawmakers would wear on neck-chains as a sign of solidarity with Brooks.

In the side room, Brooks's colleagues helped him wash a small cut he had suffered above his eye, caused by the recoil of his cane during the savage beating. Minutes after his cut was bandaged, Brooks and Keitt had left the Capitol and were walking down Pennsylvania Avenue.

A witness to the attack, William Leader of Philadelphia, who was making his first visit to Washington and had ventured into the Senate chamber just prior to the assault, later testified that the beating was "one of the most cold-blooded, high-handed outrages ever committed." He did not know Sumner and belonged to a different political party, and thus had "no prejudice in his favor." Leader believed that had Sumner "not been a very large and powerfully built man," the caning would have killed him. "No ordinary man could possibly have withstood so many blows upon his bare head," Leader said.

Within moments, Charles Sumner regained consciousness, his bleeding head resting on the knee of Edwin Morgan. A few colleagues helped the bewildered and wobbly Massachusetts senator from the floor. A page gave him a glass of water, and he heard a voice suggest that he be carried to a sofa in the anteroom. Sumner asked that someone find his hat and take care of the papers at his desk, then leaned on Morgan and, face covered in blood, staggered toward the anteroom.

On the way, he passed Louisiana Senator John Slidell, who moments earlier, when informed that Sumner was being beaten, confessed he felt "no particular emotion" at the news. When Slidell saw the bloody Sumner, he expressed no sympathy either, and "did not think it necessary . . . to make any advances toward him," admitting that he had "no associations or relations of any kind with Mr. Sumner," and had not spoken to the Massachusetts senator in two years.

Colleagues gently lay a stunned Sumner on the lobby sofa to rest. Sumner later said he recognized Morgan's voice as he lay on the floor of the Senate chamber, but he had "no recollection" of who had helped him to the sofa. Lawmakers quickly summoned Dr. Cornelius Boyle, who treated Sumner in the anteroom, stitching his wounds, which were still bleeding profusely. Boyle noted that both head gashes Sumner received had split through the scalp to the bone, "laying it bare," and that he suffered defensive wounds and bruises on his hands, arms, and shoulders.

Friends then helped Sumner into a carriage and accompanied him to his nearby Sixth Street lodgings. Upon arrival, they assisted Sumner, still in a stupor, to first undress and then get into bed. Sumner's shirt near the neck and collar was soaked with blood. His waistcoat and trousers were streaked red. Sumner was not aware of the condition of his clothing at the moment, but he examined it later and would recall: "The broadcloth was covered with blood on the shoulders so thickly that the blood had soaked through the cloth, even through the padding, and appeared on the inside. There was also a great deal of blood on the back of the coat and its sides."

As soon as he reached his bed, Sumner, likely suffering from a concussion, told Wilson that he wished to continue his crusade against slavery as soon as he could return to the Senate. "When I recover I will meet them again, and put it to them again," Sumner reportedly told Wilson. A patient Wilson did not respond directly, but urged Sumner to try to relax.

About an hour later, Dr. Boyle arrived to make a more thorough examination and told Sumner's friends that the senator's condition was such that it was "absolutely necessary that he should be kept quiet," since he could not determine the "extent of his injuries at that time." An exhausted, injured, pained, shocked, and bewildered Charles Sumner could only remark before falling asleep: "I could not believe that a thing like this was possible."

News of Sumner's beating consumed Washington and raced across the nation like a giant brush fire. Both antislavery Northerners and proslavery Southerners pounced on the caning to support their own views: the North to argue that the South could no longer be reasoned with on the most important issue facing the country; the South to declare that Sumner's reckless Kansas speech had unmasked the North's true goal, which was to destroy slavery, and with it, the South's economic system and its way of life.

In the short term, the caning sent explosive shock waves across the country: outrage in the North; jubilation in the South. In Kansas, it contributed to savage murders by abolitionist John Brown; in Illinois, it inspired a young Republican lawyer named Abraham Lincoln to deliver a speech that held listeners spellbound, so much so that no one took notes to record the full text of his words for others to read. Those who were in the audience for the so-called "lost speech" declared it among the finest they'd ever heard.

The caning left Charles Sumner debilitated and infirm, but it also solidified his role as the North's great martyr; it caused Preston Brooks to fear reprisals, including assassination, but elevated him to Southern hero. It forced the United States Congress to conduct a full investigation. It inspired some, angered some, and frightened others. The caning evoked raw emotion and action from newspapers, politicians, abolitionists, fire-eaters, speechmakers, and perhaps most notably, ordinary Northerners and Southerners.

Almost overnight, the caning crushed any hope of conciliation between North and South and galvanized both sides. It transformed slavery from a legal, political, and economic issue to a titanic moral struggle, replete with religious overtones—and it established Sumner and Brooks as Antichrist figures to their opposing sides.

In the near term and long term, the caning would carry more tragic consequences. Sectional clouds, already dark, thickened ominously as word of the caning spread. The steady chill in North-South relations over the years suddenly intensified, fostering extremism and obliterating compromise.

Preston Brooks's attack on Charles Sumner, start to finish, consumed somewhere between sixty and ninety seconds, but its tremors would reverberate across North and South for years to come. A line had been crossed on May 22, 1856, and there was no going back.

TWELVE

A DIVIDED RESPONSE

"Every Southern man is delighted and the Abolitionists are like a hive of disturbed bees," wrote Preston Brooks to his brother Ham the day after the caning. "I expected to be attacked this morning but no one came near me."

Preston Brooks had already been arrested for assault, but was immediately released on $500 bail after pledging to return for trial whenever the court requested. Earlier he had shared with Laurence Keitt that he wanted his friends to understand "precisely what I have done and why I did it." Charles Sumner's speech, he said, was "an atrocious libel on South Carolina, and a gross insult to my absent relative, Judge Butler." Once Sumner had delivered the offending oratory, Brooks was determined to punish him for it.

To his brother, Brooks acknowledged that the House already was considering his expulsion and the debate was now "very animated on the subject." He urged Ham to remain calm and not to be alarmed by any reports he should hear. And while he felt he was in danger from potential assassins, he cautioned that Ham "must not intimate [this] to Mother."

Brooks's beating of Sumner released at least two years of pent-up fury in the Southern congressman. His letter to Ham expressed both excitement and bloodlust. After recounting the assault and explaining that his cane had splintered, Brooks boasted that "the fragments of the stick are begged for as *sacred relicts* [*sic*]." He also issued a warning that the attack on Sumner might not be the last: "It would not take much to have the throats of every Abolitionist cut."

If Preston had any misgivings about the deed he did not express them, and Ham's response provided immediate vindication. Ham reassured his brother that his actions were justified and that Sumner deserved the long-overdue beating. "You did *perfectly right*," Ham exclaimed. "I have not been more delighted for years & only wish I could have *participated* with you. I am more proud of you than ever! I believe I love you better!" Ham told Preston that he was willing to help him pay his fine, and provide any other assistance his brother needed. "If they fine you a thousand dollars, if I were you, I should regard it as money well invested," Ham said. He described everything about the caning as "glorious"—Preston's initial approach, the weapon he selected, the manner in which the cane was applied, the outcome, and the cause for which Preston struck. Ham joked that he would have changed only a single detail: "I might have substituted the cow-hide [cane] for the Gutta percha, but the difference is too small to complain."

Ham's endorsement and enthusiasm were reflective of the combined glee and righteousness that swept the South. Preston Brooks had done what so many wished to do, and, in the process, had covered himself and his region in glory.

"Hit him again," crowed the *Edgefield Advertiser* in its editorial saluting Preston Brooks for his drubbing of Sumner. "We feel that our Representative did exactly right; and we are sure his people will commend him highly for it." Sumner had left Brooks with little choice, the newspaper asserted. What else could the Massachusetts scoundrel senator expect? In alliterative style, the paper recounted that Sumner had "emptied one of his vials of vile vituperation on the head of Senator Butler," who was absent from the chamber at the time. A beating was the appropriate punishment for this offense, and even more appropriate was the fact that it was a "thorough one." The *Advertiser* heard reports that Brooks had thrashed Sumner fifty times, but believed the number was exaggerated; "we very much doubt if the Captain cared to exceed the legal number of thirty-nine, usually applied to scamps."

Damn any long-term ramifications of Brooks's action, the newspaper suggested: "We have borne insult long enough, and now let the conflict come if it must." In fact, the *Advertiser* took joy in the fact that an "immense and greedy audience" witnessed Sumner's caning, implying that future beatings could occur if Southern slaveholders' rights continued to be eroded.

Brooks's hometown paper reflected the widespread opinions of Southern newspapers and Southern citizens. "Well done!" declared the Yorkville, South Carolina, *Enquirer*. "No better or more gallant man could have been selected to begin the argument [between North and South] . . . we give him unstinted commendation." Sumner's speech had rankled the South to such an extent that Brooks's response was seen as not only suitable, but necessary. The *Federal Union* of Milledgeville, Georgia, called Sumner's Kansas speech "one of the most malignant and indecent tirades ever uttered in the Senate Chamber . . . much more dishonorable to a nation than the chastisement inflicted upon the perpetrator."

Southern papers and slave-owners expressed hope that the attack on the notorious Sumner would be a lesson for all hated abolitionists. *What to do with men like Sumner?* asked one Southern publication. "Nothing in this world but to cowhide bad manners *out* of him or good manners *into* him." The attack was a righteous example of the actions required to combat the increasing Northern disrespect for Southern values. "The vulgar Abolitionists are getting above themselves," the *Richmond Enquirer* declared. "They have grown saucy, and dare to be impudent to gentlemen. . . . They must be lashed into submission. Sumner, in particular, ought to have nine-and-thirty every morning."

Other publications called Brooks "chivalrous" for avenging Sumner's outrageous attack on Butler and Southern honor. One compared his actions to patriots who had seized tea and threw it

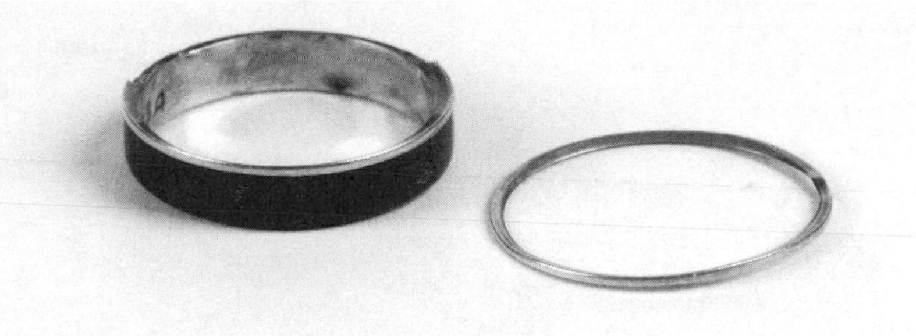

Gold-lined rings fashioned from pieces of Brooks's cane that splintered during the Sumner beating. In the days and weeks after the caning, in a display of solidarity with Brooks, Southern congressmen wore the rings on chains or rope draped around their necks. (*McKissick Museum, University of South Carolina. All rights reserved.*)

into Boston Harbor to protest British tyranny eighty years earlier (though the paper was quick to note that Sumner and other Boston antislavery fanatics had little in common with the brave Boston patriots of the Revolutionary era). In the same way those gallant men acted without official authority to advance a higher cause, Preston Brooks acted according to "his own brave heart" and in so doing, "he will be recognized as one of the first who struck for vindication of the South." That fact alone would place Brooks "among the heroes and patriots of his country." Another paper described Brooks as a "conservative gentleman" seeking to restore to the Senate the dignity and respectability from "which the Abolition Senators are fast stripping it." Furthermore, his fine example was worth emulating "by every Southern gentleman whose feelings are outraged by unprincipled Abolitionists."

Ordinary Southerners also rallied quickly and passionately to Brooks's side. At a pro-Brooks rally in Washington, D.C., one banner carried the inscription: "Sumner and Kansas: Let Them Bleed." Celebrations were held across the South, and James H. Adams, the governor of South Carolina, announced a fundraising effort to present Brooks a silver pitcher, goblet, and stick. When the governor went to the Exchange Bank in Columbia to establish the fund, he was besieged by contributors. "Before I got to Hunts Hotel I had 94 dollars paid up," he wrote to

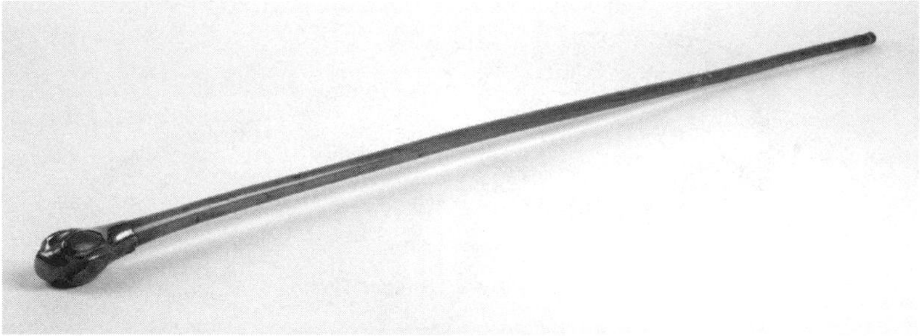

One of hundreds of canes Preston Brooks received from supporters. (*McKissick Museum, University of South Carolina. All rights reserved.*)

Brooks in Washington, "some wanting to give 5 and some 10. I was invited to a room by a friend to take a drink and on counting the money it appeared that I lacked [only] 6 dollars of the one hundred I started out to raise." Governor Adams assured Brooks: "I am satisfied I could have raised a thousand dollars just as easily as I did the 100."

Brooks received hundreds of canes as gifts from well-wishers, and Charleston merchants contributed to buying him a cane inscribed "Hit him again." At a huge May 24 public meeting in Newberry, South Carolina, Brooks's constituents voted to present a gift to their congressman—a "handsome gold-headed cane"—and fully endorsed his actions. Attendees at a large rally in Fairfield passed a resolution approving of Brooks's "administering to Charles Sumner of Massachusetts a wholesome and richly merited castigation." A group of businessmen set out from North Carolina to Washington, D.C., with a new gold-headed cane for Brooks, with one member of the group saying he would be "sorry for the abolitionist's head that shall come in contact with this cane. It will be very likely to crack." University of Virginia students arranged to send Brooks a cane that "should have a heavy gold head, which will be suitably inscribed, and also bear upon it a device of the human head, badly cracked and broken," according to the *Richmond Enquirer*.

Nor was it only white men who supported Brooks. One of "Carolina's truest and most honored matrons" wrote to Brooks assuring him that "the ladies of the South would send him hickory sticks, with which to chastise Abolitionists and . . . Republicans whenever he wanted them." Slaves in the South Carolina capital of Columbia collected money to buy him "an appropriate token of their regard."

Letter writers to Brooks echoed newspaper reactions and the brotherly sentiments of Ham Brooks. "I am so delighted with your cool, classical caning of Mr. Sumner," wrote W. F. Holmes of Newberry County, South Carolina, on May 27. "You have immortalized yourself in the opinions of your immediate constituency." Holmes said Brooks would be long remembered for his heroic act. John Swanson of Columbus, Georgia, likely pleased Brooks when he wrote: "For your beating of that Damn Rascal, liar, and tory Sumner you deserve all the honours your country can bestow," and he assured Brooks, "I would this day vote for you or Mr. Butler for *any* office." Brooks had set an example that other Southern men should follow, Swanson added: "If . . . all would treat the Rascals as you have, we would have had peace long ago and heard very little of abolition in Congress." One South Carolina citizen was glad Brooks refrained from murdering Sumner, not for Sumner's sake, but so that Brooks could avoid the death penalty. "If you were seventy-five years old, I would say 'kill him.' But as you are not half that old, I wish you to live and continue to *serve* and *honor* your country."

Others sought to inform Brooks of how news of the caning had excited the South. "The cry of 'well done' has already echoed from the seaboard to the mountains," wrote a Georgetown, South Carolina, admirer. Letter-writer Seaborn Jones added: "You have the good wishes of everyone I have heard speak on the subject—and everyone is full of it. *Nothing else* is talked of." Of the Sumner caning itself, Jones asserted: "It is what the Rascal has wanted a long time, & he has only received a small portion of what he deserves." One anonymous South Carolina letter-writer directed his correspondence to Sumner: "If you infernal abolitionists don't mind your own business . . . and let ours alone, the People of the South . . . will go in mass to the Capital—and tar and feather—horse-whip & expel every rascal of yours." Sumner would be wise, the writer suggested, to "learn a useful lesson from what you have received."

Seaborn Jones also assured Brooks that Southerners would support him in the event Sumner filed a lawsuit against him; such support would leave abolitionist sympathizers with few options. "While there is a dollar left in South Carolina, they will never hurt you in a pecuniary way, and they can do nothing else!" Jones said.

Not all of the Southern response unanimously supported Brooks. Some newspapers, especially, condemned his actions because they took place inside the Senate chamber and others questioned the chivalry of attacking Sumner while his legs were pinned under his desk. But these criticisms were relatively mild, and most were leveled by writers in border states such as Kentucky, Maryland, and Missouri.

For the most part, throughout the Deep South, the near universal reaction of ordinary people was best summarized by the words Louisiana's Braxton Bragg wrote to a friend: "Were I in the House I should certainly propose a vote of thanks to Mr. Brooks. You can reach the sensibilities of such dogs only through . . . their heads and [with] a big stick." And if such dogs could not be reached, Southerners had little recourse. The *Richmond Enquirer* warned of the potential consequences: "Sumner and Sumner's friends must be punished and silenced. Either such wretches must be hung or put in the penitentiary, or the South should prepare at once to quit the Union."

As Southerners gathered in their fields, their parlors, and their town squares to discuss and celebrate Preston Brooks's attack on Charles Sumner, Northerners clustered on city street corners, in factories, and in offices, abuzz with disbelief and outrage about the events in Washington, D.C.

Whereas jubilation was the prevalent emotion in the South, Northerners were horrified and angry, their reaction almost universally in stark contrast to their fellow Americans who lived below the Mason-Dixon line. Indeed, as in the South, the catalysts for the enormous uproar in the North initially were press accounts and editorials about the event; but the true measure of the caning's almost immediate impact in Northern states was best reflected by the groundswell of rage that poured forth from prominent officials and ordinary citizens.

Hundreds of Northerners from across the political spectrum wrote Charles Sumner to convey their sympathy, anger, shock, and indignation. Even those who disparaged Sumner's fanaticism and provocative political style, even those who protested the acerbic tone of "The Crime Against Kansas" speech, voiced their condemnation of Brooks's attack and their genuine concern for the senator who had suffered physical pain, cruelty, and distress at the hands of the slave power's representative.

Brooks's attack convinced thousands of moderate Northerners almost overnight to embrace the opinion that abolitionists had held steadfastly for years: that proslavery Southerners—stripped of their gentlemanly finery and veneer of cloying politeness—were little more than savages. Even the governor of New York wrote to Sumner, commending him for persevering in the face of the "barbarous and brutal assault" by the "sneaking, slave-driving scoundrel Brooks."

Like their Southern counterparts, Northern newspapers entered the fray quickly and set the tone for the debate, most vilifying Brooks—"a cowardly scoundrel"—for resorting to violence inside the venerable Senate chamber, and suggesting that the South Carolina congressman's actions were emblematic of the South's approach to the slavery debate. Many quickly labeled the caning as one of the nation's most infamous events. "The outrage in the Senate, on Thursday last, is without a parallel in the legislative history of the country," noted the Republican-leaning *Boston Atlas* in an editorial. "Never before has a Senator been struck down in his seat, and stretched, by the hand of a lawless bully, prostrate, bleeding, and insensible on the floor." The normally staid *Illinois State Journal* called the Brooks assault "the most direct blow to freedom of speech ever made in this country." What made Brooks's attack so dastardly, the press pointed out, was that it was part of a Southern conspiracy to destroy free speech; restrictions on abolitionist speech and writing had spread rapidly across the South. Now, apparently, those restrictions extended to the Capitol Building in Washington, D.C.

To explain why the Sumner caning had aroused "a deeper feeling in the public heart of the North than any other event of the past ten years," the *New York Times* said: "The great body of the people, without distinction of party, feel that *their* rights have been assailed." The symbolic offense against the body politic was not just the beating itself, but the location in which the attack occurred. "The blow struck at Sumner [took] effect upon Freedom of Speech in that spot where, without freedom of speech, there can be no freedom of *any* kind," the *Times* noted.

Virtually every Northern paper agreed that the caning's impact was shocking, widespread, and unprecedented in American history. This was not a duel between gentlemen, with their seconds waiting alongside in case they were needed; this was not a fistfight between equals in which each party removed his waistcoat, rolled up his sleeves, and waited for the other to announce his readiness; this was not even an emotional outburst that could be forgiven once flared tempers cooled and handshakes signaled an end to tensions. Brooks's caning of Charles Sumner was premeditated (planned for nearly two days), devious (Sumner had no idea it was coming), unfair (Sumner's thick legs were trapped under his desk when Brooks struck), shocking (because it occurred in the Senate chamber), and unmerciful (Brooks struck again and again despite Sumner's obvious helplessness).

As they castigated Brooks, many called for violent reprisals against him. The *Boston Bee* spared no language on how the "bully Brooks" should be dealt with: "[He] ought to be . . . mercilessly kicked from one end of the continent to the other." In a similar vein, the zealously Republican *Pittsburgh Gazette* printed one of the most aggressive responses to the caning, arguing even that the Christian duties to "turn the other cheek" or offer "forgiveness" no longer applied in dealings with the slave power.

Rather, the *Gazette* thundered, "these cut-throat Southerners will never learn to respect Northern men until some one of their number has a rapier thrust through his ribs, or feels a bullet in his thorax." Brooks was nothing more than a bully "who lacked even the courage of the duelist, and [instead] displayed the meanness . . . [and] malice of the assassin." In language that proved prescient, the *Gazette* declared that the caning "has done more to alienate the hearts of the North from the South than any other event that has happened since the republic was founded."

Editorials in Boston and across the North repeatedly stressed that one of the most significant impacts of Brooks's attack was the chilling effect it could have on future debates. Senators fearing physical reprisals would be less likely to express themselves, fearing, in the words of one editorial writer, "that what a single creature has done today, a hundred, equally barbarous, may attempt tomorrow." What did the future hold for the country, if "by the persuasive arguments of the bludgeon, the bowie knife, and the revolver, [a member could] . . . refute and silence any member who may dare to utter . . . his personal convictions?"

Some publications echoed the sentiments of the Republican-leaning *Evening Journal* of Albany, New York, which argued that Brooks's attack had less to do with his "injured vanity" and more to do with answering Sumner's arguments against slavery, especially in Kansas. The paper asserted that the South proposed to debate the question of self-government in the Western territories with "ball cartridges and bayonets." Southern tactics were appalling, most editorials asserted, and their most "repulsive illustration" was the Brooks attack on Sumner. The entire nefarious character of Southern debate differed radically from the North—"we do not think it necessary to shoot, to slash, or to stun the man with whom we may differ," the *Atlas* opined—and must be vociferously condemned and assailed. Despite the Brooks attack, perhaps because of it, the Senate must remain "virtuous and firm" in its effort to "strangle this serpent of Slavery Extension." Otherwise, Brooks's violence would occur again and again to antislavery Northerners under the guise of states' rights. "State liberty can not long survive the extinguishment of Federal freedom," the *Evening Journal* warned. That

Brooks felt comfortable assaulting Sumner inside the chamber was even more chilling: "Is the Senate of the United States no longer free to the North?"

Many publications pointed out that the South's widespread support of Brooks provided ample evidence that his actions could not be viewed as an isolated event. In an editorial entitled "Stupidity of the South," the *New York Times* condemned the "fatuous blindness" of Southerners in approving Brooks's attack, calling it a form of "madness that must lead to their utter defeat."

An outraged William Cullen Bryant, editor of the widely read and influential antislavery *New York Evening Post*, warned: "Violence is the order of the day; the North is to be pushed to the wall by it, and this plot will succeed if the people of the free States are as apathetic as the slaveholders are insolent." Apathy was *not* an option, asserted the Pittsburgh *Gazette*, nor were insipid calls for calm, reason, or cooler heads: "Blow must be given back for blow," the paper railed, "and if our present Representatives will not fight when attacked, let us find those who will."

Notwithstanding the inflammatory language used by Northern newspapers, it was Northern citizens who were most aghast and offended by the caning.

Preston Brooks's action was deemed heroic by Southerners because it represented a boiling-over of an entire region's deep rage and disgust with self-righteous, hypocritical abolitionists; however, Northerners reacted with equal and opposite fervor. Charles Sumner's vicious beating unleashed a fury in the North that had been brewing through years of increasing Southern brutality in its efforts to perpetuate slavery. It had been going on for far too long; beginning in earnest with debates over the Fugitive Slave Law in 1850, intensifying during the Kansas-Nebraska debate in 1854, and becoming intolerable to Northern sensibilities in the latest struggle for Kansas's future.

Preston Brooks's devious attack had pushed most Northern citizens to the edge. Anger pulsated across the North, from the

East Coast cities of Boston, New York, and Philadelphia, to the mining towns of western Pennsylvania and the Ohio valley, to the fertile farmland that carpeted Indiana and Illinois, to even more remote settlements in places like Wisconsin.

In the few days following the caning, Sumner received hundreds of letters; not surprisingly, Boston and Massachusetts were well-represented, but residents of many states expressed their stunned outrage. Sumner received more letters from Illinois than from any other state; perhaps its close proximity to Kansas coupled with the presence of a fledgling Republican Party and an emerging Abraham Lincoln sensitized its residents to the issues raised by the caning. One Illinois writer, representative of Sumner's indignant correspondents, told the senator that "the blood boils in my veins as I read the telegraphic dispatch . . . of the cowardly brutal assault on you in the Senate by the *fiend* from South Carolina." Portending the dreadful events to come, he added: "I feel as though no other provocation was needed to justify the North in shouldering the musket and fighting the battles of the revolution over again."

Even children were appalled. "The instant papa told me," one Massachusetts girl wrote about the attack, "it seemed exactly as if a great black cloud was spread over the sky." Little Mary Rosamond Dana, daughter of Sumner's friend and confidant, attorney Richard Henry Dana, wrote with a mixture of childlike innocence and a thirst for revenge: "Mr. Brooks is a very naughty man and if I had been there I would have torn his eyes out, and so I would do now if I could." She assured Sumner that her classmates were equally outraged at Brooks's attack, noting that the "school boys in Cambridge . . . have each made an image of Mr. Brooks, laid it down on the ground and let the dogs and carriages run over him and whipped and beat him." The boys also created a hay-stuffed version of Brooks's personage, dressed it in a black coat, and hung it in effigy from the flagpole. In fact, the entire Dana family was traumatized by Sumner's attack. "I think of you every hour of every day," Richard Henry Dana wrote on May 27. "You haunt me. Mrs. Dana cannot sleep because of you and my children cry tears of anger and pity."

Northern letter writers did more than express anger and sympathy; perhaps more satisfying to Sumner, they also lauded the Massachusetts senator for his courage, his steadfast and vociferous leadership, his moral virtue on antislavery issues, and, indeed, the martyrdom he had attained as a spiritual representative of the entire Northern antislavery movement. His caning brought him a level of affection and admiration from Northerners that he had long sought, but which always seemed to elude him.

Unsurprisingly—and unlike Preston Brooks's brother Ham—Sumner's siblings offered no written words of support to their brother after his beating. Instead, hundreds of Northerners assumed the role of Sumner's extended family, offering comfort to a man whose injuries and suffering elicited feelings of pity, outrage, and sectional pride. "We are all not only shocked at the outrage committed upon you," wrote prominent educator Horace Mann, "but we are wounded in your wounds, & bleed in your bleeding." Boston resident James Stone, who attributed his relatively short letter to the fact that he was an "invalid and could write no more," assured Sumner: "Indignation at the brutal attack upon you is on every lip, and fills every heart." Stone also found some positive news in Sumner's beating, pointing out that Northern slavery supporters had their beliefs shaken by the attack: "It seems to be the last feather that breaks the camel's back of their sympathy with slavery." This was God's way of turning the "wickedness of our opponents" into "food [for] our great cause."

Many letter writers picked up on Stone's theme that the caning had elevated Sumner's status and his cause. Charles Cleveland, a teacher from Philadelphia, first told Sumner he wished he could have been in Washington to prevent the attack. Short of that, there was reason to celebrate Brooks's "brutal and cowardly" assault: "I have a wife and five children and fifty pupils looking up to me; but you have the eyes of every true heart—every freedom-loving heart throughout the country looking up to you." A Dedham, Massachusetts, letter writer declared that the North harbored "united, implacable scorn" for Brooks but added: "That blow, no thanks to him, was struck for freedom." S. R. Phillips, writing from Kenosha, Wisconsin, said Brooks's attack was inevitable due to the "cruelty and brutality" of Southern slave-owners, adding that the "nation is on the brink of civil war." It was Sumner who could rally the North to destroy the South once and for all, Phillips said. It was Sumner who could command Northerners to follow him until the last "Border Ruffian" had been killed.

After New York's William C. Russell read Sumner's speech and then read it aloud to his wife—a South Carolinian "who loves the South"—neither could find anything in it that would have inflamed Brooks. By refusing to stoop to Brooks's level, Russell believed Sumner "may do a real good, which may penetrate further and last longer than your most brilliant speeches."

Sumner's dear friend Henry Wadsworth Longfellow agreed with these general sentiments. Sumner's wounds and his bleeding had "torn the mask off the faces of traitors, and at last the spirit of the North is aroused."

While Sumner lay bedridden and alone in Washington, thousands upon thousands of his fellow Northerners swarmed to rallies to show support for the Massachusetts senator and disdain for his South Carolina assailant. Throughout late May and early June, huge public gatherings and "indignation meetings" would be held in New York, Philadelphia, Boston, Albany, Cleveland, Detroit, New Haven, Providence, Rochester, and virtually every city and small town East and West—including places like Berea, Ohio, Rahway, New Jersey, and Burlington, Iowa—to protest the caning. Attendees of all political persuasions jammed into halls and churches, stomped their feet, cheered speeches, roared their approval for Sumner, and shouted their denunciations against Brooks, the South, and slavery. In many places, Brooks was hanged in effigy.

Further, when word started reaching the North and East about the pillaging of Lawrence, Northern Republicans and other antislavery factions quickly began linking "Bleeding Kansas" and "Bleeding Sumner" in the public's mind. In both instances, harm had been inflicted upon those whose voice opposed slavery and all its evils. Yet, for more than a year, antislavery advocates, including Republicans, had tried to grab the attention of Northerners about the outrages in Kansas, without success. News from Kansas was sporadic, fragmented, confusing, and often contradictory. Who could say exactly what was true and what was exaggeration? Who could say which side engaged in excesses and why?

But the caning of Charles Sumner, the deliberate attack upon a United States senator, was concrete, shocking, unprecedented, and easily understood. Even among Southerners, there was little dispute about the facts of the incident. "[The caning] was much more ominous and threatening than events in a distant, sparsely settled territory," historian William E. Gienapp wrote.

Republicans would eventually exploit and capitalize on the caning by linking the Sumner and Kansas events during the 1856 presidential campaign, but during the late spring and early summer of 1856, the antislavery party initially sought to avoid blatant partisanship as Northerners expressed themselves at indignation meetings. Republicans did play a part in encouraging the giant rallies behind the scenes, but generally stopped short of organizing them or delivering overtly partisan speeches.

In New York City in late May, a huge crowd of nearly five thousand people jammed the Broadway Tabernacle to overflowing—thousands more stood on the surrounding streets, unable to squeeze inside. The size and vociferous nature of the crowd was striking; New York City had never been a strong antislavery bastion, and in fact, its businessmen had often sought accommodation with Southern planters and farmers. But at this rally, it was well-known conservatives—lawyers, merchants, bank presidents, educators—who addressed the crowd and criticized Brooks and the South. The crowd roared when attorney Daniel Lord denounced the South for failing to uphold the principles of free speech through its endorsement of Brooks's caning. Columbia College President Charles King said it was time for the North to act as well as talk, Reverend Henry Ward Beecher spoke about the cowardice of the assault on Sumner, and former Whig Samuel Ruggles asserted that if Congress could not maintain its own decorum, "then force must be met by force."

Whenever resolutions were read to the crowd, it erupted in "cheer after cheer . . . like the discharge of heavy artillery" when Sumner's name was mentioned, and let loose with a "spontaneous outburst of groaning and hissing" whenever Brooks's name was uttered.

Describing the New York meeting to Sumner afterward, publisher George Putnam called it "the most remarkable & significant assembly I ever attended; 4000 of the most substantial citizens of N. York spoke as *one man* in terms and tones," with enough volume and conviction to "make Southern sneaks and bullies tremble in their shoes." Putnam stressed that the feeling among the big crowd was "deep, calm, but resolute," and concluded that "no public demonstration has ever equaled this denunciation of the alarming crime." Another attendee observed that the crowd consisted of men who normally did not get involved in political affairs, noting that the staunch support for Sumner was noteworthy since the throng was led by men "not given to fits of enthusiasm or generous sympathy."

Observers, reporters, speakers, and audience members in New York were struck repeatedly by the remarkable turn in public sentiment. Men who had always been "conservative and cotton loving to the last degree," the *New York Tribune* pointed out, were now denouncing slavery and the slave power for the use of wanton violence. "A *new era* is inaugurated," George Putnam declared. He had never seen such excitement and earnest determination, and all of it fomented by Brooks's uncontrolled attack. Perhaps the loudest cheer of the event occurred when Reverend Beecher boomed: "The symbol of the North is the pen; the symbol of the South is the bludgeon."

Not surprisingly, Boston, perhaps most aggrieved by the caning, held its own boisterous meeting on May 24, when a crowd of five thousand people crowded in and around Faneuil Hall. For the moment, at least, past differences between Sumner and many in the merchant class were set aside. Governor Henry Gardner asserted that he would "rise above party feeling and party bias" and stand by Sumner as a son of Massachusetts "in this, his hour of trouble." Sumner's long-time, but also long-estranged, friend George Hillard called Brooks's attack "the act of an assassin," and drew prolonged cheers when he said the caning was "not only a cowardly assault upon a defenseless man, but a crime against the right of free speech and the dignity of a free State."

The shock to Northern sensibilities led to powerful language at virtually every rally across the North. In Cambridge, Massachusetts, Professor C. C. Felton accurately informed the crowd: "The telegraphic nerves are trembling all over the country every moment with . . . the expression of public opinion on this great outrage." Later, he labeled the caning "an act without a parallel in the civilized world—nay, almost without example in savage life." Exaggerations or not, the crowd soaked up the words with unbridled enthusiasm. Felton said he regretted not being a member of the legislature that could vote for Sumner's reelection in January 1857, but elicited thunderous applause when he added: "But if I had five hundred votes, every one should be given to send him back again." At Howard Hall in Providence, Rhode Island, Professor William Gammell captured the feeling of the entire North when he reminded the crowd that the "dastardly outrage" was directed not simply against Charles Sumner. Brooks's blows also "fell on the head of this Republic. They descended on the honor and dignity, the peace and security of the American people—of you and me, fellow citizens."

As part of this brutal attack, Preston Brooks should be branded as a pariah, Gammell said. "Let all men avoid him, and turn away from him, in the halls of the Legislature, in the marts of business, and in the circles of society." Another Providence speaker echoed Gammell's theme when he urged that Brooks "should . . . be forever banished from the Capitol he has so fully dishonored. This barbarian must be purged from the houses of Congress."

Indeed, the most significant aspect of the reaction that raced through the North was that virtually every Northern man—however much he disapproved of Sumner, his speech, or abolitionists—expressed cutting condemnation of Brooks. For example, Democratic strategist Benjamin Butler, certainly no friend of Sumner's, paid a visit to the convalescing senator on his way to the Democratic National Convention in Washington, D.C. in late May. He praised Sumner, perhaps for the first time, as a "chivalric citizen of the Puritan commonwealth," and denounced Brooks as a "coward and an assassin."

Years later, historian Allan Nevins described Northern animosity in the days following the caning: "Looking at Kansas and the Senate Chamber, freesoilers of the North felt that the peaceful processes of American democracy were being supplanted by a regime of terror." Newspaper editorials, letters from citizens, and indignation rallies were powerful examples of the caning's sweeping impact, but there were others in the days immediately following the attack.

In two separate incidents hundreds of miles from Washington, D.C., the caning shaped events that further widened the chasm between proslavery forces and those who either opposed its extension or favored outright abolition. In one place, Preston Brooks's attack inspired soaring rhetoric and a call for unity and Union among Northerners. In another, the beating of Charles Sumner triggered yet another shocking and bloody act of violence that further weakened the nation's fabric.

THIRTEEN

ENTER JOHN BROWN

Deep in troubled Kansas, news of the caning rocked the plains and contributed to disastrous repercussions. It did not precipitate John Brown's anger, but it infused him with a rage that exploded into unspeakable violence—unprecedented in American antislavery activism—and forever changed the Southern perception of abolitionists.

He was not yet the legendary and often caricatured John Brown, the confrontational, enigmatic Moses-like giant whose flowing beard, mercurial disposition, and antislavery fanaticism branded him indelibly—to some, as a towering crusader for justice; to others, as a dangerous, wild-eyed madman. John Brown the legend would not appear for several years, but even in 1856 Kansas, a portrait of Brown shows the darkness that haunted him and would one day strike fear into his proslavery opponents—the deep furrowed brow, the sneering, contemptuous turned-down mouth, the lines etched in his face like dried parchment, and most chilling, the cold, hard, steel-blue eyes.

Brown was incensed even before he received word of the caning. On the evening of May 21, more than 750 Missouri border ruffians, laid low for months by the brutal Kansas winter, had finally sacked and pillaged antislavery Lawrence, swarming virtually unchallenged into the town. They burned and looted homes, ransacked the offices of antislavery newspapers and hurled their printing presses into the Kansas River, and destroyed the Free State Hotel. They carried the South Carolina flag and banners with inscriptions that included: "The Supremacy of the White Race," "Alabama for Kansas," and "You Yankees Tremble and Abolitionists Fall; Our Motto is, Southern Rights to All."

Proslavery forces in Kansas were jubilant. Samuel J. Jones, a sheriff who had been shot and wounded by a New York Free-Soiler, called the attack on Lawrence "the happiest moment of my life. I determined to make the fanatics bow before me in the dust, and kiss the territorial laws; and I have done it—by G—d, I have done it." A proslavery newspaper said of the destruction of Lawrence, and particularly the demolition of the hotel: "*Thus fell the abolition fortress* and we hope this will teach the [New England Emigrant] Aid Society a *good lesson for the future*."

Frightened Lawrence residents who watched the onslaught could hardly believe their eyes, but had agreed not to resist, lest they feed into claims of their disloyalty to the country. Still, they witnessed destruction that left them shaken. O. E. Learnard wrote to his friends that Lawrence had suffered a "fearful disaster" and believed the attack on the peaceful city was "unparalleled . . . in the history of this country." Ruffians did not stop at the hotel and printing presses, he recounted, but "every house in town was plundered and the women and children driven off." Exhaustion prevented Learnard from writing in great detail, but he assured his friends that, far from discouraging Free-Soilers, the attack had filled them with resolve. "We are more confident than ever," he wrote, though he warned in a later letter that the slavery debate would soon cause the country to be "embroiled in civil war."

John Brown, his sons, and other antislavery men heard about the raid on Lawrence too late to do anything about it, and were outraged by the destruction. "Something is going to be done now," he told his colleagues. "We must show by actual work that there are two sides to this thing and that they cannot go on with impunity." His son, John, Jr., pleaded with him: "Father, be careful and commit no rash act."

If there was any chance that his son's warning would deter Brown from violence, the possibility evaporated when Brown's party received word by messenger, probably on the afternoon of May 23, of Preston Brooks's attack on Charles Sumner the previous day. News of the caning was "the final spark for his murderous violence," according to Brown's biographer, David Reynolds.

Brown's other son, Jason, never forgot the reaction of his father and his followers when they heard about Sumner's beating. "At that blow, the men went crazy—*crazy*," he said. "It seemed to be the finishing, decisive touch." Brown ignored yet another plea to exercise caution, saying: "I am eternally tired of hearing that word caution. It is nothing but the word of cowardice."

On the bright moonlit night of May 24, bent on revenge, Brown and his party savagely murdered five proslavery men in Pottawatomie, Kansas, including three members of one family, a father and two grown sons. The enraged Brown group dragged the men from their beds and their cabins, despite desperate pleas from wives and younger children. The slaughter that ensued forever linked John Brown with deranged violence, a reputation that would haunt him for the rest of his life.

Brown and his men used heavy swords to hack their victims and then finished them off with gunshots. In a sworn affidavit, John Doyle, the youngest son of James and Mahala Doyle, described the grisly discovery of the bodies of his father and older brothers on Sunday morning, May 25: "I saw my brother, lying dead on the ground . . . his fingers were cut off; and his arms were cut off; his head was cut open; there was a hole in his breast." He then spotted the body of his other brother, William, whose "head was cut open, and a hole was in his jaw, as though it was made by a knife, and a hole was also in his side . . . my father was shot in the forehead and stabbed in the breast." James Harris, who found victim William Sherman dead in a creek near his house, dragged the body from the water and examined it: "Sherman's skull was split open in two places and some of his

A photograph of John Brown taken in the early 1850s. (*Library of Congress*)

brains was washed out by the water. A large hole was cut in his breast, and his left hand was cut off, except a little piece of skin on one side. We buried him."

When Brown and his men burst into the cabin of Allen and Louisa Jane Wilkinson after midnight, Louisa begged Brown and his men to spare her husband, since she was suffering with the measles and needed Allen to care for her. "I was sick and helpless and could not stay by myself," Louisa recalled. Brown ignored the plea. "You have neighbors," he said, and the group took Allen Wilkinson away. The next morning, neighbors found him dead about a hundred and fifty yards from the house, his throat slashed and gashes in his head and side. They refused to let the ill Louisa see the body "for fear of making me worse."

Upon learning of the discovery of her husband's body, Louisa fled "for fear of my life," to her father's home in Tennessee, convinced that Brown and his party "would have taken my life to prevent me from testifying against them for killing my husband."

John Brown went in and out of hiding during the summer of 1856, but vigilante justice still ruled in Kansas and he was not punished for his crimes. But in the weeks after Pottawatomie, retribution for the "abolitionist murders" resulted in widespread violence and the deaths of more than two hundred people across the Kansas Territory.

Press reports about the atrocities fueled the hysteria. Some papers swelled the number of those killed by Brown's band. The *St. Louis Morning Herald* offered an inflammatory description typical of general accounts: "The blood-curdling story of the murder by night of five men who were at the time quietly sleeping, thoughtless of danger, in their own homes, is fully confirmed. . . . The accursed wretches *mangled and mutilated the bodies they had slain!*" Other writers embellished the slaughter, as though it was not gruesome enough; one essayist reported that Allen Wilkinson was "flayed alive, his nose and ears were cut off, his scalp torn from his head."

What the proslavery press succeeded in doing was defining the actions of Brown and his men as an organized effort by abolitionists to perpetuate violence and mayhem, rather than presenting Pottawatomie as the anomalous event that it was among antislavery supporters. Unlike their Southern proslavery opponents, abolitionists rarely engaged in outright violence; the Brown party's savagery was virtually unheard of.

But now, Brown, like Preston Brooks, had changed the nature of the debate. As Brooks had crossed a line of violence among slave-owners, Brown had redefined the reputation of abolitionists, who were once known as passive resisters. Proslavery men now feared Northerners in a way they had not before. "There is no one for whom the [border] ruffians entertain a more wholesome dread than Captain Brown," said one Kansas writer. "They hate him as they would a snake, but their hatred is composed nine-tenths of fear."

As author David Reynolds concluded, before Pottawatomie, abolitionists were considered "laughable cowards who either shirked war . . . or could be whipped into submission, as in the case of Sumner. After it, they seemed like ferocious criminals intent on attacking Southern institutions."

The caning of Charles Sumner ignited the rage of John Brown at Pottawatomie and both events dramatically altered the perceptions of Northerners and Southerners toward each other. The caning convinced Northerners that barbarous slaveholders could never be reasoned with; John Brown's killing spree, whose wanton violence was directly fueled by Preston Brooks's actions, sobered the South's attitudes toward abolitionists—they were now dangerous fanatics who must be eliminated. Within days, in Washington and Kansas, the caning had redefined the sectional and national political landscape.

On May 29, the caning's impact would reach Bloomington, Illinois. There, passion, but not violence, would rule the day. That passion would give rise to a new, bold, unmistakable, inspirational voice that would one day electrify both North and South, causing one region to burst with pride and admiration, the other to boil with hatred and disdain.

A tall, lanky lawyer rose from his chair amid the assemblage in Major's Hall, a gathering room located over a store near the courthouse square in Bloomington. The occasion was the fledgling Illinois Republican Party's state convention. As they had converged on the town by train, carriage, and horseback, delegates were well aware of the deep national crisis sparked by Charles Sumner's vicious beating in Washington and the suffering of John Brown's victims in Kansas. Telegraph and newspaper reports had covered both events in lurid detail, and were now reporting fresh outbreaks of violence in Kansas in the aftermath of the Pottawatomie murders.

Addressing the convention, the tall man began to speak from his seat, but members of the crowd cried out, "The Platform! The Platform!" Abraham Lincoln, who had come to the convention as a delegate from Springfield at the urging of his law partner, ascended the stairs amid deafening applause, and when he began to speak, "he wrought in that crowd of men with wildly differing views and objectives an almost miraculous change," in the words of one historian. Biographer Benjamin Thomas later wrote of Lincoln: "Outwardly calm, inside he was on fire."

A towering figure, rising to his toes so that he "looked seven feet tall," according to some crowd members, he seemed to grow even larger by the power of his words. With indignation, he spoke of the beating of Sumner and the sacking of Lawrence, but he urged the crowd to avoid violent retaliation. According to one report that paraphrased a portion of Lincoln's words, he implored the audience: "Let the legions of slavery use bullets; but let us wait patiently until November and fire ballots at them in return." That would be the retribution, when opponents of slavery, galvanized by the attack on Sumner and the destruction in Kansas, could show their strength.

The audience sat transfixed by his words; even reporters neglected to write down exactly what he said, so that no complete and authentic record of what may have been Lincoln's greatest speech has ever been found. Subsequent claims by some that they had fully recorded his remarks, as well as published accounts of the full speech, have been mostly debunked.

What is known from piecemeal published accounts is that when Lincoln finished speaking, men erupted in wild cheering and applause, stood on their chairs, threw hats in the air, and waved handkerchiefs, so "caught up" were they in a "tremendous unanimous enthusiasm." In Lincoln's voice, they had heard a strong condemnation of slavery and a clarion call for the Union.

Historian Paul Wellman noted that on the day Abraham Lincoln delivered what has become known as his "lost speech," "Lincoln welded many divergent elements into a party; a party with strong, sober, and intelligent purpose; a party that would uphold the Union to the end." And throughout the summer of 1856 and beyond, that party—the Republicans, led by Lincoln and others—would seize on the caning of Charles Sumner to swell its ranks, advance its cause, solidify its power, and transform a nation.

On the same day that Abraham Lincoln left his indelible stamp on the Republican state convention in Illinois, Preston Brooks, without atoning for his actions, issued a written apology to the United States Senate for attacking Sumner inside the chamber. Two factors triggered what some called the rashness of his act. First, he claimed he had little choice but to assault Sumner where he did, since, despite his best efforts over two days, he had been unable to confront the Massachusetts senator elsewhere on the Capitol grounds. Second, Brooks pointed out, "the Senate had adjourned for more than an hour previous to the assault."

Brooks stressed that he had "little choice but to act as I did," in the wake of Sumner's caustic words about Butler, as well as his sharp criticism "upon the history and character of South Carolina." He regretted that what he had intended as "a redress of a personal wrong" had been construed as a "breach of privilege of the Senate." In fact, Brooks emphasized in his letter, he had nothing but "high respect" for the Senate, and disclaimed any "design or purpose . . . to offend its dignity."

Brooks's letter of apology culminated an eventful week following the caning. John Brown's murderous rampage and Abraham Lincoln's soaring oratory occurred in conjunction with lively debates and important decisions in both the United States Senate and the House of Representatives. Caning fever had gripped Washington, D.C.—the city buzzed about it and concerned itself with little else.

"The seat of my colleague is vacant today," said an emotional Henry Wilson, Charles Sumner's fellow senator from Massachusetts, on Friday, May 23, one day after the attack. "The seat is vacant today for the first time during five years of public service." Wilson reminded his colleagues that Sumner was "beaten upon the floor of the Senate exhausted, unconscious, and covered with his own blood." The affront to the Senate was unprecedented, Wilson argued, noting that it would be a grave offense to assault a U.S. senator anywhere. "But," Wilson concluded, "to come into this Chamber and assault a member in his seat until he falls . . . senseless on this floor, is an offense requiring the prompt and decisive action of the Senate."

But Wilson's plea left the Senate unmoved. No one stepped forward following his impassioned speech, and the Senate was about to move on to other business when an angry William Seward rose and virtually demanded that a committee of five senators be appointed to investigate the caning. The Senate agreed, but decided that the committee would be elected by members, not appointed by the Senate president—and that both Seward and Wilson would be excluded from consideration. Much to the chagrin of Sumner's two allies, the resulting committee not only did not contain a single Republican, but was composed entirely of senators who had either consistently opposed Sumner's politics, or objected forcefully to his language in "The Crime Against Kansas" speech.

Within days, the Senate committee concluded that the caning was "a breach of the privileges of the Senate," but, since Preston Brooks was a member of the House, the Senate had no jurisdiction over punishment. Brooks could only be "punished by the House of Representatives of which [he] is a member." With no debate or dissent, the Senate committee report was adopted, thus ending the Senate's discussion on what to do about the vicious physical beating of one of its members.

On the same day the Senate formed its committee, the House did the same by a vote of 93 to 68. The five-member committee included three Northern Republicans—Lewis Campbell of Ohio, William Pennington of New Jersey, and Francis E. Spinner of New York. In addition, Southern Democrats Howell Cobb of Georgia and Alfred Greenwood of Arkansas rounded out the bipartisan membership.

The House committee got to work almost immediately, gathering on Saturday morning, May 24, to appoint a clerk and discuss its rules and points of procedure. Georgia's Cobb convinced the committee that Preston Brooks be informed officially that the House investigatory committee had begun its work, and that he would be granted the privilege of attending sessions and questioning witnesses. (Brooks declined, replying to the committee's "polite note" that "I know of no witnesses to the affair but Hon. Mr. Winslow of North Carolina.")

The House committee notified Charles Sumner's attending physician, Dr. Cornelius Boyle, that it planned to hear from the Massachusetts senator first—"the sooner the better, if, as a physician, you deem it proper," and if possible, on Monday, May 26. Pennington, who wrote the letter to Boyle, said, "I have not seen [Sumner] since I saw you dress his wounds on Thursday, and have heard rumors that there is danger of inflammation of the brain, etc. For this cause, I deem it discreet to send this communication through you."

On Monday morning, Boyle and Pennington conferred and Pennington visited Sumner at home. He notified the committee that Sumner was not physically fit to leave his lodgings to travel to the Capitol, but had agreed to testify if the committee "might be willing to wait on him." Pennington said Sumner would be ready to see the committee at his home at 1:30 P.M. Given the circumstances, members agreed to the unusual request.

On their way to Sumner's lodgings, committee members dispatched Ohio's Campbell to locate Preston Brooks and invite him to the proceedings. Brooks declined the invitation.

In the first few days after the assault, Charles Sumner seemed to be recovering fairly quickly. His brother, George, traveled from Boston to act as a nurse and assist Dr. Boyle. Though Sumner remained bedridden, Boyle would tell House investigators later that Sumner was "doing very well" in the days after the attack and that his injuries were "simply . . . flesh wounds—nothing but flesh wounds. . . . Mr. Sumner might have taken a carriage and driven as far as Baltimore on the next day [after the beating] without any injury."

While Boyle's words would later do further damage to Sumner's reputation in the South, his general diagnosis was initially confirmed by Dr. Marshall S. Perry, a Boston physician hired by a Republican manufacturer to ensure that Sumner was receiving the finest possible care. Perry arrived in Washington and found Sumner in satisfactory condition on Sunday, May 25. Perry said that the wound on the left side of Sumner's head had nearly healed, but "in the one on the right there was perhaps an inch, or three quarters of an inch, which had not adhered." Bothered by a "pulpy feeling" on the right side of Sumner's head and by his patient's "unnaturally excited state," Dr. Perry recommended that the senator remain quiet and get complete rest. "His nervous system [had] received such a shock that I told him he should be very careful," he recalled.

By the time the House committee arrived at his quarters on Monday afternoon, Sumner apparently was still making progress, although his head wound still leaked pus, he was wracked with pain, and his exhaustion persisted. Sumner recounted the events of May 22, reaffirmed that he had never met Brooks prior to the assault, had no suspicion of an impending attack, and insisted that he was unarmed and totally unprepared for the confrontation.

"I had no arms or means of defense of any kind," he testified indignantly. "I was, in fact, entirely defenseless at the time, except so far as my natural strength went. I had no arms either about my person or in my desk. Nor did I ever wear arms in my life." In a swipe at the Southern members of the committee, Sumner added: "I have always lived in a civilized community where wearing arms has not been considered necessary."

Senator Cobb repeatedly engaged in questioning that was designed to suggest that Sumner could not have been totally surprised by Brooks's attack, pointing out that Sumner's colleagues offered to walk him home after "The Crime Against Kansas" speech and urged him to be careful, fearful that he had outraged Southerners. Sumner said he treated his friends' warnings as "trifling" since he "suspected no danger"—because of that dismissal, he had no hint that an assault was forthcoming. "I had not the remotest suspicion of it until I felt the blow on my head," Sumner asserted.

Sumner also dismissed suggestions that his speech was unduly inflammatory or insulting to Senator Butler or his home state. "I alluded to the State of South Carolina, and to Mr. Butler, but I have never said anything which was not in just response to his speeches or to parliamentary usage; nor anything which can be called a libel upon South Carolina or Mr. Butler."

Their questioning concluded, members of the House committee left Sumner's lodgings and returned to the Capitol.

That evening, Dr. Boyle applied collodion, a syrupy surgical dressing, to Sumner's wounds to prevent "the escape of pus."

Dr. Perry noticed a dramatic change in Charles Sumner's condition on the evening of Tuesday, May 27, observing that Sumner's skin was hot to the touch, that the senator was feverish, and that his pulse was racing to over ninety—"a very different state of things from what he had had before." Overnight,

Sumner experienced "great pain" in the back of his head, his neck glands were swollen, and his fever increased. By morning, Perry sent for Dr. Boyle, whom he still considered Sumner's attending physician.

The two doctors closely examined Sumner's wounds and found that they had both closed over. Boyle admitted that the collodion he had applied had blocked the escape of pus, as he had intended, but in so doing, had caused Sumner "to be excited and restless." The senator's head wounds were hot and his pulse hit one hundred and four. The doctors opened the wounds, Perry noticed a "table-spoon of pus discharged," which provided Sumner with relief from the "extreme suffering he had during the night" and enabled him to get several hours of sleep.

Perry told congressional investigators one day later that Sumner's wounds should be considered extremely serious. "Any blow received upon any part of the head with sufficient force to cut through the scalp down to the bone . . . would [present] a great deal of danger to life," he said, either from brain trauma or through the possibility of severe infection. He said Sumner was in no condition to leave his lodgings.

During Perry's questioning, Congressman Campbell held up a hickory stick and asked: "With a cane of the specific gravity of this stick, would blows indiscriminately dealt about the head of a person be safe against death?" Perry answered starkly: "Such blows would certainly endanger the life of the subject."

Perry's opinion came on the heels of testimony from House doorkeeper Nathan Darling, a former captain in the Mexican War, who had witnessed and treated wounded soldiers. Darling helped dress Sumner's two large scalp wounds, and he concluded that Sumner was fortunate that the blows from Brooks's cane landed "on the thickest part of the crown" of Sumner's head. "I believe if the licks had been struck with half the force on another part of the head, they would have killed him instantly," Darling testified.

On the same day Dr. Perry testified before the House committee, Charles Sumner's brother George dismissed Dr. Boyle, unhappy at the treatment he was providing and likely miffed that Boyle had referred to the senator's injuries as mere flesh wounds (Southerners would later claim that Boyle was dismissed because he would not exaggerate Sumner's injuries). Dr. Perry took over Sumner's care and he brought in Dr. Harvey Lindsly, a Washington physician, as a consultant. They allowed Sumner's wounds to suppurate freely, which relieved his pain and settled his emotions. He was "more calm and composed than he had been."

On May 29, a week after his brother's beating, George Sumner wrote to Henry Wadsworth Longfellow: "The crisis has passed and our noble fellow is safe." So it seemed.

FOURTEEN

HEATED DEBATE IN THE SENATE

On Monday, June 2, ten days after the caning and following a week of dramatic testimony from twenty-seven witnesses, the investigating committee recommended the expulsion of Preston Brooks from the United States House of Representatives. The committee also called for the censure of Congressmen Henry Edmundson and Lawrence Keitt, who knew of Brooks's intentions, though not the exact time and place he would act on them.

The 3-2 committee vote broke strictly along party and sectional lines. The two Southern Democrats, Cobb and Greenwood, dissented, insisting that the House had no jurisdiction over an attack that took place in the Senate; thus, it should "remain silent" on the matter, lest the opinion of lawmakers unduly influence the judiciary in Brooks's upcoming court case in which he faced assault charges for his attack on Sumner. Indeed, the minority report stated, by acting prior to Brooks's court appearance, the House committee was violating the jurisprudential precept of presuming a person innocent until proven otherwise: "We are at a loss to understand why it is that members of Congress cannot . . . enjoy the same privileges and the same protection which is guaranteed to every other citizen of this land."

Nonetheless, much like the Northern press, the majority report upbraided Brooks for his premeditation ("of at least two days"), his confronting of a defenseless Sumner ("the senator was in a sitting position"), his choice of weapon ("of deadly character . . . a large and heavy cane"), and the brutality of his attack ("the blows were indiscriminately dealt . . . repeated with great rapidity and extreme violence . . . at the hazard of the life of the assailed"). The report's conclusion left no doubt about the majority's position on the caning or the narrative that would play out in the North over the coming weeks and months: "The wounds were severe and calculated to endanger the life of the Senator, who remained for several days in a critical condition."

Moreover, Brooks's claim that the attack was a legitimate response to Sumner's speech was dismissed by the committee, which noted that "The Crime Against Kansas" was "lawfully spoken in debate" while the Senate was in session. Further, the speech was never ruled out of order by the Senate president, nor objected to by any senator as "violative of the rules" established by the Senate.

The majority report acknowledged that "beyond the character of the attack," there was no evidence to indicate that Brooks intended to kill Sumner, but simply to punish him. Regardless, the committee declared that the assault was a "most flagrant violation" of the privileges of both the Senate and the House, and of Sumner's personal rights. Perhaps worst of all, because Brooks's attack was an "aggravated assault" on freedom of speech guaranteed by the Constitution, the caning violated the "rights of [Brooks's] constituents and of our character as a nation."

Left unchecked and unpunished, Brooks's actions could spark "anarchy," which would bring with it "all the evils of a reign of terror." The Republican majority members felt they had little choice. The committee's official resolution to the full House read: "Resolved, That Preston S. Brooks be, and he is forthwith, expelled from the House as a Representative from the State of South Carolina." The full House scheduled debate on the resolution for July.

As restless indignation grew in the cities and towns of the North, and as the South celebrated the thrashing of Charles Sumner by one of its favorite sons, debate raged in Washington; indeed, in every sense, the caning had shifted the nation's eyes and attention from Kansas to the nation's capital.

On June 12, the United States Senate galleries again were filled to overflowing, this time to hear South Carolina Senator Andrew Butler deliver his first major speech since his honor and reputation were tarnished *in absentia* by Charles Sumner three weeks earlier. Butler purported to speak about the extraordinary resolutions delivered to Congress by the Massachusetts legislature. It was virtually unheard of for a state legislature to directly petition Congress, but Sumner's home state lawmakers had blatantly ignored the unwritten rule. The joint House-Senate resolves stated that Massachusetts "approved of Sumner's manliness and courage . . . [in] his defence of human rights and free territory." Further, the sharply worded resolution labeled Brooks's attack "an assault which no provocation could justify, brutal and cowardly in itself, a ruthless attack upon the liberty of speech." Perhaps most significantly, the legislature asserted, the caning was not simply an attack upon Sumner, but "an outrage of the decencies of life, and an *indignity to the Commonwealth of Massachusetts.*"

Butler rose to his feet, first to condemn the Massachusetts Legislature's breach of protocol. But he quickly shifted focus by declaring that Preston Brooks's detractors were overreacting and that Charles Sumner had suffered mere flesh wounds "which ought not to have detained him from the Senate." Vanity, perhaps, had kept Sumner from his Senate duties in the days since the caning, but little else. "Being rather a handsome man, perhaps he would not like to expose himself by making his appearance," Butler said. Indeed, he argued, had Sumner been in the Army, there was no reason "he should not go to the field the next day [after the caning]; and he would deserve to be cashiered if he did not go."

Infuriated, Sumner's Massachusetts colleague Henry Wilson had heard enough from Butler. Wilson had clashed with the South Carolina senator in the days immediately following the caning when he had expressed his sympathy and deep support for Sumner and had endured repeated slings from Southerners. When he declared in a May 27 speech that Sumner had been struck down "by a brutal, murderous, and cowardly assault," Butler—who had arrived back in Washington that very morning after an arduous trip from South Carolina—stood and shouted: "You are a liar!" Butler's colleagues convinced him to withdraw his impulsive remark (the words were stricken from the official record), but the damage was done—emotions again were inflamed throughout the halls of Congress.

Wilson was enraged at Butler's epithet, and the Massachusetts senator's anger intensified when Preston Brooks, through an intermediary, challenged him to a duel after hearing the nature of Wilson's remarks, especially his reference to Brooks as a coward. A resolute Wilson refused to withdraw his comments and declined Brooks's challenge, sending back a note that said in part: "I have always regarded dueling as the lingering relic of a barbarous civilization, which the law of the country has branded as crime." His duty as a senator to uphold the law and his overall opposition to duels "forbid me to meet you," he told Brooks.

Now, two weeks later, Wilson had listened over a two-day period "with painful and sad emotions" to Butler's scathing condemnation of Sumner and spirited defense of Brooks, and he no longer could remain silent. He felt it his duty to refute Butler's outrageous claims that Sumner was exaggerating his injuries and his condition. In a long and impassioned speech, Wilson beseeched his fellow senators to sympathize with Sumner's current physical infirmities ("For more than three weeks he has been confined to his room upon a bed of weakness and pain"). He reminded his colleagues that during Sumner's more than four years in the Senate, he had been "systematically assailed" for his antislavery views by Southern senators—with Butler leading the way. Butler's repeated verbal attacks against Sumner were "calculated to wound the sensibilities of an honorable man, and to draw down upon him sneers . . . and hatred, in and out of the Senate." The continued assaults on Sumner were unworthy of the Senate and "unparalleled" in its history, Wilson said.

As for Butler's criticism of the Massachusetts legislature for sending direct resolutions to Congress, Wilson said Sumner's home-state lawmakers were only expressing the fervent views of the Massachusetts citizenry. "The sentiment of Massachusetts, of New England, of the North, approaches unanimity," Wilson declared. With few exceptions, Massachusetts residents looked "with loathing and execration upon the outrage . . . [against] their Senator and the honor of their State." Butler certainly had the right to criticize the Massachusetts resolutions, but, Wilson said, they reflected the will of the people, "and from their verdict there is no appeal."

One other speech, one other challenge, epitomized the powder keg that threatened to explode in Congress in the weeks after the caning. Massachusetts Congressman Anson Burlingame—a friend of Sumner's, at once ambitious and politically vulnerable, and a shrewd judge of the direction and power of populist winds—delivered a provocative speech on June 21. His most controversial language came when he accused Brooks of sneaking into the Senate, a place that had until that point "been held sacred against violence," walked up to Sumner, "and smote him as Cain smote his brother." South Carolina's Keitt, offended by the biblical comparison, shouted from his seat: "That is false!" Burlingame refused to "bandy epithets" with Keitt and held firm, announcing he would stand by his words.

Burlingame closed with a crescendo, saying he denounced the caning in the name of the Constitution, in the name of Massachusetts, and in the name of civilization, "which is outraged." Brooks's attack was not only dastardly, it was cowardly, a violation of "fair play." The Edgefield congressman had beaten Sumner while he sat at his desk with his legs pinned. "In what code of honor did you get your authority for *that*?" Burlingame sneered.

Preston Brooks, furious at Burlingame's evocative language and religious reference, immediately challenged the Massachusetts lawmaker to a duel. Unlike Wilson, Burlingame promptly accepted, insisting upon the following terms:

"Weapons, rifles; distance, twenty paces; place, District of Columbia; time of meeting, the next morning."

But the acceptance was largely a piece of political gamesmanship by Burlingame, who was facing a tough reelection bid for his Boston seat in the fall. A friend, who would serve as his second and actually fight the duel, quickly substituted as the location for the confrontation the Clifton House in Niagara Falls, Canada, in place of Washington, D.C. Brooks and his advisors decided against participating in the duel, believing—most likely accurately—that a trip to Canada would be dangerous for Brooks. He was now so despised in the North that he ran the risk of being attacked and killed en route to the duel, perhaps by mobs in Boston, New York, or Philadelphia. Burlingame and his colleagues certainly knew this and skillfully backed Brooks into a corner; he could not follow through on his own challenge. Brooks was humiliated, Burlingame was widely criticized in the South for the sham of "accepting" a challenge from which Brooks would have to stand down, and both sides dropped the matter.

Northerners used the derailed duel to draw a contrast between the inner strength and depth of character of Sumner and the shallowness of Brooks. Sumner, who lay injured in his quarters, was enduring great suffering in defense of free speech, itself an act of courage. Brooks, on the other hand, was a coward—when Burlingame had accepted his duel challenge, he showed his true colors and dodged the confrontation. The *New York Evening Post* summarized the North's reaction to the Brooks-Burlingame dustup with this ditty:

To Canada, Brooks was asked to go,
To waste a pound of powder or so,
But he quickly answered, No; No; No.
They might take my life on the way, you know.
For I'm afraid, afraid, afraid.
Bully Brooks's afraid.

The *Post*'s levity aside, the situation in Washington was dire. The inflammatory language, the clashes, the duel challenges, the opposite reactions to the caning among Northern and Southern lawmakers—these all reflected the mood of the entire country and signaled a divisiveness that bordered on the irreparable. Violence and bloodshed, once a product of the Kansas plains, had stormed their way into the United States Senate chamber. Perhaps more frightening, the response to that violence spoke volumes about the chasm between the two sections: abhorrence and condemnation in the North; jubilation and approbation in the South. When it came to the caning, the two sides spoke entirely different languages and stood on opposite sides of a fault line. As Ralph Waldo Emerson wrote on June 6: "I do not see how a barbarous community and a civilized community can constitute one state. I think we must get rid of slavery, or we must get rid of freedom."

FIFTEEN

AN OPPORTUNITY FOR THE REPUBLICAN PARTY

Philadelphia crackled with anticipation and excitement as the first Republican National Convention opened at Musical Fund Hall on June 17, 1856.

As the more than six hundred delegates and one hundred newspaper reporters made their way into the convention hall, all were aware that the events of the previous weeks—the caning, the Pottawatomie murders, the harsh debates in Congress—had generated at once both a state of national crisis and golden opportunity for antislavery Republicans. A month earlier, Republicans had considered a presidential victory in November as a distant long shot. But these dramatic events, none more so than the caning, had altered the political landscape and their outlook.

Who would they nominate as their first-ever presidential candidate? Who would take on proslavery James Buchanan, whom the Democrats had recently nominated in Cincinnati? Buchanan was now the standard-bearer of a party that vowed to resist "in renewing in Congress or out of it, the agitation of the slavery question." The Republican Party, of course, was founded and built on the agitation of the slavery question. It was clear that the positions of the two parties were at the extremes of the most important issue facing the nation; it was also clear that those positions were intractable. No wonder, then, that the Republican Convention's presiding officer, Col. Henry Lane of Indiana, asserted: "We have assembled at the most important crisis in our post-Revolutionary history."

The Republicans were certainly a regional party—almost exclusively from the North and West, though a handful of men from border states and even the South did attend. The *Evening Bulletin* declared that it was "somewhat astonished" by the attendance of delegates from Kentucky, Delaware, Virginia, and North Carolina. "We had supposed in accordance with the popular impression that there would be *no* delegations from any southern or slave states," the paper opined.

Delegates got down to business quickly on the first day. Edwin D. Morgan of New York, chairman of the Republican National Committee, called the convention to order and addressed the delegates, reminding them of the high purpose for which they had gathered and the expectations the country had for the fledgling party. "You are here today to give direction to a movement which is to decide whether the people of the United States are to be hereafter and forever chained to the present national policy of the extension of human slavery," Morgan said. The issue was bigger than sectionalism, he asserted, bigger than whether the North or South would rule the debate. The question the Republicans would help decide was "whether the broad, national policy our fathers established . . . is to be permitted to descend to her sons." Regardless of the ultimate votes they would cast, delegates should "avoid all extremes," Morgan urged. "Let us plant ourselves firmly on the Platform of the Constitution and the Union, and only adopt positions consistent with our consciences, our country, and our mankind."

With the backdrop set, delegates adopted their platform on the first day; unsurprisingly, among its key planks were the party's firm opposition to the "barbaric" extension of slavery into the territories and the specific resolution that Kansas be admitted to the Union as a free state. But the highlight of the first day was not the platform adoption. Just prior to adjournment, Henry Wilson, the U.S. senator from Massachusetts, was invited to address the convention. As he ascended the platform, delegates erupted into a "perfect storm" of wild cheering and applause, "again and again renewed."

Wilson, who had helped Sumner through his ordeal, who had defended Sumner's right to speak, who had vociferously condemned Brook's attack on his colleague, had much to say to Republican delegates. Weeks of pent-up emotion tumbled forth and Wilson held nothing back in his efforts to inspire the Republicans. Never known for his soaring oratory, Wilson delivered a speech punctuated with evocative imagery, powerful language, and clarity of purpose, remarks interrupted many times by thunderous applause and delegates leaping to their feet.

"Our object is to overthrow the Slave Power of the country, now organized in the Democratic Party," Wilson said to tumultuous cheers. It was the slave power that had generated fear and divisiveness across America, whose members had placed lovers of freedom in peril. "Look now at our friends in Kansas," Wilson said, "who lie down at night with the conviction that their little dwelling may be burned over them before morning, or they themselves may be murdered because they love liberty." It is those men, Wilson said, whom the Republicans needed to fight for and represent with strength and conviction. Delegates roared when Wilson said: "I would sacrifice any man and any friend on earth to unite American Freemen for the rescue of the American Government of the United States from the power of slavery."

Wilson saved his most pointed and scalding attacks for the current administration of President Franklin Pierce, who, he asserted, bore the most responsibility for the country's condition. Pierce, Wilson said, dared to show himself at the Democratic Convention "with the light of the burning dwellings of Kansas flashing upon his brazen brow . . . with the blood of the murdered freemen of Kansas dripping from his polluted hands." Delegates again responded with loud and sustained applause.

But Wilson's most passionate language, and the delegates' largest roar, came during his references to the caning. "A Senator from a sovereign state . . . for denouncing the crime against Kansas, has been stricken senseless on the floor of the American Senate," Wilson reminded the delegates. At this point, he was interrupted by a voice from the audience who shouted: "*Three cheers for Sumner!*" Delegates in the crowded hall responded with rousing cheers, over and over again. Then, another voice rang out: "*Three groans for Brooks!*" and delegates unleashed a storm of groans, hisses, and epithets. When Wilson resumed, he told delegates that Southerners had made threats against other antislavery men and the audience shouted in response: "Let them dare! Let them dare!"

As Wilson reached the end of his speech, enthusiasm in the hall swelled to a frenzy. "In God's name, gentlemen of the North, resolve to do your duty and to blot out the Slave Power of the country. We can do it . . . I believe in my soul we can do it." Millions of people across the country were looking with "trembling anxiety" at Philadelphia, with the hope that Republicans would band together and nominate a formidable candidate for the presidency. "Disappoint them not, gentlemen, by any petty little interest," he warned, an admonition to resist the urge to break into factions. "Nominate a man upon whom you can unite with the most votes, and who is true to your principles." And whomever the Republicans nominated, Wilson reminded them that the party's mission was the "cause of liberty and the cause of patriotism . . . the party of the Constitution and of the Union."

Amidst a tremendous ovation, a spent but satisfied Henry Wilson returned to his seat. Moments later, delegates adjourned the first day's proceedings and voted to resume work at ten o'clock the next morning.

On day two, they would get about the task that Wilson had charged them with and inspired them to do: nominate a man for President who shared their principles, and, by seizing on the electrifying excitement the caning had generated, one who could win in November. Only a month ago, the possibility had been almost unthinkable.

The convention's second day was filled with speeches and jockeying for position—the delegates had not fully abandoned their agendas or political favorites in exchange for party unity—but in the end, the Republicans nominated a national hero who embodied the boldness and grandness of the American spirit.

Forty-three-year-old John C. Frémont had painted an adventuresome, swashbuckling, risk-taking life story across the broad canvas of two of America's most cherished milieus: the frontier and the military.

Born in Savannah, Georgia, the son of a refugee from the French Revolution, he gained his fame as "Pathfinder of the West" for his many successful surveying expeditions and explorations. As a young man, he helped map the region between the Mississippi and Missouri rivers, and later explored along the Des Moines River. He then solidified his position as a nationally famous explorer and frontiersman by undertaking three great expeditions that contributed significantly to knowledge of the American West—explorations of the Oregon Trail, the Sierra Nevadas, and the Sacramento valley, during which he crossed the formidable Rocky Mountains five times. Adding to his reputation as an intrepid adventurer was the fact that he was accompanied at times by legendary scout Kit Carson.

Frémont also served in the Mexican War, and although he was court-martialed and convicted in a command dispute between a Navy commodore and an Army general—again, contributing to his status as a rogue with an independent streak—his sentence was suspended by President James Polk. He resigned from the Army, settled in California, and, amazingly enough, promptly struck gold, again adding to the Frémont legend. After California was admitted to the Union, he served briefly (1850–1851) as one of the state's first two U.S. senators.

Now a retired Army officer, Frémont had two main characteristics that endeared him to Republican delegates: first, he was personally opposed to slavery and politically opposed to its extension into the territories (Frémont did not favor outright abolition in places where slavery existed, believing this to be a matter for states to decide); second, his name recognition and reputation would make him a favorite in both the North and the West.

A banner for Republican candidates John C. Fremont and William L. Dayton produced for the campaign of 1856. (*Library of Congress*)

Frémont received 359 votes for the Republican presidential nomination, followed by John McLean of Ohio with 100 votes. Charles Sumner received two votes for the nomination. Former New Jersey senator William Dayton was nominated as the Republican's vice presidential candidate, besting his nearest rival, Abraham Lincoln of Illinois. Though Sumner had delivered word to the convention that he did not wish to be considered for vice president, he still received thirty-five votes. When Massachusetts delegate Samuel A. Eliot announced, "Massachusetts could not afford to lose Charles Sumner from the floor of the Senate," delegates again responded with resounding cheers.

When the votes were counted and the nomination complete, workers unfurled a large white banner that read: "John C. Frémont for President of the United States." The convention erupted, as delegates flung their hats across the floor and cheered wildly. Workers quickly displayed Frémont banners in the windows to notify crowds in the streets outside, and spectators soon joined in the celebration.

Building on the momentum of Frémont's nomination and the convention's exhilaration, organizers again asked Henry Wilson to address the crowd just before adjournment, and the Massachusetts senator did not disappoint, leading the crowd in a full-throated exchange that left him flush and the delegates delirious:

Wilson began: "We have a glorious ticket. And now, all that is required is that we . . . place that ticket in power. Are you gentlemen for free speech?" There were cheers and shouts of "Aye! "Aye!" Wilson continued, "Then vote for John C. Frémont!" More cheers. "Are you for a free press—all over the North?" The crowd shouted: "Yes, Yes!" "In Kansas?" "Of course, Yes!" "Everywhere in the territory of the United States?" Wilson's words were again met with cheers and shouts of "Aye." "Then vote that ticket! Are you for free Kansas?" "Yes!" "Do you want to bring that young sister of ours, now in a condition of civil war, into the galaxy of free confederacies?" Loud cries of "Yes! Yes!" Wilson concluded: "Aye, gentlemen, [then] let our motto be, Free Speech, Free Press, Free Men, Free Labor, Free Territory, and Frémont! For victory!"

As they had on day one, delegates responded to Wilson's remarks with overwhelming affection and cheers. He had identified the ticket's campaign slogan and they recognized its power. As the caning had been an affront and an attack on free speech and free expression by the slave power, the Republicans would use the nearly eponymous name of their nominee as a reminder of the freedom they cherished and the South disdained.

They would sound that theme repeatedly during the summer of 1856, contrasting the hope that they offered for America's future with the small-mindedness that had mired Southern slave-owners in the past—and left them with little to offer the country beyond the barbarism that led to the beating of Charles Sumner.

SIXTEEN

TWO MARTYRS

By late June, as bitter debate still consumed Congress, as anger swept across North and South, as Republicans reveled in their nomination of John C. Frémont and dreamed of success in November, Senator Charles Sumner had endured weeks of pain, misery, and deep melancholia.

While thousands thronged halls, churches, and town squares to either praise or denounce him, while dynamic speakers electrified crowds by declaring him either a courageous defender of freedom's principles or an unsalvageable reprobate, Sumner remained mainly confined to his room and his bed, lonely and debilitated.

Much of the time he was unable to think clearly, and even when he was lucid, he despaired at his inability to partake in the monumental debate that swirled around him, though he occupied its center. Slavery was still the underlying issue, but the caning of Sumner had gripped imaginations and poisoned debate like nothing ever had—not the Fugitive Slave Law, not the Kansas-Nebraska Act, not the Missouri ruffians who crossed the border to terrorize Lawrence and Topeka.

"My fingers are quite unused to the pen," Sumner wrote in a shaky hand to Henry Wadsworth Longfellow on June 13, but Sumner said he could not let another day go by without thanking Longfellow for his friendship. He had longed for the companionship of friends during his suffering, whose support he welcomed with a "throbbing grateful heart."

He certainly had been heartened by well wishes from friends, colleagues, and like-minded citizens. One supporter thanked him for a "glorious speech," and the Colored Citizens of Boston, who gathered at the Twelfth Baptist Church, offered their sympathies and condemned the "brutal, murderous assault" against a "statesman" who had long offered his services "in our behalf." A grateful Sumner nonetheless declined an offer by the Commonwealth of Massachusetts to assume his medical expenses. Responding on Sumner's behalf, Rep. Anson Burlingame wrote that the matter should "not be pressed" and instead proposed: "Whatever Massachusetts can give, let it all go to suffering Kansas." Similarly, when a prominent lawyer proposed a fundraising testimonial on Sumner's behalf, the senator acknowledged his thanks but gratefully declined. "I trust you will not deem me too bold if I express a desire that the contributions intended for the testimonial to me may be applied . . . *to the recovery and security of Freedom in Kansas*," Sumner wrote.

Sumner was trying to press on, but in the weeks following the caning he was weak and disoriented. Longfellow wrote to him on June 24: "And how is it with you? Are you making the best of it? Are you getting well?" Dr. Perry reported that his patient complained of "oppressive weight or pressure of the brain," which intensified when he engaged in conversation or became excited. It often came on in waves—a sullen Sumner described it as a "fifty-six pound weight" upon his head. At the same time he lost both "flesh and strength," his appetite was irregular, and he often lay awake all night in terrible pain. "Increased sensitivity of the spinal cord" and "weakness in the small of his back" made his walk unsteady. "Every step he took seemed to produce a shock upon the brain," Dr. Perry said. "After slight efforts he would lose almost entire control of the lower extremities."

To escape Washington's June heat and aid his recuperation, Sumner was able to move to his friend Francis P. Blair's home in Silver Spring, on the outskirts of Washington. For nearly four weeks, he lay "22 hours out of 24 on my back," but by June 23, though he was "still very feeble," he could "totter a mile around the garden . . . hoping daily for strength which comes slowly." On the same day, he felt strong enough to write to Richard Henry Dana, thanking his friend for his speech at the Cambridge indignation meeting and asking him to pass along Sumner's thanks to Dana's daughter for her expressions of sympathy. He also apprised Dana of his condition, pointing out that his head and back injuries had caused his "whole system to be overthrown & I am obliged to keep on my bed much of the day." Sumner lamented that, since the caning, he had written "only *five* letters" and only two on public matters. "When this will end I know not," he fretted.

Silver Spring proved too close to the action in the nation's capital. Numerous visitors called on Sumner at Blair's house, exhausting the senator. A weary Sumner went to Washington on June 25 in answer to a summons to appear before the grand jury sitting on the Brooks assault case. When Sumner finished his testimony, he felt a little better and decided to return to work. He remained in Washington for three days, wrote and dictated letters, and visited with friends who called upon him (including Dana, who was about to sail for England). This overexertion led to a serious relapse. Exhaustion consumed him and he returned to Silver Spring; for a week his doctors prohibited visitors as Sumner fought fever and his wound again suppurated. Dr. Lindsly, after examining the pale Sumner, wrote that Sumner should refrain from any public duties for "some time to come." Lindsly also advised Sumner to "go into the country [to] enjoy fresh air."

On July 4, New York Senator William Seward was allowed to visit Sumner at Silver Spring and he found the patient bedridden and lethargic, "like a man who has not altogether recovered from paralysis, or like a man whose sight is dimmed and his limbs stiffened with age." Sumner was able to converse and expressed curiosity about goings-on in the Senate, but even he admitted that his "vivacity of spirit" was gone.

Seward was deeply concerned about Sumner's condition. It had been more than six weeks since Sumner's beating and his colleague not only seemed devoid of energy, but had turned into a sickly old man virtually overnight. "He is much changed for the worse," Seward wrote on Independence Day of 1856. "It is impossible to regard him without apprehension."

There was little doubt that Charles Sumner needed more peaceful surroundings. On July 7, he arranged his affairs in Washington and headed north for further rest. In the coming months, he would stop in Philadelphia, then Cape May, New Jersey, and later, venture high into the mountains of Cresson, Pennsylvania, desperately seeking the restoration of his full health.

One of his last acts before leaving Washington was to write to District of Columbia U.S. attorney Phillip Barton Key, informing Key that he would not be available to testify at Preston Brooks's trial in U.S. Circuit Court. Key had written to Sumner twice about arranging a voluntary appearance on behalf of the prosecution, believing there was no "impropriety" in doing so; perhaps it would even help the case against Brooks. Sumner had fulfilled his legal obligation when he had testified before the grand jury, and, particularly in his current state, that would have to suffice. "I repeat now what I expressed to the Grand Jury," Sumner said, "I have no desire to take any part in this proceeding."

On July 7, 1856, Preston Brooks appeared before Judge Thomas H. Crawford in the Circuit Court of the District of Columbia to stand trial for the caning of Charles Sumner. He was charged with assault by the U.S. attorney, rather than a more serious crime such as attempted murder, one of the several prosecutorial decisions Phillip Barton Key made that benefitted Brooks. Those decisions are best understood in the context of Key's Democratic background.

Key, a strong states'-rights Democrat, was the son of Francis Scott Key, author of "The Star-Spangled Banner" but also the former U.S. attorney for Washington, D.C., under President Andrew Jackson. Phillip Key's sister was married to a prominent Ohio Democratic congressman, and his uncle was Supreme Court Chief Justice Roger B. Taney, who one year later would become famous for a landmark and controversial decision in support of slavery and the slave power. Like Taney, Key had little sympathy for Sumner and his abolitionist friends, and admired noble, wealthy planters such as Brooks and the Southern way of life they defended.

It is difficult to say for certain how much Phillip Barton Key's personal beliefs entered into his approach to the case against Brooks. However, as historian Williamjames Hull Hoffer notes, in addition to charging Brooks with a lesser crime, Key insisted on reading into the record his exchange of letters with Sumner in which the Massachusetts senator explained that his continued illness prevented him from appearing in court to offer testimony. Some Sumner supporters would say later that this was a tactical error, perhaps deliberate on Key's part, that made Sumner appear both arrogant and exaggerative of his incapacity. In his own testimony later, Brooks objected to Sumner's absence and hinted that his victim had overstated the severity of the attack.

Brooks also had a strong defense team, who put Southern lawmakers on the stand to testify that Sumner had engaged in his own premeditated offense—delivering "The Crime Against Kansas" speech. What had the abolitionist senator expected as a response?

One day after the trial began, on July 8, a sympathetic Judge Crawford found Brooks guilty (there was no jury) and sentenced him to a fine of $300, significantly less than the $1,000 fine he had predicted he'd receive. Sumner supporters were incensed, claiming the "paltry fine" clearly showed the proslavery temperament of the federal courts in the District of Columbia and the overall proslavery leanings of Washington, D.C., in general. Brooks paid the fine and walked out of court. Later, his supporters in the South raised the money to reimburse him. The legal proceedings of the caning incident were officially concluded. The next day, Preston Brooks would face a congressional jury of his peers—the full House of Representatives was scheduled to begin deliberations on whether he should be expelled.

Brooks was ready. "I can't fight every body who denounces me," he wrote to his brother, Ham, "[but] I shall do my full duty [and not] shrink from any issue which involves a yielding of the constitutional rights or a taming of the lofty spirit . . . of the southern portion of the Confederacy." Brooks sought to allay his brother's concerns that he might face physical harm once the full House hearings began, assuring him that he was always armed "and will use my weapons if attacked." Nor would he hear of Ham traveling to Washington to defend him. "You . . . must not think of [it]," he wrote. "I have as many friends as I want and never intend to permit a friend to be involved on my account." Brooks's confidence was bolstered by his belief that, despite the threats he had received, his enemies did not have the stomach for a physical confrontation. He reassured Ham: "The dogs may bite when I kick them but, will never dare assail me, though I have fifty letters saying I shall be killed."

His bravado aside, Preston Brooks was beginning to feel the pressure that accompanies fame or infamy.

To the entire North, he was an object of scorn, representative of the incivility and increasing barbarism of slave-owners. To his beloved South, he wore the mantle of courageous hero, someone with the guts to finally silence the arrogant abolitionists after their years of insolence and repeated interference in Southern affairs. Brooks was not comfortable in either role. "The responsibility of my position is painfully heavy," he admitted to his brother, Ham, "for I have lost my individuality in my representative capacity." In his new role as "exponent of the South," Republicans—"Black Republicans" as the most radical abolitionists were labeled by Southerners—were "war[r]ing in my person." It pained him that Northerners considered him "a fair sampling of every slaveholder" or "the type, the result, of the effect of slavery." Later, he would say with regret: "I feel that my individuality has in great measure been destroyed."

This would not change when the full House took up the investigating committee's recommendation to expel Brooks. The brazenness and ferocity of the caning had awakened long-buried, almost primal responses from Congressional members, and they would direct either their fury or their jubilation not toward Brooks the man, but toward Brooks the symbol: diabolical miscreant to the North, avenging angel to the South. The political order in Washington was unraveling. Debate had deteriorated, mistrust had multiplied, and compromise was no longer seen as a sign of political virtue and maturity, but merely as weakness.

The tension was palpable when members crowded into the steamy House chamber on July 9 to debate Preston Brooks's future. To consider expelling a member was weighty enough, but every representative knew that the debate over the next few days was about far more than a lone man's fate; the nation's future could hang in the balance. Congressmen were well aware that whatever their decision, one side would be angry, perhaps irreconcilably so. Voting to expel Brooks would satisfy the North and infuriate the South; letting Brooks retain his seat would send renewed outrage through the Northern states.

Despite the stakes and the hot weather ("I feel very languid and indisposed to exertion" admitted Thomas L. Clingman of North Carolina), representatives did not shy away from the chamber or the debate. One after another, members of the House stood and delivered lengthy speeches, in part to educate their colleagues and in part to ensure that their remarks were reprinted in the more than three thousand newspapers that Americans relied on to get their information.

Their positions were predictable. One Tennessee congressman claimed that Brooks, "instead of deserving punishment, merited the highest commendation." Sumner, he said, "did not get a lick more than he deserved," and that he, as well as some members of the House deserved "a good whipping." Through the course of their speeches, Southerners generally agreed with Rep. James L. Orr of South Carolina, who argued that Brooks felt he had a "high and holy obligation resting on him to step forward and repel the insult made on the character of his state and his relative." Orr parroted the Southern belief that Brooks had little choice but to assault Sumner, that Sumner's intentional provocation in "The Crime Against Kansas" demanded nothing less, and that Sumner's injuries were far from serious.

Orr also accused the North and the Republicans of using the caning for their own political purposes. He noted that eighty members of the House had voted that very morning to reprint a hundred thousand extra copies of the House committee report investigating the caucus—"one third of which is the offensive speech in full." Why would they do so? "It is intended as an electioneering document for the Republican Party . . . part of a systematic effort to mislead and inflame the public," Orr said.

Northerners disagreed vehemently on all counts. New Jersey's Alexander Pennington said Orr's "arrow" was "pointless, though poisoned, and fell wide and short of its mark." Setting the tone for the remarks of virtually every other Northern member, Pennington called the caning "a gross and unparalleled outrage committed upon the Constitution." While he ascribed "no murderous purpose" to Brooks, he believed the "deadly weapon [was] wielded in a murderous manner." This could not stand in a nation that cherished the right of free speech. If individuals were protected by the First Amendment against lawsuits, fines, and imprisonment for speaking out, was it not also reasonable to protect them against the "bludgeon of the bully, the ruthlessness of the ruffian, and the assaults of the assassin?"

And on and on it went, for nearly six full days inside the sweltering House chamber, with neither side offering quarter nor compromise. Every Northern representative sounded themes similar to Pennington—that the caning was an attack against the laws of the nation. Orr spoke for virtually all Southerners (though three Southern lawmakers did agree that the House at least had jurisdiction to censure Brooks)—they maintained that Brooks's action was in retaliation for personal insults against his relative and his region. These arguments spoke volumes about how far apart North and South were on this issue, and by extension, on the issue that lay at the root of the caning: slavery. Debate did not soften battle lines between sections; instead, the two sides dug in and reinforced their positions.

When debate was exhausted, House Speaker Nathaniel Banks

of Sumner's home state of Massachusetts requested a roll-call vote on the committee's motion to expel Brooks from the House. For one of the first times in recent memory, the slave power was outnumbered, but not by enough. A two-thirds majority vote was required to pass the expulsion resolution, and Preston Brooks knew the Republicans did not have the votes. Three weeks earlier, Brooks had predicted that about 120 members of the House would vote in favor of his expulsion and 70 would vote against the measure; while those numbers would fall short of the two-thirds majority required to expel him, he admitted such a margin would be "censure enough for me." Brooks actually had underestimated his support.

After nearly a week of debate, the House voted 121 to 95 to expel Brooks, a full 23 votes short of the necessary two-thirds majority. All but one of the majority votes were from the free states. Thirteen free-state Democrats voted with Southerners against the expulsion resolution. The House also fell short of the necessary two-thirds majority to officially censure South Carolina's Lawrence M. Keitt, and the vote to censure Henry Edmundson was defeated outright.

Immediately after the humiliating though mostly symbolic July 14 vote, a proud and wounded Preston Brooks requested and was granted permission to address the House.

Brooks had remained silent during the debate about his future, trusting his defense to his colleagues and friends "who are abler and more learned than myself." He believed the issues under discussion transcended his particular interests and deed, and affected his constituents, the House, and "the Constitution itself." Now, though, it was time.

Flanked by Senators Butler and Mason, who remained seated, Brooks stood tall and surveyed the packed House galleries, his neat wavy brown hair, natty goatee, piercing eyes, and defiant demeanor all reflecting his position as a Southern gentleman and a proud representative of Edgefield and South Carolina.

He began, as his Southern brethren had argued, by insisting that the caning was a "personal affair," carried out in retribution for Sumner's attack on Butler and South Carolina. Had he not responded, Brooks believed he would have forfeited his own self-respect, "and perhaps the good opinion of my countrymen." By taking actions into his own hands, Brooks said he meant "no disrespect" to the Senate nor to the state of Massachusetts.

But beyond those acknowledgments, Brooks expressed no contrition for his attack against Sumner, nor did he believe the House had any authority to censure him, let alone vote on expulsion. Interrupted by both applause and hisses—Speaker Banks threatened to clear the House galleries of spectators—Brooks argued that if he had committed any "breach of privilege," it was against the Senate and not the House, yet the Senate had chosen not to act on the issue. The House's argument that its authority extended to every member regardless of where transgressions occurred was absurd on its face, Brooks said. "How far does your authority extend?" he asked. "Across the Potomac? To my own home?" Would Brooks be punished by the House if he returned to South Carolina, found that "one of my slaves had behaved badly in [his] absence," and ordered the slave flogged?

Of course not, Brooks argued. The Constitution itself provided him with the authority to "inflict [punishment] upon my slave, who is my property." Thus, the House's claim that it had the power to wield authority over the behavior of its members *outside* the chamber was irrational, immoral, and unconstitutional. "If your authority goes into the Senate Chamber, even when the Senate is not in session, why should it not go into the ante-rooms and down the steps of the Capitol?" Brooks wondered sarcastically. "Why not pursue me into the Avenue, into the steamboat, to my plantation." And yet, Brooks argued, that's exactly what his House colleagues had done, and in so doing, his peers had judged him "to posterity as a man unworthy . . . of a seat in this Hall. And for what?"

Brooks scoffed at Pennington's assertion—even while he insulted him personally for his girth—that the attack on Sumner had carried with it "an intent to kill." Nonsense, Brooks declared. "If I desired to kill the Senator, why did I not do it? You all admit that I had him in my power." Brooks reiterated that it was precisely because he wanted to spare Sumner's life that he chose an "ordinary cane" as his weapon. Otherwise, he might have committed a murderous act that he would have "regretted the balance of my natural life."

Disgusted with most House members who voted to expel him, Brooks said he had been pursued with "unparalleled bitterness," and yet he would not give them the satisfaction of renouncing his actions in any way. "If they are satisfied with the present condition of this affair, I am," he said. He thanked his friends and especially offered his gratitude to colleagues from non-slave-owning states who voted against his ouster. Even a few of those who voted to expel him likely "have been extorted by an outside pressure at home," rather than holding the genuine belief that Brooks should be removed against his will from the House. And while he "owed respect" to those who voted against him without resorting to personal attacks, Brooks hoped they would understand that, from this moment forward, "my self-respect requires that I shall pass them as strangers."

Preston Brooks knew how the vote would turn out. He knew Republicans would lack the two-thirds majority to expel him, but he was deeply rankled and insulted that a simple majority of members would declare him unfit to serve in the House any longer. He had "long foreseen" the outcome, was "altogether prepared for it," and as such, had ten days earlier placed a letter announcing his resignation with the governor of South Carolina, "to take effect the very instant that I announce my resignation upon this floor."

Defiant and unbowed, Brooks finished his remarks before the House with an expected but still dramatic flourish: "And now, Mr. Speaker, I announce to you and to this House, that I am no longer a member of the Thirty-Fourth Congress." Brooks strode from the House chamber, and, after being thronged at the doorway by sympathetic Southern women who embraced and kissed him, left the Capitol building.

Preston Brooks's absence from the House of Representatives was short-lived. On July 28, South Carolina held a special election in Brooks's congressional district to fill the seat he had resigned. Legally eligible to seek reelection, Brooks did so (as did Keitt, who, two days after Brooks, resigned in the wake of his own censure). He urged his loyal constituents to return him to office "with an unanimity which will thunder into the ears of fanaticism the terrors of the storm that is coming upon them."

He ran without opposition and remained in Washington in the weeks prior to the election, two factors that would normally depress turnout. Instead, his constituents turned out in huge numbers to show their support—Brooks received nearly eight thousand votes, 30 percent more than his 1854 regular election total.

On August 1, he returned to the House chamber, approached the rostrum, and Speaker Banks administered to him the oath to support the Constitution of the United States. Three weeks after his dramatic resignation, Congressman Preston Brooks resumed his seat as the representative of South Carolina's Fourth District.

Even more remarkably, in the regular Congressional election in the fall of 1856, though some of the initial excitement of the caning would subside, Brooks would again run unopposed and carry the day without a single dissenting write-in vote in the entire congressional district. "For inflicting merited punishment, the entire South has applauded and commended me, and placed me in the position as representative," Brooks would assert.

Such universal adulation incensed Sumner's supporters, but at the same time, Brooks's meteoric rise to fame in the South provided powerful fuel to stoke the fires of the Republican Party sweeping across the North.

SEVENTEEN

SHAMMING ILLNESS

Abolitionist and women's rights advocate Jane G. Swisshelm was shocked at Charles Sumner's condition when she met with him in late August: "When he rises from his chair, he takes hold of the table," she wrote. "His gait, at a first glance, appears that of a man of ninety years of age." He walked like a man "creeping through a darkened chamber under the influence of a paroxysm of nervous headache."

The description was part of a long letter Swisshelm wrote that was published by the *New York Times* on August 23, 1856, an update to readers on Sumner's convalescence. Swisshelm had visited Sumner at the health resort of Dr. Robert M. Jackson, a physician in the town of Cresson, Pennsylvania, high in the Allegheny Mountains, where Sumner had retired for rest, fresh air, and exercise. While Sumner assured Swisshelm that he was improving, she feared the Massachusetts senator was deluding himself by his insistence that he would return to Washington in two weeks. "Ever since his injury, he has been going to be 'quite well' in two weeks," she wrote in her letter, "[yet] sometimes he feels a pressure on the top of his head, and [his injury] appears to hurt him when he walks; but he [still claims he] will be 'ready to go' to Washington 'in two weeks.'" Swisshelm was deeply concerned: "Mr. Sumner crowds everything from my thoughts just now," she wrote.

With the exception of brief intervals of improvement, Sumner had suffered badly through most of the summer. In addition to intense pain, he was beset with fear, feebleness, fever, and frustration. From Cape May, New Jersey, he wrote to Samuel Gridley Howe in late July: "I feel as if [I'm] composed of gristle instead of bone, and am very soon wearied by walking, which induces a pressure on the brain." Frustrated and demoralized by his debilitating condition, Sumner exerted the additional strain on himself for being absent from the Senate "at a moment when more than ever in my life I was able to wield influence and do good. This has been hard to bear."

Upon his move to the Alleghenies, Sumner showed initial improvement, writing exuberantly to Ralph Waldo Emerson on August 16: "At last I am physically convalescent. Three times, in this mountain air, I have ridden on horse-back, & I begin to feel returning strength." Later in the month, he informed Salmon P. Chase that he was becoming stronger and had ridden horses for ten consecutive days. He wondered when his physician would consider it "safe . . . to make any mental effort." But then he suffered another setback and Sumner's doctor urged the senator to remain in Cresson for at least another month. Sumner longed to be heard on the issues of the day. "I have felt this divorce from my public duties at this time keenly," he confided to Chase. Sumner was so dispirited that his injuries had prevented him from speaking his mind during such a crucial period in history that he said he would trade his entire political future for "three weeks of strength" near the close of the congressional session.

Sumner's friends and fellow Republicans urged the senator to show restraint and patience, and indeed, to rest for the remainder of the session; otherwise they feared a severe relapse and potentially deadly consequences. "You will lose everything if you quit that invigorating mountain air," wrote the Rev. William H. Furness from a stifling Philadelphia, "and [you] run the hazard of being an invalid for months to come." Former Boston mayor Josiah Quincy concurred: "I entreat you, my dear friend," he wrote to Sumner on August 22, "not to think to act on public affairs until your health is *firmly* restored."

But the isolation of his Allegheny retreat weighed heavily on Sumner—acute loneliness gripped him. In addition, his debilitating headaches, lack of focus, and inability to sleep at night all contributed to a fear that he might be losing his mind. The concern was compounded when one of his doctors admitted that he was not sure whether Sumner's brain "was deranged *organically* or only *functionally*." Sumner expressed his dread of the former. A permanent brain injury would be unbearable. If Brooks's cane had inflicted lasting damage, then "death would have been my best friend." To Theodore Parker, he invoked a biblical reference when he said he wanted to leave Cresson earlier, "setting my face Eastward," but his physicians advised against it. "I [still] feel [the pain of] a short walk and any mental exercise on my brain," he said. "This must not be. The object now is to banish these tendencies, that they may not be *chronic*." Sumner confessed to his good friend that, for the opportunity to make one speech during the current Senate session, he would have "bartered a good slice of [my] life that remains."

Finally, after a month in Cresson, Sumner could not tolerate the insularity of the mountain locale any longer; against his doctor's advice, he traveled to Philadelphia, hoping to get some work done. Again, his condition worsened and rendered him incapacitated. "I left the mountain prematurely," he confessed, "before my nervous system had hardened into health." To an attorney friend he admitted: "My nervous system has suffered sadly . . . and it is now all jangled." All he could do was "pray for health, which comes slowly, very slowly."

Newspaper reporters followed Sumner from location to location during the summer of 1856 and wrote about his condition; Americans North and South were able to pay close attention to the state of the senator's health, and most were not shy about expressing their opinions. One of those opinions, repeated again and again, filled Charles Sumner with anger and stung him almost as painfully as the caning itself—this was not an assault on his person, but on his character. As though his physical and mental maladies were not difficult enough, Sumner now tried to fight through bitterness over what he considered the most egregious insult of all. Plain and simple, Southerners believed he was faking.

"While suffering for more than four months," Sumner wrote in September, "I have been charged with the ignoble deed of *shamming illness.*" He had heard these charges expressed throughout the summer, and though they weighed heavily on his mind, he had remained silent until he crafted the sentence in a letter to a friend.

Most Southerners thought Sumner's injuries were minor and that both Sumner and Northerners were exaggerating and exploiting the effects of the caning to build political momentum for the Republican Party and abolitionism in general. The shamming charges began early, when the *Whig* of Richmond, Virginia, published a piece titled "Possuming" on May 31: "For our part, we never had believed that Sumner was sufficiently hurt to make it necessary for him to take to his bed at all." The paper scoffed at the notion that the "well deserved" caning was so severe that it could "detain him in confinement for more than a week." More likely, the paper said, Sumner's absence from the Senate and reports of his serious injuries were part of a "miserable abolitionist trick from beginning to end," designed to encourage sympathy and strengthen resolve among Northerners.

Attacking Sumner's manhood, the *Whig* added that "nigger-worshipping fanatics of the male gender, and weak-minded women and silly children, are horribly affected at the thought of blood oozing from a pin scratch." The way to scare Sumner back on his feet, the paper declared, was for the Senate to appoint a committee of "one Southern man" to assess Sumner's condition. In fact, the mere sight of a "hundredth part of a Southern man" would be enough to "impart to the possuming wretch the strength to enable him to take up his bed and walk—yea, walk even to Boston!"

Throughout the summer, these sentiments took hold and blossomed, convincing Southerners that the North had resorted to the most dastardly and dishonest tactic of all: exploiting Sumner's assault for political reasons. Did this not provide the freshest and most compelling evidence to date of the Republicans' shallowness and, even more distasteful, their lack of integrity and honor?

Sumner was not helped by Dr. Boyle's "flesh wound" remark shortly after the attack, nor by his constant relocating during the summer, which, while purportedly to seek relief and comfort, suggested to the South that Sumner was perfectly fit to travel. These issues were compounded in July when the *Washington Union*, an unabashed supporter of the proslavery Pierce administration, reported that Sumner's wounds were entirely healed, but that he refused to resume his seat in the Senate due to "his wounded pride and his irrepressible anger and indignation." By the fall, the *Union* went one step farther, printing the accusation that Sumner's physicians were "nursing the disease, lest it should die a natural death." Sumner, the paper said, was resolved not to recover until after the next senatorial election in Massachusetts.

Even some Northern publications shared these feelings. The Democratic *Boston Post* suggested that Sumner's doctors were conspiring to portray him as an invalid until just before the elections, when he would suddenly appear triumphant and healthy, thereby energizing and exciting voters.

In early September, Republican strategists, alarmed about this stubborn and relentless drumbeat, urged Sumner's other four doctors (Wister, Perry, Lindsly, and Jackson) to put the "shamming" issue to rest by issuing sworn statements on the extent of his illness. Dr. Perry, one of Boston's most esteemed physicians, said Sumner was so terribly injured that mental or physical exertion could cost him his life. In his sworn affidavit, he said Sumner was "in that state of extreme nervous exhaustion from which men are months, and at times even years, in being fully restored." Dr. Jackson, a Democrat, stated that Sumner was "extremely unwell" when he arrived in Cresson, and that he left the mountain town—prematurely and against doctor's orders—"still an invalid." He said Sumner was unsteady on his feet, languid, pale, displayed a weak pulse, and even the slightest mental effort, like "writing a common letter of business," produced pressure on his brain and a "dull throbbing pain in the head." Jackson, who was also postmaster in Cresson, was removed from the position by the Pierce administration for issuing a sworn statement that Sumner was an invalid.

Sumner's behavior and correspondence in the late summer and early fall repeatedly appeared to confirm the severity of his condition. He turned down an invitation to appear at the Republicans of Rhode Island convention, telling the invitation committee that he was still under orders from physicians not to exert any "public effort." He apologized for turning down similar invitations from the Republicans of Illinois (citing his "long-continued disability") and the Republicans of Hudson River Counties in New York (pointing out he was "too feeble for any exertion").

When he missed a long-scheduled freedom rally in Cincinnati in September, many of the tens of thousands of attendees went away disappointed. Sumner was crushed. "With sorrow inexpressible," he told organizers, "I am still constrained to all the care and reserve of an invalid." The exertion he would require to reach Ohio, most of the distance by "slow stage[coach]," would almost certainly trigger a relapse. "This is hard, very hard, for me to bear," Sumner despaired, "for I long to do something at this critical moment for the cause. What is life without action?"

To abolitionist Lydia Maria Child, he explained that even when he felt marginally better, "some slight excess of exertion seems to undo everything" and he wondered "when this doom will close." To John Bigelow, he admitted that he was "still an invalid," that he faced "weeks, if not months, of seclusion," and that his "only chance of cure [was] repose." He was perhaps most honest with Samuel Gridley Howe when he described the peaks and valleys of his health on September 11: "This is my best day. But yesterday was a disheartening day; I seemed to be going back." And this: "Two nights of this week I have passed without closing my eyes for five minutes—literally hearing the clock strike every hour till daylight, while my legs and arms seemed all jangled." A disappointed Sumner told Howe that doctors advised him against "anything except amusement till cold weather." And to virtually all of these correspondents, Sumner reminded them that his infirmity was so serious that he lacked the strength to return home to Boston, though he had been away for ten months.

None of this evidence, from doctors, journalists, or Sumner himself, dissuaded Southerners. At large rallies and small meetings, in letters and newspaper articles, they repeatedly accused Sumner of shamming. They challenged his masculinity and, by extension, the character and toughness of the entire North. They dismissed with laughter the claim that a gutta-percha cane—one that had shattered to splinters in the attack, no less—carried the heft to incapacitate Sumner for so long. While Northerners expressed outrage at Brooks's savagery, and viewed him as representative of the Southern brutality that was a necessary characteristic of slave-owners, Southerners rejected the assertion outright. They adamantly depicted the caning as a personal incident, designed to avenge a personal insult, by a means that was common among gentlemen of the South.

No historical evidence suggests that Sumner was faking. Indeed, the evidence is weighted heavily in the opposite direction. Throughout the summer of 1856, Sumner's feeble condition and intense suffering are documented—by Sumner himself, by virtually all of the medical professionals who treated him, and by all of his friends and visitors. As Sumner biographer David Donald concluded, if there was a plan for Sumner to feign illness, others would have been part of the conspiracy—"and if there was a plot, it was one of the best kept secrets in American history."

Nonetheless, the chasm between North and South on the issue of "shamming" further reinforced the sectional battle lines that were hardened by the caning itself. Reason no longer seemed to matter. Sworn testimony was rejected outright and documentation was suspect. Across both North and South, any facts that challenged the story line were discredited, discouraged, or dismissed altogether.

On Friday, August 29, at 8 o'clock in the evening, throngs of Columbia, South Carolina, residents jammed the street in front of the city courthouse to see and hear from their newly crowned hero, Preston Brooks.

The Edgefield congressman was making his way home from Washington for the first time since the caning. In town squares along the way, Southerners had gathered to cheer and thank him for—in the words of one newspaper reporter—"the prompt and appropriate manner in which he chastised the notorious Charles Sumner for his wanton abuse and cowardly assault upon . . . Andrew Butler, and the fair fame of his state." Now, in the South Carolina capital, Columbia Mayor Edward Arthur presented Brooks with a silver pitcher, a beautifully crafted silver goblet, and one of the "finest hickory canes with a handsome gold head," both to reward his beating of Sumner and his display of "honorable conduct" in the stressful days and weeks that followed. The goblet was engraved with the inscription: "To Hon. Ps Brooks from Citizens of Columbia, May 22, 1856." It was no small fact that the goblet was engraved not with the date of the rally, but with the date of the caning—Columbia citizens recognized its singular importance in the swirl of events that were gripping the nation. For his actions on that fateful day, Preston Brooks was embraced by South Carolina's capital city as one of "Carolina's noblest sons."

Columbia residents had been waiting to fete Brooks since May, but felt the celebration would be far more meaningful if he could attend personally; now their patience had been rewarded. Befitting Brooks's newfound stature, his admirers in Columbia had even arranged for a handsome coach, drawn by four "neatly decorated" horses, to transport him from the train station to City Hall. But celebrations in South Carolina's upper districts had delayed his arrival in Columbia; rather than his train pulling into the depot the previous afternoon, where a large crowd had gathered to greet him, it did not reach the station until 4:00 A.M. At that time, all was quiet in Columbia.

But a couple of respectful hours later, a committee of citizens called on Brooks, notified him of the planned rally, urged him to stay over one night in Columbia despite his desire to get home, and suggested he speak at 8 P.M. Brooks agreed to the invitation, saying it would give him "great pleasure" to speak.

After Mayor Arthur congratulated Brooks for his "triumph over the malignant slanderers" from the North, Brooks advanced to the front of the portico, amid roars of approval from the crowd. He thanked them for their support and attendance, and told them he had been met with kindness from the South "every foot of the way" from Washington. Brooks told the gathering that he attacked Sumner thanks to a "high sense of duty," and that his attack was an "ordinary castigation." What had resulted was that abolitionists, seeking excuses for their "vile slanders," had made the caning a pretext for more fanaticism. Brooks said he felt as though he had done as much as any one man to "concentrate the feeling of the South." If the South could not live in equality in the Union, then its only course was to dissolve it. "With right upon our side, we could meet and conquer them," Brooks said.

Brooks then turned his attention to the upcoming presidential election, urging his fellow South Carolinians to vote for Democrat James Buchanan, not because Buchanan was his "first, second, or third choice, but [because he was] my last." He would rather have seen Franklin Pierce or Stephen Douglas nominated, but he reminded the crowd, "there must be compromise everywhere," and Buchanan and the Democrats represented a proslavery platform that was "the right one for the South."

Conversely, Brooks warned, a Frémont victory in November would be a disaster for the South. In fact, if Republicans were successful in their bid for the presidency, Brooks said Southerners should march to Washington on inauguration day and seize the archives and the government treasury. "We should anticipate them, and force them to attack us," he told the cheering crowd.

If the caning had dramatically changed Charles Sumner's life, it had also transformed the once moderate Preston Brooks into the South's chief symbol of defiance and even secession.

Several weeks after the Columbia rally, in early October, Brooks appeared before a massive crowd in the village of Ninety Six in Edgefield. The *New York Times* estimated the gathering at ten thousand people, the largest assemblage ever in the village, and the glorious culmination of the dozens of Southern celebrations to honor Brooks. Special trains were run from Greenville and Columbia, carrying dignitaries and ordinary citizens alike, all with a desire to bask in the energy and excitement that Brooks's presence generated. Senator Butler was there, as was Georgia's Robert Toombs, and the South Carolina governor presided. A band played music, a military color guard raised South Carolina's flag, and Brooks was once again presented with goblets and canes (one report said he received a wagon load of canes to replace the one he had shattered over Sumner's head).

The fanfare was beyond impressive, yet the enormous rally would best be remembered by Brooks's fire-eating remarks. The South Carolina congressman—who once said that disunion would be a "fearful catastrophe" and its prevention was "the highest duty of every patriot"—thrilled the thousands in Edgefield when he declared: "I have been a disunionist since the time I could think!" He went one dramatic step further and brought the crowd to a state of delirium when he asserted: "The Constitution of the United States should be torn to fragments and a Southern Constitution formed in which every State should be a slave state."

Even some Southerners gasped at Brooks's inflammatory remarks, which were quickly reprinted and repeated across North and South; they attached themselves to Brooks's historical legacy with almost as much tenacity as the caning itself. The incendiary language was out of character for the Edgefield congressman, but then, so was the beating of Charles Sumner. Had the pressure of the caning and all it wrought—the trial and hearings, Brooks's near expulsion from the House and his "loss of individuality," the notorious reputation he had developed in the North, the political exploitation by Republicans—clouded Brooks's judgment? Did his new status as Southern hero and iconic representative of Southern thought and lifestyle convince him that frenzied anti-Unionist proclamations alone would satisfy his countrymen? Did his Edgefield speech reflect a radical change in his thinking or was it merely his way of telling the audience what it wanted to hear?

Some in the South believed the latter. The Charleston *Courier* described Brooks's remarks as the result of this "national and union loving" man being "frighted . . . from his propriety." Virginia Congressman J. M. Botts, who had actually denounced the assault on Sumner, said the "compliments he [Brooks] had received from his warmhearted, enthusiastic but injudicious friends in the South," coupled with the "taunts and abuses heaped upon him" by the North, had combined to "bewilder and mislead his judgment in much that has transpired since." Historian Robert Neil Mathis pointed out that, considering Brooks had emerged as a "symbolic defender" of all Southern grievances, it was remarkable that the Edgefield speech was the only public instance after the caning that his "nationalism faltered."

Without question, Brooks had become the most popular and admired man in South Carolina, and probably across the South as well; some suggested he run for governor and others wanted him as "the first President of the Southern Republic." However, Mathis pointed out, after his extreme language at the Edgefield rally, Brooks made no more disunionist speeches, nor did he "seek further personal aggrandizement." He also continued to support the Constitution. Notorious villain or honorable knight, Preston Brooks had become a national figure, and his name was synonymous with a remarkable attack that resonated with symbolism across a divided nation. One contemporaneous Southern journal jubilantly and accurately proclaimed: "His name [has] now reached nearly every fireside in the land."

EIGHTEEN

THE EMPTY CHAIR

Throughout the summer and fall of 1856, Charles Sumner's continued struggles to regain his health, combined with Preston Brooks's overwhelming celebrity in the South, provided antislavery Republicans with a perfect scenario as the November election approached.

From the beginning, Republicans linked the caning with the crisis in Kansas. One day after the caning, Nathaniel Clover wrote to Sumner: "The crisis has come. Your blood in the Senate Chamber mingles with the blood of the helpless dweller in the jungle of Kansas." The "Bleeding Kansas–Bleeding Sumner" theme became a critical part of the Republicans' campaign platform for 1856. In Indianapolis, for example, Republicans organized a parade complete with floats that dramatized the assault on Sumner and the Southern brutality in Kansas. For the North to witness "one of its best men butchered in Congress," one supporter wrote to Sumner, offered an opportunity to see the aggression of the slave power in action. "Had it not been for your poor head, the Kansas outrage would not have been felt at the North."

Republican strategists took full advantage of popular indignation across the North, distributing more than one million copies of Sumner's "The Crime Against Kansas" as a thirty-two-page pamphlet. They delivered speeches, deploring the fact that Southern Democrats were using the caning as a rallying cry, even as Republicans adopted the exact same strategy. They condemned celebrations across the South that lionized Brooks. One wealthy lead-pipe manufacturer in Boston, a conservative who had little in common with abolitionists, was inspired by the assault on Sumner and put all his energies and his considerable funds into making Kansas a free state. Historian Allen Nevins recounted that in five months, George L. Stearns raised $48,000 for the Massachusetts State Kansas Association, while his wife collected between $10,000 and $30,000 in clothing and supplies.

Brooks's attack and the Southern response to it were also seen by Northerners as a frontal assault on their section after years of the South's back-room political machinations and manipulation in its efforts to protect and perpetuate slavery. "We all or *nearly* all felt that we had been personally maltreated and insulted," one Boston man wrote to Sumner.

This perceived attack on the entire North provided the momentum behind the biggest benefit Republicans enjoyed from the caning: the flood of moderate and even conservative Northerners who joined the party. Most of these people had no great sympathy for the abolitionist cause, and even objected to the outright abolition of slavery; many Northern businessmen worried about severe economic repercussions if the flow of cotton and other products from the South was disrupted. Yet, no reasonable Northerner could condone either Brooks's action or Southern support of it; most Northerners, regardless of their political persuasion, viewed the caning as a violent trampling of free-speech rights. One Boston businessman said that Brooks's assault "proves to me a lower civilization [in the South] than I would ever before believe," adding that he had previously and unwisely ignored abolitionists' insistence that this was the case.

The caning offered Republicans the opportunity to attack the South without attacking slavery, thereby making an argument that was far more palatable to moderates. In essence, the Republican argument became: If the caning has unified the South, must not the North also unify to protect its interests and its constitutional rights? One Northern Democrat who joined the Republican Party after the caning did not support the abolitionist cause and continued to believe that blacks were inferior to whites, but he could no longer tolerate Southern brutality, as exemplified by the caning, to make the proslavery case. "Had the slave power been less *insolently aggressive*, I would have been content to see it extend . . . but when it seeks to extend its sway by fire & sword . . . I am ready to say hold enough!" To a longtime Democratic associate, he added: "Reserve no place for me. *I shall not come back.*"

Historian William Gienapp points out that Democrats were alarmed by the intensity of anti-Southern feeling they observed in the North. One Illinois Democrat informed the party's presidential candidate, James Buchanan, that "there is a terrible rancor in the public mind against the people and the institutions of the south—a rancor utterly uncontrollable and I do not know but it is bound to be perpetual." In fact, Gienapp notes, conservatives were *most* aroused by the assault and were vehement in their denunciations of the South.

The South's reaction to the caning fueled the rancor and played right into Republican hands. Had Southerners repudiated Brooks's actions, or even remained silent, Northern Republicans would have been left with a single isolated incident that could have been attributable to one congressman who lost his temper. But the South's overwhelming approval fundamentally altered the dynamic—the congressional debate over the caning, the expulsion vote along sectional and party lines, the multitude of pro-Brooks celebrations across the South, and Brooks's overwhelming reelection all stunned Northerners. These events provided demonstrable and indisputable evidence that the South endorsed this brutality, and thus the entire South was tarred by Brooks's action.

Republicans portrayed Brooks as every Southerner, and Sumner and the North as every Southerners' victim. Each time a news account depicted Southerners rising to Brooks's defense, Republicans reinforced the image of Southerners, slave-owners

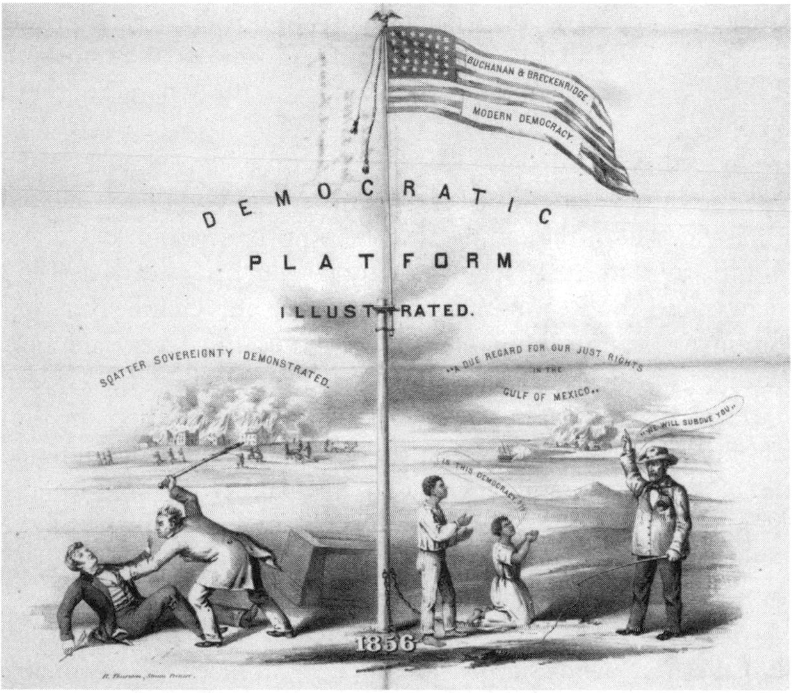

A political poster criticizing the 1856 Democratic platform of James Buchanan and John C. Breckinridge as pro-South and proslavery. To the right, two slaves are chained to the flagpole of "Modern Democracy," while on the left, Preston Brooks beats Charles Sumner. (*Library of Congress*)

in particular, as brutal and violent, and Southern society as backward and barbaric. In the opinion of the *New York Times*, the caning confirmed the impression that the South "will stop at no extremity of violence in order to subdue the people of the Free States and force them into a tame subserviency of its own domination."

Throughout the summer, conservatives begged Southern congressmen not to publicly endorse Brooks's action, but Southern support of the caning continued to be a gift to Republicans. One prominent Southern banker, doing business in New York City, warned Howell Cobb, the leading Southern member of the House investigating committee, that Brooks's assault could not be justified, and that any attempt by the South to condone it "will prove disastrous in the extreme." Another

New York conservative explained: "It was not the act itself (horrible as it was) that excited me, but the tone of the Southern Press, & the approbation, apparently, of the whole Southern people."

Indeed, well-known and staunch conservatives, who often despised the fanaticism of abolitionists, had completely altered their views after the caning and the Southern response. George Templeton Strong, a New York City lawyer, had as early as 1855 denounced the Republicans as a threat to the Union. But after Sumner's beating, he wrote: "I hold the anti-slavery agitators wrong in principle and mischievous in policy. But the reckless, insolent brutality of our Southern aristocrats may drive me into abolitionism yet." Indeed, after the Republicans nominated Frémont, Strong announced that he planned to vote for the Republican ticket. "I belong to the insurgent plebians of the North arming against a two-penny South Carolina aristocracy," he wrote.

Strong's conversion was repeated again and again by Northerners who simply could not stomach the violence endemic to Brooks's attack. A New York Democrat warned Stephen Douglas that the caning was doing the party "vast injury," and added: "You can scarcely imagine how much steam they [Republicans] are getting up on the subject." One Northern Democratic observer believed the caning would cost the Democratic Party 200,000 votes in the fall election; other key Democrats thought that the losses would be even greater.

Millard Fillmore, who was running for the presidency as a member of the American Party (a combination of Whigs and Know-Nothings) against Democrat Buchanan and Republican Frémont, saw his chances for victory dwindle as these moderate and conservative Democrats switched to Republicans. Fillmore desperately needed these voters—he portrayed himself as a middle-ground candidate for those who did not sympathize with the proslavery Buchanan, but were also wary of the ardently antislavery Republicans.

But the caning so altered the landscape that the middle ground was shrinking rapidly, and Fillmore recognized it: "Brooks's attack upon Sumner has done more for Frémont than any 20 of his warmest friends [in the] North have been able to accomplish," he said. "If Frémont is elected, he will owe his election entirely to the troubles in Kansas, and the martyrdom of Sumner." He added grumpily: "The Republicans ought to pension Brooks for life."

The single most important symbol that bolstered the Republican cause during the summer and fall of 1856 was not the deep wellspring of Southern support for Preston Brooks, nor was it Brooks's unanimous reelection to Congress following his dramatic resignation, though these were clearly beneficial to the Republicans' efforts to draw moderates and conservatives to the party.

The most visible, understandable, and emotionally charged symbol that benefited Republicans was Charles Sumner's vacant chair in the United States Senate chamber. Sumner's continued ill health and his prolonged absence from the Senate—more than five months as the November elections approached—enabled Republicans to keep the caning issue front and center. They recognized how deeply the caning had touched Northern sensibilities; Sumner's well-chronicled, highly publicized, and as-yet unsuccessful efforts to regain his health and resume his duties only heightened the caning's already powerful impact across the North. As one of Sumner's friends assured him in early October, the caning "has sunk deep in many minds, whom political tracts and politicians never reach." Republicans inherently understood this, fully grasping that the caning, in the words of a Boston minister, raised to new heights "the greatest moral struggle of our Age and Country in the contest between American Freedom and American Despotism."

For this reason, Republicans were in no hurry for Sumner to return to his duties. Perhaps the greatest irony during the early months of Sumner's convalescence was the senator's earnest struggle to get well even as his political allies viewed his absence as far more advantageous to the future of the Republican Party. When Sumner wrote to Wendell Phillips and said he longed again "for my place in the Senate, where I was struck down,"

Phillips replied: "Your empty chair can make a more fervent appeal than even you." Each time Sumner's doctors ordered bed rest and forbade public appearances, Republican strategists applauded. While Sumner lamented how "very hard [it was] to be . . . shut out not only from the duties of life, but also from the world & its society," Republican leaders believed Sumner's continued absence from the public square offered them their best chance for success. A wounded Sumner was far more politically beneficial to Republicans than a fully recovered Sumner could ever be.

At some level, Sumner may have appreciated the symbolic value of his vacant chair to the Northern Republican cause, but his writings reflected the opposite sentiment. Sumner continued to despair at his inability to speak publicly and return to work. Though he wanted to stump for Republican candidates, Sumner's physicians prohibited such strenuous activity. "Never before could I exert so much influence by speaking," he wrote in October, "and now nearly five months have been consumed—a large slice of human life—and I have been compelled to silence."

Even in his reclusiveness, though, Sumner resumed his passionate writing, focusing mainly on the dire situation in Kansas. He urged Republicans to work hard for Frémont's election and the utter defeat of Buchanan, lest the nation surrender "complete control of the National Government" to "347,000 slave-masters" who sought to form a "dominant Oligarchy." He pressed the Republicans of Rhode Island to "rise up as one man" and insist that Kansas be admitted as a free state. He contributed one hundred dollars to the *New York Tribune*'s fundraising effort for the "relief and liberation of Kansas." He urged the Young Men of Massachusetts to rally for the protection of liberty in Kansas, and for the "overthrow of the oligarchical Tyranny which now degrades our Republic." He implored New York Republicans to speak out and fight against the "countless atrocities" in Kansas, which Southerners saw as a "stepping stone to the enslavement of the whole country." Sumner urged them not to hesitate. "Freedom requires [your] vote. Is not this cause worth living for? Is not this cause worth *dying* for?"

But even here, Republicans were grateful that Sumner's writings would only reach individuals or small groups that were the recipients of his private letters. His insistence on making Kansas the center of the debate ran contrary to the Republican campaign strategy as the November election drew near; political operatives wanted the focus on Sumner himself, his ongoing debilitating condition and the brutal attack that left him an invalid. As historian David Donald noted, by stressing the Brooks assault, Republicans believed Northern differences of opinion could be minimized, and the "instincts, passions, and sense of liberty of the free states [could be] roused against the enormous pretensions and villainous acts of the South."

His vacant chair in the Senate rendered Sumner despondent and Republican managers buoyant and hopeful for November. Months earlier, a presidential victory seemed unattainable for the fledgling party; now, with the caning and all its repercussions the top-of-mind issue in the North, a Frémont win looked more than possible. "I long to do something," Charles Sumner wrote in mid-October, but Republicans knew another Sumner observation in the same letter was the key to their November aspirations: "My only chance of cure is repose." The Republicans' hope was the Democrats' fear: that a silent, still recovering Sumner would elicit maximum sympathy among Northern voters.

More than one thousand men on horseback marched in columns, accompanying a procession of nearly twenty carriages, the whole assemblage stretching for more than a half mile along downtown Boston's Washington Street. Thousands of spectators lined the street, the men cheering and brandishing their hats wildly, the women tossing bouquets, and hundreds of residents leaned out the windows of their homes, shouting and waving handkerchiefs madly; all of these Bostonians showered praise upon the haggard and pale man who sat in an open carriage drawn by six magnificent gray horses.

After nearly a year, Charles Sumner had returned home. And on an overcast but unseasonably warm Monday afternoon in November, his fellow citizens of his beloved city turned out to pay him tribute in a remarkable display of affection and solidarity.

Sumner had arrived a day earlier at his friend Longfellow's house after a tough trip from Philadelphia. Against the advice of doctors and despite entreaties from his friends not to make the long trip—"I beseech you not to come," Samuel Gridley Howe telegraphed Sumner on October 31, "most certainly not publicly"—Sumner was determined to return to Boston to cast votes for Frémont for president and for Anson Burlingame in his congressional reelection bid.

Early Monday morning, he was driven to the home of Amos Lawrence in Brookline, and from there traveled by coach through the town of Roxbury and to the Boston line, where hundreds of citizens and mounted riders, as well as scores of dignitaries, gathered to greet Sumner. He acknowledged their cheers, but spoke only a few words, his voice weak and lacking its usual sonorous power—only those near the carriage could hear him, and many of those who saw him up-close were overcome with emotion at his pallid condition and lack of vitality. He said his suffering was "not small" but was "little . . . compared with the suffering of fellow citizens in Kansas." He felt pride that his wounds had been incurred "in the performance of duty," and believed that together, the forces of freedom would enjoy a "final triumph."

Then the procession made its way toward downtown Boston, picking up horsemen along the way, joined by a carriage carrying Boston Mayor Alexander H. Rice. Sumner was overwhelmed by the crowds along the route, overcome by the hundreds of flags, streamers, and banners as his carriage wound through Washington Street, Newton Street, Shawmut Avenue, Dover Street, Tremont Street, Boylston Street, Charles Street, and Beacon Street on its way to the State House. "Massachusetts loves, honors, will sustain and defend her noble Sumner!" announced one banner that was strung high across Newton Street. "Welcome Freedom's Defender!" said another on the side of a building, and plastered across a Dover Street home was another: "Resistance to tyrants is obedience to God." On a house at the corner of Shawmut Avenue and Waltham Street was a sign wreathed in black that reminded all of the fateful day in the Senate Chamber: "May 22, 1856."

Longtime friends, Charles Sumner and Henry Wadsworth Longfellow, photographed by Alexander Gardner. (*Library of Congress*)

Sumner, normally aloof and often icy even with close friends and family, was most touched when his carriage approached the Boston Female Orphan Asylum on Washington Street, where young girls were lined up in front of the building waving handkerchiefs and displaying on a white banner a wreath of evergreen covered with flowers, along with a sign that read: "We weave a wreath for Charles Sumner." This was the only point along the route where Sumner rose to his feet in gratitude. "The kindness of these orphaned ones so touched his feelings, that he could not help acknowledging it in this way," one account explained.

And so it continued, with the signs and the banners becoming more frequent and more expressive as Sumner's entourage moved closer to the State House: "No bludgeon can dim the luster of our champion of Freedom" and "Welcome home! The sons and daughters of Massachusetts greet her noblest defender" and "Infants welcome him whose name lives immortal in the hearts of his countrymen." And from a group of women on a sidewalk: "Massachusetts's most honored son. If the ladies could vote, he would be the next President."

The turnout, the written sentiments, and the unabashed displays of affection were all amazing—but ironic too. Charles Sumner, who had sought adulation for most of his life but found it frustratingly elusive, was now being showered in it, but his physical condition rendered him unable to enjoy it fully. Charles

Sumner, who relished the role of martyr, and often anointed himself when the term did not apply, was now unable to appreciate his newfound status when the label truly was appropriate.

Still, as Sumner approached the State House, the scene must have left him awestruck. One account called it "beyond description." Between five thousand and seven thousand citizens crowded Beacon and Park streets and the long set of stairs that led to the state capitol building itself; building rooftops were packed with thousands more. The crowd greeted Sumner's arrival with long, sustained cheers, and roared even louder as Sumner and other invited guests ascended the steps of a hastily erected platform.

Massachusetts Governor Henry J. Gardner, who had months earlier proposed that the commonwealth assume the costs of Sumner's medical expenses, now urged the crowd to help him welcome Sumner, "the eloquent orator, the accomplished scholar, and the acknowledged statesman . . . the earnest friend of suffering humanity and of every good cause." He reminded the crowd that, once the reception had ended, they should refrain from disturbing Sumner in his own home, but reminded them also that Sumner was "the successful defender of honor and integrity of Massachusetts," and pledged that the state would stand by him "today, tomorrow, and forever."

When Sumner finally began speaking, it was with great difficulty and in a feeble voice. He was able to continue for barely a minute before his strength failed him, and then he handed his prepared remarks to a reporter. Nonetheless, the crowd cheered wildly as Sumner sat down. His written manuscript, published in many places afterward, expressed his deep appreciation to Bostonians and paid tribute to his fellow senator from Massachusetts, Henry Wilson. But he also recalled his painful five months of disability and expressed his sorrow that he had been unable to partake in the slavery debate during a critical moment in history. He sought only "the triumph of truth" and pledged to continue his fight against the slave power: "Show me that I am wrong, and I stop at once; but in the complete conviction of right I shall persevere against all temptations, against all odds, against all perils, against all threats—knowing that whatever will be my fate the right will surely prevail."

He also made the veiled case for his own reelection as U.S. Senator when the Massachusetts legislature considered the matter in January 1857; he said he expected soon "to be permitted, with unimpaired vigor, to resume all responsibilities of his position." And, unbowed and undeterred despite his poor health, he lashed out at opponents of the Republican Party in Massachusetts. These misguided souls were "in sympathy, open or disguised, with the vulgar enemy, quickening everywhere the lash of the taskmaster, and helping forward the Satanic carnival" of slavery.

It was close to five o'clock in the afternoon when a weary Sumner was taken to the family home at 20 Hancock Street on the back side of Beacon Hill. After he entered the house, throngs of people gathered out front on the narrow street and cheered repeatedly, too excited to remember Governor Gardner's plea to allow Sumner his privacy.

Finally, in response, Sumner and his mother appeared at a window, and bowed in acknowledgment to the crowd—after more cheers, the people began to disperse. Charles Sumner would need his rest in anticipation of the critically important Tuesday that was only hours away. November 4, 1856—election day in Massachusetts and across the nation.

On Tuesday, as the nation prepared to vote, a weary but gratified Charles Sumner received letters of support that kept alive the warm spirit of the previous day's reception. "A weight has been taken from my heart by hearing that you are better today, thank God," Samuel Gridley Howe scribbled. "As a friend, I shall keep away from you until you say it would be well for you to see me." Lois Caswell, secretary of the State Normal School, bid Sumner a "grateful and joyous" return to Boston, explaining that the entire school had followed his recovery anxiously "[from you] uncertain steps to the sea-shore and on the mountain-top." Carola Wildgrove penned a lengthy poem welcoming Sumner home as Massachusetts's "champion of freedom," and identifying him as a "martyr in a sacred cause." One important stanza alluded to the long-term positive impact the caning might portend for Sumner and the North:

Each blow the demon's fury sped
To fall upon thy classic head,
Still deeper in a nation's heart
Engraved thy Heaven-lighted name
And carved for thee a higher fame

Newspaper accounts of the Sumner reception must also have pleased the recovering senator. Many of them contrasted Sumner's magnanimous comments with the mocking, defiant tone Brooks exhibited at rallies in his honor. The event was, "in every respect, a noble one," the *Boston Daily Atlas* declared. One writer concluded that the reception represented the "unaffected homage of a humane and enlightened people to a faithful and fearless defender of human rights." This was vastly different from the Brooks rallies, both in the "tokens of honor bestowed, and in the temper and spirit of the people." Indeed, more than anything, "the two occasions typified the two civilizations, which confronted each other."

While this summary was rife with flowery language and Northern bias, the reception honoring Sumner clearly illustrated one indisputable fact: the collective joy and love expressed by thousands of attendees meant that a plethora of political opinions, a multitude of special interests, and a cacophony of voices all spoke as one, banding together to celebrate Sumner's return. The caning had succeeded in accomplishing something Sumner and his antislavery acolytes could not do by themselves—unify a previously divided Boston, wild-eyed abolitionists and staid commercial merchants alike, against what its citizens now saw as the common enemy of Southern barbarism.

Their fellow Northerners would weigh in when they cast their ballots.

NINETEEN

THE ELECTION OF 1856

For North and South alike, the most shocking, significant, and prophetic outcome of the 1856 election was not that Republican John Frémont was defeated in his bid for the presidency, but that he received as many votes as he did. The new Republican Party, which did not even exist in several Northern states only a year earlier, made a resounding statement in its first bid for the nation's highest office, and in the process, threw a scare into Southerners and Northern Democrats.

The message of the 1856 election was clear: Bolstered by the caning and its aftershocks, the new antislavery party had made an astounding showing across the North, and while it had fallen short of its ultimate goal, voting trends clearly infused Republicans with momentum for 1860. Almost overnight, the tremors from the caning had begun shifting national power in profound ways.

Frémont won eleven Northern states, all but five in the section, and collected more than 1.3 million popular votes and 114 electoral votes. Democrat Buchanan, who won every Southern state, plus Pennsylvania, California, New Jersey, Illinois, and Indiana, garnered 1.8 million popular votes and 174 electoral votes. At first glance, the Buchanan margin seems comfortable, but his weakness is more apparent when third-party candidate Millard Fillmore's popular vote total is tallied. While Fillmore won only one state (Maryland), more than 870,000 Americans voted for him and it is likely that the majority of his votes would have gone to Frémont. Indeed, many of those who did vote for Frémont would once have supported Fillmore, since Know-Nothings were considered the main alternative to Democrats; had several thousand more made the switch to Frémont, he might have claimed victory. The most ominous sign for Democrats to consider in any future two-person race was that the combined popular vote total of Frémont and Fillmore exceeded Buchanan's by a significant margin.

There were other signs. Frémont's victory across New England was not a surprise, but his vote total was astonishing. He received more than 300,000 votes in the six-state region, while Buchanan and Fillmore combined got fewer than 200,000. In the sixteen Northern states collectively, Frémont's vote exceeded Buchanan's by more than 100,000, and the fact that Buchanan won only five of them was a stunning development for Democrats to ponder.

Looking even deeper into the election results, one state in particular illustrated the perilous situation for the South and the Democrats—Illinois, home to Democratic icon Stephen Douglas, architect of the divisive Kansas-Nebraska Act. Douglas had boasted in late 1855 that Illinois would furnish a huge Democratic majority, perhaps by as many as 40,000 votes. But the caning had disrupted the landscape dramatically. Buchanan won Illinois, but his margin of victory was razor thin—only about 9,000 votes more than Frémont (of nearly 240,000 cast), and the combined Frémont-Fillmore total trounced Buchanan by nearly 30,000 votes. A switch of a few thousand votes would have swung Illinois to the Republicans, which would have utterly embarrassed Douglas and the Democrats.

Moreover, historian Allan Nevins points out that, within Illinois, the North-South schism is starkly illustrated: the state's five pro-Southern districts voted overwhelmingly for Buchanan and the four pro-Northern districts gave Frémont a huge majority. It also illustrated a larger Southern problem: the northern part of the state was increasing in population much more rapidly than the southern region, causing Douglas and the Democrats deep concern about future voting patterns in Illinois.

In all, while Buchanan's election indicated that the majority of voters chose a safe, "Union-saving" course (the South's threats to secede if the Republicans won did sow fear in some Northern states), Frémont had carried a remarkable 60 percent of the Northern popular vote. Three Northern states had won the election for Buchanan, and all of them—Pennsylvania (Buchanan's home state), Illinois, and Indiana—were increasingly Republican. In Pennsylvania and Indiana, the combined Frémont-Fillmore vote nearly equaled Buchanan's total, and in New Jersey exceeded it. More warning signs for Democrats: Buchanan had won just 45 percent of the total popular vote and became the first man in American history to win the presidency without carrying a preponderance of free states.

The heavy vote for Frémont in the North and West alarmed Southerners for the future it suggested: "The strength developed by Frémont portends the continued agitation [against] slavery," the *New Orleans Bee* said on November 8. Had Frémont been trounced, Republicans would have slunk away, discouraged and dispirited, but his formidable showing would convince the antislavery element "to renew their exertions, to organize their forces for another contest, and to keep up the struggle with energy and perseverance." The fight would go to the bitter end. The election results had revealed that the North and South were enemies; they were "countrymen only in name." It now appeared that white Southerners would have to choose "*between submission and dissolution*," warned South Carolina Congressman Lawrence Keitt. Another prominent Southerner disgustedly declared that the Republicans had fomented a "complete revolution" in the North, replacing honest government with "sheer despotism" and warning that the new Republican congressional delegation was "vulgar and fanatical, hating us and hating our institutions."

The *New Orleans Daily Crescent* best expressed the Southern conservative reaction to the election by saying the Northern voting results were a "stunning shock" and, as a result, the paper no longer "laughed at those who hinted at the . . . possibility of disunion." The *Crescent* voiced its outrage that Frémont, "the candidate of the . . . abolitionists and haters of the South generally, has received the electoral votes of a large majority of Northern people!" The Republican candidate had won the North based upon a platform "which would inflict immeasurable degradation upon the Southern people," one which would "strip them of respect at home and abroad and render them the laughing stock." Worse, the 1856 results had occurred with a Republican Party that was barely organized. What could the South expect in another four years? The handwriting was clear.

Historian Eric Walther points out that had Frémont carried Pennsylvania or the combination of New Jersey, Illinois, and Indiana (he carried all the other free states except California), he would have won a clear victory without a single ballot from Southern states. The frightening future for the South to contemplate was that, in the realm of presidential politics, the South needed the North and the North could ignore the South. A "solid North" could win the Presidency outright—the South did not have enough electoral votes or population to achieve the same result with one of its candidates. What the South feared most was that any solid North in the future would undoubtedly sweep into power the despised anti-slavery Republicans.

Far from being disappointed at Frémont's defeat, Republicans expressed hopefulness and even a measure of glee about the Presidential results. "Republicans are reveling in the conviction that they have suffered a victorious defeat," crowed W. H. Furness of Philadelphia succinctly. "They have not got a President, but they have what is better—a North." In a letter to Sumner, William Jay added: "The news from Michigan and Illinois is glorious." For his part, Sumner repeatedly referred to the Republican election defeat as "our Bunker Hill," the Revolutionary battle in which an overmatched colonial army surprisingly inflicted heavy losses on British regulars before finally succumbing. As Bunker Hill helped colonists measure their progress, the presidential election result was an indication of Republican strength "and gives assurance of speedy triumph." Sumner described the election results as "the beginning of the end" of the slave power's stranglehold on Congress, the presidency, and the nation. "All New England, with New York, Ohio, Michigan, Wisconsin, and Iowa, constitute an irresistible phalanx for Freedom," he wrote.

More moderate Northerners recognized that the election results signaled the end of a middle-ground political position in the North. Before the election, Massachusetts statesman and orator Edward Everett had observed, "There is really no ground left on which a northern conservative man can stand," and this argument was validated by Frémont's strong showing and Fillmore's feeble one in the free states.

Without question, Northerners and Southerners identified the caning as playing the key role in the Republicans' election outcome. One worried Southern Democratic activist noted to Buchanan: "The Club which broke Mr. Sumner's head has . . . turned more votes than all other causes that were at work." Robert Winthrop suggested that Preston Brooks and Stephen Douglas "deserve Statues from the [Republican] Party. The cane of the former and the Kansas bill of the latter . . . have secured a success to the Agitators which they never could have accomplished without them."

Historian William Gienapp, who has done extensive research and analysis on the timing of thousands of new Republican supporters, points specifically to Connecticut as an illustration of the caning's impact. In the last election before the caning—the spring of 1856—Republicans did no better than they did in the previous fall's election, polling about 11 percent of the vote. Yet, Frémont easily defeated Buchanan in Connecticut, polling more than 53 percent of the vote. The caning had shifted Northern voters' feelings, immediately and irrevocably, and also highlighted the vast gulf between North and South. Gienapp points out: "Because of the Sumner assault, the common values of the two sections seemed fewer, and increasingly less important."

Or, as Pennsylvania Republican Alexander K. McClure, who visited Sumner at Cresson, wrote nearly fifty years after the caning, Brooks's attack caused thousands of Democrats with natural "anti-slavery proclivities" to sever their ties with the Democratic Party and unite in support of Frémont. McClure wrote: "The most effective deliverance made by any man to advance the Republican party was made by the bludgeon of Preston S. Brooks."

Despite what both men could consider at least some good news—for one, Frémont's outstanding showing; for the other, Buchanan's victory—neither Charles Sumner nor Preston Brooks appeared to enjoy any personal happiness after the 1856 presidential election.

Brooks, like many Southern lawmakers, remained subdued and avoided public controversies when he returned to Congress in the fall of 1856. Republicans had become much bolder—they had carried the House and were soon to have twenty senators (of thirty-two total)—and Southern congressmen were much less aggressive. The notion of Kansas becoming a slave state had largely dissipated as a result of the election. Brooks made one major speech when the session resumed after the election, a measured oration in which he addressed the issues in Kansas. In a remarkably conciliatory tone, he announced that he was ready to vote for the admission of Kansas "even with a constitution rejecting slavery." Northerners were astonished and Southern proslavery radicals were disappointed with the tone of Brooks's remarks.

In fact, by the winter of 1856, Brooks apparently was growing weary of the public attention that centered upon him and was hurt by the hostile attitudes of former friends from the North. Though never doubting the justice of the caning, he confided to fellow South Carolina Congressman James L. Orr that he was "tired of his new role" and "heartsick of being recognized the representative of bullies, the recipient of their ostentatious gifts, and officious testimonials of admiration and regard." Northerner Julia Ward Howe's contention that Brooks displayed "an evil expression of countenance" when she spotted him at a Washington hotel was not an unusual reaction; without knowing or ever meeting Brooks, the abhorrence of his deed was enough for many to categorize him as a despicable human being. The *New York Times* had picked up similar reactions from its sources: "We have heard that in conversation Colonel Brooks more than once deplored his conduct as the blot and misfortune of his life."

Any regrets Brooks felt about the caning's aftermath were moot. For the entire nation, he and his deed had come to define the persona of the entire slaveholding South: aghast Northerners decried the belligerence and the violence that Brooks and the caning represented; proud Southerners reveled in his courageous defense of honor, order, state, and region. The 1856 presidential election results had merely painted a clear picture of an already unmistakably divided land.

For Charles Sumner, while he was heartened by the results nationally and in Massachusetts (Republicans swept the state and Burlingame was reelected in a close race), his ill health and slow recovery dominated his thoughts and actions during the fall and winter of 1856–57. He again suggested that "at last we may have seen the beginning of the end of our great struggle," noting the election had made it clear that the North had "assumed an attitude which it cannot abandon . . . our duty is clear, to scatter everywhere the seeds of truth." But Sumner would not be the one to sow those seeds, at least not publicly.

He did not go to Washington for the fall session, but remained at Longfellow's home, attempting to clear his head and regain his strength. Longfellow noted in his diary on November 2: "Sumner . . . looks well in the face, but is feeble, and walks with an uncertain step." And again on November 14, he noted that, while Sumner rode "horseback every forenoon, and [took] a walk in the afternoon," Longfellow feared his friend had "a long and weary road before him."

Sumner spent the weeks after the election reading and corresponding with friends and colleagues, often from bed. "I am a convalescent invalid," he wrote in December, adding unhappily that his doctors believed he was months from a "complete recovery." Dejected and lonely, he took great solace from the kindness of friends. A verse from abolitionist poet John Greenleaf

Whittier made the fragile Sumner's "pulse beat quick and my eyes moisten with tears." At the same time, he confided to Whittier, he could not bear the thought that he might "survive with impaired powers, or with a perpetual disability."

A disheartened Sumner, who was scheduled to stand for reelection to the U.S. Senate in the Massachusetts legislature in January 1857, even considered resigning his seat for health reasons, but again, his friends and fellow Republicans opposed this move on political grounds. Although the presidential campaign was over, they believed Sumner's vacant chair served as a powerful symbol that would enable them to continue to recruit new members into the party. John A. Andrew, who would soon become governor of Massachusetts and was never one for nuance, unambiguously summed up the point when he wrote to Sumner in December: "Sit in your seat if you can. If you can't let it be *vacant.*"

While Sumner desperately desired to speak on the issues of the day, he was discouraged by his physicians from doing so; his doctors ordered him to "take my seat and be quiet." On one hand, perhaps this was a blessing, Sumner said, because had he spoken his heart, he feared being shot by Southern slave sympathizers. Yet his inability to return to work had drained him of energy and left him dispirited. "My chief sorrow," he admitted to Whittier, "has been that I have been shut out from the field of action. . . . I long to speak and liberate my soul."

As Christmas of 1856 drew near, both Charles Sumner and Preston Brooks, like the rest of America, wrestled with deep discouragement and, during the season of peace and goodwill, found neither.

TWENTY

THE MOST POPULAR MAN IN MASSACHUSETTS

The State House in Boston hummed with anticipation when lawmakers gathered on January 9, 1857, to reelect Charles Sumner, a testament to how much had changed in six years.

When Sumner was first chosen to serve in the United States Senate by the Massachusetts legislature in April 1851, his election was marred by acrimony and controversy. Sumner, then an arrogant, radical, self-centered, if principled, political novice, emerged as an unlikely compromise candidate only after a grueling political process—he was finally elected by a single-vote majority on the twenty-sixth ballot. Some lawmakers were satisfied, others were outraged, but none was ebullient. The general consensus, even among many of his supporters, was that Sumner might make a passable senator, but would never come close to filling the giant shoes of his predecessor, Daniel Webster. And for members of the Boston business community, Sumner's election elicited glowering disapproval on good days and uncensored cursing on bad ones.

The caning had changed everything. Sumner was still the uncompromising abolitionist, still the imperious egotist who sneered at lesser intellects and ridiculed political opponents, still the implacable narcissist who felt it his birthright to secure a revered place in the pantheon of great statesmen.

The caning had also transformed him into a symbol—of unrepentant Southern violence and barbarism aimed at destroying free speech, and of Northern solidarity aimed at counteracting Southern aggression and preserving the Union. This time, when Charles Sumner finally agreed to stand for reelection, even as he struggled to get well, lawmakers drew on a reservoir of deep affection for their wounded senator, rallying around him with a near-religious fervor fueled by his martyrdom, and borne of sectional pride and a sense of mission that transcended partisan politics and petty agendas.

Massachusetts abolitionist Lydia Maria Child typified the Northern adoration for Sumner when she wrote to him in early January begging that he send her a lock of his hair. "I do want a few hairs from your head, and if you will grant me that favor, I will not expose you to similar requests by telling of it," she wrote, adding that Sumner could simply place his hair in a plain envelope and mail it to her. "It is no childish whim, I assure you," she added. "You can form no adequate idea of the affectionate reverence with which I regard everything connected with you." Child admitted that, upon meeting Sumner earlier, she had wanted to simply ask if she could clip a lock of his hair, "but that noble head, which had suffered martyrdom for Freedom, seemed too sacred for me to touch." She assured Sumner that "God and good angels" guarded him when he ventured among slaveholding "barbarians," who, in their "best state, are utterly incapable of appreciating a nature like yours." Though more measured and less beatific in its description, the *New York Times* nonetheless confirmed that Child's overall affection for Sumner had infused the general population: "We need not, in view of recent events, point out the change which has taken place in the public sentiments of Massachusetts. It is not too much to say that Mr. Sumner is at this moment the most popular man in the state." Prior to the caning, the newspaper's observation and the level of support for Sumner would have been unimaginable; in January 1857, it was, perhaps, inevitable.

The Massachusetts House of Representatives made Sumner's reelection its first order of business in the new year, even before receiving the governor's inaugural message (which lawmakers feared might spark arguments that would distract them from selecting Sumner). Without debate or suspense, the clerk called the roll and when he had finished, Charles Sumner had received an astounding 333 of the 345 votes cast; the 12 other votes were divided across nine other candidates. Sumner's victory in the House was fast and overwhelming, and was met with thunderous applause.

Four days later, the Massachusetts Senate met and unanimously cast their votes for Sumner. He would begin his second six-year term in the United States Senate when the new session began on March 4.

Massachusetts officials and newspapers recognized the dramatically altered political landscape that propelled Sumner to a second term. The *Boston Atlas* noted that his election was virtually unanimous and occurred only three days into the legislative term, contrasted with his razor-thin victory in 1851, a full 114 days into the term. Six years earlier, votes were cast in a sealed envelope, while in this latest election "every member [spoke] aloud his vote." Six years earlier, Sumner was part of a Free-Soil Party that drew about 26,500 votes in the previous election; in 1857 Sumner was part of a Republican Party that drew more than 108,000 votes in the previous election, about two-thirds of the entire vote. And finally, whereas only two or three others shared his political sympathies in the U.S. Senate after his first election, Sumner was going back to a Congress in which Republicans had a majority in the House and 25 percent of the Senate.

All of this, the *New York Times* said, bestowed upon Sumner "a crown of honor which may well assuage the hope deferred of a tardy convalescence." His friends congratulated him for his victory as well, recognizing that the overwhelming consensus of the Massachusetts legislature was virtually without parallel in the nation's history, especially in the midst of deep political upheaval. "No one can say now that you have not a constituency behind you," wrote Richard Henry Dana. "Where is there a senator who holds such a tenure? The day has come we have all hoped and labored for—the day of something like unanimity in New England." Seward commended Sumner on his "majestic success" and said it made him proud of Massachusetts and the abolitionist cause. J. C. Weilling wrote from Washington that Massachusetts "has honored herself again . . . and shown due homage to herself and you . . . by investing you with the senatorial robe." George Baker congratulated Sumner on his "triumphant re-election" and added: "Nothing but the election of a Republican President could give me greater pleasure." Sumner's Senate colleague Henry Wilson said that Sumner's acclamation by the state legislature "is an illustration of the progress of our cause in our country. . . . How hopeful it is!" But Wilson also cautioned against Sumner returning to Washington "unless you are well. . . . Take time and get well before you take your seat."

Indeed, just days after his resounding victory, Sumner confided in a letter to Abraham Lincoln's law partner, William Henry Herndon, that his "prostration has been great . . . I am still obliged to take to my bed at the beginning of the evening." If at all possible, Sumner said, "My hope is to reach Washington before the [current] session closes."

As Sumner said in his acceptance of the senatorship after he was reelected, he wanted to return to Washington as quickly as possible to perform his duty and live up to the trust the people of Massachusetts had placed in him. His near-unanimous reelection was a sign that the people of Massachusetts had forgotten their "ancient party hates" and instead had at last come together "in fraternal support of a sacred cause." Thus, Sumner said, regardless of his personal suffering, his home state expected him to ensure that, whatever else happened, "freedom shall prevail. I cannot neglect this injunction."

If the overwhelming election of Sumner offered evidence that Boston and Massachusetts had become antislavery hotbeds, other activities also illustrated the fact.

On January 15, abolitionists and other antislavery factions gathered at a convention in Worcester, about fifty miles west of Boston, to consider "the practicability, probability, and expediency of a separation between the Free and Slave States." The so-called Disunion Convention was the brainchild of Thomas Wentworth Higginson, who had recently returned from Kansas territory and hoped to unite both violent and nonviolent abolitionists in an effort to dissolve the union and create a slave-free nation from among the Northern and Western states. The thirty-three-year-old Higginson was energized by his quest, saying he felt younger now than when he was "eighteen or twenty, and I doubt if I shall ever feel any older." Higginson admitted that he was so consumed by the separation plan that, while trimming his tree over the Christmas holiday, he thought about "[writing] letters to Kansas and dissolving the Union."

The Worcester convention was a sign of just how fractured North-South—or, more accurately, free-slave—relations were after the events of a tumultuous 1856. Higginson and his fellow zealous Massachusetts abolitionists no longer talked of voting or political negotiations as a way to end slavery. "Disunion," he wrote, "is our only hope."

And while Higginson's views, the Disunion Convention, and Sumner's overwhelming reelection provided public confirmation of the changing sentiments sweeping across Massachusetts, it was a series of secret January conspiratorial meetings occurring in shadowy Boston offices and parlors that provided an equally ominous harbinger of the nation's future.

John Brown was in town seeking weapons and money—as much as $30,000—in the short term for the defense of Kansas against continued attacks from Missouri, but also laying the groundwork for his long-held personal dream, a planned invasion of the South to wipe out slavery forever. Brown envisioned a force of well-trained guerrillas, made up of his most rabid freedom-fighters, who would conduct lightning-quick strikes against plantations to free slaves and help them escape to the North.

While the Massachusetts legislature was fully endorsing Charles Sumner, Brown skulked from one clandestine Boston meeting to another seeking support. Still a hunted criminal in the West for the murders in Kansas, Brown was viewed by Massachusetts abolitionists and intellectuals as a symbol of the self-reliant and unjustly persecuted antislavery crusader; they either overlooked or were unfazed by the deadly violence Brown and his band perpetrated in Pottawatomie. Departing Kansas in the fall, Brown dodged federal authorities through Nebraska and Iowa, before finally arriving on safe ground in Ohio, where Governor Joshua Giddings presented him with a letter of introduction to potential contributors. Brown then stopped in New York to consult with antislavery philanthropist (and Sumner correspondent) Gerrit Smith, before arriving in Boston in early January.

His first stop was the office of Franklin B. Sanborn on School Street. The secretary of the Massachusetts State Kansas Committee, Sanborn was impressed by the "tall, slender, and commanding figure" in his presence. Brown possessed a "military bearing" and at the same time expressed a religious fervor that surrounded him with the unique aura of "the soldier and the deacon," Sanborn wrote. So impressed was Sanborn that he quickly introduced Brown to Higginson and another of Boston's militant abolitionists, Theodore Parker, who invited him to a private reception to meet William Lloyd Garrison (Brown preferred the disunion politics of Higginson and Parker, who, unlike Garrison, did not object to violence to achieve their ends). From there, he also met Boston abolitionists Amos Lawrence (of the New England Emigrant Aid Society), George Luther Stearns (who raised the $48,000 for supplies to Kansas), and Sumner's dear friend Samuel Gridley Howe.

These contacts would open the door for Brown's weapons-gathering efforts and fundraising activities that would, in a few short years, lead to his raid on the federal arsenal in Harpers Ferry, West Virginia. Stearns, Smith, Higginson, Howe, Parker, and Sanborn would become known as the mysterious "Secret Six" who financed the raid (Frederick Douglass, who knew about the scheme, was actually the seventh). Higginson, particularly, supported Brown's violent brand of abolitionism wrapped in the cloak of religious extremism, describing Brown's Kansas activities as "beginning with prayers every morning, [he] then sallies forth . . . wherever duty or danger calls . . . swallows a Missourian whole, and says grace after the meal."

By mid-January, after several successful meetings and assurances of support for his crusading antislavery army, Brown was ready to leave Boston and continue his fundraising efforts in New York. But he had one more stop to make.

Reformer and Unitarian minister James Freeman Clarke remembered the January night vividly. He had stopped by Charles Sumner's Hancock Street home to visit, where he found Sumner resting in an easy chair and talking with three other guests. Sumner introduced Clarke to one of the men, whom he identified as "John Brown of Osawatomie." Clarke then listened as Sumner and Brown talked about Preston Brooks and his savage assault.

Sumner said to Brown: "The coat I had on at the time is hanging in that closet. Its collar is stiff with blood. You can see it, if you please, Captain." Clarke recounted the scene that followed. Brown arose, went to the closet, slowly opened the door, and carefully took down the coat. He then stared at it for several minutes "with the reverence with which a Roman Catholic regards the relics of a saint." There was no doubt in Clarke's mind that Sumner's bloody coat had a profound impact on Brown. "It may be the sight of that garment caused him to feel a still deeper abhorrence of slavery," Clarke wrote, "and to take a stronger resolution of attacking it in its strongholds."

And there was also no doubt that the coat reminded Brown—as well as Sumner and Clarke—of the righteousness of their cause. Staring at the coat, Brown likely shared Clarke's reverential conclusion that "the blood of the martyrs is the seed of the church."

TWENTY-ONE

THE FIRST CASUALTY

Of all the stunning news that surrounded the Brooks-Sumner affair, beginning with the attack itself and its aftermath—John Brown's gruesome murders in Kansas, the vitriolic debate in Congress, the reactions of citizens North and South, Sumner's lengthy convalescence, the Southern accusations of shamming, the explosive growth of the Republican Party, Brooks's dramatic expulsion hearing and trial, his later resignation and unanimous reelection, the impressive showing by Frémont and the Republicans in November, Sumner's near-unanimous reelection in early January—of all of these, none startled the nation more than the dramatic telegraphic news from Washington on the morning of January 28, 1857.

Preston Brooks was dead.

The thirty-seven-year-old congressman had died in agony the previous evening in his quarters at Brown's Hotel in Washington, D.C. While a howling blizzard and frigid temperatures paralyzed the nation's capital outside, several of Brooks's colleagues, including Lawrence Keitt and James L. Orr, watched helplessly at their friend's bedside as Brooks clawed at his throat and struggled in vain to breathe. Two other friends and three doctors were with Brooks as well, including Dr. Cornelius

Boyle, who, ironically, had first treated Charles Sumner after the caning and later announced that Sumner had suffered only a "flesh wound."

His friends were stunned at the downturn in Brooks's condition. Five days earlier he had developed a sore throat and then a severe cold, and had taken to his bed on January 25. By late afternoon of the twenty-seventh, Boyle felt that the South Carolina congressman had passed any crisis and was, indeed, on the road to recovery. In a letter to Brooks's wife, James Orr said: "We thought he was decidedly better. I remained with him near half an hour, talking most of the time and admonishing him not to talk, but to listen." Orr later withdrew to the parlor of Brooks's quarters, and "I never for an instant supposed he was in any danger." Brooks's friend and predecessor in Congress, John McQueen, told his son that Brooks's death was "as unexpected as it could be, until but a few moments before he died." Keitt concurred saying later that Brooks's demise was "so swiftly fatal . . . that not even [his] medical advisers believed him to be in danger," until moments before his death. "Science availed not; skill availed not; delicate assiduous attention availed not," Keitt lamented.

In fact, just ten minutes before he expired, Brooks had told the group that he was feeling better. But suddenly, McQueen noticed the "violent heaving of [Brooks's] chest and lungs," as Brooks seemed to be suffering a "perfect stoppage of the windpipe" that allowed "not one particle of breath" into his body. His doctors quickly applied poultices of mustard and cornmeal, but to no avail. One South Carolinian angrily wrote later that some in the room advised doctors to try a treatment of "leeching and blistering his throat" to clear his breathing passages, but the medical men declined. He added: "Brooks ought not to have died; my own opinion is that leeches freely applied would have saved him." Instead, in the last moments of Brooks's life, his doctors called for warm water and salt, presumably to induce vomiting in an effort to relieve pressure on his throat, but it was too late. No one could help Brooks, who, in his final seconds, "endeavored to tear his own throat open to get breath," seized violently, and died.

Boyle later ruled the cause of death as acute inflammation of the throat (probably some kind of esophageal infection), which resulted in Brooks's near strangulation in the final moments of his life. "He died a horrid death, and suffered intensely," noted the official telegram announcing his demise.

Shortly after Brooks died, McQueen watched as Senator Andrew Butler, the object of Charles Sumner's scorn and Preston Brooks's vengeful chivalry, came into his second cousin's bedroom, threw himself on top of Brooks's body, "and wept like a child, until a heart of stone might bleed." Like Butler, presumably, McQueen could not come to grips with his friend's death. "I never saw a death so sudden and difficult to realize," he said, wondering how Brooks's wife and mother would handle the news.

Brooks's initial illness was not made public, which made his sudden death a complete surprise to the nation. Orr told Martha Brooks that his friends were "appalled" as word spread throughout Washington that Preston was dead. "Not one in five hundred knew of his illness," Orr points out. "He was in the House on Saturday last." Massachusetts Senator Henry Wilson wrote to Sumner on January 27: "A few moments ago the city was startled by the announcement of the death of Brooks. It came upon us all unexpectedly, and it will startle the country." Referring to the caning, Wilson added, "He has gone to his Maker to render an account for his deeds," and pointed out that "his enemies cannot but feel sympathy for his fate. What a name to leave behind him!"

Just eight months after Preston Brooks's brutal attack on Charles Sumner had shocked a nation, the announcement of Brooks's death did the same. "If he had been struck by lightning," one Northern correspondent noted, "the announcement could not have been more unexpected."

Still recuperating at Longfellow's, Sumner did not comment publicly on his assailant's death. Longfellow wrote in his journal: "I do not think Sumner had any personal feelings against him. He looked upon him as a mere tool of the slaveholders, or . . . of the South Carolinians."

Years later, Sumner seemed to confirm Longfellow's 1857 assessment when he did finally speak of Brooks: "It was slavery, not *he*, that struck the blow." In 1872, Sumner was walking with a friend in the Congressional Cemetery when his companion pointed out to him the cenotaph of Brooks, of which Sumner was not previously aware. Sumner stared at the monument for several moments and then uttered: "Poor fellow, poor fellow." When his friend asked how he felt about Brooks, Sumner replied: "Only as to a brick that should fall upon my head from a chimney. He was the unconscious agent of a malign power."

Considering that less than one year before his death Preston Brooks was a backbench legislator, the elaborateness and pageantry of his funeral services were nothing short of extraordinary. The national notoriety he had achieved as a result of the caning accorded him hero and statesman status upon his demise. Southern members of Congress and other public officials with proslavery leanings mourned and eulogized Brooks with reverential obsequies and lofty hosannas more often reserved for deceased kings and other heads of state than two-term members of Congress. Ordinary people wept when they heard the news and craved as many details as possible about the circumstances of Brooks's death and the tributes planned for him.

Brooks's friends dressed him in a black suit and braved the elements to move him to the Ladies Parlor at nearby Brown's Hotel. "Excepting for his palor [*sic*], his features [were] composed and natural," Orr wrote to Brooks's widow. "He looks as if he was sleeping a gentle sleep." A wreath of white flowers encircled Brooks's head and a bouquet was set upon his chest. "He looks so natural," Orr wrote, "that I felt as if he would speak." Orr assured Martha Brooks that friends had clipped a few locks of her husband's hair to send to her. While laid out at Brown's, hundreds of mourners visited "to take a last look at the face of their departed friend."

On January 29, two days after his untimely death, despite horrible weather conditions in Washington, thousands made their way to the Capitol to attend the funeral. The galleries and rotunda leading to the House and Senate chambers were "almost blocked up by the living mass" of people who came to view Brooks's body, which lay in the Capitol. The House chamber and galleries were so full that the House set aside its rules to allow women on the floor. Virtually all of the country's leaders were in attendance, including President Franklin Pierce, President-elect James Buchanan, members of the cabinet, and members of the Supreme Court.

McQueen was impressed with the intrepid nature of visitors who somehow "got into the Capitol notwithstanding the depth of the snow" and the freezing temperatures, which had plunged to five degrees below zero. The turnout provided some consolation to his friends, as did the fact that Brooks's suffering was short-lived. "Still," McQueen wrote, "the fact stands up too truly that we shall see him again no more." McQueen had paid for the undertaker to travel to Baltimore to retrieve the "handsomest metalic [*sic*] coffin there, the longest in Baltimore . . . plenty long for the body," sturdy enough to withstand the long trip back to Edgefield that Brooks's family had planned.

Both the House and Senate agreed to forego business for the day in honor of Brooks's memory, and in both chambers, members recounted their affection for the South Carolinian. Most were stunned and deeply affected by his sudden death. "Had he fallen in the evening of life, or had he even sunk down under the gradual inroads of disease," Keitt said he could have accepted Brooks's death more readily. "But for his sun to set while in its noonday blaze, it is hard to feel that it will rise no more." Georgia Senator Robert Toombs acknowledged that "many of us have lost a friend [and] the country a patriot statesman," and when Toombs reached the point in his remarks where he referred to Brooks's grieving mother, wife, and children, the senator was overcome with emotion. He signaled a colleague that he was unable to proceed. South Carolina Senator Josiah Evans said that the more he had worked with Brooks "the higher has he risen in my regard, and the deeper is the distress and affliction which I feel for his early death." Like Keitt, Evans focused on the suddenness with which Brooks died. "When a man, in the prime of life, in the midst of his hopes, is suddenly cut down . . . it is an event which strikes deep into the human heart," he said.

Even Northern representatives spoke favorably of Brooks, most notably Ohio's Lewis Campbell, who had been a member of the House committee investigating the caning. Campbell called Brooks both "generous and brave" and said he merited the confidence of his constituents "because he was the faithful advocate of their political sentiments, and the jealous guardian of their interests and their honor."

Virtually everyone avoided references to the caning. The tearful Toombs alluded to it in the Senate when he said that Brooks "had come among us in evil times," when the leaders and ideas of one section "were objects of the bitterest vituperation and invective by the representatives of the other." Only one Southern House member, Representative John Savage of Tennessee, overtly mentioned the attack, favorably equating Brooks's caning of Sumner to that of Brutus assassinating Julius Caesar. Outraged Republicans left the House in protest as soon as Savage stopped speaking. "To prevent further controversy, Senator [Andrew] Butler had Savage's remarks omitted from the published proceedings," historian T. Lloyd Benson noted. Nonetheless, the damage was done. Henry Wilson wrote to Sumner: "Savage uttered the secret feelings of the Southern gang of Negro decriers."

After the eulogies, at just before 2:00 P.M., Brooks's body was brought into the House, the coffin placed immediately in front of the clerk's desk. With the full array of political dignitaries gathered solemnly, Rev. Daniel Waldo conducted services. When he finished, the remarkable procession made its way outside in the freezing cold to the Congressional Cemetery—led by the chaplains of both houses of Congress and followed by Brooks's attending physicians, the pallbearers carrying Brooks's coffin (including his friend Rep. Henry Edmundson), Brooks's family and friends, House and Senate officers, President Pierce, cabinet members, the Supreme Court, the diplomatic corps, officers of the Army and Navy, and even the mayor of Washington, D.C. Hundreds of "citizens and strangers" brought up the rear of the procession.

Additional prayers were recited at the cemetery, and a cenotaph placed, but Brooks's body was then transported to the

Congressional mortuary to await a contingent from Edgefield who would carry him to his final resting place.

If the pageantry of Brooks's Washington funeral was remarkable, what followed was the stuff of legend, a pilgrimage during which the name and historical standing of Preston Brooks was elevated in the South from revered icon to a giant figure of Shakespearean, even mythical proportions, a reputation he enjoys to the present day.

His attack on Charles Sumner, coupled with his sudden death at such a youthful age, branded Brooks a tragic hero and endowed him with a status that few Southerners have ever attained. Some historians may argue that John C. Calhoun or Robert E. Lee approached or even exceeded Brooks's exalted position, but a powerful argument can be made that the long, mournful return of Brooks's body from Washington, D.C., to Edgefield solidified a unique place for Brooks in the vast pantheon of Southern antebellum and Civil War history. It was a journey that was documented, almost breathlessly, by virtually every newspaper in the South, and in dozens of letters and diaries. It inspired poetry, tears, editorials, homilies, and the sad gathering of thousands of citizens at large cities and small towns across the South. "Our village bells are now tolling . . . their slow and melancholy tones," the *Edgefield Advertiser* wrote. "Never have we witnessed such a deep gloom over our community."

Edgefield quickly organized a committee of twenty-six men—"intelligent and substantial men," according to one account—to travel to Washington to retrieve Brooks's body. The arduous journey took ten days, eighty-eight hours by train from Charleston alone, but all along the way the South Carolina committee was treated to hospitality and generosity from hotel proprietors, tavern owners, and train conductors. The committee was touched to its "heart's core," for example, when the adjutant of Newton's Hotel in Alexandria, Virginia, treated members to "bed and board" on the evening of February 9, while expressing his admiration for citizens of the Palmetto State as they "[paid] the last worldly honors to one of her most favorite sons." The owner of the carriage line between Alexandria and Washington also transported the South Carolinians free of charge.

Once in Washington, the committee collected Brooks's remains and set out quickly, beginning their return trip at just after 5:00 P.M. on February 10. The steamer took more than five hours to plow through the ice in Acquia Creek and into northern Virginia, which delayed its eventual arrival in Richmond, causing it to miss the train that would take members deeper South. The Richmond mayor, James Mayo, urged the committee to allow the city to pay homage to Brooks with a brief ceremony, and then transported the body to the state capitol for safekeeping. The city then paid for meals and lodging for the South Carolina committee.

At 5:00 A.M. the following morning, a detachment of the Virginia militia, accompanied by a military band, escorted the hearse that carried Brooks's body to the railroad depot to board the train that would carry the group into the Carolinas. The Edgefield committee and Brooks's body stopped in the North Carolina communities of Goldsborough, Wilmington, Charlotte, and Raleigh, before moving into South Carolina and stopping at Branchville, Charleston, Abbeville, and Hamburg, crossing over into Georgia to allow the citizens of Augusta to view Brooks's body, before moving to the final stop—Brooks's home of Edgefield.

All along the way, mayors and townspeople paid tribute with speeches and prayers and eulogies and remarkable symbolic gestures; church bells were rung, regular business stopped, and stores closed. In Charleston, the harbor master requested that all vessels in port lower their flags to half-staff (every ship complied), guns were fired when Brooks's train arrived, and church bells tolled throughout the city as the procession wound its way through the city streets. In Augusta, officials removed Brooks's body—still virtually frozen—and placed the remains in the Council Chamber at City Hall, where it was viewed by "hundreds of . . . citizens, anxious to testify . . . their respect for the memory of the lamented dead."

Even in places where Brooks's body did not pass through, Southerners commemorated his death. In Columbia, where citizens were disappointed when a failure to make a train connection caused the Brooks procession to skip the capital city, hundreds still gathered to hear Mayor E. J. Arthur express "the sorrow that pervaded the whole state," and mourn a man who was "known and loved" throughout South Carolina. In Milton, Florida, residents gathered and passed resolutions honoring Brooks, saying that his death "cast a gloom, not only over his native state, but upon every portion of this Confederacy." These events occurred as the Edgefield contingent escorted Brooks's corpse home.

Finally, after the Augusta ceremonies, a hearse drawn by four large horses began the final leg of the journey, transporting Brooks's body to nearby Edgefield, just across the state line; along the way the streets were jammed with people anxious to view the procession and pay their respects. On Friday, February 12, Brooks's funeral procession took place in Edgefield. A signal gun was fired to announce the assembly of the procession on a vacant lot at the fork of the Columbia and Hamburg Plank roads. A slew of military, fraternal, municipal, legal, congressional, and university dignitaries—followed by "strangers and citizens generally"—formed under the command of Major S. S. Tompkins. The solemn line of marchers, accompanied by the mournful toll of church bells, moved up Main Street to the Edgefield Court House. "There the body lay in state, uncovered, that his friends, relatives, and devoted slaves might look their last on the beloved form," one reporter noted. He also described the beatific condition of Brooks's body, "frozen for more than two weeks and perfectly preserved," which gave his "noble, youthful face" the appearance of being "celestially beautiful."

Afterward, Brooks was delivered to a guard of honor at the Episcopal Church and carried to Willowbrook Cemetery. Brooks was buried beneath a fourteen-foot-tall marble obelisk-shaped tombstone, a favorite shape for recognizing heroes, especially after the geometric shape was adopted for the Washington Monument in the 1840s. The stone, which had been crafted in Charleston and transported to Edgefield, was adorned with laurel wreaths, long-time classical symbols of honor and distinction. Part of Brooks's epitaph read:

Ever Able, Manly, Just and Heroic
Illustrating true Patriotism
By his devotion to his Country;
The whole South unites
With his bereaved family
In deploring his untimely end.

And further along, the inscription promised:

Preston S. Brooks will be Long, Long Remembered;
As one in whom the virtues loved to Dwell
Tho' sad to us, and dark this dispensation.
We know God's wisdom
Orders all things well.

Seventeen days after suffering a sudden and agonizing death, Preston Brooks, Southern hero, finally rested in his beloved Edgefield.

For many Republicans, abolitionists, and Northerners, Brooks's death was regarded as a providential act. Charles Francis Adams wrote in his diary that while some believed Brooks's death was a "just visitation" from the Almighty, he felt Brooks had been "a simple, good natured creature" who had been brutalized through his association with slaveholders. While he found any attempt to "canonize an assassin" distasteful, he wished "peace to his ashes." In a speech at Boston's Faneuil Hall, Massachusetts Congressman Anson Burlingame said Brooks had a "larger heart than many in the North . . . and was a braver man than the men that incited him" to attack Sumner. "Let all the hostility of the past go down into the grave, where he sleeps his last sleep," Burlingame urged the crowd. "He is with his God, who will deal mercifully with him. Let us try to be merciful here."

Sumner's correspondents were not so forgiving. In addition to Senator Henry Wilson's assessment that Brooks would be held accountable for his deeds by his maker, the Massachusetts lawmaker spent time during Brooks's funeral thinking of Sumner's long suffering. "I could not but feel . . . that God had avenged the blows of last May," Wilson wrote of Brooks's death. Others adopted similar tones of divine righteousness. "God has caused judgment to be heard from heaven," one man wrote. "Everybody (north) was quoting scripture . . . 'Vengeance is mine saith the Lord: I will repay.'" One abolitionist editor eschewed any heavenly references or charity for the deceased when he simply branded Brooks a symbol of an ever-decaying Southern society: "treacherous, insolent, imbruted and tryrannical."

Conversely, the South, and South Carolina in particular, treated Brooks's death as a sectional catastrophe. "The arm that was so lately raised in defense of his beloved state, is rigid in death," the *Advertiser* noted. "Sad is the mournful event that has deprived the State and the South of such a champion." The *Sumter Watchman* noted "the sensation of burning regard" for Brooks, as well as the "affection, and almost . . . worship." The *Yorkville Enquirer* declared that Brooks would be mourned "as nations lament the death of the great," and the citizens of Abbeville greeted Brooks's body as it passed through on the train to Edgefield with the reverence "awarded to a Roman General." Women across the South penned poems and submitted them to local papers, stanza after stanza of grief-filled verse filled with religious allusions and tributes to Brooks's valor and honor as a statesman.

In death, Preston Brooks had finally realized the crowning glory that had eluded him on the battlefields of Mexico and elsewhere. He was not slain by bullet or bayonet, but he died for the South nonetheless, defending causes greater than all others—the protection of slavery, family, sectional honor, and his region's way of life.

Ironically, too, when Preston Brooks expired on a blizzard-choked, bone-chilling January night in Washington D.C., he snatched the martyr's mantle from Charles Sumner. Suddenly it was Brooks, not Sumner—the attacker, not the victim—who elicited deep and powerful sympathy from his region. Suddenly, it was the South that felt victimized and deprived of one of its strongest, unwavering voices, just as the North had during the previous eight months, when Sumner's injuries prevented him from taking his seat in the Senate.

For Brooks, death also brought a measure of peace. Branded by the North as the epitome of Southern barbarism, anointed by the South as its quintessential proslavery representative, Brooks had wilted under the pressure from both sections. He was a changed man during his last few months in Congress, less outgoing, more furtive, skittish, and withdrawn, reviled by half the country and glorified by the other half. With all eyes upon him, the intensity of the scrutiny filled him with unease and the heavy burden disrupted and all but unraveled his orderly life.

There is no hard evidence that any of this stress contributed directly to Brooks's fatal illness, but there is no doubt it took a heavy toll on his daily existence. In many ways, Preston Brooks was the South's first casualty of a civil war that loomed, a war that, fittingly enough, his actions had drawn perilously close to reality.

TWENTY-TWO

A MISCAST PRESIDENT

Two weeks after Preston Brooks was buried, a fatigued and unsteady Charles Sumner arrived in Washington with every intention of resuming his duties in the United States Senate. He would last less than one day.

There was some question about whether Sumner should have ventured into the nation's capital at all. He had received tremendous support in Massachusetts and across New England after his reelection—even the Vermont legislature had approved an early February resolution fully, if belatedly, supporting his "Crime Against Kansas" speech and calling him a "fearless advocate of the rights of man"—but the mood was vastly different in the Southern-leaning District of Columbia. Sumner's friends and colleagues had urged him to stay away from Washington in the immediate days following Brooks's funeral, suggesting that his presence would further heighten tensions and perhaps precipitate violence. A. B. Johnson even suggested that Sumner absent himself "for some weeks" to allow the highly charged emotions that accompanied Brooks's funeral to dissipate. A newspaper reporter who visited him in Boston commented on Sumner's "sad weakness," though he was heartened by the senator's ability to bear up and put his condition in perspective, quoting

Sumner as saying: "The poorest slave is in danger of worse outrages every moment of his life."

Finally, Boston and New England manufacturers had prevailed on Sumner to return to the Senate sooner to vote on a tariff bill that would reduce the duty on manufactured woolens and eliminate a duty on the raw wool they needed for their factories. Sumner took his seat at 2:00 P.M. on February 26, 1857, for the first time since May 22 of the previous year. Republican colleagues greeted him warmly, but most Democratic senators ignored him completely. "God be thanked you are in your place once more!" declared Theodore Parker in a letter. "There has not been an antislavery speech made in the Congress . . . since you were carried out of it—not one. I hope to hear a blast on that old war trumpet which shall make the North ring and the South tremble."

However, Sumner lacked the energy and spirit that Parker longed for, and in fact, quickly suffered another relapse. Too weak to remain in his seat—he nearly passed out—he returned to his lodgings, leaving instructions to be called as votes came up on the tariff bill. Sumner returned to the chamber at 9:00 P.M. and cast seven votes on various amendments before leaving the Capitol at 2:00 A.M., completely exhausted.

On March 1, Sumner wrote despondently to Parker: "I have sat in my seat only on one day. After a short time the torment of my system became great, and a cloud began to gather over my brain. I tottered out and took to my bed." Sumner confided that he desperately longed to speak, but was not capable of doing so. He also noted that his Boston-based physicians warned him against public speaking and exertion, lest he face further brain injury and possibly paralysis. He would heed their warnings, since it was clear to him that, while he had improved, the "complete overthrow of my powers organically" meant he could hope to recover "only most slowly." His pent-up desire to speak "must stand adjourned to another day. Nobody can regret this so much as myself." For one of the first times, Sumner mentioned the current state of his health and his own mortality in the same breath. "I may die," he wrote Parker, "but if I live a word shall be spoken in the Senate, which shall tear Slavery open from its chops [cheeks or jowls] to its heel."

Sumner decided to travel to Europe to restore his health, believing that further rest and relaxation, rather than medical treatment, would make him well. He remained in Washington only until March 4 to take the oath as senator for his second term, the same day James Buchanan was sworn in as America's fifteenth president. Three days later, in New York, the forty-six-year-old Sumner boarded the steamship *Fulton* bound for Paris, a city he had visited as a young man twenty years earlier. As the vessel departed, a large crowd of friends and political acquaintances cheered Sumner, and the New York Young Men's Republican Club fired a gun salute in his honor.

The last two letters Sumner had written before leaving—one to the governor of Vermont and the other to an attorney friend—both focused on his fervent desire for a free Kansas. "With a farewell to my country . . . I give my last thoughts to suffering Kansas," he wrote to lawyer James Redpath from the *Fulton*'s pilot house, "that she may be lifted into the enjoyment of freedom and repose."

For now, though, Charles Sumner would hold no direct political influence over events in Kansas or anywhere else. As it had been for nine months, his Senate chair was vacant once again.

Unlike the mood of the country, the weather for James Buchanan's March 4 inauguration was calm and sunny, and for a short time, at least, the cheering thousands who lined Pennsylvania Avenue to witness the inaugural procession appeared united in both spirit and hope. After a brutally divisive 1856, during which the caning and its aftermath had split North and South, perhaps a new president could patch together some semblance of peace, however strained and fragile.

Proslavery Congressman John A. Quitman of Mississippi led the procession, which included an open carriage carrying outgoing President Franklin Pierce, to the National Hotel, where president-elect Buchanan lodged. Buchanan and his niece, Harriet Lane (Buchanan was the only president never to marry), joined Pierce in the carriage and rode toward Capitol Hill amid hearty approval from the crowd.

A photograph of James Buchanan's inauguration taken by John Wood on March 4, 1857. This first-known photograph of an inauguration shows Buchanan taking the oath on the east portico of the Capitol. Note the scaffolding surrounding the dome under construction. (*Library of Congress, Manuscript Division*)

Hailing from the Commonwealth of Pennsylvania, sixty-five-year-old James Buchanan (he would be America's last president born in the eighteenth century) within moments would become a Northern president with Southern sympathies, or perhaps more accurately, with a view on slavery that favored the South. While he personally opposed the institution ("I believe it to be a great political and a great moral evil"), at one time in his political life going so far as to purchase slaves in Washington, D.C., so he could bring them home to Pennsylvania and set them free, Buchanan firmly believed slavery was rooted in the Constitution and could not be legislated out of existence. States and territories could and should decide for themselves whether slavery would be permitted. "I thank God my lot has been cast in a state where it does not exist," he once wrote.

When Buchanan arrived on the stand in front of the east portico of the Capitol, he stood in the shadow of a spiderweb of construction scaffolding that encased the building's unfinished great dome. It was a perfect metaphor for an America still unfinished, a country consumed and divided by a debate over slavery that had been part of the national dialogue since the Constitution's ratification nearly seventy years earlier. In various periods over the past seven decades, anger had bubbled up from one region or another, to one extent or another, but never had it heated to the point it reached in 1856. Buchanan was assuming the country's highest office in the midst of a firestorm.

Supreme Court Chief Justice Roger Taney administered the oath of office to the new president. Legend has it that Taney, who would become the center of another national controversy within days, whispered to Buchanan how the Supreme Court would soon decide in the highly anticipated case in which a slave named Dred Scott was fighting to be declared free. In truth, Buchanan had known about the decision a week earlier when Justice Robert C. Grier, who was also from Pennsylvania, sent him a confidential letter in response to Buchanan's query on the leanings of the Court. Though worried about Buchanan's meddling in the Court's affairs, Grier informed the president-elect of the way the Court—which was dominated by Southerners, including the fiercely anti-abolitionist Taney—would rule: that slavery was constitutional and that the federal government had no authority to dictate whether states or territories allowed it. Sharing those same beliefs, Buchanan had urged Grier and other justices to go along with the majority, further interference that would prove detrimental to his presidency.

Buchanan began his inaugural address with another damaging move. At the outset of his remarks, he announced that he would serve only one term. He believed this would convince the nation that he had "no motive to influence my conduct . . . except the desire to ably and faithfully serve my country." It was a terrible miscalculation. His declaration that he would not seek reelection in 1860 immediately weakened him politically, just when the country needed a strong leader to bring it together.

Following the surprising remark about his political future, Buchanan labored through a largely pedestrian and uninspired inaugural address, though Southerners were pleased with its tone and it was not without controversy. He decried the "long agitation" against slavery, expressed his desire to see the agitation end, and hoped that the "geographical parties to which [the agitation] has given birth . . . will speedily become extinct." Indeed, he said, the antislavery extremism of Republicans and abolitionists had produced "no positive good to any human being; it has been the prolific source of great evils to the master, the slave, and to the whole country." The activities of antislavery zealots had "alienated and estranged the people of the sister States from each other, and has even endangered the very existence of the Union."

In addition, Buchanan warned, this continued agitation could eventually endanger the personal safety "of a large portion of our countrymen where the institution exists." It was the job of every Union-loving man to suppress antislavery agitation. He foreshadowed the Dred Scott decision in his remarks, feigning ignorance of the Supreme Court's deliberations, but promising to adhere to the Court's will. "To their decision," he told the crowd at the inauguration, "I shall cheerfully submit," adding that he firmly believed "nothing can be fairer than to leave the people of a Territory free from all . . . interference, to decide their own destiny for themselves, subject only to the Constitution of the United States."

While Southerners may have applauded, the *New York Tribune* blasted Buchanan in an editorial the following day: "*You* may 'cheerfully submit' . . . to whatever five slaveholders . . . on the bench of the Supreme Court may be ready to utter on this subject. But not one man who really desires the triumph of Freedom over Slavery in the Territories will do so."

Buchanan's inaugural plea for an end to agitation about slavery illustrated not so much his moderate temperament as his tone-deafness about the mood of the nation; indeed, he was exactly the wrong man for the presidency in March 1857.

Though he was an experienced politician, he had been away from the country for much of the previous two years as minister to Great Britain. Thus, he did not possess a clear, hands-on understanding of the fundamental change that the caning had brought to the tenor of the slavery debate. When he spoke of "agitation" against slavery, he seemed oblivious to the new Northern reality that had emerged in the wake of Sumner's beating; moderates, even conservatives, no longer considered "agitation" a dirty word. Indeed, the vast majority believed the agitation Buchanan cautioned against was the only way to combat the unchecked aggressiveness of the South. Even the meteoric growth of the Republican Party seemed to elude Buchanan, despite the election he had just survived and the large number of Northern states he had failed to carry.

In addition, Buchanan was a deliberative consensus builder at a time when the country needed boldness and certitude. He was often hesitant to lead decisively and forcefully on policy matters. A longtime friend recalled that "even among close friends he rarely expressed his opinions at all upon disputed questions, except in language especially marked with a cautious circumspection almost amounting to timidity."

All of this, coupled with his own self-imposed lame-duck status that he announced in his inaugural address, meant that Buchanan's administration was shaky from the start. As though to foreshadow the difficulties he would have, immediately after his inauguration, he was victimized by a malady that again would serve as a metaphor for his presidency. Buchanan, his niece's brother Elliot Lane, John Quitman (who led the inaugural procession), and hundreds of other people, mainly Southern sympathizers, who had lodged at the National Hotel in the days and weeks prior to the inauguration all became extremely ill. Rumors abounded that abolitionists had tried to poison Buchanan.

The National Hotel, a large, rectangular, five-story, two-hundred-room structure on the corner of Pennsylvania Avenue and Sixth Street, was one of the District's most luxurious hotels, and had long been a favorite venue for Southerners. Buchanan had stayed there in January, became ill, and was urged by his physician to avoid the hotel when he returned in the weeks prior to the inauguration. Buchanan ignored the advice, and late on Inauguration Day, he and other hotel guests began suffering diarrhea, fever, chills, and terrible gastric pain—all symptoms of heavy-metal poisoning. Buchanan's physician, Dr. Jonathan Messersmith Foltz wrote that there were "intimations of a deliberate attempt to poison 'by some fanatical abolitionists.'" The *New York Times* published a story weeks later saying that the outbreak, which became known as National Hotel Disease, was part of the most "gigantic and startling crime of the age . . . there is abundant ground for suspecting that the disease is the result of poison administered in the food of guests of the hotel."

Beyond the symptoms, evidence of a murderous plot was lacking, but the combination of the National Hotel's pro-Southern clientele, a president-elect with proslavery sympathies, and the North-South tensions of the past year kept the story alive. Even when the Washington Board of Health investigated the outbreak and concluded it was the result of a combination of "trash and filth" near the building, "rat droppings" near the hotel's water supply, and "foul air and noxious gases" in the sewer pipes under the hotel, rumors of the devious abolitionist plot persisted. Several years later, the Confederate spy Rose O'Neal Greenhow described how Union troops confiscated her private papers when she was captured. Among those documents her captors examined was "a full and detailed account . . . of the appalling attempt of the Abolition party to poison President Buchanan, and the chiefs of the Democratic party at the National Hotel." Greenhow noted that "one story [was] that rats, which were very troublesome, had been poisoned and had fallen into the tanks which supplied the hotel with water." She discounted the theory, pointing out that the tanks were all emptied of water, "and no rats could be found."

Whatever the cause of the outbreak—modern accounts suggest the disease was caused by a bacterial infectious agent—its effects were devastating. Quitman never recovered and died the following year. Eliot Lane died the same month, and newspaper accounts estimated that between thirty and forty others also died within weeks. Buchanan remained ill until mid-April, and spent numerous days in serious condition. Greenhow wrote that Buchanan later told her "that he was obliged to drink several tumblers of unadulterated brandy, to keep himself from entire physical exhaustion."

Though Buchanan fully recovered, his presidency never experienced good health, let alone vitality. He would deal with continued struggles in Kansas that exacerbated sectional tension, a near-crippling economic recession in 1857, corruption and disloyalty in his cabinet, Southern secession near the end of his term, and a general miasma that gripped his administration and rendered him nearly paralyzed to deal with the great events facing the country. "My dear sir," he said to his successor Abraham Lincoln in the White House in 1861, "if you are as happy on entering this house as I on leaving, you are a very happy man indeed."

And Buchanan's woes started immediately. The Supreme Court, led by the pro-Southern majority, spoke loudly and broadly on the *Dred Scott* case on March 6, 1857, just two days after the new president took the oath. Buchanan knew what was coming, had surreptitiously lobbied for it, in fact, and felt sure that the Court's ruling would put an end to the "slavery agitation" he had spoken of in his inaugural address. It was the greatest, most naïve miscalculation Buchanan would make during his presidency, and it—and the events that followed—assured that his administration would be branded an utter failure by contemporaries and historians alike.

Coming on the heels of the caning, *Dred Scott* did more than stir up "agitation" about slavery. It unleashed yet another ferocious firestorm that swept the land and threatened to scorch, and ultimately lay waste to, any last bit of common ground shared by North and South.

Part
IV

TWENTY-THREE

DRED SCOTT

No direct documentary evidence exists to suggest that the United States Supreme Court's landmark decision in the *Dred Scott* case—perhaps the most controversial American judicial decision in history—followed directly from Preston Brooks's savage beating of Charles Sumner nearly ten months earlier. There is no long-lost diary entry or scrap of a letter from Chief Justice Taney, or any other justice, admitting that the Southern-leaning court issued its decision to spite and antagonize the North in retaliation for Republican exploitation of the caning, or ruled in favor of slaveowners to help them regain their equilibrium in the wake of abolitionist attacks on the South following the assault in the Senate chamber on May 22, 1856.

But to the extent that history can be analyzed as resulting from a domino effect of causal events, it would be foolhardy to ignore the caning's clear influence on one of the most divisive and sweeping—"far-reaching" is perhaps more accurate—Supreme Court decisions in American history. Not only was it the first instance in which the Supreme Court invalidated a major piece of federal legislation, it was also the Court's most noteworthy attempt to settle a seminal national issue—in this case, slavery—through judicial fiat.

But rather than dousing the smoldering slavery debate with water, as the Court apparently had hoped, *Dred Scott* poured gasoline on the controversy; the decision, which legitimized and encouraged an expansion of slavery, reeked of partisanship and bitterness, damaged the Supreme Court's reputation for decades, and forever marred the legacy of Chief Justice Taney. Abraham Lincoln later called the court's shocking decision "an astonisher in legal history," and one historian called it an example of judicial failure and "the most frequently overturned decision in history."

As the caning had, *Dred Scott* infuriated the North and delighted the South. Neither side contemplated the decision in a vacuum, but each viewed it as yet another domino bumping against a whole series of events in the slavery debate.

The North interpreted *Dred Scott* as yet another abuse perpetuated by an out-of-control and belligerent slave power that controlled the federal government apparatus—the latest outrage in a string of sinister actions that began with the annexation of Texas and the war with Mexico; continued with the Compromise of 1850; was made worse with the passage of the Kansas-Nebraska Act in 1854 and the subsequent violence by proslavery Missouri border ruffians in Kansas during 1855 and 1856; and reached a crescendo when Preston Brooks attacked Charles Sumner in the U.S. Senate chamber.

For the South, *Dred Scott* validated not just slavery itself, but the constitutionality of slavery; Southerners viewed the decision as judicial confirmation of the Founders' wishes—that because slavery was not prohibited by the United States Constitution, it was therefore just, legal, and permissible anywhere in the country. Moreover, the South viewed *Dred Scott* as a moral and legal bulwark that protected its way of life against the increasing encroachment of the North and the radical assaults by ever-emboldened abolitionists.

In essence, Southerners believed that the Supreme Court had validated, with its pen and its voice, the actions Preston Brooks took with his cane against Charles Sumner on May 22, 1856.

As broad and complex as the Supreme Court's decision was, the facts of *Dred Scott v. John F.A. Sandford* are fairly simple and not in dispute.

Dred Scott was the slave of Dr. John Emerson, an army surgeon who lived in St. Louis, Missouri. In the 1830s, Emerson had taken Scott on tours of duty to Illinois and the Wisconsin Territory, regions that had been made free-soil by the Missouri Compromise of 1820. In 1838, Emerson returned to Missouri, where he died in 1843, leaving his property—including Scott—to his widow. When she later moved to Massachusetts, Mrs. Emerson transferred ownership of Scott to her brother, John F. A. Sanford (the Supreme Court misspelled Sanford's name in its official citation).

In 1846 Scott sued for his freedom in Missouri state court, arguing that he had become free when Emerson had moved him to live in free territory. The legal process at the state court level dragged on for years, with alternative trials and appeals producing judgments for and against Scott, until the Missouri Supreme Court ruled against Scott. Then, with the backing of a group of antislavery lawyers, Scott sued as a citizen of Missouri in the federal circuit court. Sanford, in response, argued that because Scott was a Negro, he could not be a citizen of Missouri and thus was not entitled to sue in federal court.

In March 1854, the federal circuit court in Missouri found for Sanford and Scott's lawyers appealed the case to the United States Supreme Court. The high court had three key issues before them: whether Scott was a citizen (only citizens could sue in federal court); whether the time Scott lived on free soil rendered him a free man; and finally, the constitutionality of prohibiting slavery in parts of the Louisiana Purchase that were governed by the Missouri Compromise of 1820.

The Court heard early arguments and conferred on the case between February and April 1856, and at that point, only a few newspapers had recognized the potential significance of *Dred Scott v. Sandford* (by this time, Sanford was stricken with mental illness and would be confined to an insane asylum by year's end). The *Washington Star* declared on February 12: "The public of Washington do not seem to be aware that one of the most important cases ever brought up for adjudication by the Supreme Court is now being tried before that august tribunal." Finally, though, on May 12, less than two weeks before the caning, the Supreme Court ordered that the case be reargued the following term, in December 1856, with attention paid to specific legal points. Northern skeptics, including Abraham Lincoln, argued that the Court's decision was purely political, an attempt to delay what would be a proslavery decision until after the November presidential election, which would mean that Buchanan and other Democrats would not have to face tough questions about the Court's actions.

In any case, after a tumultuous summer that featured Brooks's resignation and reelection to Congress, Sumner's highly publicized convalescence, and a ferocious battle for the Presidency, the Court heard new arguments in December. Over the next couple of months, Chief Justice Taney and his fellow jurists—with occasional meddling from President-elect Buchanan—worked on their opinions. There was no doubt that Taney would write the bulk of the majority opinion, and that his words would carry the greatest weight in the Dred Scott case.

On March 6, 1857, around 11:00 A.M., the Chief Justice and the eight other black-robed judges appeared before a crowded Supreme Court courtroom deep within the Capitol. Congress had adjourned on March 3 and President Buchanan's March 4 inauguration ceremonies were over; now it was the nation's third branch of government, the judiciary, that would make its voice heard on the slavery debate. Journalists and spectators packed the room, which was unusual for the normally staid and formal Supreme Court proceedings. But by now, most of America was familiar with the Dred Scott case and its implications.

The aging Taney, who would turn eighty in eleven days, waited for the murmuring to die down, his shaking hands clutching the fifty-five-page manuscript that contained his decision, and in a hoarse, barely audible voice—weakened from exhaustion due to his attention to and writing of his majority opinion over the past two weeks—began to read.

Later, spectators and journalists alike commented on how they strained to hear Taney's voice during his two-hour oration, how they often missed lengthy passages or were confounded by the chief justice's impenetrable prose, how they failed to pick up any telltale inflections in his weak monotone. At first there was confusion among the audience on exactly what Taney said and, thus, what the Court decided, and even newspaper articles in the following days often contained mistakes, gaps, or outright contradictions.

But soon the audacious, sweeping nature of the Court's decision, shaped in great part by Taney, became clear. One historian said Taney's words bristled "with uncompromising defiance of abolitionists, free soilers, and Republicans." Another called Taney's opinion "a work of unmitigated partisanship . . . more like an ultimatum than a formula for sectional accommodation." Without doubt, Taney's opinion was a stark example of unbridled judicial activism.

First, the former slaveholder (he had freed the slaves he inherited years earlier) espoused the Court's opinion that no Negro, slave or free, could be classified as a citizen of the United States. Citizenship was derived from the federal government, and it had never belonged to Negroes, who were regarded "as beings of an inferior order and altogether unfit to associate with the white race, either in social or political relations." Indeed, he added, Negroes were "so far inferior that they had no rights which the white man was bound to respect." The "fixed and universal" opinion in the civilized white race was that the Negro could be "bought and sold, and treated as an ordinary article of merchandise and traffic," and that he might "justly and lawfully be reduced to slavery for his benefit."

The slaveholding states, Taney asserted, never would have agreed to the Constitution if the word "citizens" included free Negroes. If Negroes could become citizens, Taney argued, that meant they could travel where they pleased "at every hour of the day or night," hold public meetings on political affairs, express their right of free speech, and even carry arms. Allowing Negroes these rights would "inevitably [produce] discontent and insubordination among them, and endanger the peace and safety of the State."

Hence, because Negroes could never be citizens—as one historian noted, "the only people on the face of the earth who (saving a Constitutional amendment) were forever ineligible for American citizenship"—Dred Scott had no right to file suit in federal court.

Nonetheless, despite Scott's lack of standing, Taney and the Court still ruled on the other issues before it. As to whether Scott's residence on free soil made him free, Taney said it did not, arguing that it was Scott's owner who brought him to Illinois and then returned him to Missouri. Therefore, "[Scott's] status, as free or slave, depended on the laws of Missouri, and not of Illinois."

Thus it was clear that Scott, who could never be a citizen, who could not file suit in federal court, and who was still considered a slave by the nation's highest court, had lost his eleven-year quest for freedom.

Had Taney stopped there, the Supreme Court's decision would still have unleashed a firestorm in the North, but it was the third major component in the case—whether Congress could *prohibit* slavery in territories—that elicited howls of protest and cries of judicial misconduct and malfeasance from Republicans and other Northerners.

In a stunning ruling, Taney declared that the Missouri Compromise restriction on slavery north of the 36° 30′ parallel was flatly unconstitutional. The Fifth Amendment clearly stated that no one could be "deprived of life, liberty, or property without due process of law." Since slaves were considered property, how could Congress prohibit owners from taking slaves into a federal territory? Taney said it could not—Congress had no more right to ban slavery in any federal territory than it had the right to deny a territorial population the right to bear arms, or the right to a trial by jury, or the right against self-incrimination. And if Congress could not do this, it could not authorize a territorial government to do so. "It could confer no power on any local government, established by its authority, to violate the provisions of the Constitution," Taney said.

With that, Taney made his historic pronouncement: "It is the opinion of the court that the Act of Congress [Missouri

Compromise] which prohibited a citizen from holding and owning property of this kind in the territory of the United States north of the line therein mentioned, is not warranted by the Constitution, and is therefore void."

By this ruling, Taney and the Court had essentially made slavery legal across any territory in the United States. And the Court's language elicited Northern fears that the spread of slavery would not stop with the territories. Abraham Lincoln warned that a future court ruling, what he called "the next Dred Scott decision," could prohibit *states* from banning slavery. In that case, Lincoln said, "we shall lie down pleasantly dreaming the people of Missouri are on the verge of making their state free; and we shall awake to the reality, instead, that the . . . Supreme Court has made Illinois a slave state."

The Northern attack against Taney and the Supreme Court was fierce and unrelenting. Republican newspapers, most notably Horace Greeley's *New York Tribune*, led the way, declaring that the decision was "entitled to just as much moral weight as would be the judgment of a majority of those congregated in any Washington bar-room." They denounced the decision as "wicked," "abominable," and "atrocious," called Taney a "cunning chief," and said his words were a "collation of false statements" that demonstrated a "detestable hypocrisy" and a "mean and skulking cowardice." Taney's ruling was shameful, the *Tribune* noted, adding sarcastically: "No wonder the chief justice should have sunk his voice to a whisper . . . knowing that he was engaged in a pitiful attempt to impose upon the public."

Republicans were apoplectic. Congressman John F. Potter of Wisconsin called the court decision "sheer blasphemy . . . an infamous libel on our government . . . a lasting disgrace to the court . . . and deeply humiliating to every American citizen." Northern legislatures controlled by Republicans formally protested the decision by Taney and the majority. The New York legislature passed a resolution calling the opinion "erroneous" and asserted that the court "had lost the confidence and respect of the people of this State." In Ohio, the legislature denounced the decision and went further by adopting measures against slaveholding or the kidnapping or capture of free blacks, and the Supreme Court of Ohio ruled that any slave brought into the state would be automatically emancipated.

Predictably, Southerners, and even some Northern Democrats, were one-hundred-eighty-degrees apart in their reaction, but this time—unlike the caning—they had the advantage of invoking their moralistic tones with the weight of a Supreme Court decision behind them. The *New Orleans Picayune* called the Supreme Court an "august and incorruptible body," which rose above parties and factions to give "the loftiest mind support to patriotism, and consolidate the Union—be it reverently hoped—for all time." More emphatic and forthright was the *Constitutionalist* of Augusta, Georgia, which summed up the *Dred Scott* case with language designed to electrify the South and chill Northern Republicans to the bone: "Southern opinion upon the subject of southern slavery . . . is now the supreme law of the land . . . and opposition to southern opinion upon this subject is now opposition to the Constitution, and morally treason against the Government." Other publications predicted that the Court's ruling signaled the beginning of the end of the Republican Party, whose entire platform rested on an end to slavery expansion and, eventually, outright abolition. *Dred Scott,* the *Constitutionalist* declared, "crushes the life out of that miserable political organization."

Like the caning, the *Dred Scott* case further polarized North and South. Rather than strengthening the Union by settling the slavery question, which Taney and the Court had hoped for, it created an uproar that further frayed the bonds tenuously holding the two sections together. Rather than bolstering the Buchanan presidency, it weakened Buchanan from the outset; when coupled with the president's own announcement that he would serve only one term and his subsequent indecisiveness, it helped render his administration ineffective at a time when the nation needed bold and unifying leadership. And rather than weakening or destroying the Republican Party, as the South had hoped, *Dred Scott* actually strengthened it further in two ways—by fracturing Northern and Southern Democrats and by encouraging still more citizens to join the Republicans in an effort to stave off slave-power abuses. Speaking to the American Anti-Slavery Society in New York, Frederick Douglass noted that the history of the movement demonstrated that "all measures devised and executed with a view to diminish the anti-slavery agitation, have only served to increase, intensify, and embolden that agitation."

In many ways, the actions of Preston Brooks and Roger Taney produced similar results. This is not surprising considering the similarities of their behavior in very different venues. As Brooks lost control of his temper and his emotions in the Senate chamber, so did Roger Taney lose control of his judicial temperament and impartiality in the *Dred Scott* case.

Sadly for his own reputation and that of the Supreme Court, there is strong evidence that Taney's majority opinion was unduly and inappropriately influenced by his strong Southern sympathies and biases, which became more pronounced amid the maelstrom caused by the caning and the agony he suffered following his own personal tragedy.

A Marylander born and raised in the Calvert County tobacco-planting tidewater strip, Roger Brooke Taney was an avid Southern Democrat and an unabashed though genteel white supremacist, with a belief in the superiority of the judiciary, a love for the South and its values, and a strong antipathy toward the North, especially Republicans. A learned, some would say brilliant, jurist, and a former member of President Andrew Jackson's cabinet, Taney was born one year after the Declaration of Independence was signed, and had once expressed personal discomfort with slavery—in 1828, he actually freed the eight slaves he had inherited. But by the mid-1850s he was a different man.

Eighty years old and suffering from health ailments when *Dred Scott* was decided, Taney had grown increasingly impatient and even intolerant of abolitionism and other attacks on the Southern way of life that he cherished. Like Preston Brooks, he worried about the fate of his section, which he believed was under constant attack from what he would one day call "free state aggression"—the Missouri Compromise, the passage of state laws defying the Fugitive Slave Act, the use of churches and schools in the North to distribute antislavery propaganda, and in the publication of *Uncle Tom's Cabin*, a novel "well calculated to rouse the morbid thoughts of fanatics, which portrayed in pictures of exaggeration the evils of slavery." He viewed Northerners, abolitionists in particular, as meddlers, who did not fathom that "a general and sudden emancipation would be absolute ruin to all Negroes."

In addition, while Taney may have had misgivings about slavery at certain points in his career, he believed strongly in its legality because it was not forbidden by the Constitution. Indeed, he pointed out more than once that when the federal Constitution was published in Massachusetts, the paper in which it was printed also contained an advertisement of a Negro for sale. He harbored particular hostility toward Massachusetts, a state that was once the center of the triangle slave trade and was now the home to fanatical abolitionists; Taney viewed the Commonwealth's position as selfish and hypocritical. As historian Don Fehrenbacher noted: "Taney, above all in the late 1850s, was fiercely anti-antislavery."

While some of these feelings could be inferred from his public writings, his fierce hostility to the antislavery movement was more evident in his private correspondence. In October 1856—just five months after the caning, in the midst of that event's fallout, and one month before the surging Republican Party hoped to win a presidential election—Taney wrote to his son-in-law: "The South is doomed to sink to a state of inferiority, and the power of the North will be exercised to gratify their cupidity and their evil passions, without the slightest regard to the principles of the Constitution." Taney saw only one course: "Nothing but a firm united action, nearly unanimous in every state, can check Northern insult and Northern aggression." Written shortly before the second round of arguments in the Dred Scott case, Fehrenbacher accurately pointed out that the letter would have caused a sensation if it had somehow fallen into the hands of a Republican journalist.

Chief Justice Roger B. Taney wrote the majority opinion for *Dred Scott*. (*Library of Congress*)

The raw honesty of Taney's letter represents the opinions of an aging, grief-stricken man who likely believed he had little to live for. The preceding year, 1855, had been one of unimaginable personal pain and heartache for Roger Taney, and his biographer, Carl B. Swisher believes the ordeal may have seriously affected his judgment in the *Dred Scott* case and thereafter.

Taney and his wife, Anne, to whom he had been married for forty-nine years, and to whom he pledged "a love as true and sincere as that I offered in . . . 1806," were accustomed to spending the summer months with their family at Old Point Comfort near Norfolk, Virginia. In 1855, Taney's youngest daughter, twenty-eight-year-old Alice, whom he adored, asked to accompany her sister and brother-in-law on their annual vacation to Newport, Rhode Island, a favorite retreat of Southerners looking to escape the summer heat. Her father disliked the idea, saying he looked upon the Southern flight to Newport "as nothing more than the unfortunate feeling of inferiority in the South, which believes everything in the North superior to what we have." While he grudgingly consented to Alice's request, he attached strict financial conditions to her travel; exasperated, she abandoned the idea to go to Newport and traveled with her parents to Old Point as always.

That summer, an outbreak of yellow fever struck across the channel in Norfolk and the Taneys found themselves in a dilemma. Should they remain on Old Point, essentially trapped if the disease made its way to their home? Or, should they risk exposure to possibly infected passengers by taking a boat back to Maryland? They remained on Old Point as the epidemic spread to other Virginia communities. In late September, Anne Taney fell ill, appearing to suffer first a mild stroke and then a more severe one. As a frantic Roger summoned a doctor from

Baltimore to minister to his beloved wife, the dreaded yellow fever gripped Alice, whom Taney described as "made up of loveliness alone."

Mother and daughter died just five hours apart on September 29–30. Taney was devastated and guilt-ridden that he had opposed Alice's request to travel to Newport. A family friend who visited him later described him as "crushed and broken in spirit." Another relative, attempting to capture the depth of Taney's grief, wrote: "He says he shall not live, that he can never take his seat on the bench again. . . . He has been in tears like an infant." Taney, he said, had given way to the most "bitter self reproaches, for keeping his family at the Point in reliance on his own judgment that they were there free from danger."

Taney was in shock and made no pretense of how he expected his terrible loss to affect him. To one fellow jurist who expressed condolences, Taney wrote in November 1855: "It would be useless for me to tell you what I have passed through." Although Taney planned to sit in the Supreme Court at the beginning of the term in December, he admitted, "I shall enter upon those duties with the painful consciousness that they will be imperfectly discharged." The next time he saw his colleague, Taney warned: "I shall meet you with broken health and with a broken spirit." Overwhelmed with grief, Taney sold his family house in Baltimore and established permanent residence in Washington, D.C. He never again visited Old Point. Friends, relatives, and perhaps Taney himself, questioned whether the chief justice wanted to live any longer.

It is clear that Roger Taney's personal tragedy, the heartbreaking near-simultaneous deaths of a wife and daughter he could not save, made him more desperate to preserve the one thing they all cherished: the Southern way of life. His deep personal pain, coupled with his age and infirmity, tore Taney free from the moorings of judicial impartiality that serve as the foundation for any Supreme Court justice. He had lost the people dearest to him, and his great fear that his Southern way of life would also disappear as abolitionists continued their relentless attacks drove him to become more extremist in his writings and his opinions, and exert greater influence over his fellow Southern justices.

The claims of Southern inferiority and fears of Northern superiority that he expressed to Alice when comparing Old Point and Newport had become even more starkly delineated in the aftermath of the caning. Preston Brooks's assault on Charles Sumner, while carried out in defense of Southern values, now threatened those values because of the caning's backlash. Northerners were furious and clamoring for revenge, the Republican Party was growing in influence, and even former moderates were now questioning the future of slavery. Taney was neither insulated nor isolated from these events, and even as he penned his majority opinion in *Dred Scott*, he was well aware of the national uproar that the caning had precipitated.

Roger Taney's majority opinion in the *Dred Scott* case was a byproduct of all that was happening around him, most of it caused or affected by the caning—and that included the emotional postscript to the caning itself, the sudden death of Preston Brooks, a new Southern hero who had perished as quickly as Taney's wife and daughter. As historian Williamjames Hull Hoffer described it: "If we cannot conclude that the majority opinions in the *Dred Scott* case were a result of the caning of Charles Sumner, we can safely assume that they were part and parcel of the phenomenon the caning revealed and helped produce." Clear parallels are evident between the actions of Taney and Brooks. Taney's extreme proslavery opinion was an attempt to stop the antislavery crusade in its tracks, much as Brooks's attack on Sumner had been, and yet, both men were deeply influenced by personal considerations: Brooks, by Sumner's attack on his kin, Senator Andrew Butler; Taney, by the hopelessness that engulfed him after his wife Anne and his daughter Alice died and the fear that the entire framework of Southern existence was crumbling.

No longer capable of a balanced judicial temperament, distraught and fearful of losing all he held dear, Roger Taney chose extreme judicial activism in a desperate effort to save his beloved South. In so doing, he tarnished the Supreme Court's reputation for the remainder of the century—and his own legacy forever.

More important, with their sweeping opinions in *Dred Scott*, Roger Taney and the Supreme Court majority—like Preston Brooks and the caning—had brought the country one step closer to civil war.

TWENTY-FOUR

FIRE TREATMENT

"My whole system is still morbidly sensitive," an exasperated Charles Sumner wrote from Paris on April 23, 1857, "and after a walk which would have been pastime once, I drag my legs along with difficulty."

Thus began a two-and-a-half-year ordeal for Sumner in a desperate effort to achieve full health, including two separate and lengthy tours of Europe, sandwiched around a frustrating and unproductive return to Washington for a four-month period at the end of 1857 and the beginning of 1858, during which he confided to a friend that he sometimes wished for death to take him.

His European trips were a bizarre mixture of immense pleasure and excruciating pain, intellectual stimulation and physical debilitation, rugged adventurism and fragile timidity, pleasant social fraternization and utter loneliness. He toured museums, cathedrals, and libraries, attended receptions, lectures, and concerts, and dined with William Thackeray, William Gladstone, and Alexis de Tocqueville. He traveled to France, England, Scotland, Belgium, Holland, Switzerland, and Italy. He "plunged into the abyss of the Louvre galleries," mingled with the intellectual elite in London, tromped through snow that was six inches deep on the streets of Munich, rode horseback in the snow-capped Pyrenees, and walked for miles through the streets of Paris and Rome. He rested a night with monks in Grand St. Bernard Pass in Switzerland on his way to Italy, admired the beauty of Lago Maggiore on the south side of the Italian Alps and Lake Leman in Geneva, and lodged with friends in a remote section of the Scottish Highlands where the hills stretched for miles and "no [other] family [lived] within 40 or 50 miles."

Yet, through all of it, his pain, his affliction, his "invalid" status as he so often referred to it, was with him virtually always. His ordeal began upon his arrival in Europe in 1857 when his injuries from the caning were exacerbated after he caught a bad cold that became influenza and "finally ripened into a furious Parisian grippe, which, finding my whole system sensitive, ransacked me." For ten days, Sumner did not leave his room. The grippe subsided, but the symptoms from the caning persisted as they had since May 22, 1856. Physically, some days were better than others and some days were terrible; virtually none was pain free. Mentally, Sumner could not shake his feeling of foreboding even during the good physical times. The days he allowed himself to hope—"I am *almost* well, my disease spins out slowly, but surely," he assured Salmon Chase in September 1857—were more than offset by despondency: "Sometimes I wish that death would come and close the whole case," he confided to Theodore Parker in April 1858, after admitting that his pain had been so disabling for several days that he had been hardly able to walk.

He sometimes derived relief from physical activities, but almost always suffered relapses when he attempted intense mental exertion. Worst of all was when he returned to Washington in December 1857 after his first European trip, despite the advice of friends who believed he was still not fully recuperated. He took his seat in the Senate, but his physical condition prevented him from participating in debates over the admission of Kansas to the Union. He attended sessions in the morning, but otherwise stayed away; protracted debates and confrontational language filled him with anxiety. "I am unhappy, and yesterday, after sitting in the Senate, I felt like a man of ninety," he wrote to Theodore Parker on December 19. "When will this end?" Just being in Washington, close to the scene of his attack, once again surrounded by harsh arguments and feeling the polarization between North and South, Sumner was unable to cope. He admitted just before Christmas of 1857: "While in Europe, without care or responsibility . . . I was not conscious of the extent of my disability. But here it is presented to me most painfully. I cannot work with the mind, except in very narrow limits."

He acknowledged that sitting in the Senate was "exhausting" despite his removal from active debating. He spent his time inspecting improvements at the Capitol, reading newspapers, and sitting quietly in his room, "often much alone." When he did try to engage in active work, he found it overwhelming. He tried his best to explain his condition to Samuel Gridley Howe: "At times I feel almost well, and then after a little writing or a little sitting in the Senate, I feel the weight spreading over my brain." To Parker he acknowledged: "This is hard—very hard. It is hard to be so near complete recovery, & still to be kept back."

Charles Sumner was nowhere near a complete recovery. He remained in the Senate until April 1858, when he suffered another relapse in what he called his "calamitous illness" that left him weak and in great pain. "I have had a pull back, which makes me very unhappy—especially because it shews me that my infirmity has not yet left me," he informed Longfellow. "I had flattered myself that I was near the end of my case." He was wracked with severe back pain, "pressure on his brain," and complete exhaustion. He could not rise from his chair or walk without pain, and, after a month with no improvement, his doctors advised him to leave Washington. "I grow old, inactive, and the future is dreary," he wrote to Longfellow, citing his "most depressing sense of invalidism." Worst of all, he wrote to Parker, his invalid status prevented him from speaking on the subject closest to his heart: "I wish I could breathe into every public servant, whether in Washington or in Massachusetts, something of my own hatred of Slavery, and of my own gulf-wide separation from its supporters."

Indeed, Sumner's anxiety and anger were heightened when he watched his Northern colleagues exchange political niceties with

Southerners, the latter the very senators who gleefully celebrated his beating. "I do not believe in friendly courtesies with men engaged in murdering [a] colleague!" he declared in a letter to Parker. "All fraternize with my assassins." Northern senators had short memories; only two years earlier they excoriated their slaveholding colleagues for creating an environment that led to Preston Brooks's assault. Now they chatted and joked amicably. And, in the House of Representatives, Sumner was shocked that one of his fellow Massachusetts lawmakers (whom he does not name) had invited the dastardly Keitt of South Carolina "to visit him on Plymouth Rock!" He expressed his bitterness at this perceived betrayal to Wendell Phillips, pointing out that he would never behave that way "if one of my associates had been brutally felled to the floor—almost murdered—and then, after a lapse of nearly two years, was still halting about . . . at each step reviving his pains." Sumner vowed that he would never have even a "small truce" with "men who seem so inhuman" either before or after such an attack. Sumner repeatedly wrote that he would have nothing to do with either Southern slave-owning congressmen or his own alleged Republican friends who "fraternize most amiably" with them, and he awaited the day his health would allow him to speak his mind fully: "The happiest day in store for me will be when I can tell them what I think of them." Acknowledging that his pain and suffering perhaps rendered him "too sensitive," Sumner nonetheless again felt totally alone among his Senate colleagues, a complete stranger in Washington.

At first unsure of what to do next, Sumner decided on a second trip to Europe in an attempt to get well. "I must regain my health or cease to cumber the earth," he asserted to Wendell Phillips. "The vacant chair must be filled." On May 22, 1858, exactly two years to the day after he was caned by Preston Brooks, Sumner sailed from New York, bound for France aboard the *Vanderbilt*; the same day, he issued an open letter to the people of Massachusetts. In it, Sumner lamented that he was struck down while in perfect health and "suddenly made an invalid." He had learned from his relapse that he was "not yet beyond the necessity of caution." He conceded that had he known the "duration of my disability," he would have resigned his Senate seat. "I did not do so, because like other invalids, I lived in the belief that I was soon to be well," he wrote. Thus, he was "reluctant to renounce the opportunity of again exposing the hideous barbarism of Slavery." In addition, he assured them that he recognized the political power of his absence to the antislavery cause: "I was . . . encouraged to feel that to every sincere lover of civilization, my vacant chair was a perpetual speech."

Privately, he wrote to Parker that he despaired of taking another trip to Europe without the same "buoyancy of youth" he had felt on his initial trip twenty years earlier and without the "assured hope . . . of a speedy restoration" that he felt the previous spring. One thing he had learned was that recovery from afflictions of his type was painstakingly slow. "The gradations of a cerebral convalescence are infinitesimal," he said. "I am sure that I shall be well at last; but I am not sure that I shall be well in six months." From the English Channel, he reiterated his thoughts to William Jay: "It is with real reluctance that I proceed on this pilgrimage, and nothing but the conviction that it is the surest way to regain my health would keep me in it." Sumner said he missed his work so much that he had little choice but to try anything to get well. He had felt miserable for far too long. "The ghost of two years already dead haunts me," he wrote to Jay.

As Charles Sumner approached continental Europe, he did not know that within days, he would willingly submit to treatments that caused near unimaginable pain in his increasingly desperate effort to exorcise those ghosts and finally achieve full health—while, back in America, newspapers North and South would once again debate the magnitude of his suffering.

The Paris physiologist and neurologist Charles Edward Brown-Séquard was a native of France who had spent time in the United States on the faculty of the Medical College of Virginia, until his strong antislavery positions forced him to leave. He specialized in treating diseases of the spine and nervous system.

When eminent Boston surgeon George Hayward, who was also visiting Paris, introduced Sumner to Brown-Séquard, the French doctor was appalled at Sumner's condition. Writing for the *New York Tribune* years later, Dr. Brown-Séquard described a Sumner who could barely walk in 1858. "When he tried to move forward, he was compelled to push one foot slowly and gently forward but a few inches, and then drag the other foot to a level with the first," the French doctor recounted, and all the while, Sumner was "holding his back . . . to diminish the pain that he had there." Only after fifteen minutes or so of this labored movement did the pain sufficiently abate to allow Sumner to walk more normally.

More foreboding, in Dr. Brown-Séquard's view, was that Sumner "could not make use of his brain at all. He could not read a newspaper, could not write a letter." Indeed, the physician wrote, Sumner was "in a frightful state as regards the activity of the mind, as every effort there was most painful to him." Sumner felt at times "as if his head would burst; there seemed to be some great force within pushing the pieces away from one another."

Brown-Séquard immediately recommended "active treatment" to cure Sumner—in the words of one account, "the application of a system of counter-irritants in order to reach the malady in the cerebral system and in the spine." In lay terms, Dr. Brown-Séquard planned to burn Charles Sumner.

Over a two-week period in June 1858, Brown-Séquard would subject Sumner to "fire" treatments that would take the senator to the limits of his physical endurance. Without anesthetic—Sumner believed the treatments would be more effective that way—Brown-Séquard six times applied a flaming compress, or "moxa," usually made of rolled cotton wool, to Sumner's bare skin, burning Sumner up and down his back and neck, tracing the length of his spinal cord. Brown-Séquard told Sumner that the treatment—nonsense by modern standards, but considered advanced for the time (though the doctor did have contemporaneous critics)—was necessary to offset the injury his spine had suffered from the nature of Brooks's caning. When a blow is struck atop the head, especially when the victim is seated,

Brown-Séquard explained to Sumner, "the shock follows the spinal column until it reaches what is termed the point of resistance. Here the shock stops, and at this point there arises the germ of future trouble." Brown-Séquard likened the sequence of events to trying to drive a nail into hard wood; the blow does not necessarily bend the head of the nail, but the weakest point along the shaft. Sumner's skull protected his brain, but the beating had injured two points along his spinal cord; an upper irritation affected Sumner's brain function, a lower irritation "caused the pain which gave the appearance of paralysis" in the legs.

Fire treatments, Brown-Séquard said, would reduce excess fluid in the brain and spinal cord, thus easing the pressure on Sumner's back. While the treatments would be intensely painful, the doctor warned that without them, Sumner would remain "a permanent invalid, always subject to a sudden and serious relapse." Sumner instantly took a liking to Brown-Séquard, who gave him "such confidence" that "I put myself at once in his hands."

Brown-Séquard's warning that the fire treatments and their aftermath would cause distress was no exaggeration. Sumner suffered unspeakable pain during his six treatments, each of which lasted between five and seven minutes. "Fire is a torment when it is on your bare skin, & also still more, if possible, in its consequences," he wrote to Howe. "I have been tormented by blisters at every gradation of inflammation and suppuration. What is life on such terms?" He added: "I walk with pain; lie down with pain; rise with pain." To Parker he said the fire left him with a "cross of blisters and inflammations."

Expressing pride that "the Dr. has never before applied the fire without chloroform" to anesthetize the pain, Sumner refrained from crying out during these excruciating treatments, instead "constraining all expressions of pain," and concentrating on the great martyrs of history such as St. Lawrence and Prometheus, "and also of many others in the list of fire-suffering," including British Protestant leader John Rogers, who was burned at the stake. Brown-Séquard was impressed with Sumner's resolve. "I have never seen a man bearing with such fortitude as Mr. Sumner has shown, the extremely violent pain of this kind of burning," he marveled at the time. Years later, the doctor told a news reporter that he had subjected Sumner "to the martyrdom of the greatest suffering that can be inflicted on modern man."

The aftermath of the burnings was almost as painful as the fire itself. After the initial six fire treatments, Brown-Séquard allowed Sumner several weeks of respite from the painful procedure, but in the ninety-degree temperatures of Paris that summer, Sumner found little relief. The open, suppurating wounds kept him in agony. "For five weeks, I have not been able to lie on my back or to turn over in my bed," he wrote to Longfellow in mid-July, adding that the fire had driven the pain into one of his legs, which he described as "sadly disabled." Sumner was disoriented, dispirited, and uncomfortable. One day in July, he admitted to Howe: "My plans are all disordered. This evening—in an hour—my doctor comes again—perhaps to burn me. But it is still unsettled how long this treatment will continue."

Later in the summer, Sumner left Paris and traveled to Aix-en-Savoie to try the famous mineral baths, a marked contrast to the violent fire treatments. "The quiet of my present retreat and my incognito is a luxury," he wrote to Charles Francis Adams in September 1858. "[The] treatment which I pursue is in entire contrast with those dismal experiences in Paris." Sumner enjoyed the "hot and cold douches" that were applied to his bath, though they exhausted him; still, despite spending anywhere from four to six hours in bed after his baths, he found time each day to "ramble in this beautiful country."

Back home, there were some in Boston who believed Sumner should resign; citizens were growing increasingly impatient with the length of his convalescence. Unwilling to resign, unable to return to his duties, Sumner in November 1858 sought to short-circuit the calls for his resignation by issuing a public statement from Brown-Séquard and other consulting physicians on the state of his health. They agreed that Sumner "was still suffering from the injuries he received more than two-and-a-half years ago." They also considered it "unadvisable for him to return to his public duties during the present winter," but they assured the Massachusetts public that they had "great confidence *that he would surely recover.*"

Sumner himself wrote in November that he "wish[ed] that I could say that I am well." While he had made positive gains, while he could now endure "a certain amount of fatigue without provoking bad symptoms," his pain was not entirely gone—not from Brooks's cane and not from Brown-Séquard's fire treatments. "I cannot express my disappointment & mortification that I find myself still halting about with a broken back," he lamented.

Sumner's literal trial by fire made for good newspaper copy back in the United States and rekindled North-South debate about just how much the senator was suffering.

Northern, primarily Republican, papers carried detailed accounts of Dr. Brown-Séquard's fire treatments in an attempt to accomplish several things: stave off Northern voices that suggested Sumner resign (how could they be so heartless while he endured such pain?), put the lie once and for all to the Southern theory that he was shamming (why would anyone subject themselves to such excruciating treatments under false pretenses?), and create what amounted to a second martyrdom for Sumner as a way to remind the country of the long-term and barbaric effects of the caning. The Paris correspondent for the *New York Tribune*, who acknowledged that Sumner's "morale is sound," also reminded his readers on July 9: "Now, fire is fire, and the quality of it is to burn, as sure as the 'property of rain is to wet.'" At the same time, that Sumner endured the fire treatments without a chloroform anesthetic was a tribute to his fortitude, the "wonderful recuperative powers of his constitution" coupled with his "vigor of will."

Southern papers did not focus so much on the "shamming" issue any longer, but simply questioned the veracity of the *reports* about Sumner's health. Southerners had developed a pattern of criticism of this nature against the North since the caning—that deception was part and parcel of the North's *modus operandi* and that the South should trust neither words nor motives of Northerners, particularly Republicans. The *Charleston Courier* questioned whether Dr. Brown-Séquard's fire treatments even occurred. "[They] are only known through the reports of anonymous and irresponsible correspondents," the paper noted. Echoing other reports, the *Courier* also expressed its disdain for Sumner's tendency to make the condition of his health a matter of public record. "The creature . . . could not deny himself the pleasure of parading his simulated sores and sorrows," the editor said.

Surely, the paper opined, even if Sumner had been injured, he certainly had regained his health by now; how else could one explain his lengthy "excursion" across Europe? The stories of his "terrible" fire treatments at the hands of Dr. Brown-Séquard, "so eloquently detailed," were exaggerated by reporters and correspondents to offset the numerous reports of the "entertainment" Sumner enjoyed while on his lengthy European stay.

The South's reaction does beg the question: If Sumner was not shamming, and there is no evidence to suggest he was, what was the nature of his malady? Why did it take him so long to get well? The answers involve a combination of physical and mental ailments that plagued Sumner following the caning.

Physically, Sumner almost certainly suffered brain trauma, perhaps swelling, when Preston Brooks beat him over and over again with his cane, as well as an infection from his scalp wounds. It also seems indisputable that he sustained a serious shock and at least a temporary injury to his spinal cord.

But these alone do not account for the fact that Sumner was debilitated for so long. The stress, headaches, and mental anguish that he complained of throughout his absence from the Senate indicates a form of psychosomatic infirmity; Sumner's biographer, David Donald, likens the affliction to what modern physicians label as posttraumatic stress disorder (PTSD). Sumner suffered his worst pain when he turned his attention to work matters, or when he visited (or got close to) Washington, D.C., and sat in the Senate chamber where he was attacked. He relapsed more than once in Washington and his condition improved after he left the city. He was able to tour Europe—hike mountains, swim lakes, walk cities—for long periods with few if any symptoms, yet he often suffered severe headaches after a single day back in the Senate chamber.

Sumner's friends refused to authorize an autopsy after his death in 1874, so the extent of the physical damage to his brain and spinal cord could never be determined. But, in the words of David Donald, "it is clear that the Brooks assault produced psychic wounds that lingered long after the physical injuries had disappeared."

While Sumner's fire treatments did nothing to improve his health, the pain he endured convinced him once again of his martyrdom status and the ultimate righteousness of his cause. Simply put, Sumner's suffering in Europe redoubled his commitment to the antislavery cause in America. "In my solitary days and sleepless nights, I have ample time to meditate on the brutality of Slavery, and the heartlessness of man," he wrote to Parker from Paris. While he despaired of his condition, he reminded himself that slaves suffered far worse every day.

He was influenced and buoyed by the antislavery sentiments he experienced throughout his European travels. Regardless of the country he visited, whether he toured galleries or museums, dined with royalty or intellectuals, attended lectures or exhibits, many of his contacts expressed astonishment that the Southern slave power held such authoritative sway in the United States, or that slavery was allowed to exist in a nation that professed liberty and equality. "This anomaly makes it impossible for the liberals of Europe to cite our example," he wrote. Instead, Sumner explained to Salmon Chase, slavery "degrades us in the family of nations and prevents our example from acting as it should. . . . Liberty everywhere suffers through us." Europeans scoffed at the American notion that "all men are created equal."

Sumner vowed that he *would* get better, would return to Washington and reclaim his Senate seat, and would continue his passionate antislavery fight with renewed tenacity. During his fire treatments, he distracted himself from the pain and drew strength from pondering how he would deal with slave-owners when he returned to Washington. "If health ever returns I will repay to slavery and the whole crew of its supporters every wound, burn . . . ache, pain trouble, grief which I have suffered," he promised Howe. "That vow is registered."

Sumner finally began to feel better late in 1858, and in March of the next year, he wrote with some trepidation to Howe: "Many gloomy hours I have passed and much pain I have endured. But I believe this is past." In April 1859, he felt well enough to visit Italy, where he toured much of the country, and over the summer spent three wonderful weeks in Rome, a city he loved. From Turin on May 18, he wrote: "I am satisfied that I have completely turned the corner. I can walk and do many things which I could not do 6 weeks ago."

He returned to Paris in June 1859, where he paused and reflected on his entire ordeal in a long letter to Theodore Parker. While expressing optimism that "my days without hope have passed," Sumner did seize upon his martyr's status and offered a piteous assessment of his recuperative efforts since the caning: "I have suffered so much, where I never took a step without an ache, a strain, or a smart." It was hard for Sumner to believe that he had experienced the passing of "3 years . . . as an invalid," years wasted thanks to, in his mind, the insensible, inexplicable, and unprovoked attack by Preston Brooks.

He had experienced firsthand the violence and barbarism he had so long publicly deplored among slave-owners. But now he felt that his pain and suffering were behind him. To Longfellow he promised: "In the autumn expect me back well—my long suffering ended—and ready for action." On November 5, 1859, nearly two-and-a-half years after the caning, Charles Sumner sailed from Liverpool bound for the United States, longing to return home and join the fight once again. During his absence, he had missed a great deal, most of it related in some way to the caning and the environment it had created.

Charles Sumner had been on his first post-caning visit to Europe and was just beginning a whirlwind tour of the French provinces when America learned of the death of Andrew P. Butler, esteemed United States senator from South Carolina.

Butler died on May 25, 1857, six months shy of his sixty-first birthday, and just over a year after Charles Sumner had made him the object of derision and insults in "The Crime Against Kansas" speech. Surrounded by friends and loved ones, Butler died peacefully at his Stonelands residence in Edgefield, where he had been born in 1796 to a father who fought in the Revolutionary War and a mother "of great strength of mind and unusual force of character." One South Carolina congressman said later that Butler's "last visions of earth were of those scenes most endeared to him by the memories of his past life."

For Edgefieldians and South Carolinians, Butler's death was a particularly bitter blow, in some ways even more devastating than Preston Brooks's demise four months earlier. Both sons of Edgefield were deeply mourned, and both deaths were viewed as harbingers of severe and unpleasant changes ahead for the South. But Brooks's remarkable popularity and heroism emanated from one gripping, flash-flood event; much, though certainly not all, of the sympathy he evoked stemmed from the suddenness of his death at such a young age, and the symbolic nature of what he and the caning represented to Southern values and ideals. Butler's death was perceived differently. He had developed a deep reservoir of genuine affection and good will over more than two decades of serving constituents. A graduate of South Carolina College and a lawyer, Butler had been named by the South Carolina legislature to a seat on the state's Supreme Court in 1833, and was elected to the U.S. Senate in 1846, joining the legendary Calhoun as South Carolina's representatives in the upper chamber.

The caning had elevated Preston Brooks to larger-than-life status, placing him upon a pedestal for the pride his actions engendered across the South and the protection the caning provided for the entire Southern way of life. Butler was beloved simply for his strength of character, his intellect, his congeniality, and his long-time distinguished service to his constituents in the Palmetto State.

It was the warmth of his personality and his sharp mind, coupled with the fact that his political ascendancy occurred during a less incendiary time, which also endeared Butler to many Northerners. Ironically, Butler and Charles Sumner became fast friends when the Massachusetts legislature sent Sumner to Washington in 1851, mainly because they shared so many common pursuits. Both men deeply respected the law and loved art and literature. Both enjoyed intellectual rigor and often made classical allusions and references in their speeches and other public utterances. Both senators relished conversation and debate. Both possessed a deep, rich passion for their positions and articulated their points of view with eloquence.

But during the heat of the slavery debate, from around the time of the Kansas-Nebraska Act in 1854, their friendship deteriorated rapidly. The camaraderie Butler and Sumner may once have shared thanks to their common ability to recite Shakespeare, quote Cicero, or appreciate Renaissance art simply was not enough to heal the deep fissure that slavery had gashed across their relationship, their states, and their sections. Ironically, again, it was their respect for the Constitution that fueled their deep and opposite beliefs: Butler embraced the long-cherished Southern view that the Constitution guaranteed slave-holding property rights; Sumner believed slavery was a violation of the spirit of equality espoused in the Declaration of Independence, which the Constitution was created to codify and protect.

In 1856, Sumner's Kansas speech and Preston Brooks's retaliatory attack on Sumner had—rapidly, finally, and after two years of erosion—washed away any common ground Sumner and Butler might have shared.

Congress was not in session when Butler died, so the remarks of lawmakers were not entered into the record until December 1857, when they returned to Washington. Sumner was back in his seat briefly when Butler was eulogized, but offered no comments. In fact, the glowing words spoken by senators and representatives likely contributed to the "pain and exhaustion" Sumner felt while in the Senate chamber. While he did not speak or write about his reactions to the tributes to Butler, he must have grimaced to hear colleagues refer to Butler as "generous, kind, and forgiving," to portray his motives as "always right," to describe his soul as "full of authentic fire," and to declare that "you could almost hear the beatings of his heart in the tones of his voice."

These encomiums Sumner believed about himself, yet they had never helped him elicit the level of affection that Butler had enjoyed among his colleagues; nor were these congressional remarks merely lofty praiseworthy exaggerations intended to honor the dead—Butler was well-liked by colleagues North and South while he was alive. Charles Sumner never was. Sumner must also have chafed, though he did not record his feelings, when one House member offered an evocative firsthand account of Butler's anguish when he entered Preston Brooks's room and realized his young friend and protégé had died. "I [saw] him in the gloomy chamber of death, gazing on the cold corpse of the friend who was dearest to his heart, writhing in his own agony, till, clasping to his bosom the lifeless form, he sobbed forth the wail of unutterable woe."

There is also no record of Sumner's reaction when one Southern congressman lauded Butler as "painfully sensitive to the sufferings of others, regardful of their feelings, attentive to their most delicate sensibilities, and [that he] cautiously avoided every topic which . . . could [cause] pain." It was a sentiment that no member of Congress could or would utter about Charles Sumner.

Just days after congressmen paid homage to the deceased Andrew Butler, a despondent and pain-wracked Charles Sumner fled Washington for the friendlier climes of New York (and eventually his second trip to Europe), and another activity took place in Edgefield, South Carolina, that stirred reminders of the caning.

The contents of Preston Brooks's estate were liquidated during a two-day sale on December 21–22, 1857; because he had died so young, Brooks left no will. Among the property for sale was Brooks's full complement of more than eighty slaves—men named "Israel" (who sold for $1,130), "Calvin" (who fetched $885), and "Henry" (who was described as "unsound" and thus brought in only $615). Women—including "Amelia" and "Hannah" and "Sophie"—sold for an average of $750 each; others were considered more valuable by prospective buyers because they were considered "hearty prime, good breeders"—for example, "Martha" fetched more than $1,200 when she was sold by Brooks's estate to her new owner. Slave children were sold for widely varying prices, including "Little Harriett" ($900), "Green" ($400), and "Fox" (a "Negro boy" who sold for $175). Preston Brooks's slaves were among his most valuable possessions. Only his 3,000 bushels of corn (which sold for $3,000) and his 46 bales of cotton ($2,070) were considered more valuable to buyers.

The men who purchased Preston Brooks's slaves in December 1857 were not the first to buy and sell human beings in Edgefield County, nor would they be the last. Slavery still drove virtually the entire economy, and at this point, the slave population in the county (more than 23,000) was almost 50 percent larger than the white population (about 15,600), according to researcher and author Gloria Ramsey Lucas.

But as the purchasers of Preston Brooks's property handed over their cash and their promissory notes to buy the men, women, and children that they would need to work their fields and plantations, they were well aware of how the caning, *Dred Scott*, and the emergence of the Republican Party were influencing the national debate. These events, plus activities that were once again occurring in Kansas, would determine the fate of the South's peculiar and essential institution. And the future of slavery would determine the fate of the American nation.

TWENTY-FIVE

THE LECOMPTON CONSTITUTION

"I tremble for Kansas, which seems to me a doomed territory," wrote Charles Sumner from Paris in April 1857. "How disgusting seems the conduct of those miserable men who thus trifle with the welfare of this region."

If Massachusetts had become the center of radical abolitionism and South Carolina the hotbed of fierce proslavery expansionism, Kansas continued to be the place where the epic battle played out. The latest fight, which Sumner watched from afar, was occurring in Lecompton, the territory's capital city (Topeka became the capital when Kansas finally achieved statehood in 1861), and carried with it enormous implications. Before the dust had cleared, President Buchanan and Congress each became involved, the controversy seriously damaged the Democratic Party, and—like the caning—the so-called Lecompton Fiasco would wind up boosting Republican fortunes.

Late in 1857, largely because the Kansas Territory's free-state majority boycotted the event, proslavery forces won control of a convention called to draft a state constitution for the territory prior to its admission as a state. Gathering in Lecompton, the convention drafted a constitution recognizing slavery as a necessary institution for Kansas. Because convention delegates feared that the free-state majority would reject the constitution, they refused to submit it for popular ratification. "Instead," historian William Gienapp observed, "voters were given the choice of voting for the constitution with the right to bring in more slaves or for the constitution with only the slaves already in the territory." No option was given to vote for a constitution without slavery, or to reject the constitution entirely.

Although he was warned by the Kansas territorial governor that the Lecompton Constitution was essentially a fraud and represented the view of a minority of Kansas residents, President Buchanan sent the constitution to Congress, urging them to approve the document and admit Kansas as the nation's sixteenth slave state—with California's admission as the sixteenth free state in 1850, this would once again balance the ledger between free and slave states. Buchanan called Kansas "as much a slave state as Georgia or South Carolina."

Buchanan lobbied heavily to push the Lecompton Constitution through Congress and the heated debate that ensued proved disastrous for his party. Democrats were split along North-South geographical lines, especially when Illinois Senator Stephen Douglas broke ranks with the Buchanan administration and opposed the Lecompton Constitution. Douglas argued his long-held view of popular sovereignty—that residents of the territory should decide fairly whether slavery should be permitted. Congressional and administration interference in this process made a mockery of popular sovereignty, which Democrats had endorsed in both the Kansas-Nebraska Act and their 1856 national platform, which had led to Buchanan's victory.

While not involved in the debate, Charles Sumner wrote of Buchanan's politicking in support of Lecompton: "His course towards Kansas is unfeeling and base . . . his party will be split and his Administration left in a minority." Sumner wrote that Buchanan was delivering a clear message with his actions; in effect, saying: "I am the tool of the South for the establishment of Sl[avery] in Kansas."

Raucous debate continued, particularly in the House of Representatives, the newspapers—Northern papers were almost uniformly opposed—and in local legislatures (Michigan, New Jersey, and Rhode Island passed resolutions against Lecompton). South Carolina's Lawrence Keitt and Pennsylvania Congressman Galusha Grow exchanged blows during one heated argument over Lecompton shortly after 1:00 A.M. on February 6, 1858. "Sir, I will let you know you are a Black Republican puppy," Keitt said to Grow. The Pennsylvania lawmaker responded: "Never mind. No negro-driver shall crack his whip over me." Keitt went after Grow, but—unlike Charles Sumner in May 1856—Grow was prepared and knocked Keitt down with a single blow to the jaw. "In an instant," the *Congressional Globe* reported, "the House was in the greatest possible confusion," as more than fifty members joined the melee.

Speaker James Orr of South Carolina furiously banged his gavel and demanded order, then instructed the House sergeant-at-arms to arrest battling members in an effort to regain control—to no avail. One report said Wisconsin Republicans John "Bowie Knife" Potter and Cadwallader Washburn ripped the hairpiece from the head of Mississippi's William Barksdale. "I've scalped him!" Potter yelled. The fight eventually petered out with no real casualties, but the brawl on the House floor again powerfully symbolized the nation's deep divisions over the future of Kansas and the fate of slavery.

About a month later, on March 4, South Carolina Senator James Henry Hammond further articulated those differences during another debate on Lecompton and Kansas. Hammond, who owned hundreds of slaves, delivered an impassioned defense of slavery and the South's contributions to the North and America. He warned the North that by continuing to wage war on the South, it was putting its own economic future in jeopardy. "No, you dare not make war on cotton," he declared. "No power on earth dares to make war upon it. Cotton is king." Hammond stressed that cotton production saved the North from economic destruction during the recession in 1857, "when thousands of the strongest commercial houses in the world were coming down, and hundreds of millions of dollars of supposed property evaporating into thin air."

And for cotton to continue to thrive as an economic engine, slavery was essential, Hammond argued. Nor should Northerners heed the call of abolitionists who argued that slavery was inhumane. "In all social systems there must be a class to do the menial duties, to perform the drudgery of life," he said. "A class requiring but a low order of intellect and but little skill. Its requisites are vigor, docility, fidelity." Without such a class, Hammond told his Senate colleagues, "you would not have that other class which leads progress, civilization, and refinement." Fortunately, the South had found such a class. "We use them for our purposes and we call them slaves," Hammond said.

The North claimed to have abolished slavery, Hammond scoffed, but it had abolished only the *name*, not the *thing*. At least Southern slaves were fed, clothed, and employed. Northern immigrants were "hired by the day, not cared for, and scantily compensated," Hammond chastised. "Why, you meet more beggars in one day, in any single street of New York, than you would meet in a lifetime in the whole South." Perhaps "ears polite" in the North and the rest of the world had discarded its usage, but "slave" was still a word the "old-fashioned" South spoke with pride.

Hammond was quite pleased with his speech, describing it as "extremely successful in the Senate and in the country," and perhaps more important, "it justified my friends and my State in sending me there—it fixed me as the Peer of any one upon the Senate floor. That was glorious to me."

Ultimately, though, neither the House brawl nor Hammond's speech could save the Lecompton Constitution. While the Senate voted 33-25 to admit Kansas under the Lecompton Constitution, the House rejected the measure—significantly, it was the South's first loss on a major slavery issue. Politicians and the press in the Deep South expressed their chagrin that eight border state lawmakers provided the difference in the House to defeat Lecompton. "None of the deserters are from cotton-growing states," noted the *Charleston Mercury*. "All represent States where slavery may be gradually and safely abolished without ruin."

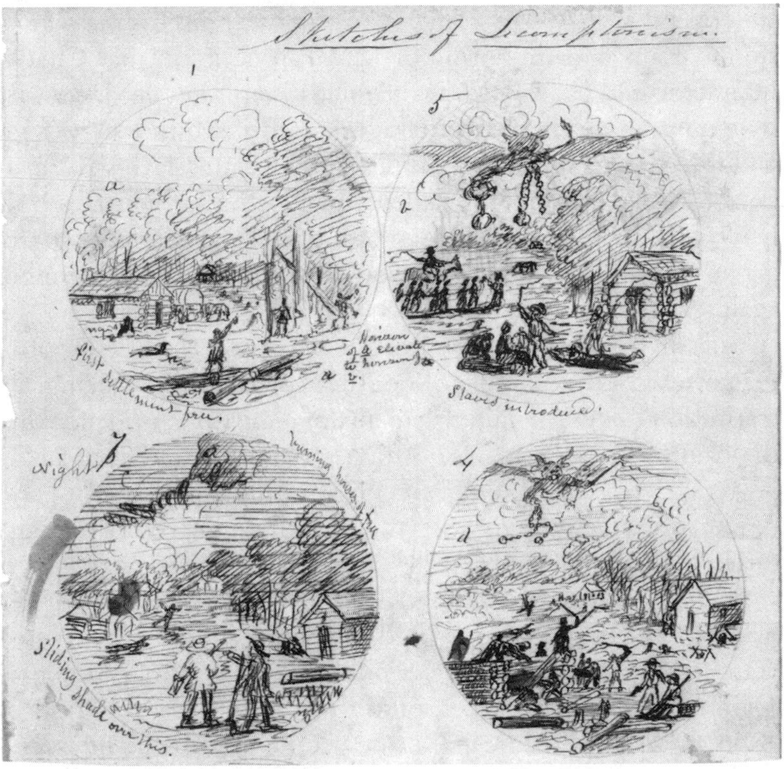

Four sketches by an unidentified artist drawn around 1857 in opposition to the proslavery Lecompton Constitution. Clockwise from the top left, the first Kansas settlements are cleared, the devil introduces slavery to the region, the devil flees as the slaves are freed, and whites burn the homes of freed slaves. (*Library of Congress*)

Moreover, Douglas's defection, which infuriated the South, split the party beyond repair. Southerners bitterly denounced him and vowed that they would never support him for president. In the election of August 1858, the voters of Kansas overwhelmingly rejected the Lecompton Constitution, 11,300 to 1,788. "The people of Kansas do not desire admission . . . with said Constitution under the conditions set forth in said proposition," declared the governor of Kansas Territory.

The vote effectively ended the Kansas controversy in national politics, and left no doubt that Kansas would be admitted as a free state as soon as the territory reached the requisite population (it did so in 1861). Congress would next discuss the admission of Kansas in the spring of 1860, an occasion that Charles Sumner would use to once again voice his opinion on slavery. By that time, ironically, with the admission of Minnesota (1858) and Oregon (1859) as free states, the "free-state, slave-state" balance had become more lopsided and Northern free states now held the clear majority; Kansas would never again be so strategic to the South, though it would continue to be a symbol against which to measure its sectional strength.

Still, in 1857 and 1858, Republicans used the "Lecompton Fiasco" as a stark example of Southern slaveholders forcing the institution upon unwilling residents of a territory, evidence that the South would stop at nothing to protect and expand its power. "Here seemed additional proof of the existence of a Slave Power conspiracy and its designs on northern liberty," wrote historian William Gienapp.

In the wake of the caning, *Dred Scott*, and the Lecompton Fiasco—the latter two supported by the President of the United States—the Republican Party would continue to make the case against the slave power conspiracy as the midterm election of 1858 approached. More and more people heeded the message.

Charles Sumner had just left France for a short side trip to Germany when, thousands of miles away, one of his Southern Senate colleagues stepped to the podium at Faneuil Hall in Boston and asked a large crowd of partisan Democrats to reject the radical antislavery message of abolitionists and Black Republicans. Jefferson Davis of Mississippi was visiting Boston, and while he did not mention Sumner by name in his speech on October 11, 1858, it was clear that his strong language referred to the Massachusetts senator and the people who shared his views.

Davis was not in Sumner's hometown by happenstance. The Mississippi lawmaker had endured a long year during which he battled a severe cold that resulted in a severe inflammation of his eye. Seriously ill for more than two months, Davis's doctor ordered him to Maine to relax and heal, and in early July, Davis and his family traveled by steamer, first to Boston and then on to Portland, where they spent a pleasant summer enjoying clambakes, parties, the Maine ocean air, and relaxed conversation. Davis gave a few speeches to friendly audiences, and his wife found the people of Portland "as kind as our own could have been." While he was roundly criticized in his home state for vacationing on Yankee soil, the respite did help restore Davis's health.

On their return trip South, Davis and his wife, Varina, expected to stop off for only a day in Boston, but they were detained when their baby, Jefferson, Jr., contracted a sudden, violent case of the croup that nearly proved fatal. While his son recovered, Jefferson Davis was invited to speak before a large gathering at Faneuil Hall, during which he launched into a rousing speech on states' rights and individual liberties. He called on Boston, as a staunch proponent and defender of the Constitution, to reject antislavery agitators, whose sole goal was "the destruction of the Union on which our hopes of future greatness depend." More than seven decades earlier, Boston patriots were willing to accept compromise to form the Union, and they championed states' rights once the Union was formed and the Constitution adopted. It was a Constitution that gave no power to the federal government to "create, establish . . . or destroy property," and thus the federal government had no power over slavery. Since abolitionists and Black Republicans could not draw on Constitutional arguments to support their cause, they wanted the "peace of the Union destroyed . . . thus it is that brother is arrayed against brother," while the antislavery agitator played the role of "vampire," clinging to the victim he wished to destroy.

Davis spoke passionately and persuasively, and touched on Boston's proud "birthplace of liberty" antecedents to bolster his case, an approach that may have worked at one time in the 1850s. But now it was too late. While some conservative Democrats and businessmen in the crowd applauded Davis lustily—after the 1857 recession, they were looking to maintain strong ties with Southern agriculturalists—abolitionist fever gripped Boston like a vice.

Charles Sumner was not around, but as a whole, his city was in no mood to hear, let alone embrace, Davis's message. His reliance on the Constitution to justify slavery rang hollow in Boston, which by now contained thousands of citizens who echoed Theodore Parker's sentiments: "I hate slavery—not merely in the abstract. I hate it in the *concrete.* I hate *Slave-hunters, Slave-breeders, Slave-sellers, Slave-holders* . . . hate them as I hate robbers, murderers, and pirates, and shall seek to rid the world of such a nuisance as fast as I can."

Davis, who in 1861 would become president of the Confederate States of America, thanked Bostonians for their hospitality, but he must have regretfully sensed that Boston and much of the North had come around to the abolitionist point of view. The caning had changed them, as had *Dred Scott* and the Lecompton outrage in Kansas. Something else had, too.

For the three months leading up to Davis's visit to Massachusetts, Northerners had watched in fascination a most extraordinary race for the United States Senate in Illinois between Democrat Stephen Douglas and Republican Abraham Lincoln, in which slavery had become the central issue. The two men had engaged in a series of remarkable three-hour debates, seven in all, across the length and breadth of Illinois, each attracting tens of thousands of voters. Hundreds of thousands more read the newspaper reprints of their speeches and comments. "Through the sheer force of their words, personalities, and ideas," one historian pointed out, "they transformed a statewide contest for the U.S. Senate into a watershed national disquisition on the contentious issue of slavery." The *New York Evening Post* captured the mood of the most heated election contest in the nation when it declared in 1858: "The prairies are on fire."

TWENTY-SIX

A HOUSE DIVIDED

The weather didn't matter—the crowds came regardless. In the parched heat of summer and into the autumn chill of 1858, on days hard-baked by bright sun or darkened by soaking, wind-swept rain, Abraham Lincoln and Stephen Douglas squared off, their ardent supporters and detractors thronging squares, halls, and fields in the Illinois county seats of Ottawa, Freeport, Jonesboro, Charleston, Galesburg, Quincy, and Alton.

More than 15,000 people jammed into Ottawa, a small town with a population of 6,000, to hear the first debate in August. Horses, carriages, military companies, and pedestrians filled the streets, while peddlers sold their wares; special trains brought visitors from Chicago and boats carried spectators down the canal leading into town. Men, women, children, and dogs made Ottawa "one mass of active life," and it became difficult to navigate through the crowd. Nor was the spectacle any less impressive later in the debate cycle. "The streets were muddy, the sidewalks slippery and things overhead decidedly damp," one newspaper reported in Quincy, Illinois, on October 26, site of the sixth Lincoln-Douglas debate. "The people kept pouring in notwithstanding the rain kept pouring down. At noon Old Abe arrived escorted by a procession *over a mile long.*"

Neither man anticipated the overwhelming popularity or the impact of the debates, and, at the outset at least, perhaps neither understood the full implications their battle would have on the nation's future. However, the Richmond *Enquirer* sensed it early in the campaign when it said the Lincoln-Douglas Senate encounter would become "the great battle of the next Presidential election."

Throughout their exchanges, the two men, both lawyers and both eloquent, made it clear that they opposed slavery extension. Lincoln, the challenger, very directly preferred an outright ban on the spread of slavery (though not its abolition), while the incumbent Douglas believed that geography and climate would confine slavery to its current boundaries, and therefore popular sovereignty—the vote of the people in new states and territories—would naturally lean against slavery when it became an issue. Douglas was squeezed by the extremists on both sides. He was scorned by Republicans and abolitionists, who believed his position amounted to support for slavery; yet the Illinois senator's arguments during the debates would cost him dearly with Southern Democrats who believed he had undercut them by not being more forceful in protecting slavery. As they had during the Lecompton furor, they vowed again that they would never support Douglas for president.

Lincoln had set the tone for his point of view before the debates, at the Republican convention in Springfield in June, when he delivered what would become known as his "House Divided" speech. He paraphrased scripture by saying: "A house divided against itself cannot stand. I believe this government cannot endure, permanently half slave and half free." Whether prescient or ironic, Lincoln's comments reflected the feeling of many in both North and South.

In at least four of the debates, Lincoln referred to the caning and mocked Douglas for holding positions similar to those of the late Preston Brooks. He reminded his audiences that, after the Sumner caning, Brooks was "complimented by dinners and silver pitchers, and gold-headed canes, and a good many other things for that deed performed by him." Yet, Lincoln noted, it was Brooks himself who had once remarked in a speech that the

Founding Fathers never expected slavery to last midway into the nineteenth century, and that the men who framed the American government were "wiser and better than the men of these days." It was only after the invention of the cotton gin in 1793 and its successful commercialization in the years following, Brooks said, that "today's men" broke with the Founding Fathers and believed slavery must continue.

Lincoln stressed to his audiences that Douglas felt the same way. "He insisted on it [slavery] being changed from the basis upon which our fathers left it," Lincoln said, "and put it upon the cotton gin basis (roars of laughter and applause from the crowd). That is the question, therefore, for him and his friends to answer—why they could not let it remain just as the fathers of the government placed it." In a later debate, he tied Douglas to Brooks more directly: "I say that, willingly or unwillingly, with purpose or without purpose, Judge Douglas has been a most prominent instrument in the changing of the basis on which our fathers originally placed it [slavery], and putting it upon *Brooks's* cotton-gin basis." Again, the crowd roared its approval.

Ultimately, Douglas was reelected to the Senate by the Illinois legislature, though the voters' enthusiasm for Lincoln's oratorical brilliance and razor-sharp arguments would have made him the clear favorite if senators were elected by popular vote as they are today. Still, the debates helped Lincoln acquire a nationwide reputation that would catapult him to the Republican nomination for the presidency two years later.

Lincoln did not refer to Sumner, Brooks, or the caning often, but considering that the assault had occurred more than two years earlier, it was remarkable enough that he referenced it at all. In fact, the Sumner-Brooks confrontation had created the environment in which Lincoln-Douglas battled; the intensity of the debates and the emotional engagement of the Illinois audiences had their genesis in a passion play that had been running for two years, a story that featured a vengeful and unrepentant Preston Brooks, now deceased, and a bleeding and long-suffering Charles Sumner.

By any measure in the 1858 midterm election, Republicans dominated across the North, as voters made their feelings known about slavery at the ballot box. Douglas retained his seat in Illinois, but anywhere the people voted directly for candidates, Democrats suffered badly. Democrats lost their majority in the federal House of Representatives, going from 132 to 83 seats. Republicans picked up 26 seats in the House, bringing their total number to 116, three short of an outright majority (they forged alliances with the remnants of the American Party and anti-Lecompton Northern Democrats). Republicans regained power in Ohio and New York, increased their hold on Massachusetts and New England, won Michigan and Wisconsin, and made substantial gains in Illinois, Indiana, and New Jersey. The New York domination was particularly impressive: Republicans swept the state, carrying even the former Democratic stronghold of New York City, and gained seven additional congressional seats. They picked up eleven seats in Pennsylvania, three in Ohio, and three in Indiana, where they also won control of the state legislature. The number of free-state Democrats in the U.S. House declined in total from fifty-three seats to thirty-two.

Republican percentages of the popular vote increased sharply compared with 1856, as they had done two years prior. In New Jersey, historian Don Fehrenbacher points out, Republicans won 28 percent of the vote in 1856 and more than 52 percent in 1858; in Pennsylvania, 32 percent versus nearly 54 percent for the same years; in Indiana, 40 percent in 1856 versus more than 51 percent in 1858. Combined, Republicans, who garnered just over 35 percent of the popular vote in 1856, saw that figure soar to more than 52 percent in 1858. When Republicans did lose, votes more often than not went to "Douglas Democrats," which did not bode well for the deep slaveholding South.

Even in the U.S. Senate, Democrats read the threatening signs. While they held onto the majority, Republicans gained six seats, a trend that, if it continued, would prove particularly destructive to slavery and Southern power as new free states (Kansas, for instance) were added to the Union, each bringing two senators into Congress with them.

In short, the 1858 midterm election was a political revolution, a triumph of Republicanism that set the stage for the presidential election of 1860. President Buchanan knew that he and the Southern Democrats had been trounced. He dined with friends as election results came into the White House and wrote afterward: "We had a merry time of it, laughing among other things at our crushing defeat. It is so great that it is almost absurd."

Can all the results be attributed to the caning in isolation? No. However, was the visceral antislavery reaction Northerners felt after Sumner's beating exacerbated by Roger Taney's astonishing ruling in *Dred Scott*? Were those feelings further intensified by the South's (and Buchanan's) heavy-handed political bullying to force the Lecompton Constitution down the throats of unwilling Kansans? Did the tone and nature of the Lincoln-Douglas debates reflect the North's evolving feelings against slavery since Brooks attacked Sumner? Without a doubt, the answer to each of those questions is a resounding yes.

Charles Sumner's "Crime Against Kansas" speech and Preston Brooks's retaliatory attack started the raging political storm between North and South, Republican and Democrat, abolitionist and fire-eater, that had consumed the nation for more than two years. The 1858 elections would further escalate hostilities as the country moved into and through 1859.

Then, in the fall of the decade's final year, another event—brazen and raw and also inspired by the caning and the issues surrounding it—rocked the country anew.

TWENTY-SEVEN

A NEW SAINT

"Today Virginia has murdered John Brown," Boston abolitionist William Lloyd Garrison declared to a crowd of more than four thousand who had jammed the Tremont Temple in his home city on the evening of December 2, 1859. "Tonight we have witnessed his resurrection."

The throng inside the temple and three thousand more outside on Boston streets had gathered to pay tribute to Brown, who had been hanged earlier in the day in Charles Town, Virginia, on charges of conspiracy to incite a slave insurrection, treason against the Commonwealth of Virginia, and first-degree murder, all related to his unsuccessful October raid on the federal arsenal at Harpers Ferry (which would later become part of West Virginia). His goal was to obtain weapons, free slaves, and—prosecutors would argue successfully, though Brown denied it—ignite a slave uprising that would bring the South to its knees.

Instead, his capture and wounding by U.S. Marines (led by Robert E. Lee), the death of half of his eighteen-man raiding party in what many Northerners believed was a righteous cause, his rapid trial, and his execution established Brown as a martyr to abolitionists and a hated madman to slave-owners. "At fifteen minutes past eleven, the trap fell," read one account of the hanging. "A slight grasping of the hands and twitching of the muscle was visible, and then all was quiet."

John Brown, whose furious reaction to the caning had provoked his slaughter of proslavery men in Kansas in May 1856, who had reached out to Boston abolitionists to fund his guerrilla army, who had touched Charles Sumner's bloody coat with awestruck reverence, was dead. Like Sumner, he was a symbol for the antislavery cause.

Brown was finally silenced, but in cities and towns North and South, there was no quiet in the aftermath of his execution.

Citizens gathered in great numbers to praise or curse his memory: to deify him as a courageous and forthright liberator, a passionate defender of human dignity and freedom, and a Christ-like martyr who had paid the ultimate sacrifice for a cause greater than himself; or to further pillory his already stained reputation by portraying him as a violent, arrogant, even insane crusader who resorted to murder with little or no provocation. Since the gruesome Pottawatomie murders, Brown's incendiary rhetoric and radical actions had galvanized abolitionists, frightened Northern moderates, and infuriated the South.

The events at Harpers Ferry further inflamed those passions. Southerners were shocked with the brazenness and illegality of the raid, and blamed it on a Republican conspiracy (though Brown generally did not like Republicans and they mistrusted him). Northerners were inspired not only by the boldness of the raid, but by the dignity Brown showed throughout his imprisonment and week-long trial—his jury only took forty-five minutes of deliberations to return guilty verdicts on all three counts. Brown's final words at his sentencing hearing were cheered in cities and towns when the Associated Press spread them across the North: "Now, if it is deemed necessary that I should forfeit my life for the furtherance of the ends of justice, and mingle my blood further with the blood of millions in this slave country whose rights are disregarded by wicked, cruel, and unjust enactments, I say, let it be done."

As he was being led from his jail cell to the gallows, officials asked if he wanted to be accompanied by a Southern clergyman. Brown scoffed and refused, declaring he would rather be joined by "barefooted, barelegged, ragged slave children and their old gray-headed slave mother." Brown said he would feel "much prouder of such an escort, and I wish I could have it." In the North, this reaction, too, served as a demonstration of Brown's courage and convictions.

That night in Boston, Brown's spiritual home and the source of his financial sustenance, it was longtime abolitionists Garrison and Lydia Maria Child who decorated the Tremont Temple platform and positioned banners and placards around the auditorium, readying the room for the Brown tribute. There would be no black crepe or funeral drapes—this was not to be a night of mourning, but of unconditional and unrestrained celebration of John Brown's life work. Soaring oratory filled the temple. Speakers read poems and recited prayers. Militant fugitive slave John Sella Martin brought the audience to its feet by charging that America had delivered up "the Barabbas of Slavery" and crucified "the John Brown of Freedom." Garrison urged the crowd, now that Brown was dead, to offer its sympathies and prayers to the "four million John Browns who serve in bondage as Southern slaves."

Boston's leading abolitionists were inextricably linked with Brown, and their voices rose in his defense, amplified by the drumbeat of religious fervor. Thomas Wentworth Higginson and Theodore Parker, part of the "Secret Six" who helped finance the Harpers Ferry raid, continued to back Brown and defend the raid even when previous supporters began to desert him after the October 16 violence at the arsenal (even Frederick Douglass, fearful of capture, had fled to Canada after Brown's arrest). Higginson called the raid "the most formidable insurrection that has ever occurred," and dared the federal government to indict him as a co-conspirator. After the raid, too, Ralph Waldo Emerson called John Brown "the new saint . . . awaiting his martyrdom, and who, if he shall suffer, will make the gallows glorious like the cross."

The "gallows glorious" phrase was published in major newspapers North and South—to praise approaching deification and howls of protest—and according to Brown biographer David Reynolds, was the most polarizing statement made about John Brown. Its impact rivaled the phrase Emerson had coined about the battle of Lexington and Concord to start the American Revolution—the "shot heard 'round the world."

Across the North, but in Boston particularly and among abolitionists most fervently, Brown was hailed as a religious and moral crusader, whose unjust death by the state of Virginia would fuel a mighty cause. Indeed, even as Brown had awaited his hanging and some called for the Virginia governor to reduce his sentence in the name of mercy, many Northerners hoped that Brown's execution would go on as planned. "Let no man pray that Brown be spared!" declared abolitionist clergyman Henry Ward Beecher in a widely circulated reprint of a sermon. "Let Virginia make him a martyr!"

After Beecher and others got their wish, Henry David Thoreau told a crowd at a Concord, Massachusetts, prayer service: "Eighteen-hundred years ago, Christ was crucified. This morning . . . John Brown was hung. These are two ends of a chain which is not without its links." Louisa May Alcott, who attended the service, later wrote: "No monument of quarried stone, no eloquence of speech, can grave the lessons on the land, his martyrdom will teach." Henry Wadsworth Longfellow noted in his diary on the day of Brown's execution: "This will be a great day in our history, the date of the new Revolution, quite as much needed as the old one." Garrison predicted that Brown's failure at Harpers Ferry nevertheless displayed boldness and courage and said that "success will grow out of the rashness of his act." Making reference to the Virginia governor who did not stop Brown's hanging, abolitionist Wendell Phillips remarked: "John Brown has twice as much right to hang Governor Wise as Governor Wise has to hang him."

Boston newspapers echoed these sentiments and their words were picked up and telegraphed southward. After the raid, the *Boston Post* admitted, "John Brown may be a lunatic," but if that were true, "then one-fourth of the people of Massachusetts are madmen." After Brown's death, Garrison wrote in his December 31 issue of the *Liberator*: "His name will echo in every hovel in the arctic midnight confines of slavery, and the motive of his actions will illuminate every heart like the blaze of a million beacons."

Across the North, reaction was similar—communities observed Brown's death with tolling bells, prayer meetings, gun salutes, and fiery speeches. Author Tony Horwitz noted that Akron, Ohio, businesses shut down and Clevelanders adorned the streets of their city in crepe. In Hartford, a statue of Liberty atop the statehouse dome was draped in black. Pieces of the rope Brown was hung with and screws from his coffin became prized relics, and after Brown's funeral, one man even made off with a lock of the abolitionist's hair. Brown's burial service was without pomp, but Wendell Phillips delivered a graveside eulogy that summarized the North's view of Brown's daring, albeit failed, raid: "History will date Virginia emancipation from Harpers Ferry. True, the slave is still there. So, when the tempest uproots a pine on your hills, it looks green for months—a year or two. Still, it is timber, not a tree. John Brown has loosened the roots of the slave system; it only breathes—it does not *live*—hereafter."

The South was thunderstruck, appalled, even frightened by the Northern reaction to John Brown's raid and his hanging.

That the North could worship and express holy reverence for a traitor and an assassin was evidence that the sectional situation had deteriorated, perhaps beyond repair, and was spinning out of control. It was bad enough that Northerners held up the loathsome Sumner as a martyr, but at least the harm he inflicted was merely with his vicious tongue, and indeed, Sumner had suffered serious injuries after being attacked without warning. Brown was a stone-cold killer, a wild-eyed lunatic who urged slaves to murder and mutilate their owners much as he had slaughtered innocent men in Kansas in 1856.

Far from Brown embodying, in Thoreau's words, "transcendent moral greatness," most Southerners believed him to be a thug and felt that comparing him to Jesus was both absurd and dangerous. "I want these modern fanatics who have adopted

John Brown as their Jesus and their cross to see what their Christ is," thundered Senator Andrew Johnson of Tennessee as the U.S. Senate was preparing to investigate the Harpers Ferry raid. "This old man Brown was nothing more than a murderer, a robber, a thief, and a traitor." It was at Pottawatomie, Johnson said, that "hell entered [Brown's] soul," when he "shrank from the dimensions of a human being into those of a reptile."

Southerners were horrified that Brown's actions and his death had seemingly provided the final strand of thread to unify the numerous Northern antislavery factions. To compare Brown to Christ would have been an anathema to the South at any time; for the North to do so in the highly charged environment of late 1859 and early 1860 was seen by many below the Mason-Dixon line as a call to arms.

Moderates in the South held little sway, so virtually the entire region was suspicious of any Northerners, but particularly Republicans, who criticized Brown. Virginia's James Mason said those Republicans who condemned Brown did so "only because it [his attack on Harpers Ferry] failed. Albert Gallatin Brown of Mississippi was equally skeptical of Northern criticism of John Brown: "Disguise it as you will," he said, "there is throughout all the non-slaveholding states . . . a secret, deep-rooted sympathy with the object which this man had in mind."

Jefferson Davis warned his Southern colleagues in a December 8 speech that, after the appalling Northern reaction to the John Brown episode, the federal government could no longer be counted on to uphold slavery's constitutional safeguards. "John Brown, and a thousand John Browns, can invade us, and the Government will not protect us," Davis said. If the South could not be protected "in our property and sovereignty," then it was released from its allegiance to the American promise and "we . . . will protect ourselves *out* of the Union." Nor was the South afraid to fight if it came to that, Davis asserted: "To secure our rights and protect our honor we will dissever the ties that bind us together, even if it rushes us into a sea of blood."

In the South's view, enough was enough. What began with Northern overreaction to Charles Sumner's beating had continued with abolitionist calls to ignore the Supreme Court's ruling in *Dred Scott*; had worsened with increased federal interference in the affairs of Kansas and the subsequent defeat of the Lecompton Constitution in the House; and had spawned lengthy and detailed debates about slavery between Abraham Lincoln and Stephen Douglas, two leading candidates for president in 1860, neither of whom represented Southern interests.

Now the culmination: Northerners had placed the messiah's crown upon John Brown, who had been feared and reviled across the South, perhaps considered even more despicable than Sumner because of Brown's long reliance on wanton violence to achieve his goals. "Abolitionism [is] a cancer eating into our very vitals," Virginia's Governor Wise told his state's assembly on December 5, 1859. The situation had deteriorated to such an extent that even President Buchanan could no longer be counted on to defend Southern rights. "We must rely on ourselves," Wise told Virginia lawmakers. "*I say then—To your tents! Organize and arm!*"

John Brown was a martyr in the North, a madman in the South. His raid, capture, trial, and execution had set up the most ominous sectional standoff yet: secessionist fury now fully swept the South, while an ardent desire to end slavery, once and for all, now unified the North.

Charles Sumner was still in Europe when John Brown raided Harpers Ferry –"the great event," as Sumner described it—but he was back on American soil and in his Senate seat in Washington shortly after Brown's execution. Sumner had arrived in Boston on November 21, relieved to be back on terra firma; he was seasick for twelve of the sixteen days of his "long and dreary" voyage. He told Samuel Gridley Howe after he reached his home: "My head still tosses and this brick house is going up and down like a ship." Overall, though, he was feeling better, telling John Greenleaf Whittier he was "at last . . . well again," though he hastened to add that his physicians urged him to use caution and gradually resume "my old activities."

Sumner's return to Washington occurred as the debate over John Brown and Harpers Ferry approached a crescendo.

Southern lawmakers demanded investigations of the raid, and warned that anyone who had assisted Brown in any way would be brought to justice. South Carolina Congressman Lawrence Keitt, one of Preston Brooks's accomplices in 1856, cut short his honeymoon in Europe when he learned of the Harpers Ferry raid, causing his new bride to complain: "Disappointed, disappointed. And the cause *Politics*. How I *hate* the word."

Upon his return to the United States, Keitt denounced what he called the "indissoluble connection" between the Republican Party and John Brown's raid. Then Keitt learned that his brother, while lying in a sickbed at his Florida plantation, had had his throat slit by one of his slaves. Keitt's brother died and vigilantes hanged his attacker on the spot. While mourning his brother, Keitt also expressed grave concerns about the confluence of events: "Our Negroes are being enlisted in politics. I confess, this new feature alarms me." He vowed to promote secession across the South.

After the Harpers Ferry Investigating Committee was established, Congress subpoenaed many Northern witnesses and supporters, including Massachusetts Free-Soil lawyer John Andrew, who was questioned primarily on his role in obtaining legal counsel for Brown. Andrew testified on February 9 that he thought Brown's raid was illegal, but so, too, was Preston Brooks's attack on Charles Sumner, which, Andrew said, had been "if not justified, at least winked at throughout the South."

Andrew's remarks reminded lawmakers and the public of the role the four-year-old caning episode played in the bitterness that consumed Washington in 1860. Charles Sumner contrasted the rancor in the nation's capital with his restful European tour. "What a difference between this place and Rome!" he lamented. He longed "for an hour, one brief hour" to stroll along Rome's streets or visit the Vatican. The situation was made worse when it became clear to Sumner that, in addition to the generally poisoned atmosphere in Washington, Southern hostility toward him personally had not abated either. Some Virginians talked of kidnapping him. Another Southern letter writer warned him that he was "spoiling fast for another licking," and told Sumner not to harbor any illusions of safety by betting that Southerners would refrain from attacking him again for fear of Northern reprisals. "What in Hell do we care for the Vengeance of the Yankees?" he asked. "Why, a dissolution and a fight is what we are after. And if giving you *another pummeling* will be the means of bringing it about, then here gos [*sic*] it."

A discouraged Sumner wrote of the nation's capital city: "This is a barbarous place. The slave-masters seem to me more than ever barbarians—in manner, conversation, speeches, conduct, principles, life. All things indicate a crisis." He wrote to a friend in January: "There is now little intercourse between the two sides . . . the bonds of union are weakening. I should not be astonished if the Gulf States went off, a Gulf squadron, and hoisted the black flag."

Politically, Sumner also fretted about his uncertain role in the Republican Party. He still desired to speak after such a long absence, but party leaders preferred that he remain silent. They felt confident about a Republican victory in the 1860 election and did not want Sumner doing or saying anything that would alienate moderates, or provide Stephen Douglas with an opening that would allow him to placate or defend the South, and thereby unify Northern and Southern Democrats. A divided Democratic Party was exactly what Republicans wanted.

Thus, even while Sumner expressed chagrin that his party now cared more about elections than principles, even while he urged his home state of Massachusetts not to take "any backward step—not an inch, not a hair's breadth" on the issue of slavery, he agreed to remain quiet at least until Republicans nominated their presidential candidate.

Yet, the decision gnawed at Sumner, precisely because the Republicans had a good chance to triumph in November—winning the election became less of a concern for him than convincing his party to remain faithful to its founding principles. Success had clouded the good judgments of many men, and Sumner sought to play the role of his party's conscience to prevent the seductive lure of national power from obscuring the clarity of the Republicans' singular vision: the abolition of slavery.

At first, Sumner found this difficult to accomplish, especially when party managers all but ignored him during the winter and spring of 1860. Sumner felt like an outcast in his own party, a party built on core beliefs that he had articulated for years. "Nobody writes to me now & I feel solitary enough here," Sumner confided to Samuel Gridley Howe in late April. Feeling more confident than ever in his unwavering antislavery views, Sumner desired again to speak publicly on the "Barbarism which I see about me, & which shews itself in speech, & sentiment." But even close personal friends like Howe and Longfellow worried about Sumner's vindictiveness, believed he was "too full of fight" for the current times, and recommended "against saying a word not qualified by benevolence and charity." Other correspondents urged him not to dwell on his sufferings when he finally did speak and to refrain from taunting his Southern tormenters and further inflaming tempers. "You have floored those dirty fellows," pointed out T. P. Chandler, "and I would not stop to piss on them while they are down."

Sumner alternated between despondency and anger at these admonitions. "I feel . . . the little faith of our own men in the true principles of our cause," he wrote solemnly to Howe, yet in a second letter to his good friend, his tone became fiery: "There is a time for everything, and when crime and criminals are thrust before us they are to be met by all the energies that God has given us." Those energies, Sumner said, included "arguments, sarcasm, scorn and denunciation. The whole arsenal of God is ours, and I will not renounce one of the weapons—*not one!*"

In May, Sumner was surprised when the Republicans nominated Abraham Lincoln for president at their convention in Chicago—Sumner and other party leaders felt all along that the nod would go to Senator William H. Seward. Nonetheless, Sumner wrote, he believed Lincoln was a "good honest anti-Slavery man," who, while inexperienced in the inner workings of government or Washington, "those who know him speak of him as a person of positive ability, & of real goodness. We think he will be the next President."

For Sumner, Lincoln's nomination meant something else. The senator from Massachusetts was no longer shackled by his promise to Republican leaders to remain silent on the slavery issue. He simply needed the right opportunity, the right occasion, the right moment to voice his opinion, to remind the Republicans and the North of their true course and their true cause.

His time finally arrived in June, two weeks after Lincoln's nomination, when the Senate took up a bill seeking, at long last, to admit Kansas to the Union as a free state. How fitting that the topic of Kansas provided the impetus. After four years of silence, Charles Sumner felt compelled to speak.

TWENTY-EIGHT

THE FINAL SPEECH

An eerie combination of déjà vu and nervous anticipation gripped the Senate chamber when Charles Sumner walked in a few minutes before noon on Monday, June 4, 1860, resplendent in formal dress—including white gloves—and clutching a sheaf of galley proofs that contained the 35,000-word text of a speech he entitled "The Barbarism of Slavery."

Four years after he was nearly beaten to death, Charles Sumner had served notice that he finally was ready to deliver a major speech—an "elaborate speech," some press reports teased—and the city was abuzz. The Senate galleries were almost full, though not as shoulder-to-shoulder jammed as they were four years earlier for "The Crime Against Kansas." But curiosity abounded in Washington.

Would Sumner have the physical strength to engage in one of his patented lengthy and impassioned orations? Would he mention his own beating and his subsequent suffering as he struggled to recover? Would he refer to the deceased assailant Preston Brooks or Brooks's second cousin whom Sumner libeled, the late Senator Andrew P. Butler? Would he moderate his position on slavery at all given the concerns expressed by Republican Party leaders? Indeed, would he be speaking for himself only or for

Abraham Lincoln and the Republicans in general? And how would the South respond?

To Sumner, the political considerations of his speech were secondary. He viewed the battle over slavery as a "solemn battle between right and wrong, between good and evil." The transcendent debate was between slavery and freedom, and that debate should not be tempered, diluted, or abandoned, regardless of politics or policy considerations. He had held these views for two decades. The debate about Kansas entering the Union as a free state provided merely an excuse. Charles Sumner was about to deliver an all-out assault against American slavery, party and politics be damned.

It is not merely that Charles Sumner refused to give an inch of ground during his four-hour address—though he certainly did not—but that he broke new ground in the annals of antislavery oration. Reading from printed galleys because he thought memorizing the speech, as he usually did, would prove too taxing, Sumner unleashed his full rhetorical arsenal. When it came to the subject of slavery, the twin political pillars of conciliation and compromise were simply foreign notions to him: he had never backed down or wavered and he would not start now.

He answered the question on everyone's mind quickly: How much emphasis would he give to the Brooks assault? "I have no personal griefs to utter . . . I have no personal wrongs to avenge," he began in a strong, moderate voice. In the only reference he made to the deaths of Brooks and Butler, he said: "The years have intervened and the tombs have been opened since I [last] spoke . . . Besides, what am I—what is any man—compared with the Question before us?"

Then, without further preliminary, Sumner launched into a searing indictment of slavery and slave-owners, a polemic unsparing in the forcefulness of content and tone, virtually every sentence and paragraph clubbing into submission the South's proslavery arguments, chastising the men who profiteered from the shackled misery of other men, and berating the Southern economic system that perpetuated such an injustice. While

Senate Republicans listened intently, if warily, Southern Democrats walked around, pretended to read newspapers, grumbled, ridiculed him, and even left the chamber in disgust.

None of it fazed Sumner. He was not necessarily speaking to his colleagues in the Senate chamber or the spectators in the gallery, but rather, to the millions who would read his speech in the coming days and to historians who would dissect his words and ideas in the years to follow. Again, his language, at once stinging and eloquent, roiled the chamber with a rancorous turbulence that had long been missing while his chair remained vacant. He summoned all the passion of the powerful Massachusetts abolitionist movement, of which he served, in practical terms if not in formal name, as standard-bearer and champion on the national level. It was as if he knew this was a speech for the ages; at the least, a clarion call to the Republican Party of Abraham Lincoln to stand up and be counted. Invoking religious themes in a way he had never done, Sumner referred to slavery as "nothing less than a huge insurrection against the eternal law of God." Between slavery and freedom, Sumner declared, there was an "essential incompatibility. . . . If you are for the one, you can not be for the other; and just in proportion to the embrace of Slavery is the divorce from Civilization."

Indeed, Sumner said, a slave society was no civilization at all; he scoffed at the slave-owners' essential argument that slavery was a beneficent institution. No, Sumner declared, far from it. "Barbarous in origin; barbarous in its law; barbarous in all its pretensions; barbarous in the instruments it employs; barbarous in consequences; barbarous in spirit; barbarous *wherever it shows itself*, Slavery must breed Barbarians," he said. The insidious, evil nature of Southern slavery was contained in the devilish laws that governed the institution. A Southern negro might be "marked like a hog, branded like a mule, yoked like an ox, maimed like a cur, and constantly beaten like a brute; all according to law," he said. Yet, "by the license of Slavery, a whole race is delivered over to prostitution and concubinage, without the protection of *any* law."

Sumner's arguments transcended the moral and the religious; the practical consequences of slavery, too, were debilitating and destructive to a society. In relentless statistical detail—a shift from his lyrical and emotional rhetoric—Sumner compared the populations of the North and South. He concluded that slavery had "stunted" progress in the South, "in population, values of all kinds, manufactures, railroads, canals, charities, the post office, colleges, professional schools, academies, public schools, newspapers, periodicals, books, authorship, [and] inventions." He could not resist singling out South Carolina for ridicule to prove his thesis, pointing out that a smaller percentage of its white population than of Massachusetts' free negroes attended school. And in what could only be a sign of the mental deficiencies of Southern slave-owners in general, they seemed to not just accept their backward situation, but to flaunt it, "to exult in [this] unfortunate condition, and to go to any lengths to protect it."

Finally, Sumner dashed the Southern argument that slavery was protected by the Constitution, claiming that this long-standing Southern canard was so unfounded as to border on the delusional. The Constitution, Sumner said, contained "not one sentence, phrase, or word—not a single suggestion, hint, or equivocation, even," to justify the South's claims. The Constitution's true purpose and principle, Sumner stressed in an argument he had made in the past, was to make "Freedom *national* and Slavery *sectional*" to establish "the law of impartial Freedom without distinction to color or race."

By the time a drained and weary, albeit triumphant, Sumner concluded his speech, his Senate colleagues, North and South, had borne witness to two simple facts: During his lengthy absence, the outspoken senator from Massachusetts had lost neither his antislavery zeal nor his ability to infuriate his opponents.

When Sumner finished, disgusted South Carolina Senator James Chesnut rose and responded to Sumner's broadside only briefly: "After ranging over Europe, crawling through the back doors to whine at the feet of British aristocracy, craving pity, and reaping a harvest of contempt, this slanderer of states and men has reappeared in the Senate." Explaining why Southern senators had listened quietly to Sumner's scathing speech (though many had not), Chesnut said he had hoped the Massachusetts senator, "after the punishment he had received for his insolence [the Brooks caning]," would have learned propriety and manners. Yet, clearly that had not occurred; Sumner had made his reappearance in the Senate none the wiser nor the better for his 1856 experience. Sumner, Chesnut said, was "the incarnation of malice, mendacity, and cowardice," though it was unlikely that Southerners would physically attack him again, since they "were not inclined to send [him] forth the recipient of punishment howling through the world, yelping fresh cries of slander and malice."

Unflappable and insufferable, Sumner replied that he planned to print Chesnut's remarks in an appendix to his speech, both to ensure that the record was complete and to dramatically illustrate the barbarism he had just recounted.

He had delivered the most comprehensive epistle against American slavery ever heard in the United States Senate; no speech had ever tackled the institution in its entirety. The *Chicago Press and Tribune* called it the "most masterly and exhaustive argument against human bondage that has ever been made in this or any other country, since man first commenced to oppress his fellow man." Sumner's speech was so comprehensive, the *Boston Traveller* wrote, "it will supersede the necessity for another." In the future, the paper said, any man who wishes to prove slavery "irrational and unconstitutional" would only need to cite Sumner's speech.

Indeed, this was not a speech merely about violence associated with the extension of slavery into the territories, nor was it a screed against the individual components of the Fugitive Slave Law, or a warning against the insidiousness of the Kansas-Nebraska Act. This speech did not simply address a small slice of the slavery debate, nor did it focus on nuance and legal technicalities.

Rather, in four hours of oratory—after four years of virtual silence—Charles Sumner had indicted and repudiated the entire system of human servitude in the American South. He had dismantled its framework and, in the process, had impugned the morality of the entire region. Sumner was the first member of Congress to do so with such intemperate thoroughness, such resoluteness, and such utter disdain for any negative political ramifications from either friend or foe.

He would also be the last. The "Barbarism of Slavery" would be the final major Congressional antislavery speech in the nation's history. In less than a year, the slavery debate would change venues once and for all, shifting from speeches in the halls of Congress to war-cries on the blood-soaked battlefields.

As they had four years earlier, Sumner's political allies feared for his safety.

From the moment he vacated the Senate chamber after "The Barbarism of Slavery" speech, his friends insisted he submit to guards and escorts whenever possible. Henry Wilson and Anson Burlingame, both armed, accompanied him on the one-mile walk to his lodging immediately after the speech. In Washington barrooms and hotel parlors, Southerners talked of new violence against Sumner for his explosive words, and across the South, the speech generated fresh fury. One newspaper said Sumner's speech "was regarded as being more offensive than the one which created such a sensation before," and if not for restraint shown by Southern slave-owners, "it might have been attended with similar results."

Some Southerners could not let Sumner's latest volley of insults stand. Four days after the speech, while Sumner was alone in his quarters, he was visited by a drunken Virginia slave-owner who forced his way into Sumner's room shouting violently that he was one of four men from his state who had come to hold Sumner responsible for his speech. Sumner ordered him from the room, but the man said he would be back with his friends to seek revenge. A nervous Sumner sent for Wilson, who immediately came to sit with him. About nine o'clock that same night, three other men came to his door, but when they learned that Sumner was not alone, they declined to enter. They left word that they would return in the morning for a "private interview" with Sumner, and if they could not have it, they would cut his "damned throat" before the next night. Faced with the threat, Sumner's friends agreed that he should not spend the night alone, despite his protests. Burlingame and another representative, John Sherman, slept in the front room that opened into Sumner's bedroom. The Virginians who threatened to cut Sumner's throat did not return the next morning.

While Sumner tried to prevent the episode from reaching the newspapers, he was unsuccessful. In Washington and throughout the country, the violent threats against Sumner prompted offers of assistance. On June 9, his friend Edward Pierce wrote from Boston: "We have just heard of the threat of violence made to you last evening. Be careful, very careful." A veteran from Duxbury, Massachusetts assured Sumner: "I am ready to shoulder my musket and march to the Capitol, and there sacrifice my life in defense of Free Speech and the Right."

Sumner's friends still feared for his safety. His personal secretary, A. B. Johnson, arranged for protection during the night at Sumner's quarters, and designated a series of armed escorts to follow closely behind Sumner, revolvers in hand, as he walked to and from the Capitol. In many cases, these armed bodyguards were citizens of Kansas, who had visited Washington for the debate on her statehood, and who volunteered to protect Sumner in return for his unwavering efforts to ensure that their land remain free.

Still, Sumner bristled at the need for protective measures and said they further illustrated the barbarism of slavery and the arrogance of slave-owners that had succeeded in poisoning the atmosphere in Washington. "All this [bodyguards and escorts] has been done without any hint from me, and hardly with my approval," he said. "Think of such precautions in a place which calls itself civilized!"

Sumner's great antislavery speech elicited raw hatred from his enemies, and it also drew initial criticism from his friends. At best, his oration received a tepid response even from Republican quarters in the North, including many newspapers, many of whom sought to distance the party from its controversial senator. When Sumner sent a copy of the speech to Abraham Lincoln, expressing his "earnest hope that what I said may help our great cause," Lincoln—ever the cagey politician—replied cautiously a week later that he had yet to read the speech, "but I anticipate both pleasure and instruction from it." Things had changed since 1856, when Sumner's beating provided the incentive and ammunition for the meteoric growth of the Republican Party. With Lincoln's nomination, and a real chance for the presidency, most Republicans feared that Sumner's remarks would alienate moderate voters. In the words of Iowa Senator James W. Grimes, Sumner's speech "sounded harsh, vindictive, and slightly brutal. . . . His speech has done the Republicans no good."

Sumner deeply resented the "cold shoulderism and heartlessness" with which fellow antislavery Republicans viewed his ideas. He felt that with all he had been through, he deserved better. "I have become so accustomed to paving-stones from friends, that I shall soon be able to bear them almost as well as the open attacks of enemies," Sumner wrote. When Republicans denounced his remarks as "ill-timed" or "in bad temper," they furnished "weapons to the enemy." Perhaps sensing that his abrasive personality contributed to the criticism, Sumner wrote: "Others, who have become equally obnoxious, have had earnest [newspaper] presses to beat back the enemy. I have none; not one that does not give the enemy something to hurl at me." Yet he was willing to accept the abuse from so-called friends: "Perhaps I deserve it. At all events, I have labored for the Truth, & I accept the consequences."

Perhaps he had developed a deeper inner strength and an even stronger belief in the rightness of his cause during his convalescence—in any case, despite the criticism, Sumner remained undeterred. Far from regretting or apologizing for his speech, he declared that he "would not have had it otherwise. Were I put back to the day when I made the speech, I would make it again." His critics needed to understand that strong language was necessary to portray slavery in its proper barbaric context. "*That* speech," he declared, "will yet be adopted by the Republican Party."

And he was right. Again, as in 1856, members of the general public became his earliest and strongest allies. In general, Sumner did not possess sharp political instincts, and his own self-centeredness usually prevented him from understanding what truly lay in the hearts of his fellow citizens, but in this case, he had spoken for a majority of Northerners. Hundreds of letters poured in from ordinary men and women in the North (450 in the first thirty days), virtually all supportive of Sumner, a groundswell that buoyed his spirit and reinforced his resolve. P. L. Page of Pittsfield, Massachusetts, summed up the general tenor when he wrote, "Notwithstanding the opinion of some politicians, [I] am glad you delivered it just as it is. It is terrible but truthful." What Sumner's speech demonstrated, Page correctly concluded, was that, "it is not this or that measure, merely, that we have to contend with, but with the Monster slavery." New York's Hiram Barney said he was "mortified" by Republican criticisms of Sumner's speech, calling it the "most valuable anti-slavery document that I have ever seen." A Pittsburgh man reassured Sumner and urged him to stand strong against the criticism: "Behind you stand a million of your fellow-citizens in whose hearts your speech finds an echo."

Without a doubt, the people of the North were far closer to Sumner in their disdain for slavery than they were to the cautious approach favored by Republican Party leaders. Even the usually unintuitive Sumner grasped this and he stayed on the offensive during the critical summer and fall of 1860.

After the Congressional session ended on June 28, Sumner spent his time addressing one Republican rally after another, writing letters condemning slavery and urging support for Republican candidates, telling voters the choice in November was between Northern civilization and Southern barbarism, between the ideas of John Quincy Adams and John C. Calhoun, between the glorious Pilgrim ship *Mayflower* and the first slave ship, "with its fetters, its chains, its bludgeons, and its whips . . . choose, ye, fellow-citizens between the two."

In an extraordinary demonstration of the support for Sumner and his recent "Barbarism of Slavery" speech, more than three thousand people jammed the Cooper Institute in New York City on the evening of July 11 to hear his remarks before the Young Men's Republican Union of New York, one of the largest crowds ever to assemble at that location. "More than one-third of the vast hall had been reserved for ladies, and it was completely filled," one account marveled. "The windows of the upper floor opening upon the basement were crammed with people." When Sumner appeared on the rostrum at eight o'clock, he received thunderous and enthusiastic applause "which defie[d] all description." One newspaper called the reception a welcome "as we have rarely seen given any man. . . . He was greeted with cheer after cheer, the audience rising and prolonging their salutations through many minutes, with continuous shouting and waving of handkerchiefs."

Sumner spoke for two hours, keeping the New York audience spellbound "without a movement and almost without a breath" throughout his oration. In his remarks, entitled "The Origin, Necessity, and Permanence of the Republican Party," he reiterated the themes he espoused in "The Barbarism of Slavery," and added political sections on the importance of supporting the Republican ticket in the upcoming fall elections. The Republicans, he stressed, were the party of the Constitution, America's cherished founding document, which slave-owners were trying to co-opt to suit their dastardly agenda. When the Constitution was adopted, Sumner said, the word "slave" was not "allowed to pollute its text; and this was in declared deference to the prevailing opinion, which regarded Slavery as temporary, destined soon to pass away." The Founders would be appalled to learn that the Constitution, "from which they had carefully excluded the very *word*, would be held in defiance of reason and common sense, to protect the *thing*" that most statesmen found offensive even seven decades earlier.

When he had finished, the crowd erupted. For Sumner, the speech was a personal triumph. The New York appearance was his first before a live audience, outside of Congress, since his beating, and the audience responded as though he were a returning hero. They longed to hear him, to be near him, to voice their unequivocal support for his perseverance; they knew how long he had suffered, and admired the fact that his pain had not compromised his principles one iota. Newspapers printed his New York remarks in their entirety, and the Young Men's Republican Union distributed more than 50,000 copies of a pamphlet edition. The New York speech was circulated as far away as California, where the Republican committee in that state published 10,000 copies in pamphlet form. William Seward wrote to Sumner: "Your speech in every part is noble and great. Even you never spoke so well." Later he called Sumner's New York address and an August address to the Massachusetts Republican State Convention "masterpieces."

Charles Sumner photographed in 1859 for the 35th Congress. (*Library of Congress*)

From a health perspective, Sumner believed that his New York speech in July, when coupled with his June oration in the Senate, proved he had turned an important corner. "I feel at last *completely restored*," he wrote to one friend. He even took the opportunity to write to Dr. Brown-Séquard, who had subjected him to the painful fire treatments in Europe, to apprise him of the "completeness of my convalescence." His June speech in the Senate had taken four hours to deliver and required intense preparation, yet Sumner endured it "without one touch of my old perverse complaints." And then he had addressed the New York audience without any symptoms aside from simple fatigue. "I think you will agree that the experiment has at last been most successfully made, and my cure completely established," he wrote to Brown-Séquard.

By late summer and early fall, thanks to the rousing popular support Sumner was receiving, Republican leaders had changed their tune. Those who shied away from Sumner in June now sought his support. The congressional Republican Committee circulated "The Barbarism of Slavery" speech as a campaign document. From New York, Illinois, Ohio, New Jersey, and Maine, Sumner received invitations to speak and stump for candidates. And if he could not personally travel afar to campaign, could he write a letter supporting Republican candidates?

Despite his newfound popularity, Sumner refused to campaign outside of Massachusetts, believing he needed to stay close to home in order to reassert his leadership among the state's Republicans. But his clear and strong voice carried throughout the North nonetheless.

At the Republican state convention in Worcester on August 29, Sumner met his Massachusetts constituents for the first time since he had resumed his duties. The Mechanics Hall audience roared as he ascended the platform and the cheers delayed his remarks for more than ten minutes. He expressed his unequivocal support for John A. Andrew as governor and Abraham Lincoln as president; Lincoln, he said, was nominated by Republicans not just because of his "unimpeachable integrity," but because "he had made himself the determined champion of the Prohibition of Slavery in the Territories . . . avowing openly his hatred of Slavery."

And on October 11, before an open-air mass meeting of Republicans in Framingham, Sumner delivered another impassioned constitutional argument against slavery and urged voters across the North not to be cowed by Southern threats to secede if Republicans were victorious in November. In a speech entitled "Threat of Disunion by the Slave States and Its Absurdity," Sumner reminded voters that the Deep South slaveholding states had threatened to secede, again and again since the nation's founding, if they did not get their way. Their threats began "even while the Constitution was under discussion. . . . The cry from these States was then, 'We will not come in [to the Union].' Ever since it has been, 'We will not stay in.'" From the Missouri Compromise to the Nullification Acts in South Carolina to the Compromise of 1850, the South had deviously and opportunistically wielded the threat of disunion as a weapon to bend the North to its will.

And they were threatening once again to leave the Union if Abraham Lincoln was elected in November. "You are called to surrender your principles, your votes, and your souls," in order to placate the South, Sumner told the audience. Whether it was true or not, Sumner said the Southern threat was absurd on its face as an argument to benefit slavery. First, much of the upper South was opposed to disunion and would likely resist it, weakening the overall Southern position. Second, if the lower South—the "Gulf Squadron" as those states were known—left the Union, how would their absence benefit slavery?

No, Sumner urged, Republicans needed to ignore Southern secession threats and stand fast for the antislavery principles upon which the party was founded; for these principles are inherent and encapsulated in the formation of the United States Constitution, as described in its preamble. Using his most powerful constitutional language yet to refute the whole notion of Slavery, Sumner said: "[The Constitution's goal] is to establish justice; but Slavery is injustice. It is to insure domestic tranquility; but Slavery insures domestic discord and insurrection. It is to provide for the common defense; but Slavery causes common weakness. It is to promote the general welfare; but Slavery perils the general welfare. Finally, it is to secure the blessings of Liberty to ourselves and our posterity; but Slavery sacrifices these blessings."

Because the Republican Party was the only party that opposed slavery, it was, in Sumner's view, by definition the only constitutional party. Republicans' first duty, then, was to "stand straight" and not wilt under the threat of disunion, whether those threats come from the South or from misguided Massachusetts politicians.

Sumner concluded his Framingham remarks with an exhortation that once again brought the crowd to its feet: "Let people cry, 'Disunion.' We know what the cry means, and we answer back: The Union shall be preserved, and made more precious by its consecration to Freedom."

Charles Sumner exerted profound influence on the slavery debate in the crucial summer of 1860. His—not Lincoln's or Garrison's or anyone else's—was the strongest, the clearest, the most unyielding antislavery voice that rang across the country since his departure from the Senate four years earlier. The 1856 caning had silenced him for a time, perhaps nearly killed him, but it failed to weaken him, his position, or his approach. In fact, it contributed to his resolve.

Without question, the ideas he promulgated, the arguments he crafted, the language he employed, formed the basis not only for the strong antislavery platform Republicans adopted, but for the similar point of view that caught fire throughout the North leading up to the 1860 election. Where others sought compromise, he remained steadfast regardless of the consequences. His combination of inspired oratory, unshakable conviction, and tenacity inspired those who agreed with him, swayed the fence-sitters, and even converted some naysayers in his own party.

Because of the caning, he was more than a senator, and more than a fiery abolitionist. His shocking beating, his highly publicized convalescence, and his triumphant return had transformed him in the North into a larger-than-life champion for a righteous cause. That he was also the most hated man in the South, a lightning rod for Southern animus, was nothing new and did not concern him; it merely bolstered his credentials in the North.

He had one more speech to deliver—this on the eve of the presidential election. Before several hundred citizens gathered at Boston's Faneuil Hall on November 5, 1860, Sumner anticipated a Republican victory and told the crowd that "tomorrow's sun will set on a day more glorious for Freedom than any anniversary since the fourth of July, 1776." He urged the group to vote for Lincoln, of course, but to also vote for Republican congressmen who would support Lincoln's agenda.

The magnitude of the 1860 election, Sumner declared, could not be overstated. "The great clock will soon strike," he said. "Every four years a new President is chosen, but rarely a new government. Tomorrow we shall have not only a new President, but a new government. A new order of things will begin, and our history will proceed on a grander scale." Citizens who voted Republican could take heart that they voted for freedom, Sumner said; indeed, it was their duty to do so. "The young man should rejoice in the privilege," Charles Sumner told his Boston audience. "The old man must take care not to lose the precious opportunity."

Still, even as he made the public comments, Sumner may have turned his thoughts to a letter he wrote just days earlier, in which his excitement about a possible Lincoln election was tempered with reality. "I do not doubt the result, Lincoln will be chosen," he predicted. "Then, however, will commence a new class of perils and anxieties. . . . Idealist as I am, I shall prepare myself in advance for many disappointments."

TWENTY-NINE

PRESIDENT LINCOLN

In what historians would one day come to call the most important and pivotal presidential election in American history, Abraham Lincoln in 1860 succeeded in accomplishing something that had eluded John C. Frémont in 1856—the Illinois lawyer won the presidency, even without carrying a single Southern state or winning a single Southern electoral vote.

Indeed, more people in the United States voted against Abraham Lincoln than for him, on the surface, at least, a less-than-rousing mandate for a man who, generations later, would be acclaimed as one of America's greatest presidents. But in a four-person race, Lincoln's 40 percent of the popular vote (54 percent of the Northern popular vote) and 180 electoral votes proved more than enough. He cruised to victory over National Democrat John C. Breckinridge (72 electoral votes and 18 percent of the popular vote), Buchanan's vice president, whom Southern Democrats nominated after bolting the convention that eventually nominated Stephen Douglas (Southerners made good on their threat to never support Douglas); Douglas, who despite capturing 29 percent of the popular vote, won only 12 electoral votes; and John Bell of the Constitutional Union Party, made up of old-line Whigs who refused to join the Republicans (39 electoral votes and 13 percent of the popular vote).

Lincoln carried every free state except New Jersey, whose electoral votes he split with Douglas. He won all the Northern states that Republicans lost in 1856, while holding all the states that Frémont had carried. In short, the Illinois lawyer won 500,000 more votes than Republicans won in 1856, which translated to an easy electoral victory. Despite winning only a minority of the popular vote, Lincoln would have triumphed even if the electoral votes of his three opponents had been combined.

In only their second national election, Republicans had captured the White House and established themselves as the most powerful party in the nation. Speaking to a crowd in Concord, Massachusetts, on the evening after the election, Charles Sumner called the Republican win "a victory not of the cartridge-box, but of the ballot-box . . . a poet, whose home is in Concord, has said that the shot fired here was heard round the world. I doubt not that our victory just achieved will awaken reverberations also to be heard around the world." In practical terms, the Republican victory meant that the "slave-trade shall be suppressed in reality as in name," Sumner said. That fact alone made the election results "destined to be ever memorable and a landmark of history." He also expressed pleasure that Massachusetts had elected John A. Andrew governor and gave their electoral votes to Lincoln by almost unprecedented majorities.

In the weeks after the election, Sumner urged "moderation" among Republicans; yes, his party had prevailed, but gloating would not help Republicans accomplish their goals. Their mission now, "plain as day and bright as the sun," was to simply stand fast by their principles—"they are of living rock, and no power can prevail against them"—never surrender to a threat of disunion, and trust the instincts of Abraham Lincoln. "He has those elements of character needed to carry us through the crisis," Sumner said. "He is calm, prudent, wise, and also brave." He would take up the Republican antislavery cause, backed by the Constitution, and, against "all menaces from whatever quarter," would speak loudly that "the Union shall be preserved and made more precious by consecration to Human Rights."

But speaking it could not make it so.

Events happened with remarkable speed following Lincoln's election and began the unraveling of the Union that Sumner loved so dearly. On November 10, South Carolina called for a state convention to meet December 17 and vote on secession. Similar conventions were scheduled for Mississippi and Alabama in January 1861. Hysteria over Lincoln's victory gripped the Deep South. Mississippi planter R. S. Holt wrote to his brother that Lincoln's election was akin to a vote to "emancipate the slaves of the South and to involve Southern States in all the horrors which that event would plainly entail." He warned of an "army of assassins" from the North who would fan out across the South, encouraging slaves to rise up against their masters, including poisoning slave-owners with "strichnine and arsenic" that had been manufactured in "special factories" expressly for this purpose. In Mississippi, the feeling was "almost unanimous in favor of an immediate withdrawal from the Union."

On November 26, Mississippi Governor John J. Pettus concurred with the sentiment and summed up the general Southern position in a speech to his legislature: "It would be as reasonable to expect the steamship to make a successful voyage across the Atlantic with crazy men for engineers, as to hope for a prosperous future for the South under Black Republican rule." There was only one "deliverance from this great danger" and that was the "reserved right of the states to withdraw from injury and oppression."

Indeed, Pettus declared, secession was the only way to avoid the blight of "Black Republican politics and free negro morals"—elements that would transform Mississippi into a "cesspool of vice, crime, and infamy." Four days later, the Mississippi legislature authorized Pettus to appoint secessionist commissioners to visit every slave state. Alabama followed with commissioners of its own. In December, as South Carolina was awaiting the secessionist convention, the state's two United States senators resigned their seats in Congress and the legislature prepared to arm a defense force of ten thousand men. In an analogy Sumner and Bostonians recognized well, the *Charleston*

Mercury proclaimed: "The tea has been thrown overboard; the revolution of 1860 has been initiated."

Charles Sumner, who, along with many Northern Republicans, misjudged the South's deep desire to secede, quickly recognized his error in a letter to Longfellow in early December: "S.C. will go out," he predicted, "then Alab & Missip; the great question is, can Georgia be saved? Some say yes; others say no. Then, if all these go, where will the contagion stop?"

Even in Massachusetts, now, the speed of events in the South made many nervous. Distinguished orator Edward Everett, a one-time Massachusetts governor, president of Harvard College, secretary of state, and U.S. senator, blamed the Republicans and their abolitionist supporters for pushing the country to the brink of a "final catastrophe." More than twenty thousand Massachusetts Unionists signed a petition favoring a compromise on slavery and slavery expansion and delivered it to Congress. Sumner dismissed it as "all wind" and ventured that it was far too late for compromise. "There must be no yielding on our part," he wrote. "We are on the eve of great events."

On December 20, 1860, South Carolina—the South Carolina that had been home to John C. Calhoun, Andrew P. Butler, and Preston Brooks—became the first state to secede from the Union.

Meeting in Charleston, secession convention delegates submitted the ordinance to dissolve the Union shortly after 1:00 P.M., and by 1:30, all 169 members had voted yes. Church bells pealed and business activity ceased in celebration. "Men rushed joyously about, whooping and shouting," historian Maury Klein wrote, "rending the air with cheers, waving palmetto flags and blue cockades that were the secessionist badge." One celebrant shouted: "The greatest enthusiasm pervades our entire community. We feel we have done right, and are prepared to defend our act."

That evening, a more solemn, formal ceremony took place at Institute Hall in Charleston, the signing of the Ordinance of

Secession. At the conclusion of the two-hour event, convention president David F. Jamison announced that South Carolina was now "an Independent Commonwealth." The immense throng that gathered roared its approval and rushed out to celebrate late into the night. One South Carolina congressman warned that "Northern invaders" would be met with "bloody flags" if they made any attempt to "conquer" his state by force.

South Carolina secession convention delegates endorsed the idea of appointing commissioners—sometimes referred to as the "apostles of disunion"—to travel to other states to discuss secession strategy and the formation of a new confederacy. Many of the names were familiar. Andrew Pickens Calhoun, son of John C. Calhoun, was named South Carolina's commissioner to Alabama (he arrived in Montgomery on January 6, 1861). Congressman James Orr, a dear friend of Preston Brooks's, was named the commissioner to Georgia, and former congressman John McQueen, Brooks's friend who was with him when he died, was selected to journey to Texas.

There is little doubt that, had Brooks still been alive, he would have been an eager and active commissioner. He would have seconded Orr's remarks to Georgia delegates: The South "had suffered indignities and insults until they were no longer tolerable." The North was in the grip of "a blind and relentless fanaticism," and a Lincoln presidency would lead rapidly to "southern degradation and dishonor." Orr, who described himself as a "conservative and Union-loving man," saw no alternative for the South save for secession.

In the North, Charles Sumner acknowledged that Lincoln's election had been followed by the "menaced storm" and that "it is clear that the South is more in earnest than ever before." Yet, despite his own desire for the Union to remain intact, Sumner refused to even consider any compromise on the slavery question. When Union-loving Kentucky Senator John J. Crittenden, Henry Clay's successor, proposed a compromise to stave off further secession (including an irrevocable constitutional amendment that would guarantee slavery in all current or future territories below the 36° 30′ latitude), Sumner was appalled. Even when Massachusetts businesses submitted petitions calling for compromise, he urged state lawmakers to stay strong in opposition. "Pray," he pleaded with Governor Andrew. "Keep Massachusetts sound and firm—FIRM—FIRM—against every word or step of concession." When outgoing President Buchanan urged Sumner to convince Massachusetts to adopt the Crittenden proposition, Sumner said the Commonwealth's people "would see their state sink below the sea and become a sandbank before they would adopt those propositions acknowledging property in man."

For weeks in late 1860 and early 1861, Congress flailed unsuccessfully trying to achieve various "peace" compromises, while in January, five more Southern states followed South Carolina out of the Union: Mississippi, Florida, Alabama, Georgia, and Louisiana. Texas voted to secede on February 1. On February 4, the seven seceded states met in Montgomery, Alabama, to form the provisional government for the Confederate States of America. While President-elect Lincoln was constructing his cabinet, "the country was falling to pieces," wrote biographer David Donald. Some congressional moderates debated admitting New Mexico to the Union as a slave state to appease the South, a move Sumner deemed "a fatal dismal mistake." Such a move would split the Republican Party just as it had ascended to power. "Nothing is gained by it," he said. "But everything is lost—our principles—the cause for which we have contended." Sumner confided to Andrew that "every word of concession" had two negative effects: first, such actions encouraged slaveholders, and second, they succeeded in "dividing and demoralizing our own friends & filling them with doubts & distrust."

Sumner was well aware of the potential consequences if there were no compromise. He detested violence, but knew that war was a distinct possibility. "Much as I desire the extinction of slavery, I do not wish to see it go down in blood," he said.

Meanwhile, as inauguration day approached, Abraham Lincoln slipped into Washington incognito aboard a secret overnight train, acting on the advice of bodyguard Allan Pinkerton, who feared a Southern assassination attempt on the president-elect's life.

On March 4, in his inaugural address, Lincoln tried to reassure the South that "their property, their peace, and their personal security" would not be jeopardized by a Republican administration., but he also warned: "No State, upon its own mere motion, can lawfully get out of the Union—that *resolves* and *ordinances* to that effect are legally void . . . and acts of violence . . . against the authority of the United States, are insurrectionary or revolutionary, according to circumstances."

He was hopeful, however, that the country could settle its differences without violence, emphasizing that the North and South were "friends, not enemies . . . though passion may have strained, it must not break our bonds of affection." In his memorable inaugural close, Lincoln predicted that the "mystic chords of memory . . . will yet swell to the chorus of the Union, when again touched . . . by the better angels of our nature."

But Lincoln was wrong. The better angels no longer exerted influence in North or South—nor would they for years to come.

THIRTY

THE INEVITABLITY OF WAR

Nearly five years after Preston Brooks's attack on Charles Sumner had irreparably shattered North-South relations and triggered a chain of foreboding events, the sky over Fort Sumter in Charleston Harbor exploded with bursts of cannon fire, signaling the dreadful, inevitable moment when America split asunder. The threats of violence and the threats of disunion had, indeed, come to pass. It was 4:30 A.M. on April 12, 1861, and the Civil War had begun.

The tension leading up to the South Carolina attack on the federal garrison stationed at Sumter had been building for more than a month. Major Robert Anderson, a Kentuckian and former slave-owner, commanded the federal troops, and his men were in desperate need of food and supplies, and could face starvation if they were not reprovisioned.

When President Abraham Lincoln had learned about the fort's supply situation just after his inauguration in early March, he faced a dilemma. He could send armed ships steaming into Charleston Harbor, ready to fight their way to Fort Sumter, which would surely provoke an attack by the newly formed independent province of South Carolina. Such overt aggression, however, would serve to unite the South—including key upper South states like Virginia, which had not yet seceded—and likely divide the North, which contained many leaders who still hoped to avoid war. He could simply withdraw Anderson's garrison and surrender the fort, but that would embolden and bolster the South in the eyes of the world, discredit the federal government, and sow humiliation across the North. It would be a defeat for Lincoln almost before his administration got started—giving up the fort would be akin to surrendering the Union, too. Or he could delay and devise a plan that could help Anderson and the North save face while still, technically at least, avoiding the first guns of war.

The new president chose the third option. He sent word to the South Carolina governor that he planned to send only unarmed supply ships—carrying mainly food—to Fort Sumter, "and if such attempt be not resisted, no effort to throw in men, arms, or ammunition, will be made, without further notice, [except] in case of an attack on the Fort."

Now the South and Confederate President Jefferson Davis faced their own dilemma. If the South attacked unarmed ships carrying food for hungry men, such an act of aggression would be seen as dishonorable; in the reverse of the Northern conundrum, it could unify the North and divide the South, whose people held deep reverence for military service and soldiers. The South would also be blamed for firing the first and unprovoked shots of war. Lincoln's deft plan had backed the South into a corner, and yet, Davis was under pressure to act in some way. "If something is not done pretty soon," said one Alabama newspaper, "the whole country will become so disgusted with the sham of southern independence that the first chance the people get at a popular election they will turn the whole movement topsy-turvy."

When it became clear that Lincoln was not going to order the evacuation of Sumter, Charleston military commander General P. G. T. Beauregard sent word to Anderson requesting that he surrender. While Anderson thanked Beauregard for the "fair, manly and courteous terms proposed," he refused the offer on the grounds that such actions would be tantamount to shirking his duty; while he and his men possessed even meager supplies, they would defend their fort. But he informed Beauregard's emissary, Colonel James Chesnut: "If you do not batter us to pieces, we will be starved out in a few days." Anderson said he would evacuate the fort on April 15, once his provisions were exhausted, which would allow him and his men to leave the fort with their honor intact. He would take this action only if the Confederates committed no hostile act against the fort or the United States flag that waved above it, and providing he received no additional provisions (or orders) from his government; if he received more food, his men would stay on at the fort.

The chess game continued. Who would make the next move and what would it be?

Jefferson Davis, his military leaders, and the South acted next. Davis believed that the North was the aggressor, regardless of whether Lincoln's supply ships were armed or not. "The order for the sailing of the fleet was a declaration of war," he said. "The responsibility is on their shoulders, not ours. . . . A deadly weapon has been aimed at our heart. Only a fool would wait until the shot has been fired." Lincoln's plan meant one thing and one thing only, Davis said: "The assault has been made. It is of no importance who shall strike the first blow or fire the first gun."

Lincoln's claim that replenishing Sumter's food supplies did not constitute an act of aggression was rejected by the Confederates, who viewed it as deceitful and underhanded. At an April 9 meeting, Davis and his lieutenants decided that they were left with only one choice to preserve their honor, blunt Lincoln's aggressive gambit, and mollify Southerners who demanded action to establish the credentials of the new Confederacy. They needed to attack and reduce Fort Sumter before the supply ships arrived in Charleston Harbor.

The ships were due sometime between April 13 and April 15, so at 3:20 A.M. on April 12, Colonel Chesnut dictated the following note to Major Anderson at Fort Sumter: "By authority of

Brigadier General Beauregard, commanding the Provisional Forces of the Confederate States, we have the honor to notify you that he will open fire of his batteries on Fort Sumter in one hour from this time."

At 4:30 A.M. the first long, arcing shell was fired at the fort, beginning a thirty-six-hour bombardment during which Confederates lobbed somewhere between four thousand and five thousand shells at the federal fort in Charleston Harbor. Charlestonians gathered on balconies, wharves, and rooftops along the Battery to watch the shelling, which illuminated the night sky with fiery red tracers and choked the daytime sky with smoke from bursting shells. "I knew my husband was rowing about in a boat somewhere in that dark bay," Mary Chesnut wrote in her diary the morning of the attack. When she heard the booming of cannon, she "sprang out of bed, and on my knees prostrate I prayed as I never prayed before."

Meanwhile, in the fort, Anderson and his men were being battered; they sustained no casualties in the attack on Fort Sumter, but hot shot rained down upon them, igniting personal effects and the living quarters, and chunks of the fort's walls and parapets were blown away by the Confederate shells. Fires broke out in several places inside the fort. Anderson did not return fire from Fort Sumter; his ammunition supply, along with his food, was nearly gone. Finally, at just after 1 P.M. on Saturday, April 13, Anderson ordered the American flag taken down.

After negotiations with Confederate emissaries that evening, arrangements were made to evacuate the fort on Sunday morning, April 14. Anderson asked for terms that included his troops being allowed to salute the flag one last time and fire fifty two-gun salutes as they marched from the fort onto waiting Confederate transport ships. Most of the evacuation occurred without incident, but toward the end, an ignited cartridge from the hundred-gun salute set off an explosion when it mixed with other ammunition. Two of Anderson's soldiers were killed and four others hurt. Anderson could hardly bear the irony of losing two men in a freak accident after protecting his entire garrison during the pounding of Fort Sumter.

With that, the Confederate and South Carolina palmetto flag were raised above Fort Sumter, to wild cheers from spectators on shore and the roar of guns fired in salute from Confederate ships in the harbor. Charleston residents celebrated late into the night, with bonfires and fireworks crackling all along the shore. They were jubilant that Fort Sumter had fallen without the loss of a single Southern soldier or sailor. "Wonderful, miraculous, unheard of in history, a bloodless victory," one woman wrote.

Later in the day, South Carolina Governor Andrew Pickens delivered a rousing speech from the balcony of the Charleston Hotel. "We have met them," he shouted. "Let it lead to what it might, even if it leads to blood and ruin. . . . We have met them and conquered them. We have humbled the flag of the United States before the Palmetto and Confederate . . . today it has been humbled before the glorious little state of South Carolina!"

An awful war had begun, one that would plunge the nation into a nightmare that would require it to pay a ghastly price for its preservation. In the words of historian Maury Klein, when America finally emerged from Civil War almost exactly four years later, "secession was dead, slavery was dead, the world of chivalry was dead, the old Federal Republic of Clay, Calhoun, and Webster was dead, Abraham Lincoln was dead, and upward of 620,000 Americans were dead, a number greater than the total of all the men who died in every other war the United States has fought."

The news from South Carolina about Fort Sumter infuriated and unified the North. "I never knew what a popular excitement can be," wrote one Harvard professor. "The whole population, men, women, and children, seem to be in the streets with Union favors and flags." In New York City, more than a quarter-million people turned out for a pro-Union rally in a place that once harbored strong pro-Southern sentiments. "The time before Sumter was like another century," wrote one New York woman. "It seems as if we never were alive till now; never had a country till now." Even Democrat Stephen Douglas got swept up in the pro-Union fervor when he told a huge crowd in Chicago:

"There are only two sides to the question. Every man must be for the United States or against it. There can be no neutrals in this war, *only patriots—or traitors.*"

On April 15, President Abraham Lincoln issued a proclamation calling on Northern states to commit 75,000 militiamen to suppress the Southern rebellion. This led to two critical moves—the mustering of troops across the North and the decision by Virginia, the most important upper South state, to secede. Otherwise, under the terms of Lincoln's order, Virginians would be asked to take up arms against South Carolinians. In May, Virginia seceded (bringing to the Confederacy a brilliant military commander named Robert E. Lee), while ardent pro-Union forces in western Virginia split off from the state, and in June, formed the Union state of West Virginia.

If South Carolina fired the opening salvo to destroy the Union, then it made sense that its alter ego in every way, Massachusetts, would be the first state to respond to Lincoln's call to begin the country's restoration. Governor Andrew quickly ordered out the first wave of troops: the Third, Fourth, Sixth, and Eighth Massachusetts Regiments. On April 17, the Sixth Massachusetts left Boston by train en route to Washington to defend an unprotected capital—huge crowds cheered as the train left, as Bostonians rushed to support the war from all quarters. Even abolitionists, who normally deplored bloodshed, saw the war as a chance to abolish slavery forever. If war put an end to "that execrable system," said William Lloyd Garrison, this war would be "more glorious in history" than the American Revolution. Charles Sumner wrote: "At last the war has come. The day of insincerity and duplicity is now passed, & *all* the cabinet is united in energetic action. It will be needed, for the Slave States will be united."

Boston's support for the war grew only more strident and united when the city received word that the Massachusetts Sixth Regiment had been set upon by a mob in Baltimore on April 19 and four of its members killed—the first battle casualties of the Civil War. Maryland was a border state and clashes between pro-Union and pro-Southern sympathizers were relatively common.

Across Massachusetts, outraged residents, newspaper editors, clergymen, and politicians focused on the historic date of the attack, drawing parallels between the actions of the Sixth and the "shot heard 'round the world" in Lexington, Massachusetts, that opened the American Revolution in the early morning hours of April 19, 1775.

Any vestige of empathy for the South, any hope that war could be avoided, was obliterated with the news from Baltimore. Militiamen and merchants alike in Boston, who were stunned by the civilian attack on American soldiers, demanded revenge and full support for the war effort. Those feelings reached a fever pitch when word arrived from Richmond that thousands of Virginians participated in a torchlight celebration to honor the heroic acts of "the gallant Baltimoreans" who had attacked the Sixth.

Across the city of Boston, young men rushed to enlist, the wealthy contributed funds to the war effort, and women signed up to aid the wounded. Governor Andrew, heartened by the response, pledged that he would always remember "that great week in April when Massachusetts rose up at the sound of the cannonade of Sumter, and her Militia brigade, springing to arms, appeared on Boston Common."

On the evening before the Massachusetts Sixth was attacked, Charles Sumner ran into his own problems in Baltimore. On his way home from Washington, he stopped in the Maryland city to rest overnight, registered at Barnum's Hotel, and walked to a family friend's house for tea.

On his way back to the hotel, around 9:00 P.M. on April 18, Sumner spotted a large, violent crowd gathered in the square in front of his hotel, shouting and shaking their fists. Looking to avoid the scene, Sumner slipped into a side door of the hotel, where he was met by a worker who delivered a shocking message: "That mob in the square is for you," he said. "They were told that you were out—that nobody knew where you were, and that you had probably left town." The pro-Southern mob was not convinced and continued to scream for Sumner, the man they held most responsible for the current Northern aggression against the South.

Sumner spoke to the owner of the hotel, who requested that he leave the premises, fearing that the mob would storm the lobby; the proprietor also said the hotel could not guarantee Sumner's safety. Sumner replied that there was nowhere else for him to go, that he refused to return to his friend's house, where the mob could bring its wrath upon an innocent person, and that the hotel had an obligation—because Sumner had paid for lodgings—to provide him with a room. The Barnum management finally relented, and tucked Sumner into a third-story room without even informing the staff of his new location. From the window of his new room, which opened on the street at the side of the hotel, Sumner could see the enormous crowd, swaying and calling for him.

Early in the gray dawn, after the mob had dissipated, Sumner boarded a train for Philadelphia. On the way north, the southbound train carrying the Massachusetts Sixth passed him, and he was "struck by the gayety of soldier life, which overflowed" as the train went by. Upon his arrival in Philadelphia, Sumner learned by telegraph of the attack upon the Massachusetts soldiers.

Shaken by his own near-miss in Baltimore and the attack on Massachusetts soldiers, Sumner felt a need to speak to other troops. On April 21, still traveling toward Boston, he met the Third Battalion of Massachusetts Rifles, commanded by Major Charles Devens, at the New York armory. Devens ordered his battalion into line, and Sumner addressed them.

Amid applause and cheers, he thanked them for their service and for the mission they were undertaking. He felt he had done his part for the antislavery cause, now the cause was in their hands. "Elsewhere it has been my part to speak," he told the troops. "It is your part now to act." He told the Massachusetts men that his "soul was touched" when he heard that members of the Sixth had fallen in Baltimore. "And yet, he added: "When I thought of the cause for which they met death, I said to myself, that, for the sake of Massachusetts, ay, and for their own sake, I would not have it otherwise." Indeed, Sumner said, the fallen heroes of the Sixth "have died well, for they died at the post of duty, and so dying, they have become an example and a name in history." The Rifle Battalion cheered wildly.

Sumner did not minimize the dangers these troops would face, "the hardships and perils in your path," but urged them to be brave in the duty for which they had been called. "And if you need any watchword, let it be, Massachusetts, the constitution, and FREEDOM!" Again the troops roared their approval and surrounded Sumner, shaking his hand and thanking him for his words and for his role in the Union cause. The United States senator from Massachusetts, who had never been elected by popular vote, was now the North's most important, powerful, and influential figure—and as they headed off to war, these Massachusetts troops let him know of their devotion and admiration.

Outside of Richmond, Virginia, on June 29, Mary Chesnut was caring for Lucius Quintus Cincinnatus Lamar (L. Q. C. Lamar), who suffered from apoplexy and had been brought from his camp to a makeshift hospital where Chesnut and other women were assisting Confederate soldiers.

Lamar, a lawyer from Mississippi, had won his first race for Congress in 1857 at age thirty-two. Like most Southern politicians of his time, he was a firm supporter of states' rights and slavery. He resigned his congressional seat in January 1861 and had written the official Mississippi Ordinance of Secession. He now served as a lieutenant colonel of the 19th Mississippi Regiment.

Now, as Mary Chesnut fanned and brushed flies away from the prostrate Lamar, the two talked of war between North and South. Lamar proffered that the hatred between the two sections had boiled over, that the fight had to come. He told Mary Chesnut that he could trace the inevitability of the war back to one event that occurred on May 22, 1856: "If the athlete Sumner had stood on his manhood and training when Preston Brooks assailed him, Preston Brooks's blow need not have been the opening skirmish of the war," Lamar lamented. "Sumner's country took up the fight because he did not. Sumner chose his own battle-field and it was the worse for us."

Lamar then succinctly summed up the impact of the caning upon the South: "What an awful blunder that Preston Brooks business was!"

EPILOGUE

In the late afternoon of March 16, 1874, Henry Wilson, vice president of the United States, stood stoically beside an open grave in the dusky shadow of a large oak tree in Mount Auburn Cemetery in Cambridge, Massachusetts. Next to him, heads bowed in prayer, stood Henry Wadsworth Longfellow, Oliver Wendell Holmes, Ralph Waldo Emerson, and John Greenleaf Whittier.

All of them had accompanied the casket from the start of the extraordinary funeral procession: from the Massachusetts State House, where the body had lain for thousands of mourners to view; to the brief prayer service at King's Chapel; and then for the trip down Cambridge Street to Beacon Street to Charles Street, across the Charles River Bridge into Cambridge; past the deceased's alma mater, Harvard College, and finally to Mount Auburn, where the cortege arrived just as the late-winter sun was setting. Pallbearers "reverently and by tender hands" placed the casket by the side of the grave, while outside the cemetery's wrought-iron gates, thousands of people clustered to glimpse the burial and honor the late statesman who had helped change the nation's history during one of its darkest periods, and had paid dearly for his efforts.

Charles Sumner was dead, and Boston and all of America were grieving the loss of the country's most passionate, vociferous, and unwavering, antislavery champion. One publication summed up the senator's accomplishments, and thus, the impact of his death: "No man in this generation has done more to advance the cause of equal liberty for mankind, . . . No death in the country, since that of Mr. Lincoln [after assassination in 1865] has caused a deeper feeling of sorrow."

The heart attack that claimed Charles Sumner's life occurred during the early morning hours of March 11, 1874, while the senator was at his Washington, D.C., home on Vermont Avenue and H Street, just across Lafayette Park from the White House. When word spread across the city that the sixty-three-year-old Sumner had been stricken, small groups of well-wishers—black and white alike—congregated quietly outside his house. With his close friends gathered at his bedside, Sumner's last phrases were, "Tell Emerson I love and revere him," and "Don't let the civil rights bill fail" (Sumner was working on a post-Reconstruction bill to advance the cause of Southern blacks that would become the Civil Rights Act of 1875). Among his deathbed visitors in Washington was the former slave Frederick Douglass, but the senator did not recognize him in the moments before his death.

At 2:50 P.M., while his old friend George T. Dowling held his hand, Sumner gave a "convulsive moment" and grasped Downing's hand so powerfully that he almost crushed it. Sumner died a minute later.

Congress voted to set aside Friday, March 13, for funeral services in the Capitol. Douglass led a "great assemblage of colored men," who followed Sumner's hearse to the Capitol, where thousands of mourners were waiting. Sumner's coffin was placed in the center of the great rotunda on the black catafalque where Lincoln's body had rested nine years earlier. "It was the first time in American history that a Senator's memory had been so honored," historian David Donald pointed out.

President Ulysses S. Grant, senators and representatives, members of the Supreme Court, and a contingent of army officers led by William T. Sherman, all gathered in the Senate chamber for services, while wives, friends, and other dignitaries packed the gallery. Every chair in the chamber was filled, save for Sumner's, which—as it had for three years after the caning—remained vacant, though this time it was draped in black.

At just before 12:30 P.M., pall bearers brought the coffin into the Senate chamber, and the entire assemblage watched in silence as it was carried to the front and placed before the main desk. "The nation in its three branches—legislative, executive,

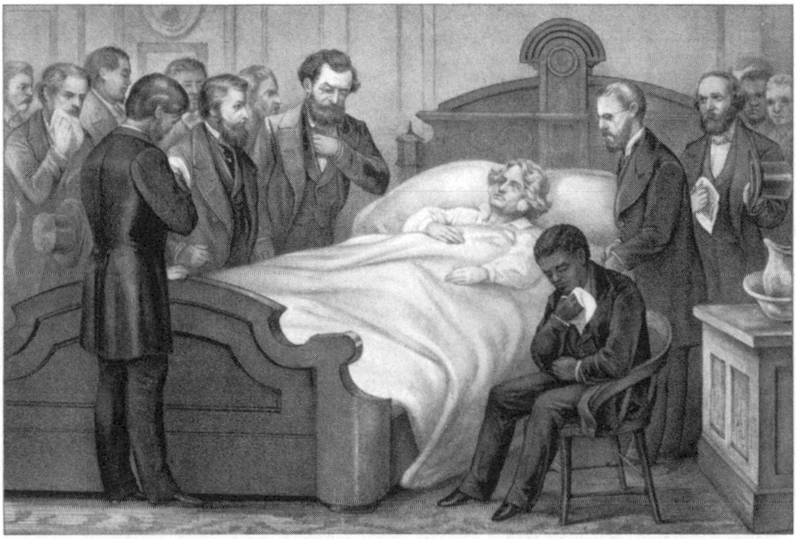

A Currier & Ives print of the death of Charles Sumner in 1874. (*Library of Congress*)

and judicial—stood around the coffin, and the people from all quarters of the land looked down upon it," one Boston newspaper reported. Religious services lasted for about a half hour, and Sumner's friend, Senator Matt Carpenter of Wisconsin, then entrusted Sumner's remains to the sergeant-at-arms "to convey them to his home, there to commit them, earth to earth, ashes to ashes, dust to dust, in the soil of Massachusetts. Peace to his ashes."

Sumner's body had been transported north by special train that left Washington around 3:00 P.M. on March 13, bound nonstop for New York (much to the disappointment of crowds that had gathered in Wilmington, Delaware, and Philadelphia), where, arriving at midnight, it halted.

The next morning it continued through Connecticut, where, one news account noted, "At New Haven and other cities, the whole population seemed to pour out to pay their last tribute to the dust of the great Statesman." And then the train crossed into

Massachusetts, where, beginning in Springfield, throngs gathered at every station to watch it rumble eastward, while church bells tolled along the entire route. Meanwhile, in Boston, thousands had filled Faneuil Hall for a public prayer meeting, and mourners poured onto the tracks to greet the train when it arrived in the early evening of March 14. Then a long procession followed the coffin, which was escorted by a mounted guard of honor from the Massachusetts First Battalion, up Beacon Hill to the State House, where Sumner's body was placed in Doric Hall "in sight of the memorials of Washington and the flags of Massachusetts regiments," and guarded by black troops.

The next day, Sunday, March 15, with an enormous crowd waiting outside—some women fainted in the tightly packed lines—the doors to the State House were opened at 10:00 A.M. for mourners to pay their respects, and the resulting turnout stunned even Sumner's greatest supporters. Somberly, silently, two or three abreast, somewhere between 40,000 and 50,000 people passed by Sumner's casket during Sunday and the early hours of Monday. The people of Massachusetts—many of whom disagreed with Sumner's inflexible tactics, imperious manner, antagonistic language, and uncompromising antislavery views twenty years earlier—today recognized the profundity of his contributions as they filed through State House halls. "Under that roof," noted the *Boston Advertiser*, "was uttered the summons of the State to him to go forth in her name to withstand the great wrong."

Those who filed by Sumner's coffin knew that America had endured a bloody civil war, the assassination of a president, a contentious and violent Reconstruction Era, and also required the passage of three constitutional amendments—the Thirteenth (in 1865, abolishing slavery), Fourteenth (in 1868, making all persons born in the United States citizens), and Fifteenth (in 1870, giving blacks and former slaves the right to vote)—to right the great wrong that Charles Sumner had fought against for most of his adult political life.

On Monday, at around 2:30 P.M., church bells tolled once again, and since virtually all of Boston's businesses suspended operations, the downtown streets were jammed with spectators and mourners. Police had to clear the roadway to allow the funeral procession to travel the short distance from the State House to King's Chapel for the Episcopal service, so chosen because it had once been the place of worship for Sumner's mother; the senator belonged to no church.

From there, the procession wound its way toward Cambridge and Mount Auburn Cemetery, closely followed by dignitaries and, perhaps more notably according to one reporter, "the representatives of the dusky race, for whom Charles Sumner battled and suffered, and in whose cause he laid down his life."

Charles Sumner is buried in a secluded spot in Mount Auburn Cemetery, far from the main entrance, on the southwest slope of a hill along what is today called Arethusa Path. His grave is marked by a coffin-shaped granite monument inscribed only with his name and the dates of his birth and death (January 6, 1811–March 11, 1874). Beside it are the graves of his family members, including those of his siblings, with whom Charles maintained little or no relationship for most of his life, marked with small white-gray rectangular stones. Sumner's marker is sturdy and significant, but relatively unpretentious compared with other large stones and obelisk-shaped monuments nearby. His gravesite certainly does not reflect the reputation, contribution, and impact of the towering nineteenth-century figure it honors.

In 1874, though, his death was marked around the world. Publications such as *Harper's Weekly* and the *New York Tribune* ran full-length tributes. Longfellow and Whittier commemorated him in poems. The New York Chamber of Commerce held a special service mourning his passing. Newspapers across the country recognized his loss as a national event and were almost united in the generous praise they offered him. And in Europe, where he had spent so much time, tributes and portraits appeared in Great Britain, France, and Sweden.

Combative until the end, Sumner had been censured in late 1872 by the Massachusetts legislature, when, as part of a politi-

The understated coffin-shaped memorial marking the grave of Charles Sumner in the Mount Auburn Cemetery, Cambridge. (*Author*)

cal dispute with President Ulysses S. Grant, Sumner introduced a Senate resolution to remove the names of Civil War battles from the Army Register or from regimental colors. The so-called "battle-flags resolution" insulted virtually every veteran, North and South, who had fought in the war, and caused a national uproar. Sumner disingenuously tried to portray the resolution as a way to put the fighting behind the nation once and for all. Ever perplexed by other people's reactions to his words and actions, Sumner wrote of the outcry: "I cannot comprehend this tempest." The Massachusetts legislature rescinded its censure in February 1874, just weeks before Sumner died.

The ideas that Charles Sumner had promulgated for so long were now more than part of mainstream opinion—they had been codified into law and written into the United States Constitution. Once derided, scoffed at, widely denounced, and beaten nearly to death, Charles Sumner could rest in peace knowing his ideas and ideals had triumphed. A deeply flawed man, Sumner's courage and leadership on the antislavery issue were indisputable and unrivaled, and in death, virtually universally acknowledged.

And perhaps no tribute offered a more profound testament of how far the country's attitudes had changed in the decade following the terrible Civil War than one that occurred upon Sumner's death, eighteen years after the caning: the South Carolina flag was lowered to half staff in his honor.

If the South Carolina tribute was startling, one other tribute to Charles Sumner bordered on the remarkable, this one occurring in Washington, D.C., a few weeks after his death.

Mississippi Congressman Lucius Quintus Cincinnatus Lamar—whom Mary Chesnut nursed outside of Richmond in 1861 and who declared Preston Brooks's assault an "awful blunder"—stood in the House of Representatives on April 25, 1874, and asked to be heard. No one was quite sure what he was going to say, but what he said echoed across the country, stunned his colleagues, and touched the hearts of every listener. Lamar, a former rabid fire-eater and slaveholder from the deep South, offered a stirring eulogy to Charles Sumner and, in Sumner's memory, made a simple plea for lasting peace and justice between North and South.

This was not an easy speech for Lamar to make. Both of his brothers and two of his law partners were killed in Civil War battles, a war that most Southerners believed was fought due to the radical antislavery policies favored by Sumner and those like him. For years, Sumner had been the South's bitter enemy, before the war, of course, but also during and after the conflict. For example, when Chief Justice Roger Taney, a Southern icon, died in 1864, Sumner wrote to President Lincoln: "Providence has given us a victory in the death of [Taney]. This is a victory for liberty and the Constitution." Later he said Taney's name should be "hooted down the page of history." Sumner then argued vociferously against commissioning a sculpted bust of Taney: "I object to that; that now an emancipated country should make a bust to the author of the *Dred Scott* decision." When the war ended, Sumner favored placing harsh and radical Reconstruction terms upon the South, part of a Northern-led federal government policy that made the postwar years a nightmare for the vanquished Confederacy. "Congress must assert jurisdiction of the rebel region & mould it into republican states," Sumner wrote in August 1865, months after the South's surrender.

And yet, despite all of this, Lamar believed it was time for North and South to heal. Lamar told his House colleagues that just before Sumner died, he believed that "all occasion for strife and distrust between the North and South had passed away, and there no longer remained any cause for continued estrangement between those two sections of our common country." Lamar asked: "Are there not many of us who believe the same thing? Is that the common sentiment, or if not, ought it not to be, of the great mass of our people, North and South?"

Americans from every region needed to view themselves as a single people, Lamar said, "bound to each other by a common constitution, destined to live together under a common government." It was time for Americans to "endeavor to grow toward each other once more in heart, as we are indissolubly linked to each other in fortune." The time was right, Lamar said, for a new understanding between the sections, especially in the aftermath of Sumner's death. Sumner was a "great champion of liberty . . . a sympathizer with human sorrow," an "earnest pleader for the exercise of human tenderness and heavenly charity." In his name, Northerners and Southerners should "lay aside the concealments which serve only to perpetuate misunderstandings and distrust, and frankly confess on both sides we most earnestly desire to be one . . . in feeling and in heart." If Sumner could speak from the dead to both sides, Lamar declared, he would say: "My countrymen! Know one another and you will love one another."

When Lamar finished, the House sat for a moment in shocked silence, and then a loud and long burst of applause rolled across the floor. "My God, what a speech!" said New York Congressman Lyman Tremaine. "It will ring through the country."

Lamar's speech marked an important turning point in the relations between North and South, and it elevated the Mississippi congressman to statesman status. The *Boston Globe* called Lamar's speech on Sumner "evidence of the restoration of the Union in the South." The *Boston Advertiser* declared it "the most significant and hopeful utterance that has been heard from the South since the war." Some Southern newspapers vigorously criticized Lamar, but he was willing to bear it. To his wife, he wrote: "Our people have suffered so much, have been betrayed so often . . . that it is but natural that they should be suspicious of any word or act of overture to the North by a Southern man. I know for once that I have done her [the South] good. I shall serve no other interest than hers." Still, if enough people disagreed with his actions, Lamar would abide by the will of his constituents and "will calmly and silently retire to private life if [the] people do not approve [of] me."

But his fellow Mississippians eventually came to understand and accept Lamar's message, or, if they still objected to it, at least respected him for speaking honestly about his feelings that Sumner's death should mark a new era in North-South relations. In 1876, Mississippi's Democratic state legislature elected him to the United States Senate; Lamar had strong support from blacks and whites, Republicans and Democrats. In 1877, when he took his seat, he became the first former Confederate leader in the U.S. Senate.

On January 29, 1887, thirty years after her husband's death, Martha C. Brooks received her widow's pension from the United States Bureau of Pensions for her husband Preston's service with the South Carolina Palmetto Regiment during the Mexican War. The total sum was eight dollars per month.

Mrs. Preston Brooks collected the pension until her death from pneumonia on March 24, 1901; she had been a widow for forty-four years. One obituary made reference to her husband's congressional service and, in reference to the caning, noted only that Preston Brooks had "chastised Charles Sumner in the United States Senate for an unkind reference in regard to the venerable Senator Butler of this state." Another called the caning "one of the thrilling episodes before the Civil War." Martha Brooks was laid to rest in Edgefield beside her famous husband.

The manner in which their two regions remember Sumner and Brooks is most intriguing. Sumner, a member of Boston's intellectual and social elite, a Harvard graduate and lawyer who traveled to most of the great cities in the United States and Europe, a Senatorial giant above and apart from the caning episode, became a living martyr to the rightness of the antislavery cause after his beating. Brooks, a respected planter and slave-owner, a son of Edgefield, South Carolina, who attended (but did not graduate from) the state university in Columbia, a backbench legislator before May 1856 who afterward was defined by the caning, became the defender of the Southern way of life and of the states' rights supporters who argued that they had the framers of the U.S. Constitution on their side.

In South Carolina today, tributes to Brooks can be found. The South Carolina State Museum at McKissick maintains in its collection the commemorative goblet, several gold-lined rings fashioned from pieces of Brooks's splintered cane, and many of the canes Brooks received from Southern well-wishers. Brooks's burial site in Edgefield is marked with a tall obelisk, and inscribed with a lengthy epitaph summarizing his virtues. His two homes, both of which I was privileged to visit, are now privately owned, but meticulously maintained and part of the historic fabric of Edgefield.

And at the South Caroliniana Library, a short walk from the McKissick Museum on the famous University of South Carolina campus "Horseshoe," a plaque honoring Brooks adorns the main lobby, across from the manuscript room in which his papers are located. The plaque, commemorated upon Brooks's premature death in 1857, had hung in the chapel on the Brooks family plantation until the church was razed around 1940. Its inscription states in part:

Gallantly has he borne himself upon the Battle Field,
And in the Council Chamber of the Nation,
Won the applause of his constituents.
The State has lost one of her most gifted and cherished sons
And his family their pride and boast.

The obelisk marking the grave of Preston Brooks in the Edgefield, South Carolina, Cemetery. (*Author*)

There is no question that the applause Brooks received in 1856 and 1857 was due almost entirely to his beating of Charles Sumner. Today, while Brooks's home state acknowledges his fame and the heroic status he attained in the years prior to the Civil War, South Carolina still seems to wrestle with exactly how to treat his controversial legacy within the context of its rich historical pantheon. Other areas of the South also pay tribute to Brooks: Brooksville, Florida, and Brooks County, Georgia, are just two places named in his honor.

In Massachusetts, Sumner's legacy is mixed. Monuments certainly celebrate the Senate giant in a stately and dignified way. In Boston and Cambridge, two statues honor the former United States senator. The first, erected just a few years after his death, is located in the Public Garden in the heart of the city. It depicts Sumner standing, overcoat askew behind him, a scroll in hand, gazing into the distance. The statue's pedestal is engraved with one word: "Sumner." At the time, no further explanation was needed. In 1902, a second bronze statue was erected in Harvard Square, near Sumner's alma mater. This visage is of a brooding, seated Sumner, coat draped over the chair, book in hand, sitting atop a pedestal that is also simply inscribed with his name.

Sumner's home on narrow Hancock Street, on the back side of Boston's Beacon Hill, is similarly easy to pass by without notice: it bears a plaque that merely lists the years (1830–1857) Sumner lived there. His monument stone in Mount Auburn Cemetery in Cambridge also lists only his name and years of birth and death. Neither his home nor gravesite bears any further inscription honoring Sumner. Again, there was a period when little else needed to be said about Charles Sumner in Boston—virtually everyone knew of his reputation and accomplishments.

Top, the statue of Charles Sumner on the campus of Harvard University; bottom, the statue of Sumner in Boston's Public Garden. (*Author*)

That is not the case today. Aside from historians and academics, few Bostonians recognize the full extent of Sumner's achievements and influence, if they recognize him at all. His home is part of a tour of Boston's Civil War and abolitionist places of interest, and an elementary school in Boston's Roslindale section is named for him, but exactly who he was and why he was important eludes most Bostonians. Some mistakenly believe that the Sumner Tunnel, which connects mainland Boston with East Boston across the harbor, was named for the Massachusetts senator (it was actually named for William Sumner, a lawyer, legislator, and general who served in the War of 1812). In 2011, the bicentennial of Charles Sumner's birth, several Boston academic and historical institutions sponsored readings, seminars, and workshops designed to rekindle interest in

Sumner, but few of these events excited the imagination of the general public. Even Sumner's massive fifteen-volume *Works*, which contains his most important writings, and whose completion he described as his reason for living in 1873, could not fully cement his legacy or sustain for him in history the celebrity status he once enjoyed.

This is regrettable and understandable at the same time. Boston prides itself on its history, of course, but mainly on being a city of the American Revolution and the emergence of the Irish politician—eighteenth-century founders John Hancock, John Adams, and Paul Revere, as well as John F. Kennedy in the twentieth century, are far better known than Sumner, though Sumner's contributions to the nation's history are comparable to theirs.

In the tempestuous nineteenth century, especially in the pivotal 1850s, Charles Sumner was liked by few, but respected by many. And no man did more to influence the slavery debate on a national scale. Southerners detested and sometimes feared him. Northerners first resisted and eventually came to revere him. But when Charles Sumner spoke, everyone listened.

A tantalizing question lurks when we consider the nation at this point in its history: Without the caning, would the Civil War have broken out?

The answer is: eventually, perhaps, but certainly not as soon as it did, and with delay could have come the possibility of compromise, however remote it may seem in hindsight. Tensions had simmered and tempers had flared between North and South on the issue of slavery since the nation's founding, but until May 22, 1856, cooler heads and determined statesmen from both regions—Clay, Calhoun, Webster, and others—had prevailed.

But Brooks's assault on Sumner, in the halls of Congress, no less, crossed the line from debate to outright violence, and sent a signal to both sides that they had few options to resolve their differences through political discourse. Bruce Catton, who called the caning the first battle of the Civil War, wrote that Brooks undeniably had done what he set out to do when he assaulted Sumner, "but the final effect was wholly disastrous." By beating Sumner, Brooks had caused "many folk in the North to overlook the provocation that the ["Crime Against Kansas"] speech had contained. The slave power (it would be said) could not be reasoned with; the man who tried it would be bludgeoned almost to the point of death." William Gienapp said simply: "The caning of Charles Sumner was a major landmark on the road to civil war." Robert Neil Mathis concurred, saying that, after Brooks's attack, "many previously uncommitted Northerners and Southerners were provoked, persuaded, or cajoled into becoming avowed abolitionists or slaveryites, therefore dangerously weakening the bonds of the Union."

And Sumner's most noted biographer, David Donald, wrote of the caning more than fifty years ago, "When the two sections no longer spoke the same language, shared the same moral code, or obeyed the same law, when their representatives clashed in bloody conflict in the halls of Congress, thinking men North and South began to wonder how the Union could longer endure."

Many beliefs and stereotypes that North and South held in 1856—indeed, many that prompted the caning and were exacerbated by it—continue to exist today. Sumner's contention that Brooks and his slaveholding colleagues were barbaric and unrefined are little different than the stereotype of the Southern redneck that many elite Northerners hold today. Brooks's feeling that Sumner was arrogant, rude, and ungentlemanly is close enough to the way many Southerners feel about people from Massachusetts and the rest of the Northeast.

The political parties have changed sides (the South is far more Republican and the Northeast heavily Democrat, though even those distinctions are in flux), but the depictions of the people have remained largely similar. Despite the ease of travel and mobility, residents of each region continue to believe the other does not understand their values. "The outgrowth of these kinds of divisions," wrote journalist Peter Cannellos in 2006, "is, inevitably, the types of misunderstandings that lead to the depiction of Southern rednecks and prissy Northeast snobs." By recognizing that these differences date back as far as nineteenth-century slavery discussions, we can better understand and deal with the depth and strength of their roots, a necessary step if we are ever to overcome them, or at the very least, simply learn to live with them.

The caning, Preston Brooks's one-minute act of aggression against Charles Sumner on the floor of the United States Senate chamber on May 22, 1856, dramatically altered the course of American history, and continues to shape it today.

BIBLIOGRAPHIC ESSAY

Preston Brooks's caning of Charles Sumner, including the events leading up to and following it, is filled with larger-than-life personalities, dramatic episodes, and far-reaching implications for America. This book is a work of narrative history that rests on a sturdy foundation of primary and secondary sources: layers of scholarship and research. This Bibliographic Essay lists my sources and how I use them, and the Acknowledgments contain additional details about my research.

I have tried to tell this rich story with as much accuracy as the historical record allows. Everything that appears between quote marks is contained in a diary, letter, government document, court transcript, piece of congressional testimony, newspaper, magazine article, journal, pamphlet, or book. I have taken no poetic license. My conclusions are based on an examination and interpretation of the sources and my knowledge of the characters and events; these also provide the underpinnings for any conjecture that I engage in (as all historians and nonfiction authors must do from time to time). In those few instances when I do speculate about people or events, I make these clear to the reader.

The source material for *The Caning* is so rich that I feel as though I've spent a great deal of time over the last few years in the 1850s, and while on my journey to the past, got to know Charles Sumner and Preston Brooks especially well.

Sumner, of course, was a prolific speaker and writer. His Pulitzer Prize-winning biographer, David Donald, estimates that Sumner's fifteen-volume *Works*, which the senator compiled in the last few years of his life, represents less than half of his public utterances. He wrote often, on broad topics, to a vast array of people. Just as rich were the thousands of letters people wrote to him during his career; those also offer a wonderful glimpse into the tenor and tone of the times. I've examined as many of Sumner's letters as possible during the time period and topics covered by this book, scores of letters he received, many of his speeches, and several volumes of his *Works*—and I've only read a fraction of his writings.

Brooks's career did not last long enough for him to be as prolific as Sumner, nor was he as naturally inclined to write as the Massachusetts senator, but his papers contain enough of his observations about the caning, slavery, his family, and his region to get a real feel for what drove him as a man, a congressman, and a Southerner. Those letters written to and about Brooks, also contained in his papers, amplified a number of these topics—the correspondence about his untimely death was particularly powerful and interesting.

Below I provide a list of primary sources and for certain ones included a brief explanation of how I used them and why they were important. I have grouped secondary sources according to topical categories when appropriate.

I have referred to the primary or secondary source (mostly newspapers in the latter case) chronologically closest to the event for greatest accuracy and veracity. For example, Sumner's *Works,* written late in his life, may, in some cases, represent what the "1870s Sumner" wished or hoped he had said in earlier years; thus, to describe, say, Sumner's convalescence in July 1856, I tried to draw on letters or other documents from that month. While this was not possible in all cases, I was able to adhere to this approach most of the time, since Sumner wrote—and was written to—so frequently, since the Preston Brooks papers contained many colorful, in-the-moment letters and documents, and because so much of the caning investigation was part of an extensive public record.

I drew on hundreds of articles from several nineteenth-century newspapers as secondary sources throughout the book. Northerners and Southerners relied on papers for their news and for interpretations of events. I mention many of these papers within the text, and I used other newspaper articles for background. The newspaper references were derived from three main sources: the New England Historic Genealogical Society's (NEHGS) wonderful collection of nineteenth-century newspapers (www.newenglandancestors.com); the Furman University Department of History *Secession Era Editorials Project* (http://history.furman.edu/editorials/see.py), a remarkably ambitious compilation; and newspaper clippings included in a scrapbook collected by Preston Brooks's great-granddaughter, which is part of the Preston S. Brooks Papers at the South Caroliniana Library at the University of South Carolina (USC).

Rather than list the newspapers separately in the topical areas that follow, I've included them here since I used them throughout the book to capture the feel of the time period. This list does not represent all the publications I referred to, but provides readers with a good sampling:

Albany Evening Journal
Atchison (KS) Union
Boston Courier
Boston Daily Advertiser
Boston Daily Atlas
Boston Daily Evening Transcript
Boston Investigator
Boston Post
Charleston (SC) Mercury
Charleston (SC) Standard
Chicago Press and Tribune
Columbian (SC) South Carolinian
Daily Lawrence (KS) Republican
Edgefield (SC) Advertiser
Illinois State Register
Jefferson City (MO) Inquirer
Kansas Crusader of Freedom
Leavenworth (KS) Times
Lecompton (KS) Union
The Liberator
Macon (GA) Messenger

Milledgeville (GA) Federal Union
Montgomery (AL) Journal
New Orleans Times-Picayune
New York Times
New York Tribune
Pittsburgh Gazette
Raleigh (NC) Register
Richmond (VA) Enquirer
Richmond Whig
Spartanburg (SC) Spartan
Springfield (IL) State Journal
Wilmington (NC) Daily Herald

A final note: When an author writes about a subject that touches the Civil War in any way—the run-up, the war itself, the aftermath—he can't help but rub elbows with some of America's greatest historians. There is no way to read or refer to all of the great books written about this momentous time period. The books I list below are but a fraction of the thousands written about the Civil War Era, but in my view, they are among the best and most important, and they provided me with invaluable material for this work.

PRESTON BROOKS, CHARLES SUMNER, AND THE CANING AND ITS AFTERMATH

Primary Sources

Charles Sumner

To understand and analyze this complex man—before, during, and after the caning episode—I drew extensively on the enormous collection of letters to and from Sumner contained in *The Papers of Charles Sumner, 1811–1874*, on 85 reels of microtext at the Boston Public Library. These comprise letters contained in the Charles Sumner Papers at Harvard's Houghton Library plus letters located in nearly two hundred other repositories in the United States, Great Britain, France, and Canada. This vast collection helped me paint the portrait of Sumner the man, as well as Sumner the antislavery crusader, and also provided an illuminating look at how American citizens viewed Sumner and the critical issues of the day.

I owe a debt of gratitude to editor Beverly Wilson Palmer for producing the masterful *The Selected Letters of Charles Sumner,* Volumes 1 (1830–1859) and II (1859–1874) (Boston: Northeastern University Press, 1990), which was my constant companion during the research and writing of *The Caning.* It is no surprise that Palmer, a Sumner scholar, chose letters that revealed Sumner's character as well as his beliefs; I found this collection particularly helpful when sketching Sumner's European sojourns.

Sumner's speeches, including "The Crime Against Kansas" and "The Barbarism of Slavery," and many other writings, are also contained in his exhaustive *The Works of Charles Sumner* (Boston: Lee and Shepard, 1875); I mainly made use of Volumes 1–7 of the fifteen-volume collection. Both major speeches were also reprinted in newspapers across the North and are available from numerous Internet sources.

I consulted both the Charles Sumner Papers and the Theodore Parker Papers at the Massachusetts Historical Society for original transcripts of some of Sumner's speeches, and a heartfelt correspondence between Sumner and Parker while Sumner was convalescing.

PRESTON BROOKS

The most complete collection of correspondence to, from, and about Preston Brooks and his family is contained in the Preston S. Brooks Papers at the South Caroliniana Library at the University of South Carolina. These include letters from Southerners to Brooks about the caning; a collection of letters about Brooks's Mexican War experience; a Brooks diary recopied by his wife Martha (which contains, among other things, Brooks's heartbreaking recollections of the death of his three-year-old daughter Yettie in 1851, and his overall feelings about family); a lengthy diary kept by Brooks's father; and a scrapbook collected by his great-granddaughter that contains newspaper clippings and other documents relating to his death (including colorful details of the long journey made by the Edgefield contingent transporting Brooks's frozen body from Washington back to his South Carolina home).

In addition, this collection contains the remarkable eight-page handwritten "Statement of Mr. Brooks on the Sumner Assault," dated May 28, 1856 (six days after the caning), in which he candidly outlines his motives and actions. It also contains poignant letters—to Mrs. Brooks and others—from those in attendance when Brooks died suddenly in January 1857.

Lawmakers' comments on Brooks's life and death are also contained in extensive testimony recorded in the *Congressional Globe* (precursor to the *Congressional Record*), 34th Congress.

I also found helpful "Speeches of the Honorable Preston S. Brooks, and Proceedings of Congress on the Occasion of His Death," in the *Southern Quarterly Review* (February 1857), which contains excerpts from his speeches and articles about his death. Brooks's speech on the Kansas-Nebraska Act (March 15, 1854) is contained in the *Congressional Globe*, 33rd Congress, 1st Session, Appendix.

The information in the book about the disposition of Preston Brooks's estate and the value of his slaves is contained in the "Inventory of the Personal Estate of Preston S. Brooks" housed at the Edgefield, South Carolina Archives, and also in an exhaustive bound collection of slave records entitled, *Slave Records of Edgefield County, South Carolina* by Gloria Ramsey Lucas (Edgefield, S.C.: Edgefield County Historical Society, 2010).

Finally, information about Brooks and the Southern planter lifestyle is captured in *Secret and Sacred: The Diaries of James Henry Hammond, a Southern Slaveholder*, edited by Carol Bleser (Columbia: University of South Carolina Press, 1988).

The Caning and Its Aftermath

Primary source material about this extraordinary event and its fallout is extensive and varied. The entire episode, including testimony of the House of Representatives investigation, follow-up speeches from lawmakers, testimony from Brooks, Sumner, and other witnesses, as well as the Brooks expulsion hearing, is contained in the *Congressional Globe*. A wealth of information is included in the *Alleged Assault upon Senator Sumner* (House Report, No. 182, 34th Congress, 1st Session, 1856), but extensive additional information appears in the appendix and other places within the *Congressional Globe*. I also consulted the *Globe* for debates and discussion on the Kansas-Nebraska Act and the tumultuous situation in Kansas that led up to Sumner's "Crime Against Kansas" speech.

In addition, the *Journal of the House of Representatives* (July 15, 1856) contains the resolution calling for Brooks's ouster and outlines the arguments of his actions.

I also examined the United States Senate report from the "Select Committee appointed to inquire into the circumstances attending the assault committed upon the person of Hon. Charles Sumner, a member of the Senate" in *The Reports of the Committees of the Senate of the United States* (First Session of the 34th Congress, 1855–1856).

The Resolutions of the Legislature of Massachusetts Relative to the Recent Assault upon the Hon. Mr. Sumner (June 11, 1856) is an interesting document sent to the U.S. Congress, expressing the Massachusetts legislature's outrage over the "brutal and cowardly" assault on Sumner.

Numerous pamphlets were published at indignation meetings in the North, summarizing the speeches and sentiments at the rallies protesting Brooks's attack on Sumner. Among others, I examined *A Full Report of the Speeches at the Meeting of Citizens in Cambridge, June 2, 1856, in reference to the Assault on Senator Sumner in the Senate Chamber at Washington*; and *Proceedings of a Public Meeting of the Citizens of Providence on the Evening of June 7, 1856*. Also, a pamphlet ridiculing Brooks for his August 29 speech in Columbia, South Carolina, was printed in Boston entitled: "Disunion Document, No. 1: Speech of Honorable Preston S. Brooks delivered at Columbia, South Carolina." The pamphlet asked the provocative question: "Which party is the sectional and disunion party?" And then it urged Massachusetts citizens: "Read the following account of the reception of the Assassin Brooks at Columbia, S.C. with his speech, and then answer the question."

For an excellent compilation of primary sources, as well as short analyses that bridge the primary documents, see Lloyd Benson's *The Caning of Charles Sumner* (Belmont, Calif.: Wadsworth, 2003), which contains Sumner's "Crime Against

Kansas" speech; letters to and from Sumner and Brooks; period newspaper editorials; and Congressional documents associated with the investigation. I found Professor Benson's work a valuable clearinghouse for some of the critical primary sources associated with the caning.

Extensive primary-source material on the caning is available as part of the excellent Cornell University Samuel J. May Anti-Slavery Collection, which I accessed frequently at http://dlxs.library.cornell.edu/m/mayantislavery.

Finally, the story about Lucius Quintus Cincinnatus Lamar expressing his opinion that the caning was an "awful blunder" for the South appears in Mary Chesnut's *A Diary from Dixie: The Civil War's Most Celebrated Journal, Written 1860–1865 During the Conflict by the Wife of Confederate General James Chesnut, Jr.* (New York: Gramercy Books, 1997, a facsimile of the 1905 edition). Lamar's tribute speech to Charles Sumner after Sumner's death is reprinted in several places. I made use of the version at www.bartleby.com/268/10/6.html (accessed February 28, 2012), and also of extensive excerpts about Lamar in President John F. Kennedy's *Profiles in Courage* (reprint, New York: Pocket Books, 1961).

Secondary Sources

Unpublished Works

For a compelling overview of the caning, particularly from the Southern sense-of-order perspective, I recommend Joel Harlan Gradin's Ph.D. dissertation, "Losing Control: The Caning of Charles Sumner and the Breakdown of Antebellum Political Culture" (University of North Carolina at Chapel Hill, 1991).

I also found helpful another paper that looked at the caning from a Southern perspective entitled: "Preston Brooks in the Verbal and the Visual: Showing Face to Save Face and Avoid Disgrace in the Antebellum South," an honors thesis for a bachelor's degree in history by Margot Bernstein (Williams College: 2010).

Articles, Essays, and Periodicals

I made use of the following in my research for Sumner, Brooks, and the caning in general:

"Charles Sumner." *United States Magazine,* 3 (July–December 1856), 355–358.

Dietrich, Ken. "Ever Able, Manly, Just and Heroic: Preston Smith Brooks and the Myth of Southern Manhood." *Proceedings of the South Carolina Historical Association* (2011), 27–38.

Fleming, Thomas. "When Politics was Not Only Nasty . . . But Dangerous." *American Heritage* (Spring 2011), 56–63.

Friefeld, Jacob. "Honor and Blood: Brooks, Sumner, and Conceptions of the Body in Nineteenth-Century America." *Historyroll.com* (September 2010), 11 pages.

Gienapp, William E. "The Crime Against Sumner: The Caning of Charles Sumner and the Rise of the Republican Party." *Civil War History* (September 1979), 218–245.

Mathis, Robert Neil. "Preston Smith Brooks: The Man and His Image." *South Carolina Historical Magazine* (October 1978), 296–310.

Slusser, Daniel Lawernce. "In Defense of Southern Honor: Preston Brooks and the Attack on Charles Sumner." *CalPoly Journal of History*, 2 (2010), 98–110.

Books

The finest biography on Sumner is the two-volume work by David Herbert Donald, and I especially consulted the first volume, *Charles Sumner and the Coming of the Civil War* (Chicago: University of Chicago Press, 1960), which discusses the caning and Sumner's convalescence in detail. I spent some time with the second volume, *Charles Sumner and the Rights of Man* (New York: Alfred A. Knopf, 1970), to understand Sumner's stances during the Civil War and Reconstruction, as well as the magnitude of his death.

I also found extremely helpful the contemporaneous four-volume work by Edward Lillie Pierce, *Memoir and Letters of Charles Sumner* (Boston: Roberts Brothers, 1878–1893), which contained many primary sources (speeches and letters) as well as Pierce's well-written—if overly charitable—narrative.

The definitive Brooks biography has yet to be written, but I consulted several books that contained references to Brooks and provided a flavor for the plantation South of which he was a part. These include: Orville Vernon Burton, *In My Father's House Are Many Mansions* (Chapel Hill: University of North Carolina Press, 1985); Lacy K. Ford, Jr., *Origin of Southern Radicalism: The South Carolina Upcountry, 1800–1860* (New York: Oxford, 1988); Daniel Walker Hollis's multivolume history of the University of South Carolina, Vol. 1, *South Carolina College* (Columbia: University of South Carolina Press, 1951), which provided primary source documents related to Brooks's rebellious days as an undergraduate student.

Also, see Alvy King's biography, *Louis T. Wigfall: Southern Fire-Eater* (Baton Rouge: Louisiana State University Press, 1970), which chronicles the feud between the Brooks and Wigfall families; Ernest M. Lander, *Reluctant Imperialists: Calhoun, the South Carolinians, and the Mexican War* (Baton Rouge: Louisiana State University Press, 1980); Lorman A. Ratner and Dwight L. Teeter, Jr., *Fanatics and Fire-eaters: Newspapers and the Coming of the Civil War* (Urbana: University of Illinois Press, 2003), which provided analyses on the power of the press in the 1850s; Charles Grier Sellers, Jr., *The Southerner as American* (Chapel Hill: University of North Carolina Press, 1960); and Steven M. Stowe, *Intimacy and Power in the Old South: Ritual in the Lives of the Planters* (Baltimore: Johns Hopkins University Press, 1987).

In addition, I found two other books helpful to gain perspective into Preston Brooks's South: (author unnamed) *The Story of Edgefield* (Edgefield, S.C.: Edgefield County Historical Society, 2010); and a short publication written by Katharine Thompson Allen and edited by Elizabeth Cassidy West, *The University of South Carolina Horseshoe: Heart of the Campus* (Columbia: Produced by the University of South Carolina Archives, University Libraries, University of South Carolina, undated).

For another short academic treatment of the caning and related issues, plus brief analyses of other major issues of the time, see Williamjames Hull Hoffer's *The Caning of Charles Sumner: Honor, Idealism, and the Origins of the Civil War* (Baltimore: Johns Hopkins University Press, 2010).

KANSAS AND JOHN BROWN

Primary Sources

As mentioned, scores of Charles Sumner's letters and multiple pages in the *Congressional Globe* deal with the debate about Kansas and with John Brown—both Brown's murderous rampage in Kansas and his raid on Harpers Ferry. This section highlights additional sources that focus on Kansas and John Brown.

There is rich and valuable information on the dire situation in territorial Kansas at www.territorialKansasonline.org (accessed frequently), which contains diaries, letters, legislative proceedings, and other primary sources.

In addition, the Assumption College E Pluribus Unum Project, a collection of documents and analyses of three American decades (1770s, 1850s, 1920s) contained some excellent primary sources that help analyze the situation in Kansas. I accessed this collection frequently at www.assumption.edu/ahc/Kansas.

Similarly, there is a fine collection of sources, including affidavits and testimony from the families of John Brown's murder victims in Pottawatomie, at West Virginia's online Archives and History site: www.wvculture.org/history (accessed frequently).

James Henry Hammond's "Cotton Is King" speech before the United States Senate in March 1858, during the discussion on the admission of Kansas, is reprinted in numerous publications and online sites. See www.sewanee.edu/faculty/Willis/Civil_War/documents/HammondCotton.html for the reference I cited (accessed February 6, 7, 2012). Senator Andrew Butler's June 12, 1856, speech on whether Kansas should form its own constitution as it prepared to enter the Union is available at www.hti.umich/edu (accessed frequently).

Senator Stephen Douglas's committee's lengthy report (March 1856) relative to the "Affairs of Kansas" is available in the *Congressional Globe* (34th Congress, 1st Session).

Secondary Sources

Unpublished Works

For an interesting and well-researched look at the relocation of New Englanders to Kansas Territory, I found helpful Tracee M.

Murphy's history master's thesis, "The New England Emigrant Aid Company: Its Impact on Territorial Kansas, 1854–1857" (Youngstown State University, 1999).

Articles, Essays, Periodicals

Of the plethora of articles on John Brown and Kansas, I found the following particularly helpful.

Harold, Stanley. "Border Wars." *North & South*, 12, January 2011, 22–31.

Horwitz, Tony. "Why John Brown Still Scares Us." *American History*, December 2011, 38–45.

Linder, Douglas O. "The Trial of John Brown: A Commentary." *University of Missouri at Kansas City* online faculty projects (www.law.umkc.edu/faculty/projects/ftrials/johnbrown (accessed several times), 2005.

SenGupta, Gunja. "Bleeding Kansas." *Kansas History* (Kansas Historical Society), 24, no. 4 (Winter 2001–2002), 318–341.

Stottelmire, Marvin. "John Brown: Madman or Martyr?" *Brown Quarterly*, 3, no. 3 (Winter 2000) (http://brownboard.org (accessed frequently)

Books

It is important to emphasize that virtually every book that deals with the runup to the Civil War deals with the Kansas issue and with John Brown—I have listed most of these in a later section of this essay.

However, I want to mention two that deal specifically with Brown that I found invaluable: Tony Horwitz's *Midnight Rising: John Brown and the Raid That Sparked the Civil War* (New York: Henry Holt, 2011), which focuses on Harpers Ferry; and David S. Reynolds's excellent biography, *John Brown: Abolitionist* (New York: Alfred A Knopf, 2005).

In addition, much of the scene in which John Brown meets Charles Sumner and touches his bloody coat in Boston is drawn from James Freeman Clark's "Charles Sumner: His Character and Career," in *Memorial and Biographical Sketches* (Boston: Houghton, Osgood and Company, 1878), a near contemporaneous account written just a few years after Sumner's death.

DRED SCOTT, REPUBLICAN PARTY, LINCOLN-DOUGLAS DEBATES

Primary Sources

Dred Scott

A wonderful digital collection of primary sources in the *Dred Scott* case is available from Washington University in St. Louis, entitled *The Revised Dred Scott Case Collection*. The collection contains more than 110 documents and is fully text-searchable. I accessed it frequently at http://digital.wustl.edu/d/dre/index.html.

Charles Sumner refers to *Dred Scott* frequently in his letters and papers, and discussion of the case also occurs in Congress and is recorded in the *Congressional Globe* (including the full 1865 debate over whether Congress should have commissioned a bust of Chief Justice Roger Taney upon his death).

In addition, documents related to the case are contained in *James Buchanan, 1791–1868*, a collection of documents and bibliographic aids, edited by Irving J. Sloan (New York: Oceana Publications, 1968).

For a document that straddles the line between a primary and secondary source, see Samuel Tyler's *Memoir of Roger Brooke Taney, LL.D.* (Baltimore: John Murphy & Co.), an 1872 account that contains numerous primary sources, including letters to and from Taney, bridged by Tyler's narrative.

Republican Party

For a fine collection of primary sources on the emergence and growth of the Republican Party, see *Proceedings of the First Three Republican National Conventions of 1856, 1860, and 1864, including proceedings of the antecedent national convention held at Pittsburg* [*sic*], *in February, 1856, as reported by Horace Greeley* (Minneapolis: Charles Johnson, 1893).

In addition, an 1856 congressionally commissioned short biography of John Charles Frémont entitled *Life of John Charles Frémont* (New York: Greeley & McElrath), provided a revealing look into the subject's life, including a collection of speeches and other writings.

Also, for a wide collection of primary sources, opinion pieces, and letters, see the contemporaneous *The Republican Scrap Book:*

containing the platforms, and a choice selection of extracts, setting forth the real questions in issue, the opinions of the candidates, the nature and designs of the slave oligarchy, as shown by their own writers, and the opinions of Clay, Webster, Josiah Quincy, and other patriots, on slavery and its extension (Boston: John P. Jewett & Co., 1856).

I also made frequent use of the University of Pennsylvania's Schoenberg Center for Electronic Text and Image collection entitled: *The Crisis of the Union: Causes, Conduct and Consequences of the U.S. Civil War,* available at http://sceti.library.upenn.edu/sceti/civilwar/index.cfm

Lincoln-Douglas Debates

The best primary sources for the Lincoln-Douglas debates are Paul M. Angle, ed., *Created Equal? The Complete Lincoln-Douglas Debates of 1858* (Chicago: University of Chicago Press), 1958, which also contains detailed newspaper accounts of the debate days across Illinois; Harold Holzer, ed., *The Lincoln-Douglas Debates: The First Complete, Unexpurgated Text* (New York: Fordham University Press), 2004; and Lincoln's own *Lincoln: Speeches, Letters, Miscellaneous Writings, The Lincoln-Douglas Debates* (New York: Library of America), 1989.

Secondary Sources

Articles, Essays, Periodicals

Again, I consulted numerous articles about the *Dred Scott* case, the growth of the Republican Party, and the Lincoln-Douglas debates. I found the following most helpful:

Denton, Sally. "Frémont Steals California." *American Heritage,* 60, no. 4 (Winter 2011), 30–39.

Fehrenbacher, Don E. "The Republican Decision at Chicago." In Norman A. Graebner, ed., *Politics and the Crisis of 1860* (Urbana: University of Illinois Press, 1961).

________. "Comment on Why the Republican Party Came to Power." In George H. Knoles, ed., *The Crisis of the Union, 1860–1861* (Baton Rouge: Louisiana State University Press, 1965).

Gienapp, William. "Formation of the Republican Party." In L. Sandy Maisel and William G. Shade, eds., *Parties and Politics in American History* (New York: Garland Publishing, 1994), 59–81.

________. "The Crime Against Sumner: The Caning of Charles Sumner and the Rise of the Republican Party." *Civil War History* (September 1979), 218–245. (See above bibliographic reference to this important article under Charles Sumner, Preston Brooks, and the caning).

McPherson, James. "Politics and Judicial Responsibility: Dred Scott v. Sandford." In Robert P. George, ed., *Great Cases in Constitutional Law* (Princeton, N.J.: Princeton University Press, 2000), 90–93.

Sunstein, Cass R. "Dred Scott v. Sandford and Its Legacy." In Robert P. George, ed., *Great Cases in Constitutional Law* (Princeton, N.J.: Princeton University Press, 2000),, 63–89.

Books

I found the following books most helpful for information about *Dred Scott*, the Republican Party, and the Lincoln-Douglas debates.

William E. Baringer, *Lincoln's Rise to Power* (Boston: Little Brown, 1937); Andrew Wallace Crandall, *The Early History of the Republican Party, 1854–1856* (Boston: Gorham Press, 1930); Don E. Fehrenbacher, *The Dred Scott Case: Its Significance in American Law and Politics* (New York: Oxford University Press, 1978), an excellent analysis of the major constitutional questions this landmark case sparked; Eric Foner, *Free Soil, Free Labor, Free Men: The Ideology of the Republican Party Before the Civil War* (New York: Oxford University Press, 1970); Mark A. Graber, *Dred Scott and the Problem of Constitutional Evil* (Cambridge, England: Cambridge University Press, 2006); and Michael F. Holt, *Forging a Majority: The Formation of the Republican Party in Pittsburgh, 1848–1860* (New Haven: Yale University Press, 1969).

Also, see Walker Lewis, *Without Fear or Favor: A Biography of Chief Justice Roger Brooke Taney* (Boston: Houghton Mifflin, 1965), a largely sympathetic work of the man whose career and historical legacy was defined by *Dred Scott*; Corinne J. Naden and Rose Blue, *Dred Scott: Person or Property?* (New York: Benchmark Books, 2005); David Potter, *Lincoln and His Party in the Secession* Crisis (New Haven: Yale University Press, 1962); and Charles W. Smith, Jr., *Roger B. Taney: Jacksonian Jurist* (Chapel Hill: University of North Carolina Press, 1936).

ABOLITIONISTS, SECESSION, SLAVERY, AND THE RUN-UP TO THE CIVIL WAR

Primary Sources

Again, these topics are covered in great detail in several of the primary sources I've already cited (Sumner papers, Brooks papers, *Congressional Globe*, numerous digital collections). The sources included in this section are additional documents that I examined in connection with this topic heading.

The postelection letter (November 9, 1860) from Mississippian R. S. Holt to his brother, Joseph, in which he warns of slaves poisoning their masters in the wake of Lincoln's election, is contained in the Library of Congress's *Joseph Holt Papers*, a copy of which was included in the *Milledge Bonham Papers* at the South Caroliniana Library. In addition, Bonham's telegraph from Washington, D.C., to Charleston (December 19, 1860), threatening to meet Northern invaders with "bloody flags," is also contained in this collection.

Jefferson Davis's October 11, 1858, speech at Faneuil Hall in Boston is available in numerous locations and repositories. I accessed it by way of the fine digital collection at Rice University, *The Papers of Jefferson Davis*, which I accessed frequently at http://jeffersondavis.rice.edu/.

The *Congressional Globe* of December 17, 1857, contains a number of lengthy tributes to Senator Andrew Butler upon his death.

For Daniel Webster's famous March 7, 1850, speech on the Fugitive Slave Law, and several responses (including John C. Calhoun's), see the appendix to the *Congressional Globe*, beginning on page 269. I also referred to two handbills that helped crystallize the debate and provide context for Sumner's viscerally negative reaction to Webster. The first, published in May of 1850 by Gideon and Co. in Washington, D.C., was titled *Letter from Citizens of Newburyport, Mass., to Mr. Webster in Relation to his Speech Delivered in the Senate of the United States on the 7th of March, 1850, and Mr. Webster's Reply.* The second, published in August 1850, also by Gideon and Company, was entitled *Correspondence Between Mr. Webster and His New Hampshire Neighbors.*

For a comprehensive look at the depth of the opposition to the Fugitive Slave Law in Sumner's hometown of Boston, I found helpful the nineteen-page Massachusetts Senate Report No. 51 (March 24, 1851), titled *Joint Special Committee on So Much of the Governor's Address as Relates to Slavery and on Petitions Praying to the Legislators to Instruct Their Senators and to Request Representatives in Congress to Endeavor to Procure a Repeal of the Fugitive Slave Law.*

For a powerful overview of the Fugitive Slave Law and the Thomas Sims case from the point of view of Boston abolitionists, see the collection of writings from Thomas Wentworth Higginson, edited by Howard N. Meyer, titled *The Magnificent Activist: The Writings of Thomas Wentworth Higginson, 1823–1911* (New York: Da Capo Press, 2000). In addition, see *Massachusetts Senate Document No. 89*, April 9, 1851, for an in-the-moment account of Sims's capture and confinement just days after his arrest.

For more about the abolitionist movement and slavery, I made use of the Frederick Douglass Papers, many of which are online from the Library of Congress at http://lcweb2.loc.gov/ammem/doughtm/doughome.html (accessed several times). I also examined the words of Douglass in his three autobiographies: *The Narrative of the Life of Frederick Douglass, an American Slave* (1849); *My Bondage and My Freedom* (1855); and *The Life and Times of Frederick Douglass* (1881). In addition, numerous writings, speeches, and illustrations of notable abolitionists and other antislavery champions are available at the Library of Congress's *The African-American Mosaic* at http://www.loc.gov/exhibits/african/afam006.html and at the Massachusetts Historical Society's *Images of the Anti-slavery Movement in Massachusetts* at http://www.masshist.org/database/essay2.cfm?queryID=70. I accessed both sites frequently in my efforts to immerse myself in Charles Sumner's world.

For the secession crisis, I relied on a number of primary sources, two of which were included as an appendix to Charles

B. Dew's *Apostles of Disunion: Southern Secession Commissioners and the Cause of the Civil War* (Charlottesville: University of Virginia Press, 2001). These included: a speech in pamphlet form titled *Address of Hon. W. L. Harris, Commissioner from the State of Mississippi, Delivered before the General Assembly of the State of Georgia, on Monday, Dec. 17th, 1860* (Milledgeville, Georgia, 1860); and *Letter of Stephen F. Hale, commissioner from Alabama, to Governor Beriah Magoffin of Kentucky*, Dec. 27, 1860.

I also looked at secession documents in *The War of the Rebellion: A Compilation of the Official Records of the Union and Confederate Armies* (Washington, D.C., 1880–1902), focusing mainly on Vol. 1, available through the Cornell University Making of America series at http://ebooks.library.cornell.edu/m/moawar/waro.html (accessed frequently). Also, see Yale Law School's Lillian Goldman Law Library's *The Avalon Project: Documents in Law, History and Diplomacy*, which includes: *Confederate State of America: Declaration of Immediate Causes Which Induce and Justify the Secession of South Carolina from the Federal Union* at http://avalon.law.yale.edu/19th_century/csa_scarsec.asp (accessed frequently); and The Civil War Trust's "Secession Acts of the Thirteen Confederate States" at http://www.civilwar.org/education/history/primarysources/secessionacts.html (accessed frequently).

Secondary Sources

Articles, Essays, Periodicals

Nearly countless articles and essays have been written about this broad topic. However, I relied on the following for direct references and background reading:

Brooks, Elaine. "Massachusetts Anti-Slavery Society." *Journal of Negro History*, 30, no. 3 (July 1945), 311–330.

Deppisch, Ludwig, M.D. "The National Hotel Disease." *The Grog Ration: A Publication of the Bureau of Medicine and Surgery (BUMED)*, 4, no. 1 (January–February 2009), 1–5.

Fellman, Michael. "Theodore Parker and the Abolitionist Role in the 1850s." *Journal of American History* 61, no. 3 (December 1974), 666–684.

Johnson, Linck C. "Liberty Is Never Cheap: Emerson, the Fugitive Slave Law, and the Antislavery Lecture Series at the Broadway Tabernacle." *New England Quarterly*, 76 (December 2003), 550–592.

Levy, Leonard W. "Sims' Case: The Fugitive Slave Law in Boston in 1851." *Journal of Negro History*, 34, no. 1 (January 1950), 39–74.

Loewen, James W. "The First to Secede." *American Heritage*, 6, no. 4 (Winter 2011), 13–16.

Pease, Jane H., and William H. Pease. "Confrontation and Abolitionism in the 1850s." *Journal of American History*, 58, no. 4 (March 1971), 923–937.

Von Drehle, David. "The Civil War 1861–2011: The Way We Weren't." *Time* (April 18, 2011), 40–51.

Vose, Caroline E. "Jefferson Davis in New England." *Virginia Quarterly Review* (Autumn 1926), 557–568, accessed February 6, 2012 at http://www.vqronline.org/articles/1926/autumn/ vose-jefferson-davis/

Books

In addition to the books already listed that cover the abolitionist movement, I found helpful Tilden G. Edelstein's *Strange Enthusiasm: A Life of Thomas Wentworth Higginson* (New York: Atheneum, 1970), a work about one of Boston's most militant abolitionists; Louis Filler, *The Crusade Against Slavery, 1830–1860* (New York: Harper and Row, 1960); Henry Mayer's comprehensive and electrifying biography *All on Fire: William Lloyd Garrison and the Abolition of Slavery* (New York: St. Martin's Griffin, 1998); my own *A City So Grand: The Rise of an American Metropolis, Boston 1850–1900* (Boston: Beacon Press, 2010); and Wendy Hamand Venet's *Neither Ballots nor Bullets: Women Abolitionists and the Civil War* (Charlottesville: University of Virginia Press, 1991).

For books focusing on secession, I relied on some outstanding works, including: Shearer Davis Bowman, *At the Precipice: Americans North and South During the Secession Crisis* (Chapel Hill: University of North Carolina Press, 2010); Steven A. Channing, *Crisis of Fear: Secession in South Carolina* (New York: Simon & Schuster, 1970); David Detzer's fast-moving

Allegiance: Fort Sumter, Charleston, and the Beginning of the Civil War (New York: Harcourt, 2001); Charles B. Dew's dramatic overview of one of America's most dramatic three-month time periods, *Apostles of Disunion* (see citation in the "Primary Sources" section of this topic); Clifford Dowdey, *The Land They Fought For: The Story of the South as the Confederacy 1832–1865* (New York: Doubleday & Co., 1955), William W. Freehling's excellent overview, *The Road to Disunion (Vol. II): Secessionists Triumphant* (New York: Oxford University Press, 2007); Maury Klein, *Days of Defiance: Sumter, Secession, and the Coming of the Civil War* (New York: Alfred A. Knopf, 1997); Nelson D. Lankford, *Cry Havoc! The Crooked Road to Civil War, 1861* (New York: Penguin Books, 2007), in which he examines the unlikely confluence of events that had to—and did—coalesce to lead to war; and Robert Rosen, *A Short History of Charleston* (Columbia: University of South Carolina Press, 1982).

I was also assisted immeasurably by comprehensive works that focused specifically on slavery. These included: John W. Blassingame, *Slave Community: Plantation Life in the Antebellum South* (New York: Oxford University Press, 1972), which discusses the rich cultural and family life that many slaves deliberately kept hidden from their masters; David Brion Davis's excellent *Inhuman Bondage: The Rise and Fall of Slavery in the New World* (New York: Oxford University Press, 2006); Anne Farrow, Joel Lang, and Jennifer Frank, *Complicity: How the North Promoted, Prolonged, and Profited from Slavery* (New York: Ballantine Books, 2005), which makes many of the same arguments as Preston Brooks and other slave-owners; Don Fehrenbacher, *The Slaveholding Republic: An Account of the United States Government's Relations to Slavery* (New York: Oxford University Press, 2001), which focuses on U.S. proslavery policies; Eugene D. Genovese's classic and exhaustive analysis of slavery, *Roll, Jordan, Roll: The World the Slaves Made* (New York: Random House, 1972); Peter Kolchin's synthesis of 250 years of slavery in America, *American Slavery: 1619–1877* (New York: Hill and Wang, 1993); and Stephen Yafa's study of the crop that made slavery's continuance possible and profitable, *Big Cotton: How a Humble Fiber Created Fortunes, Wrecked*

Civilizations, and Put America on the Map (New York: Viking, 2005).

Works by some of America's best historians provided me with insights on the run-up to the Civil War. These works included Bruce Catton, *The Coming Fury* (New York: Doubleday & Company, 1961); Catton's *This Hallowed Ground: The Story of the Union Side of the Civil War* (New York: Doubleday & Company, 1955), in which the author maintains that Preston Brooks's assault on Charles Sumner was the first blow of the Civil War; William and Bruce Catton, *Two Roads to Sumter* (New York: McGraw-Hill, 1963); and Avery Craven, *The Coming of the Civil War* (Chicago: University of Chicago Press, 1942). Also, David Donald followed his classic Sumner biography with a magnificent biography years later of our sixteenth president, simply titled *Lincoln* (New York: Simon and Schuster, 1995).

For a valuable summary on the 1856 and 1860 presidential campaigns, I turned to William A. DeGregorio, *The Complete Book of U.S. Presidents: From George Washington to Bill Clinton* (New York: Wing Books, 1993). For a discussion on how trade and production drew the nation closer to civil war, see Marc Egnal, *Clash of Extremes: The Economic Origins of the Civil War* (New York: Hill and Wang, 2009); Ernest B. Furgurson details the chaos in the nation's capital during the war in *Freedom Rising: Washington in the Civil War* (New York: Alfred A. Knopf, 2004); and I found invaluable Constance McLaughlin Green's *Washington: Village and Capital, 1800–1878* (Princeton, N.J.: Princeton University Press, 1962), to get a feel for life and conditions in D.C. during the caning years. Michael F. Holt provided political context for the slavery extension debate in *The Fate of Their Country: Politicians, Slavery Extension, and the Coming of the Civil War* (New York: Hill and Wang, 2004). J. William Jones published an 1890 family-authorized book on the president of the Confederacy that I found helpful, entitled *The Davis Memorial Volume of our Dead President, Jefferson Davis, and the World's Tribute to His Memory* (Richmond, Va.: R. F. Johnson); and Colonel Alexander K. McClure, *Recollections of Half a Century* (Salem, Mass.: Salem Press Company, 1902) offered context on America in the latter half of the nineteenth century, including the Civil War run-up and the conflict itself.

It is hard to imagine learning about the Civil War or its causes without consulting James M. McPherson's one-volume masterpiece, *Battle Cry of Freedom: The Civil War Era* (New York: Oxford University Press, 1988). Nor is it possible to overlook Allan Nevins in the pantheon of great Civil War historians. I consulted his *The Emergence of Lincoln* (New York: Charles Scribner's Sons, 1950); and his two-volume *Ordeal of the Union* epic: *Fruits of Manifest Destiny, 1847–1852* and *A House Dividing, 1852–1857* (both New York: Charles Scribner's Sons, 1947). For Boston's role in the Civil War, the standard-bearer is Thomas H. O'Connor's *Civil War Boston: Home Front & Battlefield* (Boston: Northeastern University Press, 1997).

Finally, for other fine and important books on the national run-up to war, see David M. Potter, *The Impending Crisis, 1848–1861* (New York: Harper, 1976); Kenneth M. Stampp, *America in 1857: A Nation on the Brink* (New York: Oxford University Press, 1990); Stampp, *The Imperiled Union: Essays on the Background of the Civil War* (New York: Oxford University Press, 1980); Erich H. Walther, *The Shattering of the Union: America in the 1850s* (Wilmington, Del.: Scholarly Resources, 2004); and Paul I. Wellman, *The House Divides: The Age of Jackson and Lincoln, from the War of 1812 to the Civil War* (New York: Doubleday & Company, 1966).

ACKNOWLEDGMENTS

As an author, I have been blessed in so many ways, not the least of which is the help, counsel, and support I've received from so many people throughout the course of my career. This is my fifth book and, I am profoundly grateful to those whose assistance has made my work easier and better. I've been thinking about and, in one way or another, working on *The Caning* for a long time. The drama and far-reaching implications of the event have always captured my imagination, and I've longed to move the story from my head to the printed (or electronic) page. I appreciate the contributions of everyone who has made this journey with me and helped make this book a reality.

I want to offer thanks to the staff in the Microtext Division at the Boston Public Library for their help with the Charles Sumner papers (see my Bibliographic Essay for the description on this revealing trove of documents). At the Massachusetts Historical Society (MHS), I appreciate the efforts of Peter Drummey, who assisted me with the repository's Charles Sumner Papers and Theodore Parker Papers, and Anne Bentley, MHS curator of art, who provided me with images of Charles Sumner.

A large portion of the research for *The Caning* took place in South Carolina, and I'm pleased to say that Southern hospitality is alive and well in the Palmetto State.

In Columbia, I'm deeply indebted to the staff at the South Caroliniana Library at the University of South Carolina (USC). Curator of Manuscripts Henry Fulmer, Manuscript Specialist Graham Duncan, and Electronic Access Archivist Brian Cuthrell made it a pleasure to go through the Preston Brooks Papers and Milledge Bonham Papers, and to just spend some enjoyable time in their historic and superb repository. Their knowledge was deep and they answered questions patiently and thoroughly—it is hard for a researcher to ask for more. Special thanks to Graham for his tour of the famed USC "Horseshoe" and to Brian for his restaurant recommendations.

Also, my thanks to Jill Beute Koverman, chief curator of collections and research at USC's McKissick Museum, for opening up the institution's vaults so I could get a look at the goblet that Columbians presented to Preston Brooks in 1856.

In Edgefield, the research experience was so pleasurable that I had to pinch myself to be sure I wasn't dreaming. First and foremost, my deepest gratitude goes to Bettis Rainsford, historian for the Edgefield County Historical Society, who knows more about Preston Brooks than any man alive, and is also the proprietor of a fine establishment, the Old Edgefield Grill, where I enjoyed my first delicious meal of shrimp and grits (this Bostonian is now hooked). Bettis made available to me his personal collection of Preston Brooks documents, and also offered invaluable information about Brooks and Edgefield during a lengthy tour of the town, the Willowbrook Cemetery (where Brooks is buried), and the now privately owned historic houses where Brooks and his family members lived. Bettis had no idea who I was until I set foot in Edgefield for the first time, yet he treated me as though I were an old friend and renowned historian. I am forever grateful for his enormous help on this project.

Elsewhere in Edgefield, I would like to thank County Archivist Tricia Price Glenn, who assisted me with the Preston Brooks estate documents; John Gerrard, director of the Edgefield County Discovery Center, who introduced me to Bettis Rainsford; Hugh and Lisa Bland, who now live in one of Preston Brooks's former homes (Tomkins House) and opened their doors at dinnertime for a tour; Helen Feltham, who lives at Brooks's first home (Sweetbriar), and also graciously opened her house for a visit; and Tim and Beth Worth (Halycon Grove house), who also opened their home, which was once owned by Preston Brooks's two aunts. Thanks to all of these people who helped Preston Brooks come alive for me.

As always, I am thankful for the contributions and support of so many friends and family members whose interest and encouragement keep me going and make me a better author. I wish I could list everyone, but that's impossible—for now, I need to mention three very special people for their contributions.

My dear friend Paula Hoyt, who regularly edits and proofreads my work, once again lent her outstanding talents to this manuscript. I know I am in good hands anytime Paula reviews my writing; she always makes it better, for which I am enormously grateful (as is my publisher). Paula also created, manages, and writes content for my website (stephenpuleo.com), and she is responsible for dragging me (gently) into the Facebook age (facebook.com/stephenpuleoauthor), which I've found valuable as a way to connect with readers. I'm so thankful for Paula's constancy, sound judgment, spot-on recommendations, and wide-ranging communications abilities; and much more thankful for the gift of her friendship.

It is hard to quantify the contributions of my wonderful and longtime friend Ellen Keefe, and certainly impossible to list them all here. She also reads all of my work in advance; promotes my books to her family, friends, and colleagues; supports me at my presentations; offers wise counsel on writing and virtually any other topic; helps me with research; and is always there to provide personal or professional support. For this book, Ellen took her research assistance to a new level, accompanying me on the South Carolina leg of the journey, and helping me pore through the Preston Brooks records in Columbia and Edgefield. I can't thank her enough for her contributions to my "author life," nor will I ever be able to thank her enough for the enduring love and friendship she provides to my family and me.

I was thrilled to work on this book with my wonderful niece, Rachel Brevich, who holds a degree in history and has proven to be an excellent researcher. Rachel examined hundreds of letters to and from Charles Sumner and did an extraordinary job analyzing the Sumner Papers. She brings all of the qualities of the best researchers to her work: diligence, thoroughness, perseverance, attention to detail, shrewd instincts, an understanding of the big picture, and an innate sense of what's important (and what's not). I am immensely proud of Rachel for her great work on *The Caning*, but even more so, for the intelligent, thoughtful, loving person she has become.

I want to thank my editor, Bruce H. Franklin, at Westholme Publishing, for his support for this book from the beginning. An author's life is always easier when he knows his publisher recognizes the full value of the work and is enthused about bringing it to readers. Bruce has expressed both of these sentiments throughout this project.

I am grateful to have the world's best agent, Joy Tutela, represent me. This is our fifth book together, and Joy and I have been a team for nearly twelve years. I couldn't ask for a stronger, smarter, more supportive and loyal partner and friend. Joy worked closely with me to polish the proposal for this book, and then found it a good home. She is a pro in every sense of the word and has believed in me from day one. Perhaps the greatest compliment I can pay her is this: she has helped me live my dream.

My mom, Rose Puleo, provided her constant interest, encouragement, and love throughout the writing of this book. She had to do double duty: this is the first complete project I've worked on without being able to share it with my dad, Anthony Puleo, who died nearly four years ago. Throughout the research and writing, I felt dad's comforting presence on my shoulder and in my heart, and I count my blessings that mom is able to share with me daily her own wisdom, strength, and support. For all they've done and continue to do, I will never be able to thank my parents enough.

And finally, I offer my most profound thanks and deepest love to my "First Lady," Kate, to whom this book—and my life—is dedicated. I'm an author, but I have no adequate words to describe how much she does for me or how much she means to me. As we are in most things, we are partners in book-writing: she is a sounding board for ideas, a thoughtful adviser, and a skilled editor and proofreader who also reads my manuscripts before I submit them to the publisher. On a grander scale, Kate is an inspiration to me. She welcomes new challenges (she became a principal recently after more than thirty years as a fifth-grade classroom teacher), offers remarkable support and encouragement to others, maintains a contagiously optimistic outlook on life, and loves her friends, family, faith, and me. She makes those around her (especially me) better people. She is my best friend, fills me with joy each day, and has always instilled in me the belief that anything is possible. For more than thirty years, her love has been my greatest source of strength and peace. I am truly blessed.

INDEX